Learn Microsoft Office 2019

A comprehensive guide to getting started with Word, PowerPoint, Excel, Access, and Outlook

Linda Foulkes

BIRMINGHAM - MUMBAI

Learn Microsoft Office 2019

Commissioning Editor: Richa Tripathi
Acquisition Editor: Karan Gupta
Content Development Editor: Ruvika Rao
Senior Editor: Afshaan Khan
Technical Editor: Gaurav Gala
Copy Editor: Safis Editing
Project Coordinator: Francy Puthiry
Proofreader: Safis Editing
Indexer: Rekha Nair
Production Designer: Nilesh Mohite

First published: May 2020

Production reference: 1290520

Published by Packt Publishing Ltd.
Livery Place
35 Livery Street
Birmingham
B3 2PB, UK.

ISBN 978-1-83921-725-8

www.packt.com

To the memory of my mother, Wendy Foulkes, an expert computer trainer from whom I had the privilege of learning and working. Her passion for end user training was infectious and instilled in me life-long skills of patience, dedication, determination, and confidence. If her life were not taken away so early, we would be coauthoring many books together, but I know that she is proud looking down from above.

To my three sons, Chris, JJ, and Matt, as a reminder that you only have one chance at your unique life. Use this valuable gift surrounded by family, love, and a focused passion to move forward through it with contentment. Give yourself a shake as you hit any of life's obstacles, regain a positive outlook, and continue to be the best unique you. You are my everything.

Packt.com

Subscribe to our online digital library for full access to over 7,000 books and videos, as well as industry leading tools to help you plan your personal development and advance your career. For more information, please visit our website.

Why subscribe?

- Spend less time learning and more time coding with practical eBooks and Videos from over 4,000 industry professionals

- Improve your learning with Skill Plans built especially for you

- Get a free eBook or video every month

- Fully searchable for easy access to vital information

- Copy and paste, print, and bookmark content

Did you know that Packt offers eBook versions of every book published, with PDF and ePub files available? You can upgrade to the eBook version at www.packt.com and as a print book customer, you are entitled to a discount on the eBook copy. Get in touch with us at customercare@packtpub.com for more details.

At www.packt.com, you can also read a collection of free technical articles, sign up for a range of free newsletters, and receive exclusive discounts and offers on Packt books and eBooks.

Contributors

About the author

Linda Foulkes is an L&D trainer at Knights plc. She is also a Microsoft Office Master Trainer, Microsoft Certified Educator, and Microsoft Innovative Expert Educator and Trainer with over 25 years of experience. In 2015, Linda represented South Africa at the Microsoft Global Forum in Redmond. She has certified and coached students who competed at the Microsoft Office Specialist Championships in Texas. She has published five training manuals and courseware for the Microsoft Office Specialist Certification and the ICDL Foundation SA. She has presented at conferences and webinars for SchoolNet SA, hosted TeachMeets and MicrosoftMeets, and developed e-learning paths for the Microsoft Office suite of programs, owing to her interest in e-learning.

I would like to acknowledge the Packt staff, who have displayed nothing but professionalism, coupled with a supportive and collaborative work ethic throughout the various stages of this book. In particular, Karan Gupta (Acquisition Editor), with whom it has been an absolute pleasure working. Karan, thank you for initiating the first contact and going the extra mile for me with professional care to detail and making sure everything was running smoothly across different time zones, being available 24/7; and to Ruvika Rao (Content Development Editor), who has been my right-hand woman, hot on my heels supporting and keeping me in check. Your work ethic is impeccable and I have thoroughly enjoyed my interactions with you. I would also like to thank Prajakta Naik, Richa Tripathi, Aaron Lazar, and my reviewers, Ambarish Tarte and Omprakash Pandey, for their valuable input.

About the reviewers

Ambarish Tarte is a Mumbai-based Microsoft Certified Professional and a globetrotter who conducts corporate training for various corporate giants/multinational companies across the globe. With MS Office and Office 365 end user apps being his forte, he operates as a corporate training consultant with a team of associates in almost every major city. He began his corporate training stint in 2011 and has had the privilege of training delegates of over 20 nationalities in classroom and online sessions. Being able to add a bit of humor and always keep participants active during training is a unique selling point that Ambarish has developed over the years. Ambarish is also a YouTuber and runs various social media pages.

I thank my parents for their continued support during my stint so far as a corporate training consultant. Quitting a full-time job and moving into freelancing requires support from family, and my parents left no stone unturned in doing so. I would also like to thank Mr. Saiesh G Tripathi, my colleague, for his inputs. Thanks to Ms. Pooja Vaishnav, my protégé, for the initial screening of the chapters in this book.

Omprakash Pandey, a Microsoft 365 Consultant, has been working with industry experts to understand project requirements and work on the implementation of projects for the last 20 years. He has trained more than 50,000 aspiring developers and assisted in the development of more than 50 enterprise applications, which have been his key achievements. He has offered innovative solutions on .NET development, Microsoft Azure, and other technologies. He has worked for multiple clients across various locations including Hexaware, Accenture, Infosys, and many more. He has been a Microsoft Certified Trainer for more than 5 years.

I want to thank my parents and colleagues, Ashish and Francy, for their assistance and support.

Packt is searching for authors like you

If you're interested in becoming an author for Packt, please visit authors.packtpub.com and apply today. We have worked with thousands of developers and tech professionals, just like you, to help them share their insight with the global tech community. You can make a general application, apply for a specific hot topic that we are recruiting an author for, or submit your own idea.

Table of Contents

Preface

Learn Microsoft Office 2019 is a step-by-step comprehensive journey through the Office 2019 applications, which includes visual and detailed explanations of concepts and the opportunity to practice throughout using workplace examples. It contains full coverage of the latest version of the Microsoft Word, Excel, PowerPoint, Access, and Outlook suite of programs.

Before we turn our attention to the chapter details, let's consider the organization of the book. This book is a comprehensive guide containing six main parts, allowing the user to learn about the tools common to all Office applications. The parts include common tasks across all Microsoft Office 2019 applications, Word, PowerPoint, Excel, Access, and Outlook. You will definitely want to work through all parts of this book as it will provide you with a way to work more productively and learn everything you need to be proficient in the worlds of work, study, and home.

Who this book is for

The book is a step-by-step guide that assumes no prior knowledge, providing full coverage of the Office 2019 applications from the basics to analyzing data, including common challenges for working productively in the workplace or at home. Our audience is anyone who is willing to add valuable skills, whether as a complete starter or as someone looking to develop what they already know, to their professional development path. This book will ensure that the student is equipped with workplace skills, and would be useful for those undertaking certification exams in each of these applications. It will also suit the trainer, lecturer, or organization as a whole as it contains full coverage of Microsoft Word, Excel, PowerPoint, Access, and Outlook 2019.

What this book covers

Chapter 1, *Exploring the Interface and Formatting Elements*, will make it easy for you to create, manipulate, and work with documents using Microsoft Office 2019. You'll learn about the interface layout, ribbon elements, and how to customize the default behavior. We will delve into controlling font attributes, creating a style to speed up the file formatting process, changing the spacing of paragraphs, and looking at text alignment options. You will learn how to create and print professional-looking documents.

Chapter 2, *Creating Lists and Constructing Advanced Tables*, will teach you how to create bulleted, numbered, and tabbed lists using predefined or custom symbols and how to alter the layout of lists. You will be able to easily integrate tables in documents and to modify them in different ways. We will also cover some advanced features of table creation such as sorting operations, managing a table that spans multiple pages of a document, using formulas in a table, and converting text to a table.

Chapter 3, *Creating Professional Documents*, explains that Word 2019 includes an array of features that aid in creating attractive and professional documents. This chapter will teach you how to add references such as citations, a table of contents, and a bibliography, and perform a mail merge using different methods. We will construct a form using the Quick Parts feature, insert a cover page, and get to grips with navigation techniques and working with long documents. There is also a section on troubleshooting endnotes and footnotes, headers and footers, and links in a document.

Chapter 4, *Versions, Restrictions, and Comparisons*, explains all about setting editing restrictions and passwords on all or part of a document to prevent unwanted changes. After learning how to collaborate, we will compare and combine document revisions.

Chapter 5, *The PowerPoint Interface and Presentation Options*, teaches you how to personalize the Backstage view and set various options. You will navigate the interface and perform basic tasks, including creating, saving, printing, and viewing presentations in PowerPoint 2019.

Chapter 6, *Formatting Slides, Tables, Charts, and Graphic Elements*, explains how to easily add slides to a PowerPoint presentation and use predefined options to give the slides a particular *look and feel*. In this chapter, you'll learn how to set up a basic presentation, order a sequence of slides, apply a presentation theme and slide layout, and reuse slides. You will also learn how to work with tables and charts, which make data much easier to present and add to the impact of a presentation.

Chapter 7, *Photo Albums, Sections, and Show Tools*, covers how to set up a photo album, add photos and captions, and customize the order and appearance. You will also get to know how to navigate a presentation easily using sections and rename and remove sections in presentations. You'll learn how to set up and manage slide shows, control slide timing, and master the playback of audio narration. We also cover master slides, check the consistency throughout a presentation, and look at options for hiding or showing specific slides.

Chapter 8, *Formatting, Manipulating, and Presenting Data Visually*, shows how to personalize the Backstage view and set various spreadsheet options, and distinguish between spreadsheet elements. You will be taken on a journey through formatting elements to manipulate data, and will also learn how to print elements and set print options. You will learn how to enhance Excel 2019 with decorative, professional-looking charts such as the sunburst and funnel charts. You will gain all the skills you need to format, print, and present data professionally.

Chapter 9, *Applying Formulas and Functions*, explains how to create a formula and investigate the difference between a formula and a function. You'll also learn about operators and formula construction using the correct order of evaluation. After learning the different methods of constructing a formula, you will be introduced to a number of functions from different categories located in the function library. To end the chapter, we will highlight common formula errors and learn how to use named ranges in formula.

Chapter 10, *Analyzing and Organizing Data*, covers the tools that effectively analyze and organize data within Excel 2019. We will cover summarizing data using pivot tables and charts and how to access the Quick Analysis Tools, work with maps and the new 3D map feature, use Power Pivot to effectively build and use relational data sources inside an Excel workbook, consolidate workbook data by creating a summary sheet, build a relationship between datasets for easy reporting with Excel's data model, and take a look at macros.

Chapter 11, *Exporting and Optimizing Files and the Browser View*, teaches you how to export Office 2019 documents, presentations, and workbooks using different formats. We will compress images and optimize presentation compatibility with different systems. You will also save workbooks in comma-delimited format and work with Browser View.

Chapter 12, *Sharing and Protecting Files*, explains that Office 2019 includes several features for sharing and collaborating on documents, presentations, and worksheets. In this chapter, you'll learn how to share files via different share methods and locations. We will look at the Share with People option, saving files to OneDrive, the different methods of sharing directly through email using PDF, and the attachment options. We will also look at sharing options for Skype for Business and how to present online, as well as via email and blog post.

Chapter 13, *Database Organization and Setting Relationships*, introduces database theory and distinguishes between database objects such as tables, queries, forms, and reports, and explains how to switch between them. You'll learn how to organize your table data and properties to set primary keys, thereby forming relationships between objects in a database. You will gain an understanding of the different relationship types and when they should be applied, and learn the rules for setting relationships between two or more tables in a database.

Chapter 14, *Building Forms and Report Design*, takes you on a journey through the creation of forms and reports. We will enter, modify, and format data on a form using the different views and see the impact of deleting records. You will create and modify report design, work with different report view modes, create reports based on table or query, and master report headers and footers and manipulate controls.

Chapter 15, *Constructing Queries to Analyze Data*, is the heart of Access 2019. They allow you to search and extract information from tables for analysis. In this chapter, you will learn how to construct queries using the design view to analyze data, and you will become knowledgeable about the different query types and their function.

Chapter 16, *Creating and Attaching Item Content*, takes you through the important parts of the Outlook 2019 interface and shows you how to configure objects such as mail, contacts, tasks, notes, and journals. We will set some advanced options, learn how to manipulate item tags, and arrange the content pane. Search, print, and filter tools, as well as how to configure send and delivery options to improve productivity in the Outlook application, are also covered here. Lastly, we will professionally format item content and learn how to attach content to an email.

Chapter 17, *Managing Mail and Contacts*, introduces you to best practices while working with message attachments and to keep your mailbox clean and streamlined. You will learn how to set up rules and manage junk mail options and create or modify signatures within the Outlook application. This chapter will also teach you to be proficient at creating business cards for contacts, and you will learn how to set up and manage contacts and contact groups.

Chapter 18, *Calendar Objects, Tasks, Notes, and Journal Entries*, explains how to work with calendars, appointments, and events, as well as explaining how to set meeting response options and arrange calendars and calendar groups. You will work with tasks and find out how to assign them to other Outlook users, as well as tracking them via the status report tool. A section on journal entries is included, which allow you to create and track items such as telephone calls, tasks, and documents relating to a specific client along a timeline.

To get the most out of this book

You will need the Pro version of Microsoft Office 2019 to run the code for all the applications covered in this book, as well as access to a OneDrive account if you would like to take advantage of the online sharing and collaboration features of the suite.

Software/hardware covered in the book	OS requirements
Microsoft Office Professional 2019 or the following individual applications	Windows 10 or macOS
Microsoft Word 2019	Windows 10 or macOS
Microsoft PowerPoint 2019	Windows 10 or macOS
Microsoft Excel 2019	Windows 10 or macOS
Microsoft Access 2019	Windows 10 or macOS
Microsoft Outlook 2019	Windows 10 or macOS

Alternatively, you can get Office 365 with the relevant apps as listed in the preceding table.

Download the example code files

You can download the example code files for this book from your account at www.packt.com. If you purchased this book elsewhere, you can visit www.packtpub.com/support and register to have the files emailed directly to you.

You can download the code files by following these steps:

1. Log in or register at www.packt.com.
2. Select the **Support** tab.
3. Click on **Code Downloads**.
4. Enter the name of the book in the **Search** box and follow the onscreen instructions.

Once the file is downloaded, please make sure that you unzip or extract the folder using the latest version of:

- WinRAR/7-Zip for Windows
- Zipeg/iZip/UnRarX for Mac
- 7-Zip/PeaZip for Linux

The code bundle for the book is also hosted on GitHub at `https://github.com/PacktPublishing/Learn-Microsoft-Office-2019`. In case there's an update to the code, it will be updated on the existing GitHub repository.

We also have other code bundles from our rich catalog of books and videos available at `https://github.com/PacktPublishing/`. Check them out!

Code in Action

Code in Action videos for this book can be viewed at `https://bit.ly/2WpM7iY`.

Download the color images

We also provide a PDF file that has color images of the screenshots/diagrams used in this book. You can download it here: `https://static.packt-cdn.com/downloads/9781839217258_ColorImages.pdf`.

Conventions used

There are a number of text conventions used throughout this book.

`CodeInText`: Indicates code words in text, database table names, folder names, filenames, file extensions, pathnames, dummy URLs, user input, and Twitter handles. Here is an example: "Open the workbook called `SSGRegions.xlsx`."

Bold: Indicates a new term, an important word, or words that you see onscreen. For example, words in menus or dialog boxes appear in the text like this. Here is an example: "The **Function Arguments** dialog box will appear where the user is able to enter values as cell references to construct the formula."

 Warnings or important notes appear like this.

 Tips and tricks appear like this.

Get in touch

Feedback from our readers is always welcome.

General feedback: If you have questions about any aspect of this book, mention the book title in the subject of your message and email us at customercare@packtpub.com.

Errata: Although we have taken every care to ensure the accuracy of our content, mistakes do happen. If you have found a mistake in this book, we would be grateful if you would report this to us. Please visit www.packtpub.com/support/errata, selecting your book, clicking on the Errata Submission Form link, and entering the details.

Piracy: If you come across any illegal copies of our works in any form on the Internet, we would be grateful if you would provide us with the location address or website name. Please contact us at copyright@packt.com with a link to the material.

If you are interested in becoming an author: If there is a topic that you have expertise in and you are interested in either writing or contributing to a book, please visit authors.packtpub.com.

Reviews

Please leave a review. Once you have read and used this book, why not leave a review on the site that you purchased it from? Potential readers can then see and use your unbiased opinion to make purchase decisions, we at Packt can understand what you think about our products, and our authors can see your feedback on their book. Thank you!

For more information about Packt, please visit packt.com.

Section 1: Word

Microsoft Word 2019 is included in Microsoft's latest office desktop productivity suite, Microsoft Office 2019. This part of the book introduces end users to Word 2019, identifying its new features and demonstrating how to use it to create, format, and work with documents. You will cover everything you need to know to start using Word 2019 productively in the workplace, at home, or for certification purposes.

Beyond the basics, you will cover a range of tasks, from working with graphic elements and performing picture corrections to modifying tables and adding references, such as citations and a table of contents. This part of the book also covers the many ways that Word 2019 supports real-time collaboration and the sharing of documents.

Throughout, new features of the application will be highlighted for you, and you'll learn shortcuts to speed up everyday tasks. Once you reach the end of this content, you will have grown your knowledge and skills to an advanced level and will be a pro at creating Word 2019 documents.

In this section, we will cover the following chapters:

- Chapter 1, *Exploring the Interface and Formatting Elements*
- Chapter 2, *Creating Lists and Constructing Advanced Tables*
- Chapter 3, *Creating Professional Documents*
- Chapter 4, *Versions, Restrictions, and Comparisons*

1
Exploring the Interface and Formatting Elements

Welcome to the first chapter of *Learn Microsoft Office 2019*. This chapter will show you how to create, manipulate, and work with documents using Microsoft Word 2019. You'll learn about the interface layout and the ribbon elements, as well as how to customize the default behavior.

We will look at controlling the font attributes, creating a style to speed up the document formatting process, changing the spacing of paragraphs, and looking at the text alignment options. In addition, you will learn how to use Word 2019 to create, print, and review professional-looking documents.

The following list of topics is covered in this chapter:

- An overview of the interface features
- Creating and opening documents
- Selecting, rearranging, and duplicating text
- Setting the printing options
- Formatting text, styles, and paragraphs

The skills mentioned in this chapter are important for building up your confidence to work on the later chapters of this book.

The various interface features we will talk about span across all of the Microsoft Office suite applications and can be accessed and used using the same method shown for Word 2019.

Technical requirements

To understand the contents of this chapter, you should be able to locate and launch the Microsoft Office 2019 applications from the Windows environment.

To benefit from the contents of this book, it is imperative that you are able to follow along with and work through the examples demonstrated in each chapter. The examples used in this chapter can be accessed from `https://github.com/PacktPublishing/Learn-Microsoft-Office-2019`.

An overview of the interface features

In this overview, you will learn about the elements of the interface and be able to recognize some new features that have been incorporated into the latest update of the desktop versions of Word, PowerPoint, and Excel 2019.

This topic will focus on all three aforementioned applications. The reason for this is that most of their interface features and explanations are identical. Let's browse through the environment and learn about the different elements that make up Office 2019 applications.

The title bar

The title bar area is located at the very top of each program launched on the Windows environment. This bar displays the name of the file you currently have open. Normally, when you launch Microsoft Word, the blank page displayed is titled **Document1**. This means that you have not yet saved any elements that have been added to the document.

In the following screenshot, **Document7** is printed in the title area as this is the seventh blank document that I have opened (this is the same as using the seventh piece of paper from a notebook):

You need to save the current document to keep its changes. The title bar also houses the **Quick Access Toolbar** (**QAT**) and the program manipulation icons to the right of it.

The QAT

To the left of the title bar, you will find the QAT. This toolbar contains, by default, the save, undo, and redo icons. You can easily add frequently used icons to the QAT by clicking on the small arrow icon that is always present at the rightmost end of the QAT, as shown:

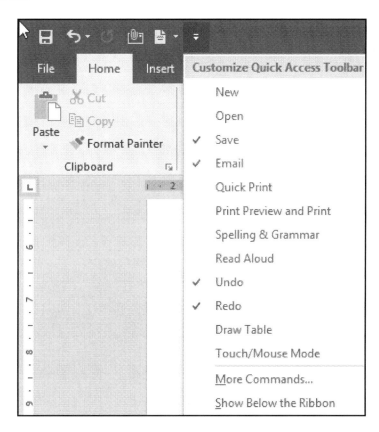

 Icons that already display a checkmark next to them indicate that the icon is already an option on the QAT. You simply have to click on the name of the shortcut that you want to add to the QAT.

You can select the **More Commands...** option, which opens a dialog box that allows you to search for any additional icons from the comprehensive list of Office 2019 commands. The **Show Below the Ribbon** option is used to change the location of the QAT to display it below the ribbon (just above the ruler bar).

Using tabs and groups

The tabs are a list of words that you can use to access the program functions. They are located just underneath the title bar and span the Office 2019 environment from left to right. These are similar to the file divider tabs that you would use in an office. There are quicker ways to complete simple tasks, either by right-clicking your mouse button or using shortcut keys, but you will always find more comprehensive options when using the tabs.

Simply click on a tab with your mouse pointer to make it active, then use the icons it offers. Familiarize yourself with the contents of each of the tabs. Knowing exactly where to go to perform a certain action in the program is of the utmost importance when taking any certification exam:

Double-clicking on a tab will collapse the groups underneath it. Simply double-click on the tab to return the groups.

You will find that when selecting a tab with a mouse click, various groups are defined on the ribbon via light separation lines that define boxes around groups of icons:

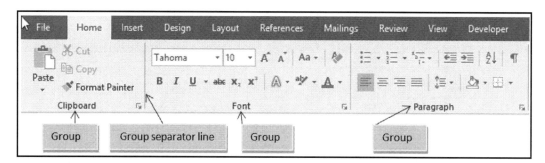

Most of the group sets in Office 2019 present a show dialog box arrow, where you can access more options relating to a group of related icons. For instance, to access the **Page Setup** dialog box within any of the Microsoft Office applications, click on the arrow, as shown:

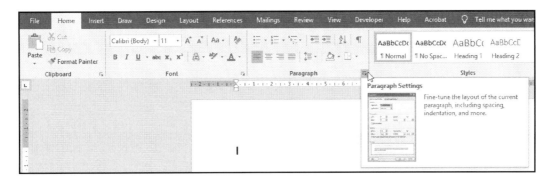

In the next section, we will look at how to access ribbon commands if your mouse stops working or you prefer using the keyboard.

Using shortcut keys to access the ribbon

Pressing the *Alt* key on your keyboard grants you access to the shortcut keys available for each of the tabs. If you look at the tab shortcuts available (see the following screenshot), you will see that the **Insert** tab shows **N** as the shortcut key:

If you press the *N* key on your keyboard, further shortcut keys will present themselves for each of the options available under that specific ribbon:

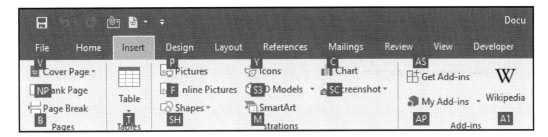

Using these shortcuts allows you to quickly access the various tabs and options without using the mouse.

Accessing the rulers

We use the ruler bars (vertical and horizontal) in Word 2019 to measure and set the distance between tabs, margins, the page layout, and the header and footer distances. You can adjust these settings using the mouse pointer or the relevant dialog box settings. Rulers can also be accessed on PowerPoint slides when you are working with bullet-pointed or numbered lists.

To remove or display the ruler bar, click on the **View** tab and then check or uncheck the checkmark option next to **Ruler**:

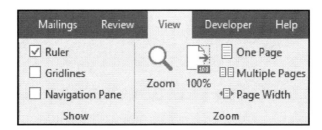

Minimizing the ribbon

To allow more space to work with documents, simply fold away or minimize the ribbon. This can be achieved in more than one way:

- Use the **Collapse the Ribbon** option (the tiny upward-facing arrow) to the right of the ribbon to hide everything on the ribbon except the tabs. If you click on a tab, it will unfold the ribbon options for that particular tab:

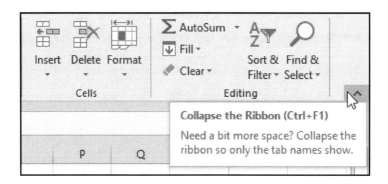

After selecting the desired options from the tab, take your focus back to the document by clicking back on the document. The ribbon will fold away again.

- To display the ribbon permanently, click on the ribbon display options icon to the left of the minimize icon on the title bar:

This drop-down list also allows you to auto-hide the ribbon and to only show the tabs. Alternatively, you can click on any tab to select it and then double-click on the tab heading to hide the ribbon; then, double-click on the tab heading again to un-hide the ribbon. The ribbon display options icon provides another method of auto-hiding the ribbon and showing the tabs and commands.

Adding items to the status bar

The status bar is located at the bottom of the Office 2019 environment. It displays information about the current file you are working on and provides quick access to some tasks. Right-clicking on the status bar provides you with a shortcut menu to make changes to it. You can add or remove items from the status bar:

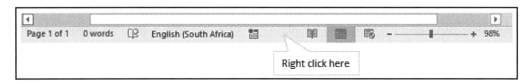

A tick to the left of an option identifies that it is already active. When we say *active* throughout this book, we mean *already selected, visible, or selected*. To add or remove an item from the status bar, simply click on the desired option in the shortcut menu:

Average, **Count**, and **Sum** are the default functions that reside on the status bar. They provide a result when selecting values on a worksheet in Excel 2019. To change how these values are calculated, right-click on them and select another function to perform. If you highlight a range of numerical values on a worksheet, Excel will display the count, sum, and average of those values on the status bar.

Using the help facility

Office 2019's help function can be accessed by pressing the *F1* keyboard key, which opens the **Help** pane to the right of the worksheet. You are able to select a topic of interest from the list provided, which offers further sub-topics until you find what you are looking for. Alternatively, you can search for a topic using the **Tell me what you want to do** feature located along the top of the ribbon at the end of the list of tabs:

1. Simply click to the right of the light bulb icon, located to the left of the empty placeholder (see the following screenshot).

2. Start typing a question and the feature will offer suggestions as you type:

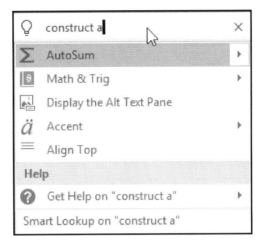

3. Click to select a topic from the drop-down list to obtain the help topic you require.

Now that we have learned how to navigate the user interface, let's learn how to create documents in the next section.

Creating documents

Opening, saving, closing, and creating new documents from templates are very similar procedures in each of the Microsoft Office 2019 applications. The Backstage view can be accessed via the **File** tab in each of the applications and requires the same steps to complete these tasks. The Backstage view is where files are managed in terms of creating, saving, printing, sharing, inspecting, and setting the interface options and properties.

In the following table, you will find the introductory steps to work with documents in Office 2019 applications:

Skill	Interface Navigation
Creating a new document	**File	New	Blank document**
Saving a document	**File	Save** or **File	Save As** (or press **Ctrl + S** on the keyboard) : • Navigate to the drive, location, or folder that your file resides in • Click on **OK** to save the document
Closing a document	**File	Close**
Creating a new document from a template	**File	New,** then select a template from the list provided, or search for templates online using the search box provided. Click to open the selected template.
Saving a document as a template	**File	Save As	Browse,** then select document template (*.dotx) from the **Save as type:** option. The folder will automatically update to the application template default. Click on **OK** to accept.
Opening saved documents	• **File	Open** • Navigate to the drive, location, or folder that your file resides in • Double–click to open the document
Closing a document	**File	Close** or click on the **X** located at the top right of the interface
Switch between open documents	Go to **View	Switch Windows**
Open a recent document	**File	Open	Recent,** then select the recent file from the list provided

A blank document in Word 2019 is a template with predefined fonts and attributes, as well as margins and page orientation settings. There are two blank document templates available—the single-spaced blank and the blank document options. The only difference between the blank document template and the single-spaced blank template in Word 2019 is the line spacing and paragraph spacing settings. Both documents are empty and have no text or objects added to them.

The following diagram displays the difference in file extensions when saving a document as a template compared to saving it as a document:

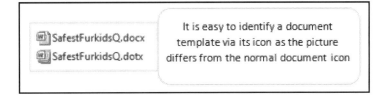

A template is a presentation with a predefined look and contains default text, layouts, and even animations. Templates are often used as a starting point for presentations, documents, and worksheets—especially in the 2019 version, as there are many professional animated effects, budgets, and reports available.

They have been created to suit the needs of the user and are often a quick way to get things done. The file extension for a template differs from that of a normal document. For instance, the file extension for a Word document is `.docx`, whereas the file extension for a Word template is `.dotx`.

When using Office 2019, you can search and download templates from the internet from within the application. Categories are available just below the search bar and guide the user when searching online. To search for templates online, you must have a working internet connection.

Setting the printing options

This section will show you how to select basic printing options for a document, specify pages to print, and set properties for a document prior to printing. There are numerous methods to achieve the same result in Word 2019. We will concentrate on the most productive methods when dealing with page setup.

Changing the page margins

1. Click on the **Layout** tab.
2. Click on the **Margins** icon located under the **Page Setup** group.

3. Select a format from the available predefined options (the default is the **Normal** setting):

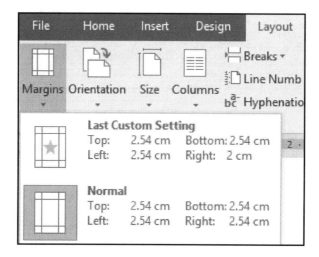

4. Click on **Custom Margins...** at the bottom of the list to control the adjustment of the margins.
5. Adjust the margins by typing a value into the placeholder or using the spin arrows to move up and down to increase or decrease the margins in centimeters.

Changing the page orientation

There are two types of page orientation—**Landscape** and **Portrait**. When you create a new document, the page orientation is set to **Portrait** by default. The **Landscape** option is often used to accommodate large tables in Word documents or Excel reports with numerous columns:

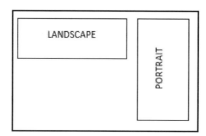

To change the orientation, follow these steps:

1. Click on the **Layout** tab in Word 2019, or the **Page Layout** tab if using Excel 2019.

2. Choose **Orientation,** then select the desired layout—either **Portrait** or **Landscape**:

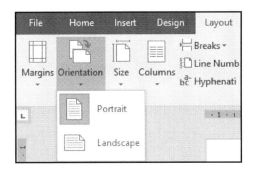

Changing the paper size

It is a good idea to check the paper size and make adjustments before creating or printing a document. Not doing so could lead to a number of formatting complications or problems when printing the document on the desired printer. Most printers use an A4 (210mm x 297mm) paper size and not **Letter**, as we will cover shortly. If your document does not print properly, always check this option first!

To change the paper size, follow these steps:

1. Click on the **Layout** tab. From the **Page Setup** group, click on the drop-down arrow below the **Size** text:

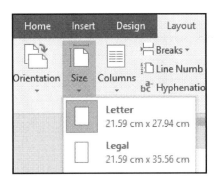

2. Choose the desired paper size from the list provided. In this case, we will choose an A4-sized paper. If you do not see your desired paper size in the list, choose **More Paper Sizes...** from the bottom of the list to access the **Page Setup** dialog box.

Changing the print options

Before printing a document, you should check the **Print Layout** view to see whether the page layout, margins, and document content looks professional:

1. Click on the **File** tab to access the Backstage view, then select **Print** from the options provided:

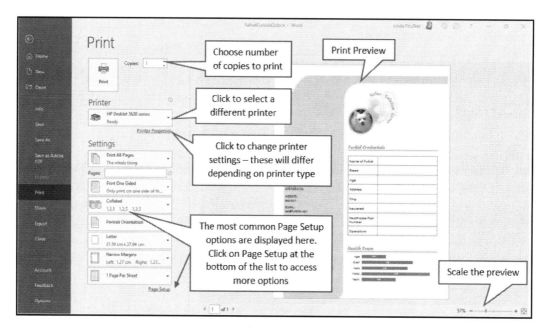

2. The settings on the **Print** backstage are the same in all of the Office applications, with only a few changes depending on whether you are printing a document, presentation, workbook, or worksheet. These are explained in the chapters dedicated to each topic throughout this book.

Setting the collate and page options

Collating is the sequence that you want multiple copies of a document to be printed in. For instance, if a document consists of six pages and you would like two copies of the document, you may wish to print page 1 of the document six times, then page 2, and so on. Alternatively, you may want to print pages 1 through 6 and then 1 through 6 again:

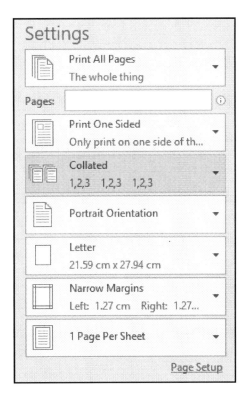

Go to the **Settings** option to instruct the document to print on both sides of the paper. This option can be accessed by selecting the drop-down arrow next to the **Print One Sided** heading. Select **Manually Print on Both Sides** from the list provided. You can also set options through the specific printer that you choose by going to the printer's options or by using the **Print** settings list, which can be accessed by going to **File | Print** within Word 2019.

Depending on the type of printer that is connected, the options will differ slightly, such as offering you the choice of printing automatically on both sides of the paper or even using different terminology for this feature, such as **duplex printing**.

Printing background colors and images

You can apply themes or include images to the background of your Microsoft Word documents. When printing documents with themes and images, you might notice that the background color or image doesn't print with the other document content. To fix this, follow these steps:

1. Go to **File | Options**.
2. From the **Options** dialog box, click on the **Display** heading.
3. Locate the **Printing options** heading and select **Print background colors and images**:

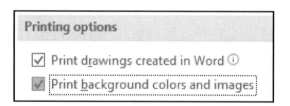

4. Click on **OK** to save the changes.

Setting pages to print

Often, you will need to fit more than one page from a document onto a landscape or portrait page. This option is great for booklet-, manual-, or brochure-type layouts. To select the number of pages to be included per sheet, go to the **Settings** section located at the bottom of the **Print Settings** list:

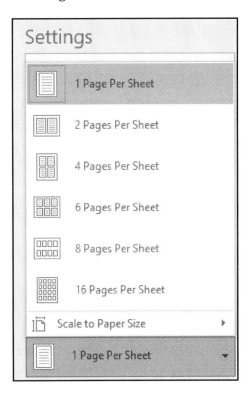

 Note that if you are using PowerPoint or Excel, the options will be slightly different.

Inserting page breaks

At times, headings (or the first line of a paragraph) end up at the end of a page. These headings or paragraphs might need to be forced to the top of the next page. If you need to leave space for a particular graphic or chart at the end of a page, you can force a break at the desired position in the document. You can insert a page break or a blank page at any point in a document by taking these steps:

1. Position the mouse pointer on the text that you want to force onto the next page. Alternatively, you can position your mouse at the start of the location where you want the space to be inserted:

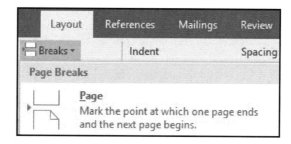

2. Click on the **Breaks** icon in the **Layout** tab or select the **Page Break** option from the **Insert** tab:

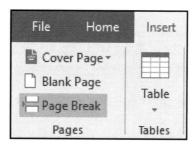

There is another method of inserting a forced page break via a keyboard shortcut key:

1. Place the mouse pointer at the desired position in the document where you want to include a break.
2. While holding down the *Ctrl* key on your keyboard, press the *Enter* key.

Formatting text, styles, and paragraphs

Formatting means changing the way your document looks. A character is a letter, number, or symbol that makes up the text of your document. We will look at the formatting of characters and paragraphs in this section.

To format text in a document, we can use the icons under the **Home** tab or the mini toolbar. Although you cannot edit through the mini toolbar, when select text in a document, it offers you the frequently used formatting options. If you rest your mouse pointer on the mini toolbar, it stays active. If you ignore it, the mini toolbar becomes transparent, disappears, then reappears when you next select some text to format:

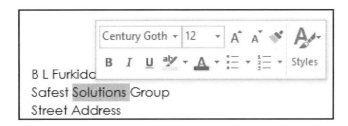

Remember that the icons in the ribbon can easily be identified by placing your mouse on the icon for a second. This presents a tooltip with a short description of the icon. We will investigate the various formatting options under the **Home** tab in the following section.

Basic text formatting

1. Select some text to format in your document.
2. Locate the **Font** group, then select the **Font** drop-down arrow.

3. A list will unfold, listing a number of fonts. Your frequently used fonts are listed near the top of the list. The list is in alphabetical order. Each font type presented in the drop-down list is written in that font, demonstrating how it will look. Select the desired font by selecting it with your mouse pointer. Alternatively, start typing the font name you want to use, then press *Enter* on your keyboard to apply it to the selected text:

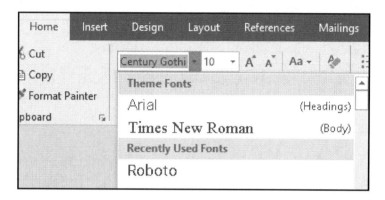

4. To select a point size to apply to the text, simply click on the tiny arrow just after the font face list. Choose a point size from the list provided or enter a font size of your own by typing it into the number placeholder provided. For example, you can type the size you require into the text area, replacing the size **11** font with size **13**. Don't forget to press *Enter* once you are done!

5. Next to the font size icon are two icons—one for increasing and the other for decreasing the font size. This is another quick method of changing the size of elements in a document:

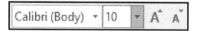

6. The bold attribute can be applied to make text bold by clicking on the bold icon on the toolbar. The procedure is the same for the italic and underline icons. By clicking on the drop-down arrow to the right of the underline icon, a list of underline styles will appear. There are also shortcut keys for all of these attributes, which are *Ctrl + B*, *Ctrl + I*, and *Ctrl + U*, respectively:

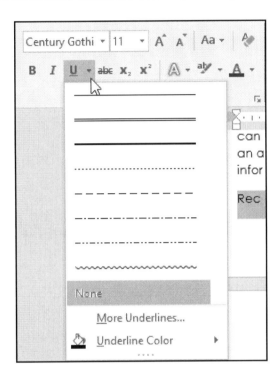

If you see that a formatting control (such as bold, italic, or underline) is selected, it means that the option is already active on the selected text or paragraphs in the document. To remove the formatting, simply select the paragraph or text that has the formatting applied to it and click on the relevant icon on the ribbon. Sometimes, there are multiple formats applied to the same selection in a document. If so, you will need to remove the formats from them individually. This concept works in much the same way as a light switch; you can switch it on and off using the same button.

Changing the font colors

1. Select some text and locate the font color icon on the toolbar:

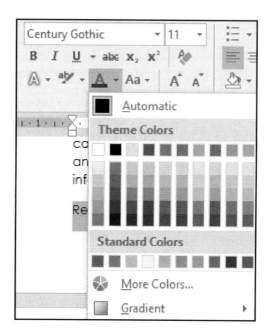

2. In the preceding screenshot, the **A** icon has a colored line directly below it. This indicates what the last selected font color was. If you select some text and then click on this icon, the selected document text will change to this color. The icon's line color is black by default. To change the color, click on the arrow next to the font color icon. A color palette will appear, where you can select a different color.

3. Click on the **More Colors...** option in the font drop-down list. A dialog box will appear, where you can select from a palette of additional colors:

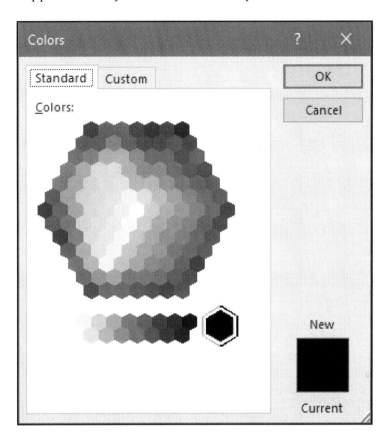

4. By clicking on the **Custom** option above the color wheel, you are able to select specific tones of color using either the **RGB** or **HSL** color models:

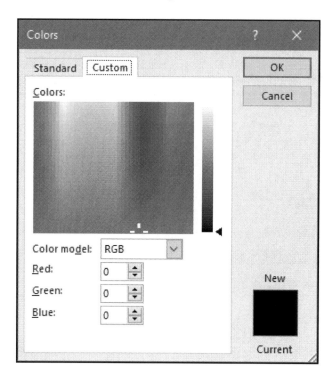

5. Once a specific shade of color is selected for a particular purpose, it is always a good idea to jot down the RGB color model numbers. This way, if you want to produce the exact same color again—for example, for some promotional material for a marketing brochure—you can type in the specific RGB colors into the relevant fields to get the same color. This is especially useful when working across multiple Office 2019 applications.

 To change a paragraph's fill color, use the fill bucket icon located under the **Paragraph** group. Apply the color to text or an entire paragraph by selecting the text. Alternatively, use the borders and shading icon, also located under the **Paragraph** group. Select the desired option in the **Apply To:** drop-down list box.

Adding text effects

The text effects and typography icon is located under the **Font** group. Simply click on the **A** icon to add some creativity to selected text or paragraph headings:

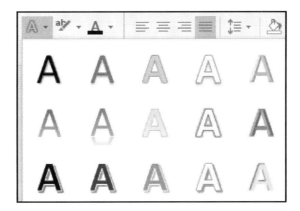

Removing text formatting

The clear all formatting icon is an excellent way of getting rid of multiple formats on selected text, as well as to return text to the plain default text:

1. Simply highlight the text that you wish to remove formatting from.
2. Click on the clear all formatting icon:

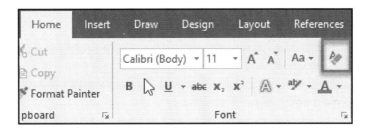

3. The text is now set to the normal font attributes.

Changing the casing of text

Word specifically provides an icon to change between different text case options. This icon is located under the **Home** tab, to the right of the increase and decrease font size icons:

1. Select some text or a paragraph.
2. From the **Home** tab, select the change case icon:

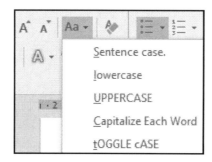

3. Select the case you would like to apply to the selected text or paragraph.
4. You can also use a shortcut key to cycle through the change case options. After selecting the text that you want to change to another case type, press the *Shift* key on your keyboard and hold it down while you press the *F3* function key (if you are using a laptop, you may need to press the *Shift* key, the *Fn* key, and the *F3* key together).

Copying multiple formats

The format painter tool allows you to copy multiple formats from selected text to other parts of a file. It is normally used to copy heading styles from one heading to another, which can save a huge amount of time instead of repeating formatting manually over and over on each individual heading:

1. Select some text to format.
2. Format the text—for instance, set it to bold or underline or change the font color to blue, the font size to **20**, or the font face to **Courgette**.
3. Make sure the text stays selected once the formatting is complete.
4. Double-click on the **Format Painter** icon located under the **Clipboard** group:

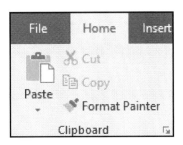

5. Double-clicking on the **Format Painter** icon allows you to copy the formatting more than once.

6. Notice that the mouse pointer changes to a brush shape when hovering over text in the document:

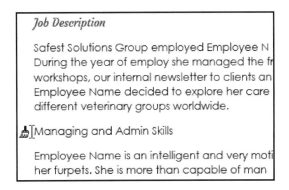

7. Select the next heading in the document to apply the format. Once this is complete, you will see that the text is now formatted in the same way as the first heading.

8. Repeat this process until each of your document headings have the new format.

9. To stop the format painter, simply put the icon back in place by clicking on the format painter icon on the ribbon. Alternatively, press the *Esc* key on your keyboard.

 The format painter icon is also available on the mini formatting toolbar.

Formatting using font attributes

Some character formats are not available through the toolbar icons. You will have to use the **Font** dialog box to access them:

1. Select the text you want to format.
2. Go to **Home | Font**, then click on the attributes below the **Effects** heading that you would like to add to the selected text:

Once you have altered the options in this dialog box, you will be able to preview the changes at the bottom of the dialog box. Be sure to go to the underlined options to see what options are available to enhance your document.

Changing the text alignment options

There are different types of alignment options in Word 2019. You will find each type located under the **Home** tab:

The alignment options are located under the **Paragraph** group, as shown. After applying each of the alignment types, you will see the following result:

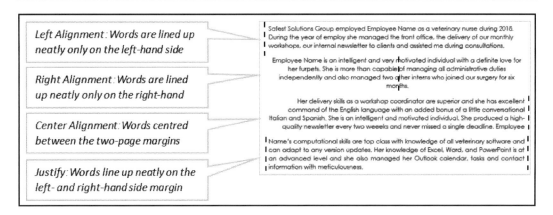

The justify option is very useful when you want to create professional documents to meet any legal formatting requirements.

Applying a drop cap

A drop cap is the inclusion of a large capital letter at the start of a paragraph. Dropped caps are usually found in children's storybooks:

1. Select the first letter of a word at the start of a paragraph.
2. Click to select the **Insert** tab, locate the **Text** group at the end of the ribbon, then click on the drop cap icon.
3. Choose a drop cap style to apply to the selected letter:

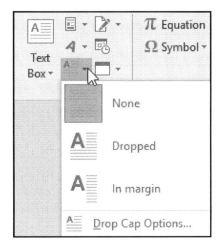

4. The drop cap is inserted into the document:

5. From the **Drop Cap Options…** option, you can edit the font face, line, or distance attributes.

Inserting special characters and symbols

1. Click at the end of a word or anywhere in a document where you need to place a symbol.
2. Click on the **Insert** tab, locate the **Symbol** group at the end of the **Insert** ribbon, then click on the drop-down arrow next to **Symbol**:

3. Your recently used symbols are listed in this list. To access more symbols, click on **More Symbols…** to populate the dialog box with a range of symbols:

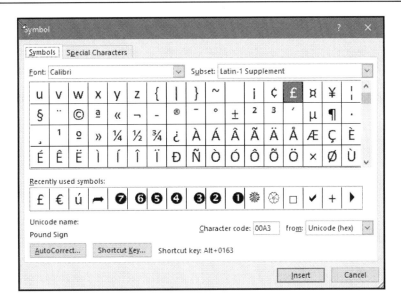

4. Click on a symbol that you wish to insert to the document. You can apply formatting options to symbols just as you would any other text.

5. Special characters allow you to insert different dash types, as well as commonly used characters such as the copyright, registered trademark, and trademark symbols:

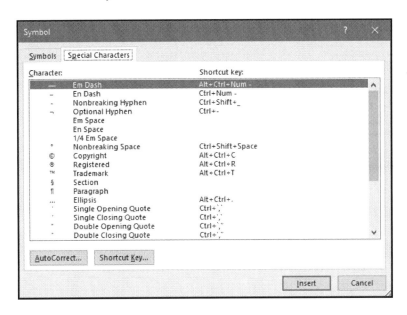

You can also use your keyboard to insert symbols to a Word document:

- To insert the copyright symbol, type (c) and you will get the © symbol.
- To insert the trademark symbol, type (tm) and you will get the ™ symbol.
- To insert the registered trademark, type (r) and you will get the ® symbol.

Indenting paragraphs

Indents are applied using various methods. The simplest method is to use the increase or decrease indent icon, which we highlighted earlier. Alternatively, you can use the ruler bar to manipulate indent icons along the ruler or go to the **Paragraph** dialog box to set indents.

On your ruler bar, you will find the indent button—it looks like an egg timer. We will use this indent button to create various types of indents in our document. Select a paragraph to indent, then click on the increase indent button in the **Paragraph** group:

- **First-line indent**: Select a paragraph to apply an indent to and drag the top slider of the egg timer to the position you want on the ruler bar:

> Safest Solutions Group employed Employee Name as a veterinary nurse during 2018. During the year of employ she managed the front office, the delivery of our monthly workshops, our internal newsletter to clients and assisted me during consultations. Employee Name decided to explore her career and spend a number of years at different veterinary groups worldwide.

- **Hanging indent**: Select a paragraph to apply an indent to and drag the hanging indent slider (the middle slider of the egg timer) to the position you want on the ruler bar:

> Employee Name is an intelligent and very motivated individual with a definite love for her furpets. She is more than capable of managing all administrative duties independently and also managed two other interns who joined our surgery for six months.

- **Left indent**: Select a paragraph to apply an indent to and drag the left indent marker (the entire egg timer) to the desired position on the ruler:

Her delivery skills as a workshop coordinator are superior and she has excellent command of the English language with an added bonus of a little conversational Italian and Spanish. She is an intelligent and motivated individual. She produced a high-quality newsletter every two weeks and never missed a single deadline.

- **Right indent**: Select a paragraph to apply an indent to and drag the right indent marker to the desired position on the ruler:

Employee Name's computational skills are top class with knowledge of all veterinary software and can adapt to any version updates. Her knowledge of Excel, Word, and PowerPoint is at an advanced level and she also managed her Outlook calendar, tasks and contact information with meticulousness.

Although it is not that important to check whether the indents are positioned at the correct position on the ruler, we need it to be accurate in the certification exam. Therefore, it is imperative that you go to the **Paragraph** dialog box and set indents with accurate measurements:

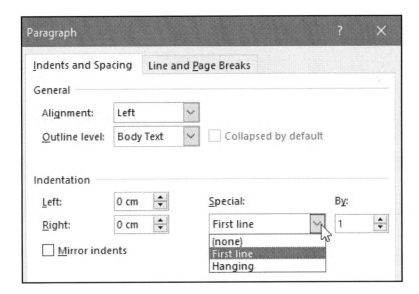

Setting spacing before or after a paragraph

You might want to automatically increase or decrease the amount of space before or after a paragraph so that the document looks consistent and flows easily. This is especially important when typing a thesis. The secret is not to format the document beforehand so that the result is consistent.

Remember that this option replaces a certain point size of space either before or after each paragraph marker. Every time you press the *Enter* key after a heading or a paragraph of text, Word automatically adds a certain amount of space either before or after the new paragraph. The amount of space it inserts is controlled by the space before or space after settings.

Follow these easy steps to set the spacing:

1. Highlight the paragraphs you want to apply the spacing to.
2. To apply or remove the spacing, use the line and paragraph spacing drop-down icon. Select the desired option at the bottom of the list. Don't add spaces between paragraphs of the same style.
3. To control the amount of space you would like either in front of or after a paragraph, go to the **Paragraph** dialog box. Right-click on the selected text and choose **Paragraph...**:

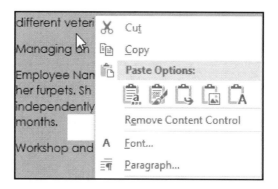

4. The **Paragraph** formatting dialog opens.
5. In the **Spacing** section, adjust the paragraph spacing options as desired by clicking with the mouse pointer on the up arrow next to the **Before:** option. In the case of the preceding example, we used **6 pt** before the paragraphs.

6. Add **6 pt** of blank space to the **After:** field.
7. Click on **OK** to save the change. Note the changes.

Here, we can see these changes applied to the preceding example paragraph:

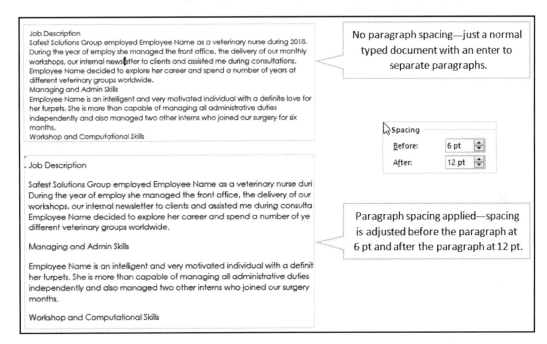

If styles have been applied throughout a document when formatting, it is important not to add a space between paragraphs of the same style. To explain further, if I applied **18 pt** of spacing (after each paragraph) to the entire document but do not wish to add any extra space after all the main headings (which I have used the **Heading 1** style for), then this option comes in handy. Adding a checkmark to this option prevents space from being added after all the **Heading 1** styles in the document:

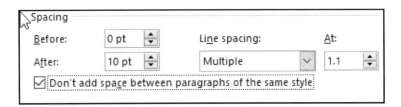

Adjusting the line spacing

To set the line spacing, try one of the following methods:

1. Click on the paragraph that you would like to set the line spacing for.
2. Click on the **Paragraph** dialog launcher to the right of the **Paragraph** group.
3. Locate the **Line Spacing** drop-down list to select the desired spacing:

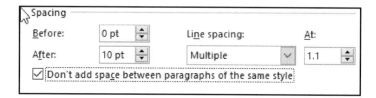

Alternatively, you can either press *Ctrl + 5* on your keyboard to set the line spacing to 5 lines, *Ctrl + 2* for double-line spacing, or *Ctrl + 1* to return it to single-line spacing. You could also use the line spacing icon in the formatting toolbar to change the line spacing.

Creating a new style

Word 2019 also offers styles, which are a named set of formatting conditions to help you create a consistent-looking document, which is especially useful for documents with more than one page. Instead of having to apply multiple attributes, such as the color, size, font, spacing, and alignment, separately on each part of your document, Word offers predefined collections of attributes that can be quickly applied to parts of your document.

The existing styles in the Word 2019 environment are located under the **Home** tab. **Title**, **Heading 1**, **Heading 2**, and **Heading 3** are the most popular options. You will also see the **Normal** style in the **Styles** drop-down list:

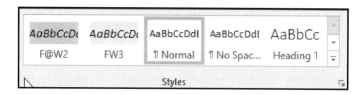

1. Select some text in the document and format the text, choosing the formats of your choice (for example, underline, dark blue color, size **12**, and the **Courgette** font type):

2. With your selected text still highlighted, click on the drop-down arrow of the **Styles** group and select **Create a Style**:

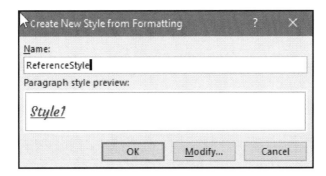

3. A dialog box will appear asking you to name the style:

4. Click on **Modify...** to access more options relating to the style.

5. Click **OK** to save the style to the gallery:

6. The new style is now visible in the **Styles** group and you can apply it to other headings or text throughout your document.

Modifying a style

At some stage, you may need to update a style, such as with a different font attribute. There are a few ways to do this. We will cover the most efficient method here:

1. Select the text in the document that already has the style applied to it.
2. Make the formatting changes to the text.
3. With the text still selected, right-click on the existing style name in the **Styles** group.
4. Click on **Update ReferenceStyle to Match Selection** (**ReferenceStyle** is the name that we chose for the style earlier):

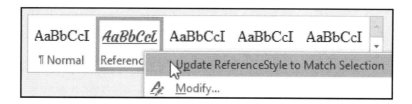

5. The style is updated to include the changes. The beauty of this tool is that any text that has the old style applied to it in the document will update automatically!

Summary

In this chapter, you learned the skills required to carry out basic tasks on Microsoft Word 2019. Although these seem very basic, they are important foundational skills to build further skills on as you work through the following chapters of this book.

The next chapter focuses on the creation of bulleted, numbered, and tabular lists. We will look at predefined or custom symbols and layouts. You will learn how to easily incorporate tables into documents and look at lots of formatting options. We will also cover some advanced features of table creation, such as sorting and converting options and how to use formulas in a table.

2
Creating Lists and Constructing Advanced Tables

In this chapter, you will be taught how to create bulleted, numbered, and tabbed lists using predefined or custom symbols, and how to alter list layout. You will be able to easily integrate tables in documents and modify them in different ways. We will also cover some advanced features of table creation such as sorting operations, managing a table that spans multiple pages of a document, using formulas in a table, and converting text to a table.

The following list of topics are covered in this chapter:

- Creating bulleted and numbered lists
- Working with tabbed lists
- Creating tables
- Editing and formatting tables
- Customizing advanced tables

Technical requirements

Prior to working through this chapter, you should be able to navigate around the Word 2019 interface, with knowledge of the parts of the screen such as the ribbon, groups, tabs, and icons. Being able to select relevant ribbon icons and being familiar with the use of the right-click shortcut menu to access formatting options is also a prerequisite.

The examples used in this chapter are accessible by visiting the following GitHub URL: `https://github.com/PacktPublishing/Learn-Microsoft-Office-2019`.

Creating bulleted and numbered lists

You will learn how to use predefined or custom bulleted lists and customize list number formats, and become a pro at working with multilevel lists. In this section, we will also work with the new math feature called **LaTeX** (short for **Lamport's TeX**).

Bulleted and numbered lists are applied to points, facts, paragraphs, or headings in documents. You can change the symbol of any characters used in a numbered or bulleted list, as illustrated in the following screenshot:

• Communication	A. Communication		
• Decision-making	B. Decision-making		
• Leadership	C. Leadership		
• Persuade, Influence and Negotiate	D. Persuade, Influence and Negotiate		
• Problem-solving and analytical skills	E. Problem-solving and analytical skills		
• Work as a Team	F. Work as a Team		
• Effective Time Management	G. Effective Time Management		
1. Communication	✓ Communication		
2. Decision-making	✓ Decision-making		
3. Leadership	✓ Leadership		
4. Persuade, Influence and Negotiate	✓ Persuade, Influence and Negotiate		
5. Problem-solving and analytical skills	✓ Problem-solving and analytical skills		
6. Work as a Team	✓ Work as a Team		
7. Effective Time Management	✓ Effective Time Management		

Numbered or bulleted lists can also be inserted into textboxes and shapes and other objects, such as tables.

Constructing a list automatically

Microsoft Word uses the **AutoFormat** feature to automatically construct bulleted or numbered lists as you type. This default setting can be disabled in the **Options** dialog box (shown later as we progress).

For numbered lists, type a 1, followed by a period, and add a space using your spacebar to automatically achieve the start of a numbered list, as shown here:

For bulleted lists, type an asterisk * followed by a space to automatically achieve the start of a bulleted list, as shown here:

Editing AutoFormat Options

It is important to know how Word 2019 works and where to adjust options within the environment. The **AutoFormat** option is located in the Word **Options** dialog box. Let's have a look at where the **Replace text as you type** option is located for bulleted and numbered lists, as follows:

1. Create a new document, or open an existing document in Word 2019.
2. Click on **File | Options**.
3. Choose the **Proofing** category on the left of the screen, as illustrated in the following screenshot:

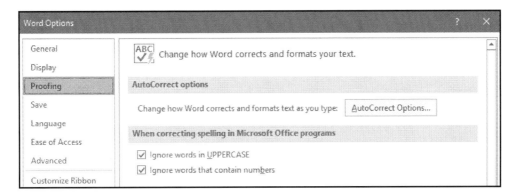

4. Click on the **AutoCorrect Options...** button to change how Word corrects and formats text as you type.

5. There are numerous tabs displayed in the **AutoCorrect** dialog box. These contain lots of options that allow you to customize the environment efficiently. Select the **AutoFormat As You Type** tab, shown in the following screenshot:

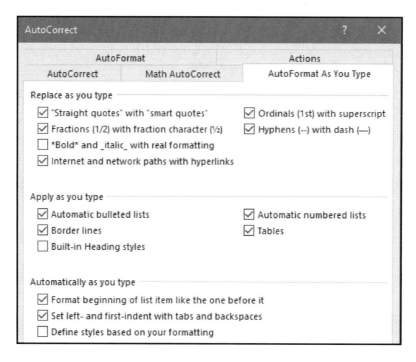

6. The options that enable automatic bulleted and numbered lists are located under the **Apply as you type** section. These are enabled, as they contain a checkmark. If you disable these two options, automatic lists will not be created as you type in Word 2019.

If any changes are made to these options, you will need to commit the changes by clicking on the **OK** button at the very bottom of the dialog box.

 Note that when changing options in the Word environment, the changes replace the default settings in the whole of the Word 2019 environment and not just for the current document.

Constructing a list manually

There are various ways to set up a bulleted or numbered list, either by typing the text first and then converting the list into a specific list type or by choosing the list type first and then beginning typing. Let's learn how, as follows:

1. Type the list shown in the following screenshot (or another list of your choice), making sure to press *Enter* at the end of each line (so that it takes you to the next line). Select the typed list, as follows:

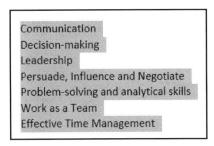

2. Choose the type of list to apply to the text by selecting the relevant icon from the **Paragraph** group, located on the **Home** tab, as illustrated in the following screenshot:

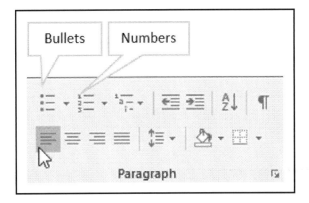

Once you have finished typing a numbered or bulleted list and would like to continue typing normally, just press the *Enter* key twice on the keyboard, and the numbering will discontinue.

Modifying a bulleted or numbered list

It is possible to customize a list by selecting different bullet styles and number sequences, and even adjusting list font types and sizes, by doing the following:

1. Select the typed list or position the mouse pointer onto the document.
2. Right-click with the mouse pointer over the selected list and choose the bulleted or numbered icon from the mini toolbar presented, as illustrated in the following screenshot:

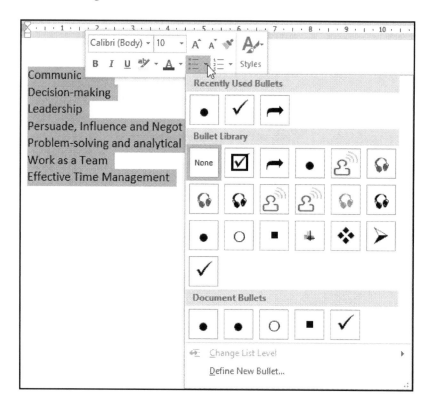

Alternatively, navigate to the ribbon to locate either the bulleted or numbered icon from the **Paragraph** group, as illustrated in the following screenshot:

3. Depending on the type of list you would like to create, select the tiny arrow to the right of the relevant icon to access the options available.

4. You can choose a bulleted or numbered list from the recently used list, the library, or the bullets used throughout the current document, or you can define a completely new bulleted or numbered list.

 Remember that you can set options prior to or after typing a list.

In the next few subsections, we will have a look at the options available for defining and customizing a bulleted list.

Defining a new bullet symbol

Let's see how we can change the appearance of the bullet, as follows:

1. At the bottom of the bullet drop-down list, select **Define New Bullet...** .
2. In the **Define New Bullet** dialog box, select the **Symbol...** button under the **Bullet character** heading, as illustrated in the following screenshot:

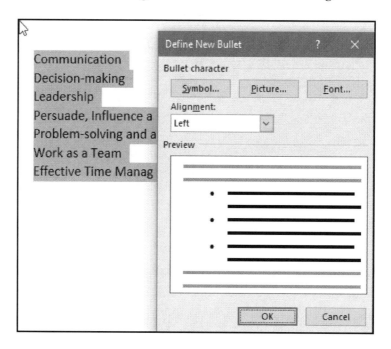

3. Scroll through the **Font:** drop-down list to select a font face. The most popular bullet fonts are **Webdings**, **Wingdings**, **Wingdings 2**, and **Wingdings 3**, shown in the following screenshot:

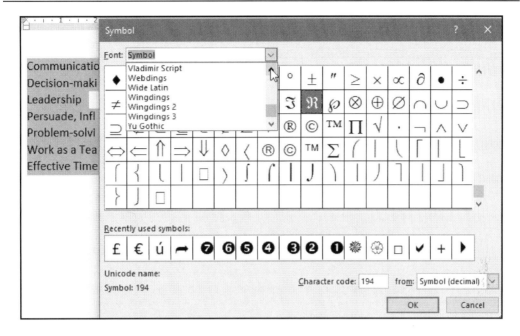

4. Browse the symbols, and choose an appropriate symbol to insert as your bulleted list icon.

5. Click on the **OK** button to commit the changes, and return to the **Define New Bullet** dialog box.

6. Click on the **OK** button again to apply the selection to the bulleted list, which should then look like this:

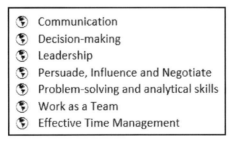

For illustration purposes, we have used **Webdings** as our bullet font in the previous screenshot.

Editing bulleted list font attributes

After a symbol has been applied to text in a document, you might find that the symbol is too small to be seen or not in alignment with the adjacent text. This is very easy to adjust using the font attributes, as detailed here:

1. Select the bulleted list.
2. Click on the drop-down arrow to the right of the bullet icon in the **Home** tab.
3. Click on **Define New Bullet...** .
4. Click on the **Font...** button, as illustrated in the following screenshot:

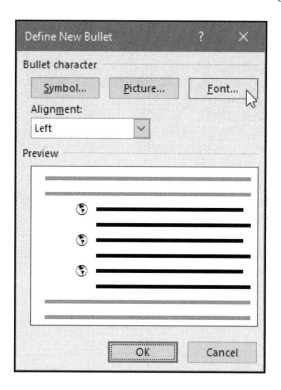

5. Use the **Font** dialog box to alter the font color, size, and other attributes to suit your bulleted list, as illustrated in the following screenshot:

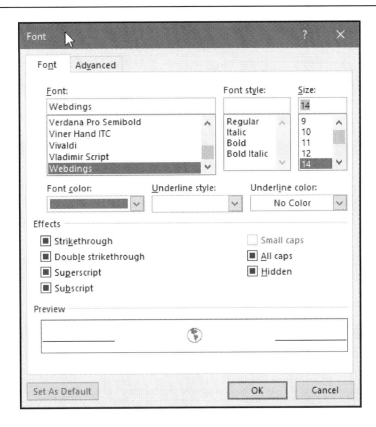

6. Click on the **OK** button to commit the changes, resulting in the following bulleted list:

Inserting a custom picture as a bullet

It is possible to use a company logo or a specific image as a symbol for the bulleted list. Follow these steps to add that extra creative flair to boring lists:

1. Highlight an entire bulleted list to apply bullets to, or start a new list.

2. Click on the drop-down arrow to the right of the bullet icon in the **Home** tab.

3. Click on **Define New Bullet…** .

4. Select the **Picture...** button to peruse the **Insert Picture** options, as shown in the following screenshot:

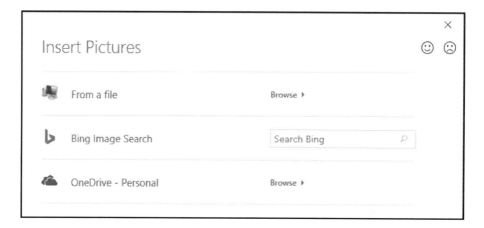

5. The dialog box that populates allows three options. The first option is to browse the computer to locate an image; the second, to conduct an online **Bing Image Search**; and the third, to select an image from a `OneDrive - Personal` folder.

6. For this example, select **From a file**.

7. Browse to select the folder that contains the image you wish to use for the bulleted list.

8. Double-click on the image to insert as a bulleted list, or select the image and click on the **Insert** button, and click **OK**.

Working with multilevel lists

A multilevel list has more than one level. This type of list allows you to keep control of chapter numbers, headings, and subheadings in a document. Multilevel lists can include bullets or numbers. Multilevel list is located just to the right of the other list icons located under the **Paragraph** group, as illustrated in the following screenshot:

Here is an example of an outline (multilevel numbered list) and how to get from one list level to another, using the mouse. Alternatively, type the list prior to converting to a numbered list, and then apply the numbered list format of your choice:

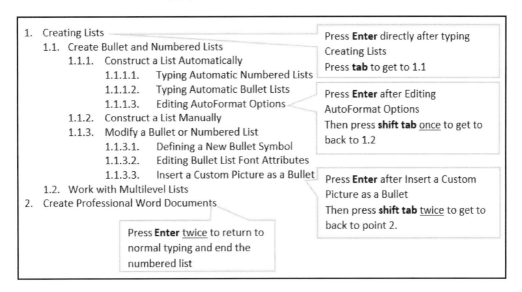

 Use the Increase Indent and Decrease Indent icons on the **Home** tab, under the **Paragraph** group, to promote and demote list levels. The **Change List Level** option at the bottom of the drop-down list (see the next screenshot) is another way to increase or decrease levels.

Creating a multilevel list

There are two ways in which we can approach the creation of a multilevel list, and these are detailed next.

Creating an outline (multilevel list) before typing a list

1. Create a new document or select an existing document to construct a multilevel list.
2. Select the **Home** tab and choose the multilevel list icon in the **Paragraph** group.

3. Select a style from the **List Library**, as illustrated in the following screenshot:

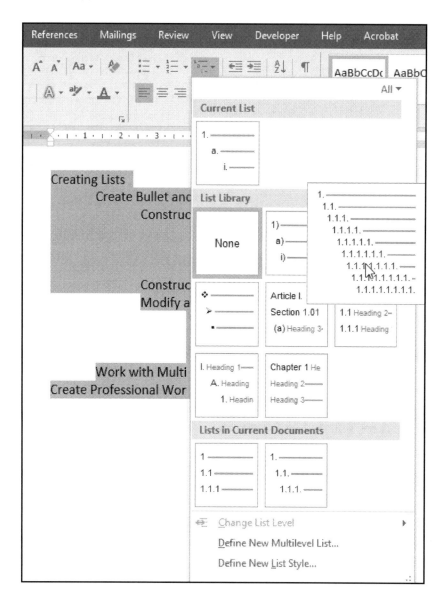

4. Type the first line of list text, and press *Enter*.
5. Use the *Tab* key on the keyboard to go to the next numbered level, or press *Shift* + *Tab* to return to the previous level.

6. Once the list is complete, press *Enter* twice on the keyboard to return to normal typing.

If your list is not looking quite as you envisaged, you will need to tweak the list by adjusting indents. The best way to do this is to select a level of your list and use the ruler to change either the left or hanging indent increments.

Creating an outline (multilevel list) after typing a list

It is beneficial to type a list using tabs to denote one level from another, before selecting the list type from the multilevel list options. At times, lists can cause a few hurdles, but if you follow the general guidelines in this section, you will become a whiz at multilevel list creation. Proceed as follows:

1. Create a new document, or open an existing document in which to insert a multilevel list.

2. When typing up a multilevel list, you will use tabs to specify the list level, and use the *Enter* key at the end of each line (see the following list example).

3. For the purpose of indicating where tabs (arrows) and paragraph markers (use of the *Enter* key) have been inserted in the document, the **Show/Hide** icon has been activated for the example shown in the following screenshot:

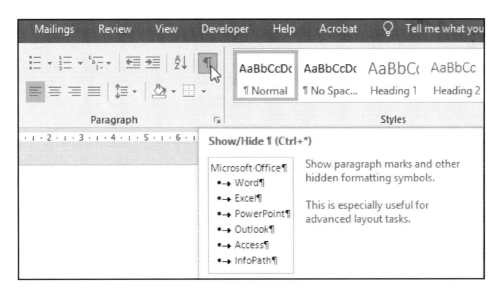

4. Type the list, as in the following example:

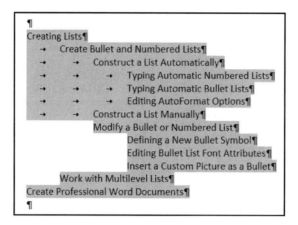

5. Be sure to highlight the entire list before converting it to a multilevel list.
6. Click on the multilevel list icon residing in the **Paragraph** group, as illustrated in the following screenshot:

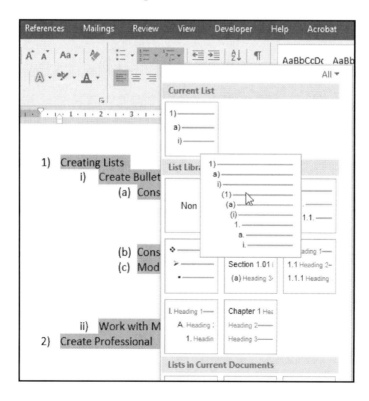

7. Select a style to apply to the highlighted list.

Removing a multilevel list

Removing a multilevel list from the text is really simple. Always make sure that you have highlighted the list prior to clicking on any paragraph icons to remove the list format. There are two methods, described as follows:

- The first is to use the numbered list icon (note that it is highlighted in the following screenshot, which means it is active). Click on the numbered list icon to return the list to normal type, as illustrated here:

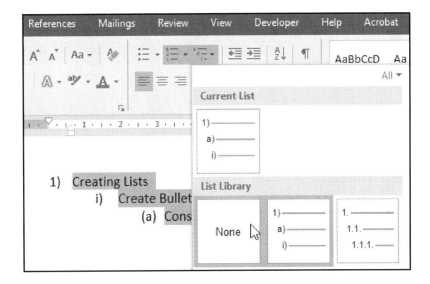

- The second method is to visit the multilevel list icon and to select **None** from the options displayed.

Restarting numbering for a new list

Scenario: You have typed a list in a document and formatted it as a multilevel or numbered list, or the document you have received from a colleague already has a numbered list set up. You would like to insert a new list directly underneath the list or at any point in the document. Word will automatically continue the numbering sequence on the new list, but you want to restart the numbering from your insertion point.

Let's see how we can do this, as follows:

1. Start a new list by choosing the numbered or multilevel list icon.
2. Let's say you notice that a **3)** appears instead of a **1)** to start the new list.
3. Right-click next to the **3)** and choose **Restart at 1** from the shortcut menu provided. Alternatively, you can choose **Set Numbering Value...** and choose a number to set your list to start at, as illustrated in the following screenshot:

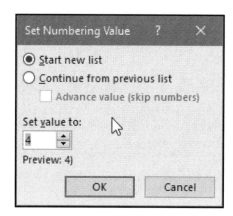

4. Click on the **OK** button to commit the change.

LaTeX math

LaTeX is a new feature in Office 2019. This feature, available at the end of the **Insert** tab on the Word 2019 ribbon, allows the user to build up LaTeX expressions in a professional format. There are a number of LaTeX expressions that are supported in Word 2019, such as vectors, boxed formula, brackets, brackets with separators, fractions, LeftSubSup, limit, matrix, nary, over/underbar, and radicals.

To construct a formula using LaTeX math, follow these steps:

1. Click on the **Insert** tab.
2. From the **Symbols** group, select **Equation**.
3. Type the LaTeX equation into the equation field provided, as illustrated in the following screenshot. You can paste an equation into the field, if you prefer, or select the LaTeX conversion icon (see the following screenshot), and then build your equation:

4. For this example, we will paste a LaTeX equation into the field provided, as illustrated in the following screenshot:

5. Click on **Convert** to access the **Professional** equation format, as illustrated in the following screenshot:

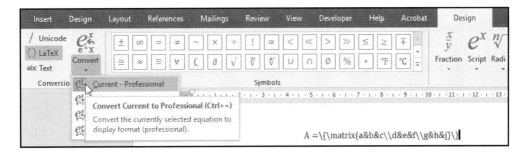

6. The **Professional** equation format is now displayed—note than you can also use the drop-down arrow to the right of the equation to change the equation format, as illustrated in the following screenshot:

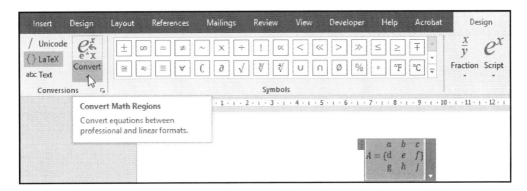

Working with tabbed lists

In this topic, we will create and adjust a tabbed list, create an aligned tabbed list, and learn how to delete or replace list tabs. When you press the *Tab* key on the keyboard, the computer automatically jumps to a certain position on the page. This position is termed the **tab stop** position and is automatically set to jump at 1.27-cm intervals when pressing the *Tab* key on the keyboard.

Sometimes, you may need to create a wider or smaller gap between tabs. Tabs are great to line up lists of things on a page. The default alignment of tabs is set to *left-align*. On the ruler bar, you have access to different tab types, which aids the user in lining up text.

The following is an example of why we need to use tabbed lists to line up text. We should never use spaces to line up items in a list as this would be a disaster if we decided to change the font face or font size, as the list would all jumble up.

Let's look at the following example:

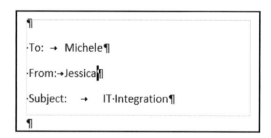

This list does not look professional as the **Subject** tab has pushed the text over too far. Therefore, we need to adjust the tab spacing so that we are able to align our list correctly. From the following screenshot, you will see that the tabs are indicated by arrows pointing to the right. These are visible only when the **Show/Hide** icon is selected to show markers in your document:

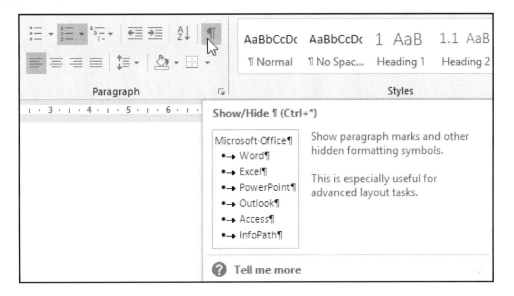

Every time the *Tab* key on the keyboard is pressed, an arrow appears in the document as a tab marker. Let's learn how to correct the list so that it lines up correctly, by following these steps:

1. Highlight the list.
2. Move your mouse to the **3** cm mark on the ruler and click.
3. A left tab marker appears on the ruler and the list is now in line, as illustrated in the following screenshot:

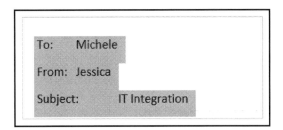

If you feel that the spacing between the document text is too small or large, you can adjust this by dragging the tab marker along the ruler to the desired position.

Selecting tab types

The **Tabs** dialog box is another method to work with tabs, giving the user many more options and the ability to set exact measurements for professional documents.

1. To access the **Tabs** dialog box, double-click on a tab indent marker on the ruler, as illustrated in the following screenshot:

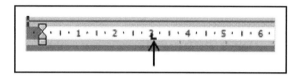

Or click on the **Paragraph** dialog box launcher located in the **Paragraph** group, as illustrated in the following screenshot:

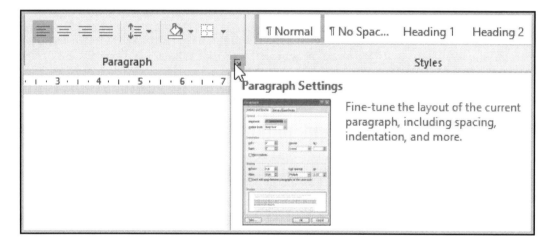

2. Click on the **Tabs...** button located at the bottom of the **Paragraph** box to access the **Tabs** dialog box, as illustrated in the following screenshot:

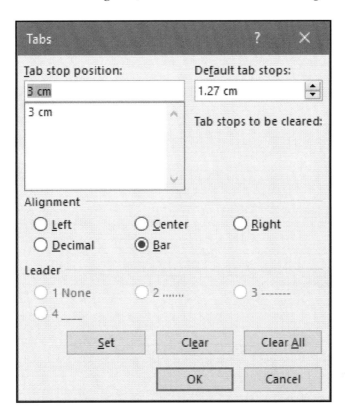

3. Note that the default tab stop is at **1.27 cm**, as per the preceding screenshot, and we have five types of alignments. Let's have a look at how each type of tab alignment appears in Word 2019, illustrated in the following screenshot:

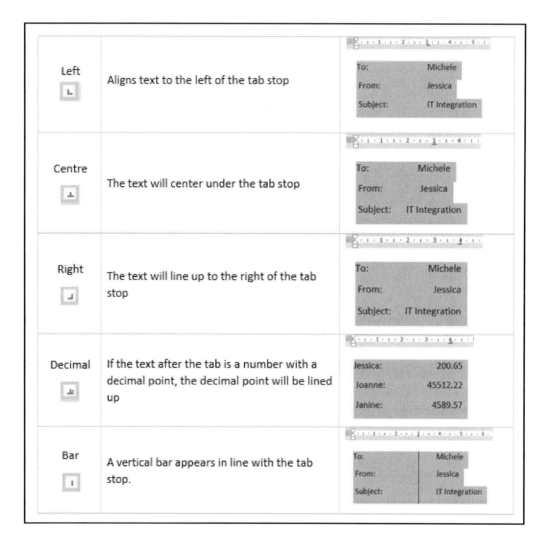

Typing a new tabbed list

There are two ways to set tabs when typing a list. Type the list first or set tabs, and then type the list thereafter:

1. Create a new Word document and type up the following list:

Fruit	Carbohydrates	Fats	Protein
Banana	Potatoes	Butter	Pork
Apple	Rice	Oil	Steak
Peach	Pasta	Avocado	Beef
Strawberry	Lentils	Margarine	Chicken

2. Be sure to press the *Tab* key on the keyboard only once after each word typed. If you are not sure whether you have done this correctly, click on the **Show/Hide** icon (in the **Paragraph** group on the **Home** tab) to show the tab markers in the document (demonstrated earlier), as illustrated in the following screenshot:

Banana·Potatoes   →   Butter→Pork¶

Apple→ Rice → Oil →   Steak¶

Peach→ Pasta → Avocado   →   Beef¶

Strawberry → Lentils→Margarine → Chicken¶

This way, you can see if you have more than one tab marker between each piece of text. If so, just delete one of the markers by using the *Backspace* or *Delete* key on the keyboard. Don't be concerned if the typing looks untidy, as in the preceding list!

1. Select (highlight) the list you have just typed.
2. Set tabs at the following positions on the ruler bar, using your method of choice:

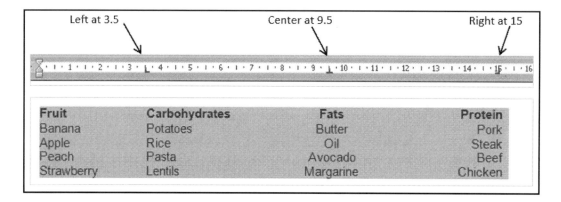

 To move a tab stop position, click on the marker on the ribbon and move it with the left mouse button along the ruler to a new position OR access the **Tabs** dialog box, clear the old position, and enter a new tab.

Creating a list using the leader dot tab

Have you ever needed to type a list that consists of leader dots—dots that separate, for instance, a name and a telephone number, or an item and a value? This topic will go through the steps to create a list using the leader dot tab.

1. Type the name of a staff member, a child in class, or a client to the left of a new document in Word 2019.
2. Locate the **Tabs** dialog box.
3. Set the following options in the **Tabs** dialog box: **Tab stop position: 15**; **Alignment**: **Left**; **Leader**: **2……..**, demonstrated in the following screenshot:

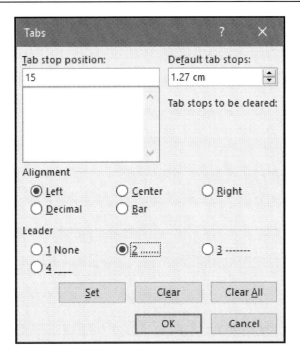

4. Click on the **Set** icon.
5. Click on **OK** to confirm, and exit the **Tabs** dialog box.
6. Position the mouse pointer directly after the name of the person.
7. Press the *Tab* key on the keyboard. Once you have done this, a leader dot tab will appear, as in the following example:

Margorie Meadows ....

8. Type the birth date of the first child, or a telephone number or an amount, and press *Enter*. The result is shown in the following screenshot:

Margorie Meadows 27
September 2019

Is your birth date wrapping to the next line, as in the preceding example? If so, here is how you fix it:

9. Click on the birth date.
10. Launch the **Tabs** dialog box.
11. Click on the tab stop in the box below **Tab stop position**.
12. Change the **Alignment** option to **Right**, as illustrated in the following screenshot:

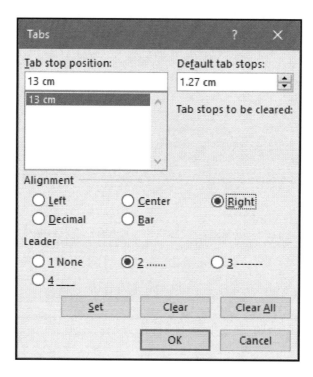

13. Click on **Set**.
14. Click on the **OK** button to commit the change.
15. Type a new line under the existing text, remembering to press *Enter* after you have typed the name of the second person in the list, then type the date. The result is shown in the following screenshot:

```
Margorie Meadows ..............................................................................27 September 2019
Janet Viljoen ...................................................................................... 4 June 2019
```

It is very important to note that tabs are set on a line in a Word document. When pressing *Enter* to move to the next line, any tabs set on the preceding line will travel with the *entry* to the next line. Always check the ruler bar for signs of any tab markers so that you are able to remove them, to continue typing normally in a document.

Always select the entire tabbed list when making changes to a list. Failure to do so will result in tabs set on individual lines and not to the whole list, and will thus cause complications.

Removing tabs in a document

Before removing tabs in a document, you need to highlight the section of the document that contains tabs. Tabs are easily discarded from the ruler by dragging the tab marker off the ruler. If you prefer to use the dialog box to remove tabs, simply access the **Paragraph** dialog box, click on **Tabs** at the very bottom of the dialog box, and choose the tab you wish to delete on the left-hand side under **Tab stop position:**, and click on **Clear**. Should you wish to remove all tabs, click on the **Clear All** icon. Don't forget to press the **OK** button to commit the changes.

Creating tables

In this topic, we will create a table and become familiar with table elements, enter text, and master table selection techniques. Tables are used to display information in a list or to organize information in rows and columns. There is more than one way to insert a table in Word. Let's review them while referring to the following screenshot:

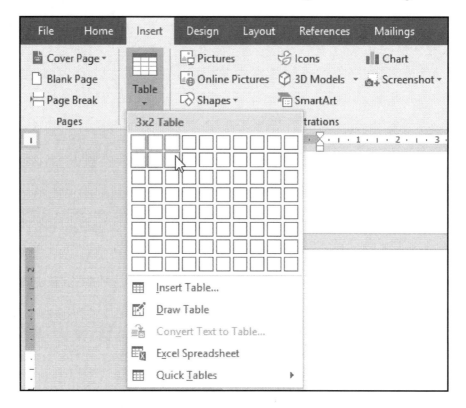

1. Using the **Table** icon from the **Insert** tab (shown in the preceding screenshot), and selecting the number of columns and rows you require by clicking and dragging the mouse pointer over the rows and columns provided.
2. Using the **Insert Table...** option from the drop-down list on the **Table** icon from the **Insert** tab, and specifying the number of rows and columns you require.
3. Using the **Draw Table** option.
4. Inserting a quick table. A gallery of table formats will appear, from which to choose styles. Adjust the content as necessary.

Make sure you are aware of the difference between a **Row**, **Column**, and **Cell**, illustrated in the following screenshot:

Row	Row	Row	Row	Row
	Column			
	Column		Cell	
	Column			

 A cell is an intersection between a row and a column. Use the *Tab* key on your keyboard to navigate from one cell to another in a table.
To navigate to a tab stop in a table, press *Ctrl + Tab*.

Selecting skills

For some formatting and editing tasks, various parts of a table need to be selected. Selecting parts of a table can be done via the **Table Tools Layout** menu or simply by just selecting with your mouse, as follows:

1. Position the mouse pointer onto the table.
2. This will activate the **Table Tools** contextual menu.
3. Click on the **Select** icon located to the very left of the ribbon, as illustrated in the following screenshot:

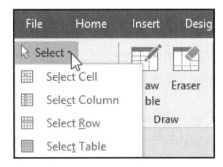

4. Alternatively, use the following selecting skills:

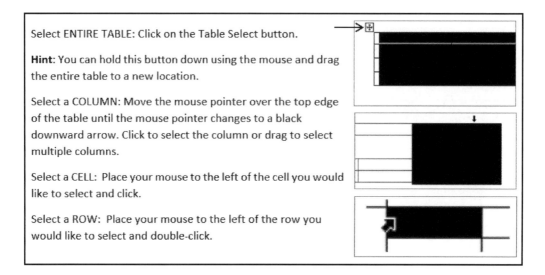

Select ENTIRE TABLE: Click on the Table Select button.

Hint: You can hold this button down using the mouse and drag the entire table to a new location.

Select a COLUMN: Move the mouse pointer over the top edge of the table until the mouse pointer changes to a black downward arrow. Click to select the column or drag to select multiple columns.

Select a CELL: Place your mouse to the left of the cell you would like to select and click.

Select a ROW: Place your mouse to the left of the row you would like to select and double-click.

Editing and formatting tables

During this section, you will learn how to autofit content and use the split and merge feature on table cells. We will also cover the alignment of text vertically and horizontally; changing text direction and applying table styles; adjusting row and column sizes; changing the direction of text; applying table styles; using the distribute options; and, finally, applying borders and shading.

Merging cells

Often, you need to combine cells together so that you can type some text across a range of cells. This is called **merging**:

1. Select (highlight) the cells you would like to merge.
2. Right-click with the mouse over the highlighted area.
3. Choose **Merge Cells**, as illustrated in the following screenshot:

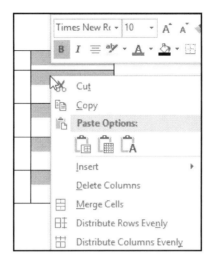

You can also use the **Merge** icon located on the **Table Tools** ribbon.

Splitting cells

Once you have merged cells, you might want to split them again, as follows:

1. Right-click over the merged cells.
2. Choose **Split Cells...** from the shortcut menu provided, as illustrated in the following screenshot:

3. Select the number of rows and columns from the dialog box to split the cell into, as illustrated in the following screenshot:

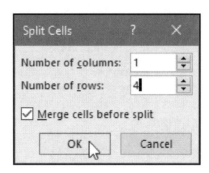

4. Click on the **OK** button to commit the changes and split the cell.

Changing row/column height or width

You can easily change the width and height of a table row or column by dragging the lines around the border of the cell/s. Simply click on the table line you wish to alter. Depress the mouse and keep it depressed, and drag the line to a new location to resize the row or column. An example of a table containing rows and columns of a different width is provided in the following screenshot:

Staff Member	Amount Paid	Contract	Contribution	Leave Taken
Dunborar, S	35000	Temporary	2%	6.5
Kourkova, A	49000	Full Time	3%	15
Pittern, B	4567	Part Time	2%	12
Barryline, D	120678	Permanent	5%	27

If you are asked in an exam scenario to resize a row or column to a certain width or height, you will need to access another method. There are always many ways to do things in the Office environment.

Alternatively, proceed as follows:

1. Select the row/column to resize.
2. Click on the **Layout** tab under the **Table Tools** option and adjust the width and/or height accordingly, as illustrated in the following screenshot:

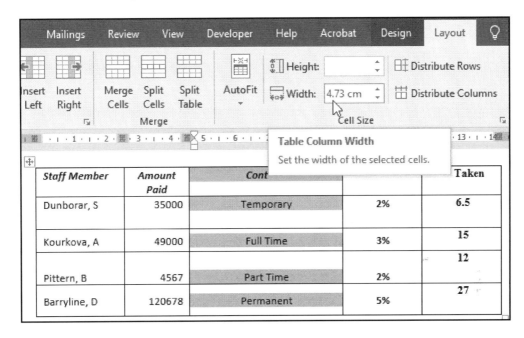

Inserting rows or columns

To insert a row in between **Kourkova** and **Pittern** (as per the preceding example data), proceed as follows:

1. Select the **Pittern** row.
2. Right-click over the selected row with the mouse pointer.
3. Choose **Insert**, then choose the desired option from the list provided to the right in the following screenshot:

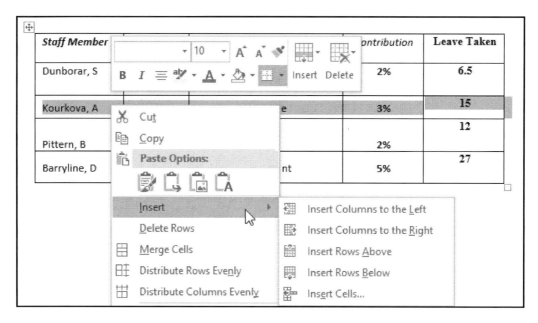

Alternatively, proceed as follows:

1. Select the **Pittern** row.
2. Click the **Table Tools** icon,
3. Make sure you are on the **Layout** tab, and then select **Insert Above**, as illustrated in the following screenshot:

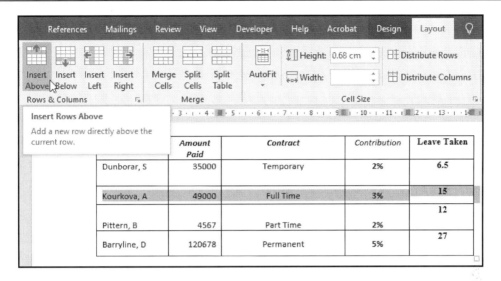

If you have more than one row selected, more than one row will be inserted.

Deleting rows or columns

The method for deleting rows and columns is exactly the same as the **Insert** methods. Simply right-click on a selected row or column, and choose **Delete** from the shortcut menu. The **Delete** option is also available on the **Table Tools** contextual menu, as illustrated in the following screenshot:

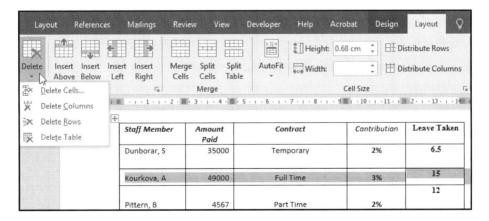

Click on the **Layout** tab to locate the **Delete** icon.

Aligning cells in tables

Aligning cells in tables is fairly straightforward, as illustrated in these next steps:

1. Use the **Layout** tab under **Table Tools** to change the alignment of text within a table.
2. Select the area of the table to change the alignment.
3. Choose from the list of alignment options available, as illustrated in the following screenshot:

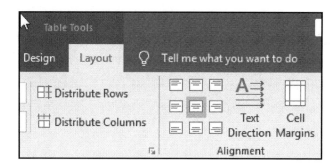

This is how the different alignments would appear in our example table when applied:

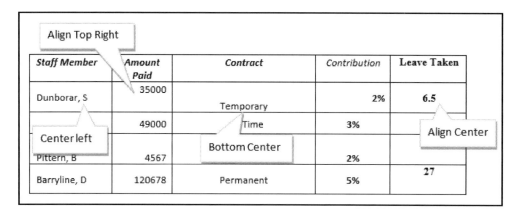

Changing text direction

Changing the text direction in a table cell might be just the thing you need to give you more space in a table to fit all the contents across the width of a page! To do this, proceed as follows:

1. Select the cell or cells to change the text direction.
2. Click on the **Text Direction** icon on the **Layout** tab under **Table Tools**, as illustrated in the following screenshot:

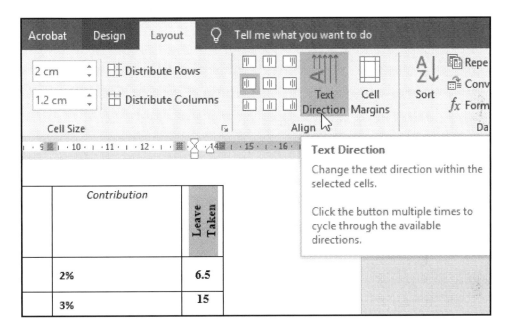

3. Different text direction options are available by clicking (cycling through) the **Text Direction** icon multiple times.

Distributing rows and columns evenly

The **Distribute Rows** and **Distribute Columns** options allow you to resize selected columns and rows evenly. At times, you will notice that rows end up with different heights when you are working. Selecting the rows of a table and applying the distribute features (located on the **Layout** tab) fixes this, creating evenly distributed rows and columns, as illustrated in the following screenshot:

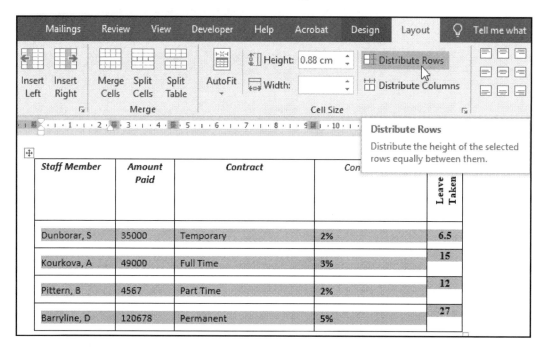

Applying borders and shading

Here is how you can apply this formatting to your tables:

1. Select the table.
2. Right-click over the highlighted area of the table and choose either **Border Styles** or **Table Properties** to access the options available.

3. To select the table styles, shading, border styles, or border options, visit the **Design t**ab of the **Table Tools** contextual menu, as illustrated in the following screenshot:

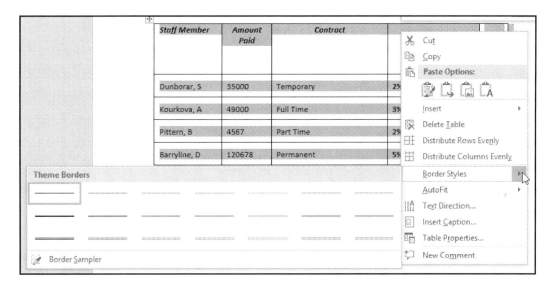

4. Experiment with the options available while the table is selected.

Customizing advanced tables

In this topic, we will learn how to convert a table to text, define the header row of a table (very important for additional applications and use of data tables), sum the cell values in a table, and sort the contents of a table.

Converting a table to text

Now that you have learned about tables, you may want to convert tabular text to a table without retyping the information. Word can convert existing text to tables—and vice versa. Follow these steps:

1. Select the table to convert to text.
2. From the **Table Tools** contextual menu, select **Layout**.

3. Under the **Data** group, locate **Convert to Text**, as illustrated in the following screenshot:

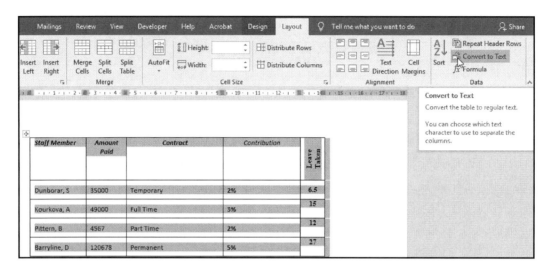

4. Select **Tabs** from the dialog box provided and click the **OK** button to commit the change, as illustrated in the following screenshot:

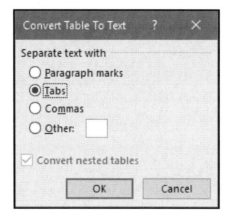

Let's go through the steps to convert text to a table. It is always easier if your text contains tabs separating the text and is consistent in that there is only one tab in between typed text. Follow these steps:

1. Select the text to convert to a table.
2. Click on the **Insert** tab.
3. From the **Table** drop-down list, choose **Convert Text to Table...**, as illustrated in the following screenshot:

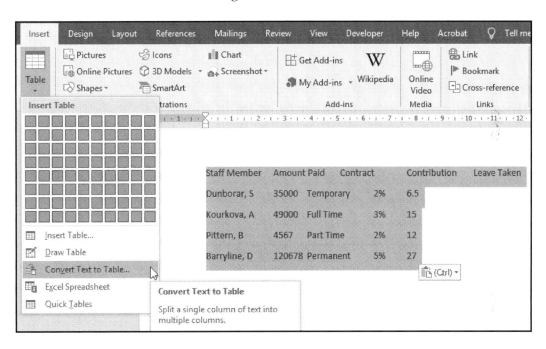

4. Choose how to split the text using the dialog box provided, as illustrated in the following screenshot:

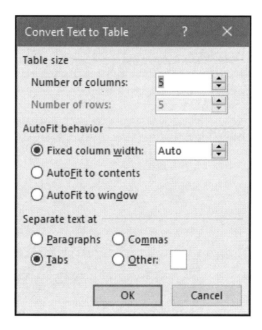

5. The options presented in the dialog box are normally correct due to Word picking up the number of columns and separation type from the text.

6. Click on the **OK** button to convert the text to a table.

Defining the header row

Setting the first row of your table as the header row has its advantages when the table is large and will span across multiple pages. Defining the header row (the first row of the table containing your headings defining the contents of the column) makes sure that the headings in the first row of the table will repeat themselves at the top of the next page, and so forth.

1. Select the first row of the table.

2. Click on the **Table Tools** tab.

3. Click on the **Layout** tab.

4. Choose **Repeat Header Rows**, as illustrated in the following screenshot:

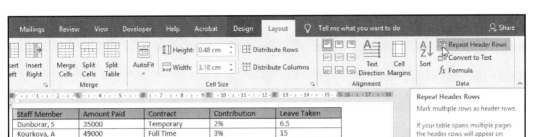

5. The header row has been set to repeat automatically at the top of each page. Any formatting change made to the first row (header row) will automatically update to each of the header rows at the top of each page.

Adding up cell values in a table

Although Excel would be the go-to application for calculating data, calculations can be performed within Word tables. We could create a formula to add sales values, work out percentage commission, or multiply values:

1. Click where you would like your answer to be (that is, place your cursor in the total cell).

2. On the **Layout** tab under **Table Tools**, choose the **Formula** icon, as illustrated in the following screenshot:

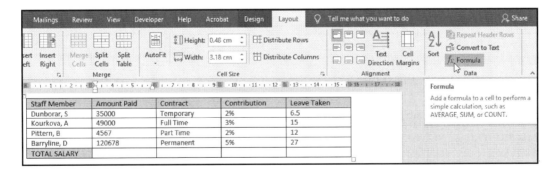

3. The **Formula** dialog box will open and will automatically enter a formula to add values in a table cell, as illustrated in the following screenshot:

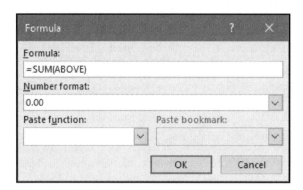

4. Check that the formula is correct. (Word automatically assumes that we are adding all the values above, which is correct in this example. Always double-check after the calculation is assumed by Word, as you may wish to alter the formula to =sum[LEFT] if you are to add all the values to the left, or =sum[RIGHT] to add all the values to the right of the formula cell.)
5. Click on **OK**.

To update a formula, press *F9* on your keyboard. If you change any of the table values, which will have an impact on any formula in the table, select the table and press *F9* on your keyboard to update the formula. Alternatively, right-click on the answer, and select **Update Field**, as illustrated in the following screenshot:

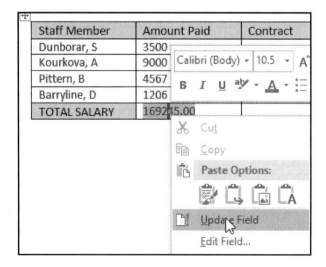

To multiply, subtract, or divide in a Word table, simply use the rows and column cell references in the formula. For example, to sum up the values **9000** + **4567** to reach a total, you would need to use column *B* and row *2* and column *B* and row *3* to identify the cell references for the cells to use in the formula to obtain the total in column *C*, row *6*.

This feature can be used for quotations, invoicing, and so on.

Sorting table contents

1. Select the column you would like to sort by (in this case, **Staff Member** was selected).
2. Click on the **Layout** tab under **Table Tools**.
3. Choose **Sort**, as illustrated in the following screenshot:

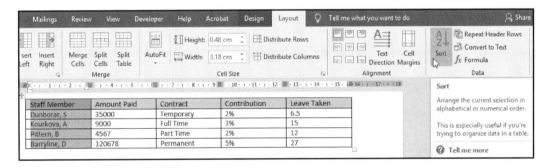

4. In the **Sort** dialog box, notice that the Word program has automatically detected that the table has a **Header row**. Choose whether to sort **Ascending** (A-Z) or **Descending** (Z-A) using the options on the right, as illustrated in the following screenshot:

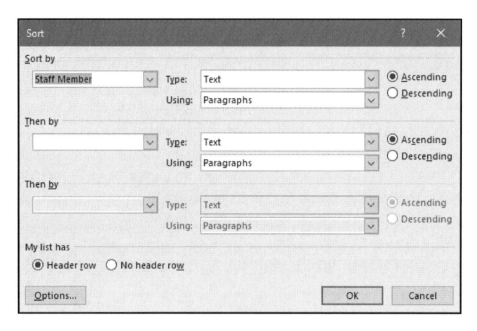

5. Click on **OK** to sort the table. The result can be seen in the following screenshot:

Staff Member	Amount Paid	Contract	Contribution	Leave Taken
Barryline, D	120678	Permanent	5%	27
Dunborar, S	35000	Temporary	2%	6.5
Kourkova, A	9000	Full Time	3%	15
Pittern, B	4567	Part Time	2%	12

Summary

This chapter has imparted important skills to use when constructing bulleted and numbered lists, with a very thorough explanation of the correct method when working with tabbed lists, including leader dot tabs. It has equipped you with the knowledge to create a table, select table elements, format a table, and apply advanced table customization such as converting tables, text, and header rows, working with table formula, and sorting data.

In the next chapter, we will concentrate on creating professional documents and forms, with a section on working with graphic content and how to work with **Paste Special** and text import.

3
Creating Professional Documents

Word 2019 includes an array of features that aid in creating attractive and professional documents. This chapter will teach you how to add references such as citations, a table of contents, add a bibliography to a document, and perform a mail merge using different methods.

We will construct a form using the Quick Parts feature, insert a cover page, and get to grips with navigation techniques and working with long documents. There is also a section on troubleshooting endnotes and footnotes, headers and footers, and links in a document.

We will cover the following topics in this chapter:

- Word-referencing features
- Performing a mail merge
- Constructing forms
- Customizing page layouts

The skills you will learn about in this chapter will allow you to create well-organized documents with easier to read navigation for readers, as well as the skills needed to apply professional features when working with long documents. You will also have the skills to prepare a mail merge document using different output requirements and compile a form to collect information from others online.

Technical requirements

As this chapter focuses on advanced concepts in Word 2019, the prerequisite is definitely being confident with the Word 2019 interface so that you can troubleshoot and produce professional documents. The examples that will be used in this chapter can be accessed from the following GitHub URL: `https://github.com/PacktPublishing/Learn-Microsoft-Office-2019`.

Word-referencing features

This section will teach you how to apply different referencing features within Word 2019 to generate a **table of contents** (**TOC**), citations to create a bibliography, and work with the master and sub-document tool when compiling long documents.

We will also add endnotes and footnotes; for example, the author's notes to referenced marks at the end of a document or on single pages within a long document.

Creating and updating the TOC

The TOC is generated using document heading styles. Once a document is formatted using heading styles, Microsoft Word uses these styles to create the table. Once the TOC has been inserted into the document, you will be able to update the table (without redoing the entire table). Word offers a gallery of *TOC* styles to choose from:

1. To follow this example, open the document called `Table-of-Contents.docx`.
2. We will create a TOC as the first page in this document.
3. Force a page break at the start of the document by pressing *Ctrl + Enter*.
4. Type the heading `Table of Contents` on the first page of the document.
5. Heading styles need to be applied throughout the report so that we can generate the TOC on the first page of the document—use **Heading 1** through **Heading 3** to format the report headings:

6. To select more than one heading in order to apply the same heading style, select the first heading, then hold down the *Ctrl* key on the keyboard. While keeping the *Ctrl* key depressed, select the next heading, and so on.

7. Once the heading styles have been applied throughout the document, we are ready to build our TOC.

8. Click in the document where you want the TOC to reside. This is normally at the very top of the document on the first page.

9. Click on the **References** tab.

10. Click on the **Table of Contents** drop-down arrow to select a built-in TOC style to use:

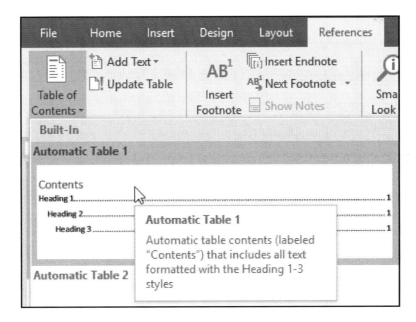

Your TOC will be generated at the top of the document. But if you need to make any changes to the existing TOC or you used the incorrect heading styles on a section of the document and need to correct this, then simply click into the TOC and press the *F9* function key to update the entire table or just the page numbering:

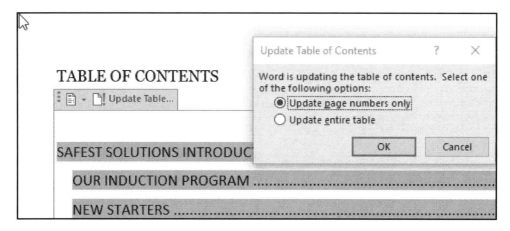

Using citations to build a bibliography

Creating citations in a Word 2019 document is really simple. Citations are references to either published or unpublished work. Citations are used to explain any reference to, for example, websites, journals, reports, artwork, interviews or authors in a Word document.

Once the source is created as a citation, you would attach it to the relevant part of the document (text, image, table, column). These sources are then generated in a bibliography at the end of your document. You can then update a single citation, by adding or removing information from the source, after which it will automatically update the bibliography.

Adding citation sources

Follow these steps to learn how to add citation sources:

1. For this demonstration, we will open the document called
   `CiteThis.docx`.
2. The first step when it comes to generating your bibliography is to *insert citations* throughout the document.

3. Position the mouse pointer either on the left- or right-hand side of the text you wish to cite to include it in the bibliography.

4. Visit the **References** tab on the ribbon.

5. Select the **Insert Citations** icon from the **Citations & Bibliography** group.

6. Select **Add New Source**...

7. Edit the source by selecting the **Type of Source** you wish to create from the drop-down list provided.

8. For this example, we will create two sources at two different points in the document:

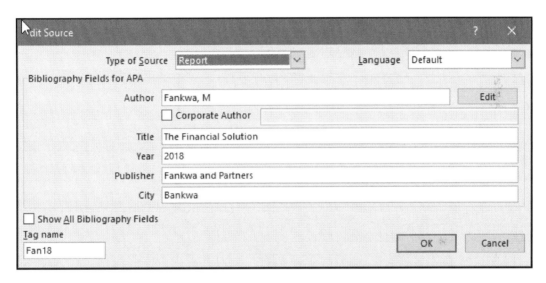

9. Fill in the details of the source, then click on the **OK** command when complete.

10. The source will be inserted at the position of the mouse pointer and will look as follows:

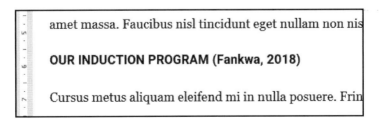

11. Move to the next position in the document to add the next new source. Change the **Type of Source**, if necessary, and fill in the details:

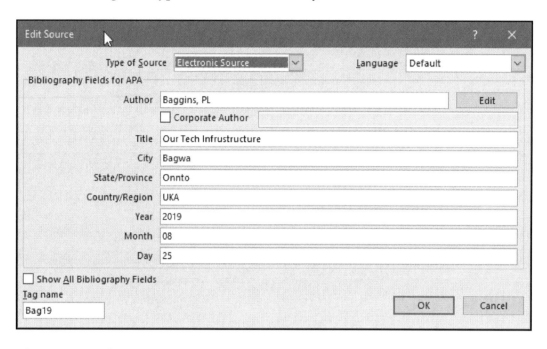

That's it. Now that you have learned how to insert citations, we will build a bibliography.

Generating the bibliography

Follow these steps to generate a bibliography:

1. As bibliographies are positioned at the end of a document by default, scroll to the last page of the document.
2. Click where you would like to insert your bibliography.
3. Visit the **References** tab on the ribbon.
4. Choose **Bibliography** from the **Citations & Bibliography** group.

5. From the list provided, choose from either **Bibliography**, **References**, or **Works Cited**. In this case, we'll be inserting the bibliography into the document:

> Bibliography
>
> Baggins, P., 2019. *Our Tech Infrustructure,* Bagwa: s.n.
>
> Fankwa, M., 2018. *The Financial Solution,* Bankwa: Fankwa and Partners.

In the next section, we will learn how to edit citations by applying a different style.

Editing the citation style

There are various citation styles to choose from, such as the popular **APA** or **Harvard**. To select a different citation style, simply click the drop-down arrow of the citation marker and choose the preferred style. Then, the bibliography will be updated automatically.

You can add page numbers to a citation marker in the document or suppress information related to the author, year, and title. Follow these steps to edit your citation:

1. Click on a citation marker in the document.
2. Choose **Edit Citation** from the list provided:

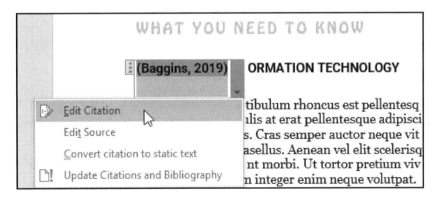

3. For this example, we will add the page number for the currently selected citation:

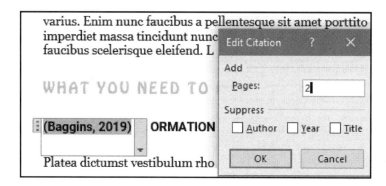

4. Type the page number that the citation refers to into the placeholder provided.
5. Click on the **OK** button to update the citation within the document.

Working with master documents or subdocuments

If you ever need to work with very long documents within Word 2019, then this feature is for you! Having a particularly long document with a huge number of pages can become difficult to edit, and you have to take into consideration whether your computer can handle the processing it has to do. You can either work with the master document feature on its own or use it in combination with the subdocument feature, where parts (for example, chapters of a book) are stored as separate files and called upon when changes need to be made.

The **Master Document** feature is the main parent and keeps all the subdocuments connected. It will continue to allow the use of features such as page or chapter numbering, styles, references, headers and footers, and so on. Let's investigate this feature.

Always keep master documents and subdocuments within the same folder. This will ensure that you have the correct file path access to all the parts of the master documents and subdocuments and that you won't have any problems locating documents when editing, which could lead to all sorts of editing and version problems!
It is always best to name your master documents and subdocuments really carefully with some naming convention order! This way, you will not have a problem locating parts of the document that need to be in a particular order.

If you are creating a master document from scratch, open a new document as usual. Alternatively, if you want to change a normal document into a master document, open the first document, which will become the main document.

For this demonstration, we will use a few documents, that is, `Master.docx`, `Sub1.docx`, `Sub2.docx`:

1. Click on **File** | **New** | **Blank document**.
2. Click on **View** | **Outline**.
3. Notice that the **Outlining** tab is now present on the ribbon. Click on the **Show Document** icon.
4. Click on the **Insert** icon to start differentiating between different parts of the document:

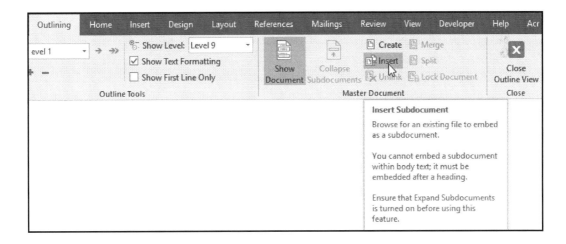

5. Insert your documents in order of the master, then visit **Insert** again separately until all the subdocuments have been added in order:

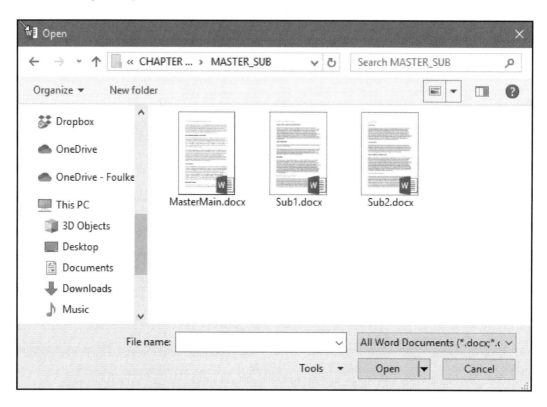

6. You will be asked via a popup message dialog whether you want to keep conflicting styles. Say **Yes to All** of these to maintain consistency with the style that will be used throughout all the documents linked to the master document:

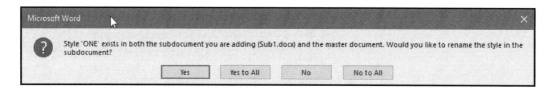

7. Don't forget to save at this point since you have created a new document consisting of different parts.

How you continue to edit after this point is entirely up to you. Each document can be worked on separately, which will update the master document upon saving it. You can *collapse* and *expand* subdocuments and remove links from documents you no longer need to keep as part of the master. The beauty of master documents is that you have the ability to print a large document without the heaviness of one very long document.

Constructing endnotes and footnotes

You use endnotes or footnotes to *reference* text in the document. A superscript number is positioned after the text and, when clicked on, it will take you to the actual explanatory note at the very end of the page, document, or section. You can convert footnotes into endnotes and vice versa in Word 2019.

Inserting footnotes/endnotes

Follow these steps to learn how to insert footnotes/endnotes in Word 2019:

1. Open the `FootNotesEndNotes.docx` document for this example.
2. Place the mouse cursor in the text where you would like to place a footnote.
3. Select **Reference** | **Insert Footnote**:

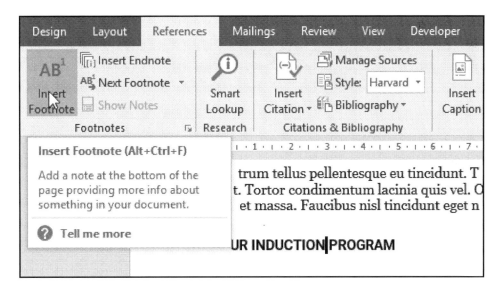

4. A *footnote marker* will appear in the document text and the footnote section will open up at the end of the page.

5. Type an explanation of the footnote into the space provided. We will type `Our Induction Booklet is downloadable from our intranet site SafestSolutionsWeb` for this example:

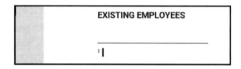

6. Navigate back to the footnote marker in the document, just after the text stating `Induction`. You will notice that when hovering the mouse pointer over the marker, it will display the text, as typed into the footnote explanation.

7. To navigate from the marker to the explanation, click on the **Show Notes** icon or double-click on the marker to move between the text and explanation.

Converting footnotes into endnotes

Follow these steps to learn how to convert footnotes into endnotes:

1. After inserting footnotes throughout a document, click on the **Footnote and Endnote** expand icon.

2. The footnote and endnote dialog box will populate. Click on the **Convert**... icon:

3. Click on **OK**, then **Close**.

4. The footnotes will be converted to endnotes at the very end of the document.

5. When you convert footnotes into endnotes, the number format changes. If you need to alter the number format for endnotes and footnotes, click on the **References** tab to launch the **Footnote** dialog box. Select the drop-down arrow next to **Number format** and choose the desired number format from the list provided.

6. Click on **Apply** to commit the changes you've made.

Inserting links in a document

A link is a piece of text, graphic, picture, chart, or shape in a document that, when clicked on, will take the user to another location! An example would be to use a link to go to a website or file from the document. Links can be used to link to other files, to external documents, to a place in the same document, or to web pages or graphics. This section will take you through a few methods you can use to insert links into Word 2019 documents. Let's go over the first method and open the document called `Hyperlinks.docx`:

1. Select some text or position the mouse pointer in the document where you would like to place the link.
2. Right-click and choose **Link**....

Alternatively, you can do the following:

1. Click on the **Insert** tab.
2. Choose the **Links** icon.
3. The **Insert Link** dialog box will populate.
4. Under the **Link to:** text at the left top of the dialog box and make sure **Existing File or Web Page** is selected.
5. Type the *link address* into the space provided in the **Address:** placeholder.
6. Click on **OK** to complete the link.
7. In the document, you will notice that the text you selected in now formatted differently. This is because it has been identified as a link. To launch the link, hold down the *Ctrl* key on the keyboard, and with the *Ctrl* key depressed, click once with the mouse. The browser will open with the relevant website.
8. To visit the link, position the mouse pointer over the linked text. Hold down the *Ctrl* key and click once with the mouse pointer. The mouse pointer will change to a *hand icon* to indicate that you are launching a link:

This procedure is pretty much the same for all types of links you wish to create in a document. You can create a link from an image or shape in a Word document. A **Screen Tip...** for the link can be added via the **Text to display:** heading at the top of the dialog. The text that's entered here will be displayed in the document instead of the entire hyperlink code and gives the user direction as to what the link might contain. This can be used as a marketing tool too.

Linking to a separate file is a popular feature as you can distribute a report in Word 2019, including a link, for example, to an Excel file to explain a certain part of the report or include links to separate documents as part of an agenda.

Note that any links to files need to be in a shared folder that can be accessed by all the recipients of the document.

When visiting the **Insert Link** dialog box, you will notice the **Place in This Document** option under the **Link to** heading on the left-hand side. This option is wonderful when working with long documents. If you have a list of headings at the top of a document and need to read additional content for one of the topics, which is located on page 101 of the document, you will need to scroll to get there, which is not ideal. Once set up, you can click on the linked heading, which will immediately take you to the topic's location in the document:

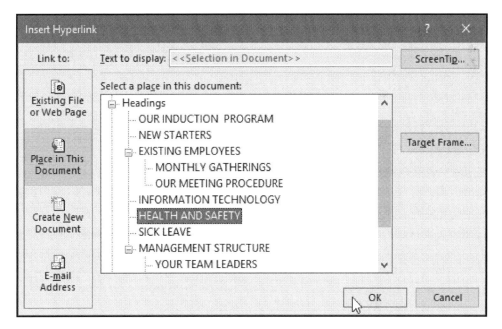

To edit a link, simply right-click on the link's text and choose **Edit Link**:

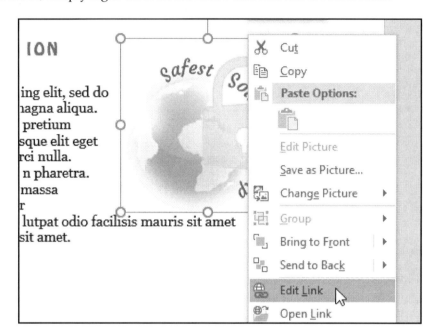

To remove the link, follow these steps:

1. Select the text that contains the hyperlink you wish to remove.
2. Right-click and choose **Remove Hyperlink** from the shortcut menu.

This way, the hyperlink will be removed from the text.

Performing a mail merge

A mail merge is a standard document that you can create and merge with a contact list to produce a merged document. A standard document could be in the form of a letter, envelope, labels, and so on. The contact list or data source contains the unique information (fields) that you can merge via merge fields into the document.

A Mail Merge has many uses for business users in that they can speed up the production of personally addressed emails to clients for direct marketing, or standard updates or notifications, for instance. This saves time and has the added feature of being able to generate E-mails, Letters, Labels and Envelopes easily from a data source such as an address list.

The mail merge feature, is accessible by visiting the last step of the Mail Merge, named Finish & Merge at the end of the Mail Merge ribbon. During this last step you are able to select to send your results to email rather than to print them out. You are also able to start the Mail Merge process by selecting the E-mail Messages option from the Start Mail Merge drop-down list.

The data source can be in the form of a Word table, an Outlook contact list, an Excel worksheet, or an Access table. In this section, we will learn how to perform a mail merge manually, as well as how to use the wizard to perform a mail merge using letters, envelopes, and labels.

Creating a mail merge manually

Follow these steps to learn how to create a mail merge manually:

1. Open a new blank document in Word 2019.
2. Click on the **Mailings** tab on the ribbon.
3. We will be creating labels in this example. Choose the **Start Mail Merge** icon and select **Labels**....
4. The dialog box will offer many options that you can use to customize labels. You can choose different **Label vendors**, such as Avery or Microsoft, as well as the most popular online vendors. You are also able to customize any selected label by visiting the **Details**... icon at the bottom of the dialog box.
5. Select the **Label** type and customize it, if necessary.
6. Click on the **OK** button when complete.
7. The label guidelines will appear on the new document.
8. The next step is to format the first label, thus creating the label template.
9. Format the first label only by adding any logos, text, and shapes that need to appear on every label. You can customize this as you wish but for this example, we are going to add a company logo.
10. Click into the first label and choose **Insert** from the ribbon.

11. Click on **Pictures**, select `SafestSolutionsLogo.png`, and click on **Insert**:

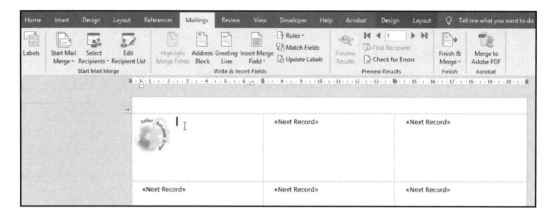

12. Resize the picture so that it fits into the first label, leaving enough space for the customer details.

13. Now, we are ready to insert our recipients (customer details).

14. Click on the **Mailings** tab once again and choose **Select Recipients** from the **Start Mail Merge** group.

15. Since we already have a recipient address list typed up in Excel 2019, we will use the customer information for our labels. You will notice, however, that there are three options:

   - **Type a New List...**: This will open a datasheet that constructs an entirely new set of data for the labels.
   - **Use an Existing List...**: This will allow you to open an already constructed data source from a location on your computer.
   - **Choose from Outlook Contacts...**: This will allow you access to your Outlook 2019 contacts so that you can use them as the mail merge recipient list.

16. Browse to find the data source on your computer (please use the Excel file called `CustomerData.xlsx` if you are following this example).

17. Open the file. The *Select Table* dialog box will open. You will need to select the worksheet that contains your data – there could be many tables (sheets) within an Excel workbook.

18. Select the `Customers` table and click the **OK** button to continue.

19. Notice the change in the label document. The ribbon has more options available and the `<<Next Record>>` field appears on each label. The recipient list is now a part of the document and the fields can be inserted into the document.

20. Position the cursor where you would like the first merge field (on the first label) to appear.

21. From the **Write & Insert Fields** group, select **Insert Merge Field**. The list of field names from the data source will appear:

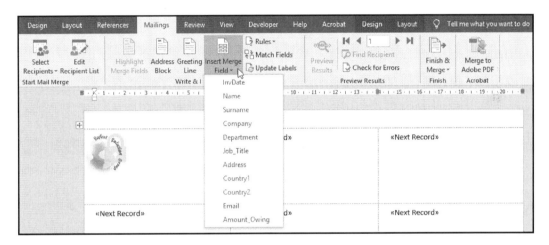

22. Click on the **Name** field name to insert the merged field onto the first label, press the *spacebar* on the keyboard, and then return to the **Insert Merge Field** drop-down list and select **Surname**.

23. Press *Enter* to move to the next line.

24. Continue adding the following fields to the label, with each on a new line: **Company**, **Address**, **Country1**.

25. Add a comma after **Country1** and then add the merge field called **Country2**.

26. The first label looks great, but we will need to update this information for every label so that the customer data will update with each label when we complete the merge:

27. Click on the **Update Labels** icon on the **Write & Insert Fields** group.
28. The labels are updated with the merge fields. Don't worry if the rest of the labels look a bit out of line compared to the first label; this is due to the `<<Next Record>>` field being inserted and will correct itself when we merge the data.
29. **Note:** Before you print or merge the information, it is a good idea to preview the results first so that any mistakes can be corrected before labels are wasted during printing.
30. Click on the **Preview Results** icon on the **Mailings** tab.
31. The labels will be updated and the fields on all labels will finally be lined up!
32. Before the merge is completed, you can set the **Check for Errors** option. By default, the middle option is set in this dialog box and will stop at each point in the merge to prompt you if an error is occurring (an example of an error would be that a merge field is not recognized).
33. If you are not comfortable just moving on, choose **Simulate the merge and report errors in a new document** first so that you can fix whatever is causing a problem before you continue with the actual merge. If you click on the **OK** button to continue at this point, the check will happen and your results will be sent to a new Word document. We will skip this step for this example.

34. Click on the **Finish & Merge** icon from the **Finish** group to complete the last step.

35. There are three options to choose: **Edit Individual Documents...** to merge the data to a new document, **Print Documents...** to send the completed merge directly to the printer without making any changes, and **Send Email Messages...** to be able to use the email merge field addresses to send emails.

 It is never a good idea to print documents directly to the printer without seeing if the merge was successful first.

36. For this example, we will choose **Edit Individual Documents....**

37. A new document will open containing the result of the merge.

38. Now, we can choose to print using the **File** | **Print** option on the Backstage view.

39. Remember to save the original merge document containing the data source as this is an important document. The resulting document can be closed once it's been printed.

Creating a mail merge using the wizard

We will use the mail merge wizard to combine an existing Word 2019 document with merge fields from an existing Excel 2019 worksheet to produce invoice letters for our customer base. Follow these steps to do so:

1. When using the **Mail Merge Wizard**, start from **New** | **Blank Document** or open an existing document.

2. For this example, we will use an existing document called `SafestInvoice.docx`. This document can be opened prior to starting the merge or as the first step of the mail merge wizard.

3. Click on the **Mailings** tab on the ribbon.

4. Click on the **Start Mail Merge** icon to access the drop-down menu.

5. Choose the **Step-by-Step Mail Merge Wizard...** option at the bottom of the drop-down list:

6. Note that the **Mail Merge** pane has opened up on the right-hand side of the Word environment and shows *Step 2 of 6* at the bottom of the pane due to the fact that we have already opened an existing document to use in the mail merge.

7. At this stage, you can open a letter you would like to use for a mail merge or type a letter on a new, blank Word document. Since the letter is a mail merge letter, we will make sure to leave spaces for the fields that we would like to insert from our address list at a later stage. The only information on the letter should be general information that's not specific to a person, place, or thing. We will add merge fields to populate specific information for each individual customer.

8. For information purposes, *Step 1 of 6* is to select a document type to create. Letters are the default document type. Please note, though, that other document types are available, such as email messages, envelopes, labels, directories, and so on. For this example, we have already moved to *Step 2 of 6* due to already having an *existing document* open.

9. Make sure that *Step 2 of 6* displays **Use the Current Document**.

10. At the bottom of the pane, click on **Next: Select Recipients**.

11. The task pane reflects *Step 3 of 6*, which allows you to choose the data you wish to merge with the **Letter** (data could be a contact list typed in Excel, Outlook, Access, or a Word table). You should also be able to type your own list if you have not created a list yet or selected one from your Outlook contacts list. For this example, we will use an already created Excel data file called CustomerData.xlsx.

12. Click on **Use an Existing list**.
13. Select the **Browse...** icon to locate the `CustomerData.xlsx` data source on your computer.
14. Click on `CustomerData.xlsx` and then choose **Open** at the bottom of the dialog box.
15. Select the worksheet you wish to use in the mail merge:

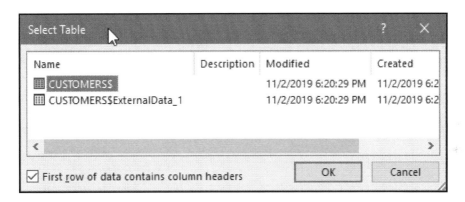

16. The mail merge recipients list will be displayed in a dialog box where you can edit, sort, filter, or include/exclude merge field recipients from the data source.
17. Click on the **OK** command when you're done.
18. The recipient list will be visible on the **Use an existing list heading in the Mail Merge** pane. Here, you can change to another list or edit the current recipient list.
19. Click on **Next: Write your letter**.
20. The task pane reflects *Step 4 of 6*, which allows us to write the letter and insert the merge fields. Since we already have our standard invoice, we can start inserting merge fields into our document.
21. Click in the document next to the word **Invoice #.** Click on the **More Items...** option to select the field names from your data source so that you can enter them in the Word document at the relevant positions. Choose the **InvNo** field from the dialog box provided and click on **Insert**.

22. Repeat this process until all the field names have been inserted into the document:

The preceding screenshot displays the fields that were inserted in the first part of the document, while the following screenshot shows the fields at the bottom of the document, for reference:

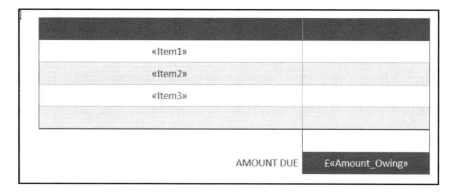

23. Click **Next: Preview** to preview your letters on the task pane, which will take you to *Step 5 of 6*. This view gives you an indication of how the document will look once it's complete and give you a chance to see if the merged fields are correct and spaced properly.

24. If any errors present themselves, return to the previous step by clicking on the **Previous:** icon at the bottom of the task pane, make the change, and then move on.

25. To exclude a recipient from the final merge result, locate the person you no longer wish to send a letter to using the back or forward recipient arrows, and click on the **Exclude this recipient** button.

26. Click **Next: Complete the merge** to move to the last step.

27. *Step 6* offers two options: one to print directly to the printer and another to edit the letters before printing. Choose **Edit individual letters...** to check that you have all your letters in order before sending hordes of incorrect information to the printer and wasting paper.

28. In the **Merge to New Document** dialog box, click **OK** to send all records to the new document.

29. A new document will open, in this case, `Letters6.docx`, containing all the merged information as unique separate letters positioned one after the other.

30. Print the letters and close the document (you don't need to save).

31. The document you need to save is the Word document with the merged fields in it (the document that you created all the mail merge steps in).

32. A mail merge document is very useful as you could use the same information to prepare and merge envelopes or labels.

33. To print the document, click on the **File** tab to access the Backstage view. Click on the **Print** option. Adjust any settings/properties and then click on the **Print** icon.

Next, we'll look at constructing forms.

Constructing forms

Forms are very useful for collecting information, thus restricting users so that they can only fill in the required information without being able to change the format of the document. To begin the process of constructing a form, you will need either a new document, an existing document, or a template to base the form on. Once the basics of the form have been entered, you will need to add content such as drop-down lists of choices, textboxes, checkboxes, date fields, and much more.

You will need to add the **Developer** tab to the ribbon to use form controls. Let's create a basic form to see how the process works!

Working with the Developer tab and form controls

The first step is to set up your *Word* 2019 environment to create forms. By this, we mean that the **Developer** tab must be visible as a tab, along the ribbon:

1. Click to select **File | Options** from the list provided. Then, click the **Customize Ribbon** icon down the left-hand side.
2. On the right, under the **Customize the Ribbon** option, make sure that the **Main** tab is selected, then locate **Developer** and ensure that the checkbox is activated to the left it. Click on **OK** to confirm this.
3. This will add the **Developer** tab to the existing ribbon.

Content controls are located within the **Controls** group on the **Developer** tab. There are two main types of controls – **content controls** and **legacy form control**s. There are more content control options than legacy controls, and they do not require any type of protection to make them active for user input.

Legacy controls need to be protected using the restrict editing option so that they are active for user input. Legacy controls are also sometimes preferred for complex documents. The reason for this is that when using the legacy controls, the form can be protected using the **Filling in forms** feature, which stops users from editing that particular area of the form:

Field	Icon	Explanation
Text Form Content Control	Aa	Used to indicate that text is required to be filled in by the user of the form
Plain Text Content Control	Aa	Allows the user to input text into the content control
Check Box Content Control	☑	This check box is used to allow the user to indicate either a yes or no answer
Combo Box and Drop-Down Content Control		Use this list to provide a few options which the user can choose to answer the question
Date Picker Content Control		Used to indicate a date must be inserted into a content control on a form
Picture Content Control		The control enables the user to add an image to a form
Design Mode	Design Mode	This icon is used to edit content controls
Properties	Properties	Make changes to the properties of content controls

In addition, macros can be used to refine input and create computations. You will learn how to protect a form later in this section.

Let's create a basic form using some of the controls located on the **Developer** tab.

Creating a basic form

Microsoft Word 2019 has a huge range of form templates you can use or edit. To access these templates, click on the **File | New** option and choose to access the templates. In the search text area, type in `Forms` to locate all the form templates within Word 2019. Follow these steps:

1. Open an existing form or create a new form. For this example, we will open an existing form and examine its contents.

2. Let's open the form called `Request for Use of Vacation.docx`.

3. To fill out this form, simply press *Tab* on the keyboard to jump from one control to another to fill in the information required.

4. You will notice that when navigating, controls are *gray* when clicked, indicating that they are content controls.

5. To view the properties of the content controls, simply click on the required control and select the **Properties** icon on the **Controls** group.

6. The **Properties** dialog box will open, thus allowing you to make changes:

7. To delete a content control, right-click the control and click on **Remove Content Control.**

8. To add a control, click into a table cell (tables are the best way to construct forms as it keeps everything in line and when in a tabular form, navigating is really easy using the *Tab* key). Let's use the cell that contained the content control we just removed.

9. Select content control from the **Controls** group. For this example, we will use the Date Picker Content Control.

10. Time for a challenge! Let's see if you are able to replicate the following form using the content controls from the **Controls** group and some table formatting:

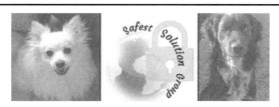

FIRST CONTACT PURPET FORM

NAME OF PURPET	PURPET BREED	NAME OF OWNER		PURPET PICTURE
Click or tap here to enter text.		Click or tap here to enter text.		
PURPET AGE	PURPET IMMUNIZATION	PURPET SEX		
Choose an item.	Choose an item.	☐	Female	
		☐	Male	
INSURANCE DETAILS	PURPET ID TAG	PURPET CHIP		CHIP NUMBER
Click or tap here to enter text.	Click or tap here to enter text.	☐	Yes	Click or tap here to enter text.
		☐	No	
OPERATIONS	SPAY / NEUTERED	ANY OTHER INFO WE SHOULD KNOW?		
Click or tap here to enter text.	Choose an item.	Click or tap here to enter text.		

Please fill out this form online and return to safestsolgrp@safest.co.il at your earliest convenience so that we can get you and your purpet/s entered on our system. Note that a new form must be filled out for each furpet.

11. You will use the following content controls – Rich Text Content Control, Plain Text Content Control, Picture Content Control, Check Box Content Control, Combo Box Content Control, Drop Down List Content Control, and Date Picker Content Control.

12. Add the following options for the Combo Box Content Control and the Drop Down List Content Control. For the **Pets Age** content control, simply add your own range of ages:

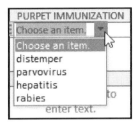

Now, you know how to insert and enter data into a content control. In the next section, we will look at legacy content controls and getting the form ready for distribution.

Adding and modifying legacy form controls

If you want to create greater protection in terms of restricting users so that they can only access certain parts of the form or be guided only from one content control to the next, then legacy form controls are the way to go. Let's take a look:

1. In a new, blank document, type in the following text, exactly as it's shown here:

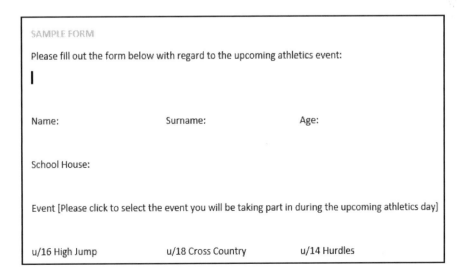

2. Save the form as `SampleForm.docx`.

3. Click the **Name:** text and use the **Legacy Forms** icon to insert the text field from the **Developer** tab:

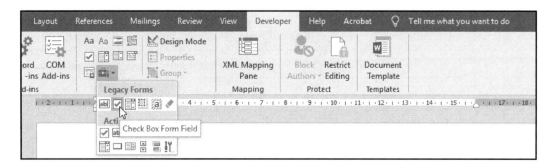

4. Do the same for **Surname: field**.

5. Click after **Age:** and insert a drop-down field.

6. Click after **School House** and insert another drop-down field.

7. After **u/16 High Jump**, insert a checkbox field.

8. Do the same for each of the other events.

9. Your form should look similar to the following example:

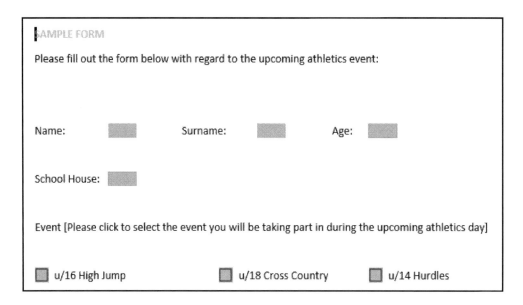

10. To investigate properties for each of the fields you have inserted, simply double-click to access the dialog box on the field you would like to edit. Fields are displayed with gray fill shading once they've been inserted into the document. For instance, the **School House** drop-down field needs to list the sports houses within the school.

11. To list the options so that the user can select an answer, double-click on the *gray field* you inserted next to **School House:**. Then, in the dialog box that appears, type **Ruby** into the text area at the top left and click on **Add>>**.

12. The text **Ruby** appears in the **Items** in the drop-down list area. Repeat this until you have entered all three houses into the list. If you prefer to have a generic item at the top of the list instead of one of the required answers, add an item called **Click** to select an answer and move it to the top of the list using the **Move** arrows to the right:

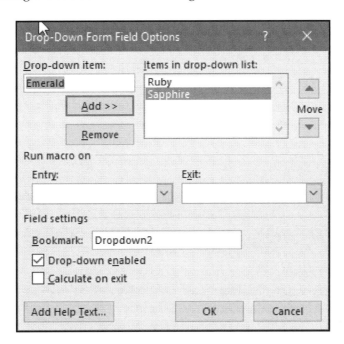

13. Click on **OK** to confirm.

14. Complete the form field options by double-clicking them, making changes, and saving.

15. The form should look similar to the following:

SAMPLE FORM

Please fill out the form below with regard to the upcoming athletics event:

Name: Enter First Name here Surname: Enter Surname here Age: Enter School Age group

School House: Enter School House here

Event [Please click to select the event you will be taking part in during the upcoming athletics day]

☐ u/16 High Jump   ☐ u/18 Cross Country   ☐ u/14 Hurdles

Your form is now complete and ready to be protected so that users cannot edit the actual text on the form and only answer the questions.

Protecting a form

Follow these steps to learn how to protect a form:

1. We will continue to use the form we created in the previous section.
2. Make sure the **Developer** tab is selected.
3. Click on **Restrict Editing** under the **Protect** group.
4. Under the **2. Editing restrictions** heading, select the checkbox for **Allow only this type of editing in the document:**.
5. From the drop-down list, choose **Filling in forms**:

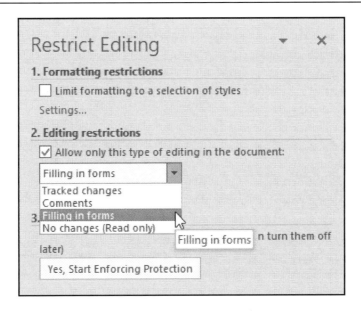

6. Under *Step 3*, click on **Yes, Start Enforcing Protection**.
7. A dialog box will present itself, asking you to enter a password (this is optional).
8. Click on **OK** to complete the protection process.
9. If your form was protected correctly, the user should not be able to edit any part of the form except the fields you inserted.
10. Click on **File | Info**. The **Protect Document** icon indicates that this document has protection applied.
11. If you need to make changes to the form, you will need to *unprotect* the form first. Visit the **Stop Protection** icon at the bottom of the **Restrict Editing** pane, then enter the password to *unprotect* the form and make the form accessible for editing. Do not forget to *protect* the form again before sharing it with others.

Customizing page layouts

In this section, we will learn how to insert a cover page quick part, convert text into columns, and insert and modify section breaks in a document. By doing this, you will be able to add a header or footer to a document; insert page numbers, images, or quick parts; work with different page headers and footers; and add a design element to your document by adding and customizing cover pages.

Inserting a cover page quick part

Cover pages make documents look professional and also offer the user an efficient way of adding a first-page introduction to a long document. There are many styles to choose from, either within Word 2019 and online, and we can control where to place the cover page in the document:

1. For this demonstration, we will open the document called `CoverPages.docx`.

2. Click the **Insert** tab.

3. In the **Pages** group (at the very left of the ribbon), choose the **Cover Page** drop-down arrow. A gallery of pages will appear:

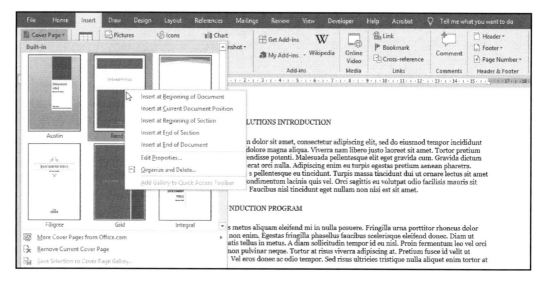

4. To view more pages, click on the **More Cover Pages from Office.com** option. Please note that an active internet connection is necessary.

5. Click to insert the desired cover page into the document or right-click to access more options to control where you would like to place the page.

6. Once the cover page has been inserted into the document, you will be able to add or format the information as desired.

7. Deleting the cover page is easy – simply access the **Cover Page** drop-down menu from the **Insert** tab and select **Remove Current Cover Page**.

Converting text into columns

Follow these steps to learn how to convert text into columns:

1. Select a paragraph in your document to convert into text.
2. Click on the **Layout** tab on the ribbon.
3. Select **Columns** from the **Page Setup** group.
4. Choose the number of columns you require:

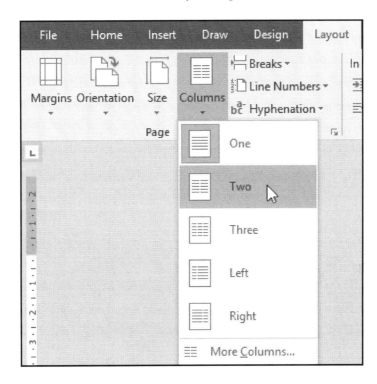

If you wish to set other options such as the line between columns or set column width, visit the **More Columns...** option at the bottom of the dialog box.

Inserting and modifying section breaks

Breaks in a document are extremely useful if you would like to have a different layout or formatting changes for a certain section of the document, a page, or pages. By formatting or layout, we mean margins; paper size or orientation; page borders; vertical alignments of text; headers and footers; columns; page numbering; line numbering; and footnote/endnote numbering. The following is an explanation of these special break types:

- **Continuous**: A continuous section break is inserted before and after a portion of text on the same page. Changing text into columns is an example of where a continuous break is used:

> OUR INDUCTION PROGRAM
>
> →············Section Break (Continuous)············
>
> Cursus metus aliquam eleifend mi in nulla posuere. Fringilla urna porttitor rhoncus dolor purus non enim. Egestas fringilla phasellus faucibus scelerisque eleifend donec. Diam ut venenatis tellus in metus. A diam sollicitudin tempor id eu nisl. Proin fermentum leo vel orci porta non pulvinar neque. Tortor at risus viverra adipiscing at.
>
> Pretium fusce id velit ut tortor. Vel eros donec ac odio tempor. Sed risus ultricies tristique nulla aliquet enim tortor at auctor. Lobortis mattis aliquam faucibus purus in massa tempor nec. Faucibus pulvinar elementum integer enim neque volutpat ac tincidunt vitae. Quis risus sed vulputate odio ut enim. Pharetra vel turpis nunc eget.
>
> →············Section Break (Continuous)············
>
> Nibh sit amet commodo nulla. Et leo duis ut diam quam nulla porttitor massa. Leo vel orci porta non. Eget magna fermentum iaculis eu non diam phasellus. Velit egestas dui id ornare arcu odio. Vitae proin sagittis nisl rhoncus mattis rhoncus. A pellentesque sit amet porttitor

- **Even Page** *or* **Odd Page**: This prepares the document for formatting changes on all the odd pages only of the document or only on all the even pages throughout the document. You might like to place a header or footer on only the odd pages in the document, and therefore would insert an odd page section break:

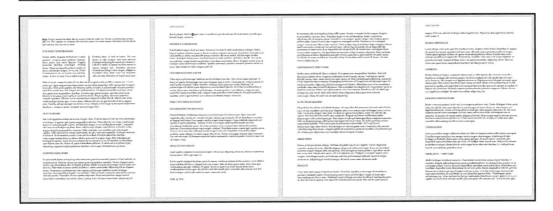

- **Next Page**: This section break being inserted instead of a normal page break (before and after the page) will control what happens on that page only. This type of section break is very useful when you want to create portrait pages followed by one landscape page, and thereafter the document returns to portrait mode. Another use for this type of break is to sort out a problem table that is too big to fit on a portrait page!

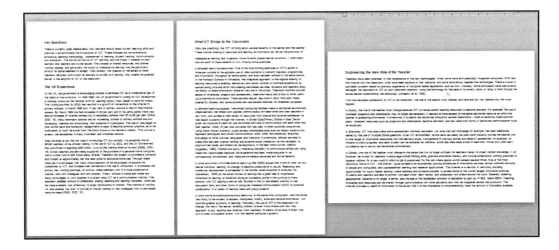

Now, we will learn how to locate and insert **Next Page** section breaks into a document to create different page orientation layouts in a single document.

Viewing section breaks

Follow these steps to learn how to view section breaks:

1. Let's open a document to work on. In this example, we will work on `SectionBreaks.docx`.
2. On *page 2* of this document, you will notice that columns have been inserted in a particular paragraph.
3. At the start of the paragraph and the end of the paragraph are section breaks.
4. These breaks are not evident in the document, but because this section of the document contains columns, we know that they are there.
5. If a document contains section breaks, they can be viewed in three ways: by changing the document view from **Print Layout** to **Outline** view, by changing the document view from **Print Layout** to **Draft** view, and by using the **Show/Hide** icon on the **Home** tab:

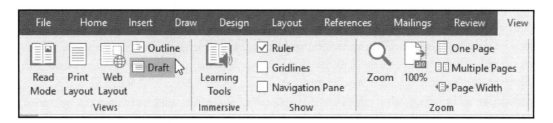

6. Click on the **Print Layout** icon to return to the normal working view.

Adding section breaks

Follow these steps to learn how to add section breaks:

1. Click into the document where the section break is required. I have continued using the same file from the previous section.
2. Insert the type of section break required into the document.
3. Here, the second page will be changed to landscape orientation. We have inserted a **Next Page** section break at the end of the first page (to show where the change must start) and at the end of the second page (to show where the change must end):

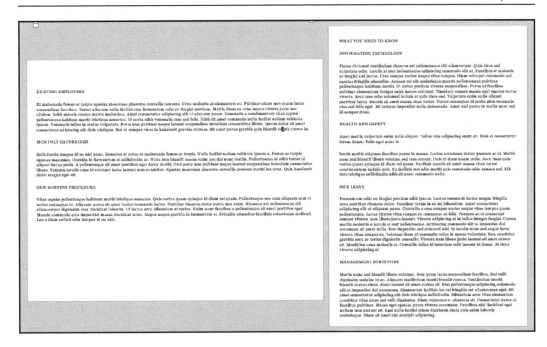

4. Let's replicate these by inserting **Next Page** section breaks into the document to create a landscape page in the middle of the document.

5. Click before the text **Existing Employees**.

6. Visit the **Layout** tab and select **Breaks** from the list.

7. Choose **Next Page** section break to insert a break before the text **Existing Employees**.

8. Move to the end of the paragraph, before the text **What You Need to Know**.

9. Insert another **Next Page** section break at the end of the paragraph.

10. Make sure your mouse pointer is clicked into the text of the page beginning with **Existing Employees**.

11. Click on the **Layout** tab and choose **Orientation**.

12. Choose **Landscape** from the list provided.

13. The page will turn into a landscape page with portrait pages on either side.

Note that this is just one example of how section breaks can transform your documents. The **Next Page** section break is really great when you need to add a complex table in the middle of a Word document.

To delete the section breaks, click on the non-printing symbols (**Show/Hide** icon) icon on the **Paragraph** group, which is located on the **Home** tab. Alternatively, change the document view to **Draft view** and click to place the cursor on the section break line in the document. Then, press *Delete* on the keyboard.

Headers and footers

A page header is an area at the top of the document where you can add text, page numbers, or logos that repeat at the top of each page of the document. A footer is exactly the same, except it resides at the bottom of each page.

The header area is located at the top of the document:

When a header exists in a document, you will notice that the information in it is grayed out when you are in **Print Layout** view. This is because the information is not *active* at the present time. To activate this area and work in it, simply double-click on the existing header. The header area will open up, as shown in the preceding screenshot, and you will be able to edit it. The same applies to the footer.

Inserting a header and footer

Follow these steps to learn how to insert a header and footer:

1. Open the document that you wish to add a header to. We will continue with the `HeadersFooters.docx` document.

2. On the **Insert** tab, locate the **Header & Footer** group.

3. Click on the **Header** icon to access the drop-down list:

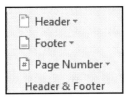

4. Choose a *built-in style* to suit your document.

5. Notice that the list contains different types of headers such as odd and even page headers and styles.

6. For this example, we will use **Blank header**.

7. Type in the text so that it appears at the top of each page in the placeholder provided. In this case, `Report on Services 2019` will be inserted. Notice that all the pages update with the header text:

    1. To type text into the center of the page, press the *Tab* key on your keyboard once.

    2. To type text on the right of the page, press the *Tab* key twice on your keyboard:

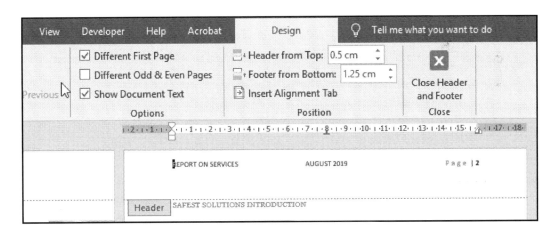

8. The footer area is also available to edit.

9. Use the scrollbar to move to the bottom of a page or click on the **Go to Footer** icon on the **Design** ribbon.

10. Using the keyboard, type the text you wish to appear on the left of the footer. In this case, we will type `Safest Solutions Group`. If you want to place text in the *center* or to the *right* of the page, simply press *Tab* on your keyboard to get there!

11. Press *Tab* to navigate the *center* of the footer.

12. Click on the **Date & Time** icon on the **Header & Footer Tools Design** ribbon.

13. Select the *date/time format* you require from the dialog box. If you would like the footer date to update automatically each time you open the document, make sure that **Update Automatically** is selected.

14. To exit your header area, click on the **Close Header and Footer** icon or double-click outside of your header, onto a page in your document.

 If a custom header already exists in the document and you select either one of the built-in styles or page number styles, it will replace the contents of the current header or footer.

Inserting page numbers

Follow these steps to learn how to insert page numbers:

1. Open the document that you would like to add page numbers to.

2. Click on the **Insert** tab.

3. Choose the **Page Number** icon under the **Header & Footer** group (alternatively, double-click into the header or footer region to edit it, then select **Page Number** from the **Header & Footer** group):

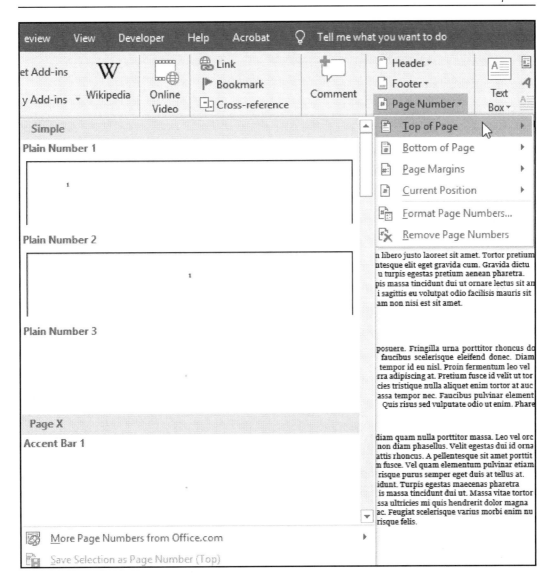

4. Choose where you would like to insert the page number (top, bottom, or current position) and choose a style from the drop-down list that appears – the current position is the position of the mouse pointer when you clicked there. Page X of Y page format is the most popular!

5. After inserting the page number in the footer, you will notice that the first page indicates page 0 of 7. Don't worry about this as it is assuming that the cover page in this document is not counted. We will fix this in the next section.

6. Formatting the header or footer is exactly the same as formatting text in a document.

Choosing a different first page

In the previous section, our page footer numbering included the first page, which is the cover page. Since we do not want a number on this page, we need to do some tweaking to remove the numbering from the first page only:

1. Double-click on the *footer* area in the document to open it.
2. Go to the **Header & Footer Options** group.
3. Select **Different First Page.**
4. With that, the problem has been fixed! Our cover page is now excluded from the header and footer entries.

Numbering from a specific page number

To continue numbering from a specific page number in the document in order to start at a particular page for a chapter of a book, do the following:

1. Open the header or footer area in a document.
2. Select **Format Page Numbers…** from the **Page Number** drop-down list on the ribbon:

3. In the **Page Number Format** dialog box, click on **Start at:** and type the number to start from. Alternatively, use the spin arrows to navigate to the number of your choice.

4. Click on **OK** to make the changes.

To remove headers, click on **Insert** | **Header** | **Remove Header.** To remove a page number, double-click on the header or footer area to access its contents manually. Alternatively, click on the **Page Number** icon from the **Insert** tab and choose **Remove Page Numbers** from the drop-down list box.

Different header and footer sections

Often, you might feel a bit restricted when dealing with headers and footers that have the same information at the top or bottom of each page in the document. With section breaks, you can fix this so that, for instance, *pages 1 and 3* can have different header content to that of *pages 2 and 4*. Follow these steps to learn how to do this:

1. Open the document called Sections.docx. Notice that the first page is excluded from headers and footers. This is because the **Different First Page** option is active in the document.

2. Also, notice that when viewing the header and footer area, the sections are the same from page 2 onward, and the **Same as Previous** option is active on each page header in the document. This means that anything inserted into a header or footer area will be repeated across all pages:

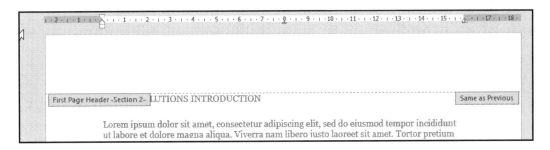

3. Insert section breaks, where relevant, into the document (for this exercise, we will insert **Next Page** section breaks at the bottom of each page to break the document into different sections).

4. As you add **Next Page** section breaks, you might find that the text on the next page moves down slightly. This is normal as the section break tends to do this. Just delete the space at the top of the document as you insert breaks.

5. Make sure you are on the first page of the document.

6. Double-click to open up the header area.

7. Type the text **Report on Services**.

8. As the second page displays **Same as Previous** to the right, any text added to the header will appear on the first page as well.

9. Click into the header area on *page 2*, then click on **Link to Previous** from the **Navigation** group – this will remove the link between the two sections and allow you to delete the header from the first page, without interfering with any text on the second page:

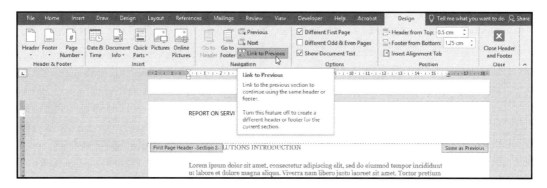

10. Move to the next page (Section 3).

11. Click on **Link to Previous** to remove the link between two sections.

12. Enter the text **Safest Solutions Group** in the center of the header area.

13. While navigating between sections, notice that the distance between the text in some sections is wider than the next – this demonstrates that you can also use formatting to denote a difference between sections in headers and footers.

14. Move to the next page (Section 4).

15. Click on **Link to Previous** to remove the link between two sections.

16. Enter the text `Report on Services`.

17. Continue in this fashion until you reach the end of the document.

18. Click on the **Close Header and Footer** icon to return to the document and view the result.

Summary

In this chapter, you have learned how to create professional documents using Word 2019. Now, you should have a firm grasp of Word 2019 referencing features, be able to perform mail merge documents manually, and be able to use the wizard with confidence. By gaining knowledge of how to customize page layouts and work with forms, you can now create stunning professional documents with ease.

In the next chapter, you will learn how to share and protect documents from unwanted editing or restrict access to content using passwords. We will look at the collaboration features within Word 2019, compare document revisions, and understand metadata. By doing this, you will be able master track changes, locate document properties, and check documents for issues.

4
Versions, Restrictions, and Comparisons

In this chapter, we will learn all about setting editing restrictions and passwords on all or part of a document to prevent unwanted changes. After collaborating on the documents, we will compare and combine document revisions.

This chapter will cover the following topics:

- Recovering draft versions
- Restricting access to documents and workbooks
- Comparing and combining documents

By the end of the chapter, you will understand the term metadata and the importance of checking for documenting properties and issues using the Document Inspector utility.

Technical requirements

Prior to going through this chapter, you should have a working knowledge of how to create professional documents, being able to save, close, and open documents. You should be familiar with document layouts and the ribbon contents offered in Microsoft Word 2019, and also know how to manipulate images. The examples used in this chapter are accessible from the following GitHub URL: `https://github.com/PacktPublishing/Learn-Microsoft-Office-2019`.

Recovering draft versions

You will learn how to recover unsaved versions of documents, allow only certain types of formatting and editing by setting restrictions, apply password protection to documents, and mark documents as final to protect users from editing the final version of a document.

If a user closes a document without saving it, the program stores a version in the temporary files list so that it is recoverable. The user usually has 4 days from the document creation date to restore the version.

Previously saved files—that have been opened and edited, but closed without saving—can be restored as an autosaved draft from the Microsoft Backstage view. These features are particularly useful if a power outage occurs or your system becomes unstable.

Please note, however, that to recover files, you must make sure that you enable the following features in the Microsoft Word environment beforehand.

Enabling the AutoSave and AutoRecover features

The AutoSave and AutoRecover tools within Word 2019 can be of great value when unforeseen computer crashes happen while you are working on documents. Steps to set up both these tools are explained here:

1. Select the File tab.
2. Select **Options** from the list provided.
3. Click on the **Save** category to display the applicable information.
4. Enable **Save AutoRecover information every 2 minutes** (you can change the time according to your usage) and **Keep the last AutoRecovered version if I close without saving** so that files can be recovered.
5. Click the **Browse...** button to choose a folder on the hard drive, which will become the **AutoRecover** file location, or leave the default folder as-is.

   Refer to the following screenshot to view the preceding information:

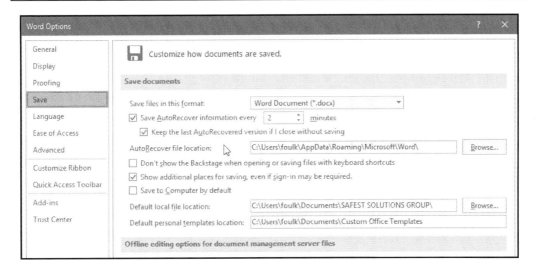

6. Click on **OK** to commit the changes.

Recovering documents

If Microsoft Word 2019 suddenly closes while working or you forget to save a document that you have been editing for some time, you will definitely want to try to recover the document. In order to do so, follow these steps:

1. Open Microsoft Word. If there are files to be recovered, they will be listed on the launch window of Word 2019, as illustrated in the following screenshot:

2. Word will notify you at the top left-hand corner of the screen if there are files that need attention.

3. Under the **Recovered** text, click on **Show Recovered Files**.

4. The Word environment will open with a new blank document, and, to the left of this, the **Document Recovery** pane will be visible, as illustrated in the following screenshot:

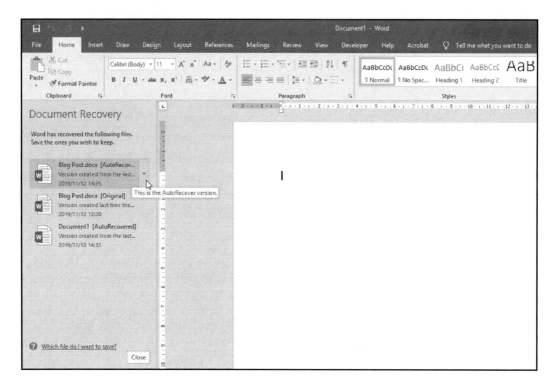

5. If you no longer need the files, click on **Close**; you will be prompted to confirm that you no longer need to keep them.

6. The times and dates of the revisions are listed under each filename in the **Document Recovery** pane.

7. Click to the right of the filename to access options about each file, such as **Open**, **Save As...**, **Delete**, or **Show Repairs** (these will only be active if there are repairs to be conducted—normally when the file is corrupt or experiences errors).

8. You will able to click on the file to view it in the **Document Recovery** pane, and then decide what to do with it, as illustrated in the following screenshot:

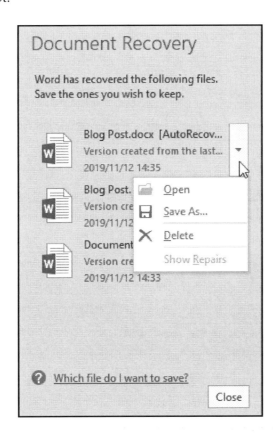

It is also possible to recover files using another method, as follows:

1. Click on **File | Info**, and the options shown in the following screenshot will appear:

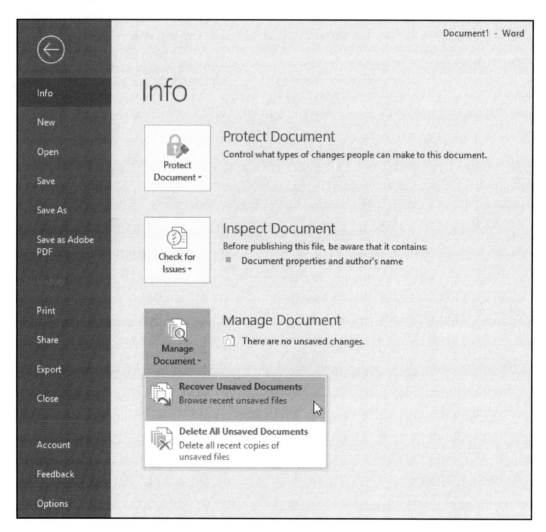

2. Click on **Manage Document** to access its options.
3. Click on **Recover Unsaved Documents**.

4. The **Open** dialog box will populate, showing the `UnsavedFiles` default folder with all the recovered files listed, as illustrated in the following screenshot:

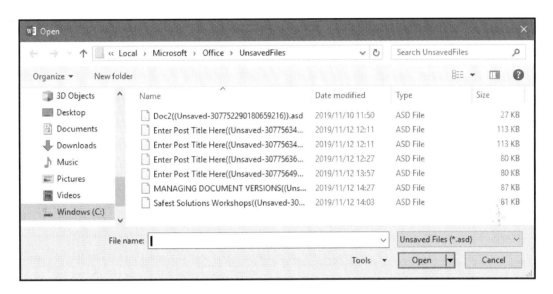

5. The unsaved document opens in Microsoft Word 2019, where you can edit, save, or close the file.
6. If you wish to get rid of all unsaved documents, click on **Delete All Unsaved Documents** from the **Manage Document** list.
7. If you still have recovered files when you close Microsoft Word, a dialog box will open, asking if you would like to view recovered files at a later stage or remove them all right now, as illustrated in the following screenshot:

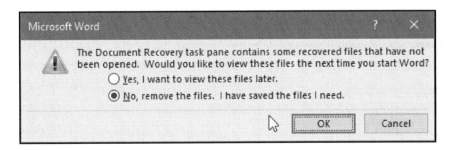

Restricting access to documents and workbooks

This section will focus on protecting documents in Microsoft Word and Excel 2019. You will learn more about the restricting of document parts from editing using the **Review** tab options.

Restricting access to document contents

We can restrict documents using a number of methods in Microsoft Word 2019. If you forget a password for a protected document you will not be able to recover it, so be very careful with this, and only restrict documents when absolutely necessary.

The entire document can be restricted, or we can select parts of the document that can be viewed but not edited. These options are explained in the following subsections. Restrictions can be set via the **Info** option from the **File** tab, or from the **Review** tab on the ribbon.

Follow these next steps to protect certain parts of a document from editing when sharing with others:

1. Open the document. We will use `Resume1Furkidds.docx` for this example.
2. Select the **Review** tab.
3. Select **Restrict Editing** from the **Protect** group, as illustrated in the following screenshot:

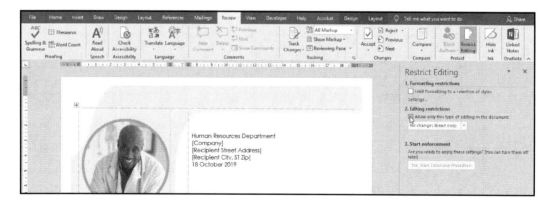

4. The **Restrict Editing** pane will now be present to the right side of your Word document (see preceding screenshot).

5. Locate the second step, **Editing restrictions**, on the Task pane, making sure that the checkbox is selected to reflect **Allow only this type of editing in the document**.

6. Click on **No changes (Read only)** from the drop-down list box.

7. Select/highlight parts of the document for which you wish to allow editing to happen. You may use the *Ctrl* key on the keyboard to select multiple parts of the document simultaneously.

8. Under the **Exceptions** option, select **Everyone** to allow any user of the document to make changes to the highlighted parts of the document.

Or you could follow these steps:

1. Click on **More users...** to type the usernames of the people granted editing rights.

2. Click on **OK** to accept the usernames, after which they will be added to the list.

3. At this point, you may select other parts of the document to allow different users editing rights.

4. Repeat this step, if required.

Refer to the following screenshot to view the preceding information:

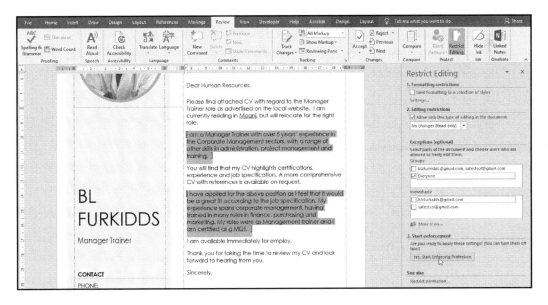

5. In the last step, click on **Yes, Start Enforcing Protection**.

6. A dialog box appears, asking for a protection method. In this case, I've chosen the **Password** option.

7. Choose a method and click on **OK** to continue, as illustrated in the following screenshot:

8. Editing is in place for certain document parts, defined for particular users, and the rest of the document will be restricted.

9. Don't forget to save the document so that the changes are intact when you share the document.

10. You will notice that if you try to delete a sentence or edit a paragraph that is protected, you will not be able to edit it until protection is removed.

11. To stop protection, simply click on the **Stop Protection** icon at the bottom of the pane, as illustrated in the following screenshot:

Note that you can also use the following steps to access the **Restrict Editing** feature:

1. Go to **File | Info | Protect Document**.

2. Select **Restrict Editing**, as illustrated in the following screenshot:

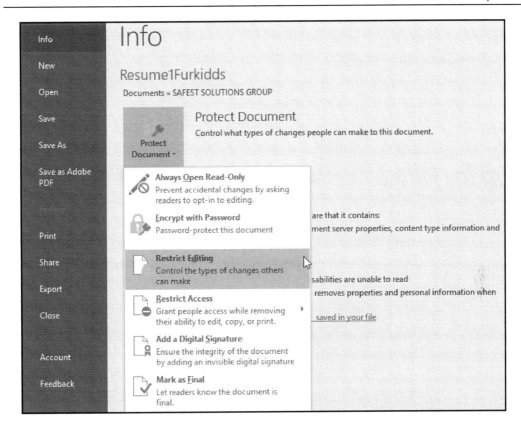

You now have the skills to protect certain parts of your document from editing using the **Restrict Editing** pane within Word 2019. The next topic will show you how to protect the entire document.

Restricting access to workbook contents

In addition to using the **File** | **Info** | **Protect Workbook** method to restrict the editing of workbooks, we can use the **Review** ribbon. We will use this option to protect different parts of a worksheet from editing.

If you are working with others on the same workbook, you may want to consider removing editing rights to parts of the workbook, especially to protect complicated formulae or functions.

Follow the instructions described in the next section to protect a certain part of the workbook from any unwanted editing.

Restricting changes to parts of a worksheet

1. Open the `YearlyProductSales.xlsx` document, in order to restrict parts of the worksheet. This tool is very useful when you do not want users to have editing rights to delete or change the formula you have constructed in certain parts of the workbook. The user can view the result of the formula but cannot edit it.

 Please note that before you can prevent users from editing locked cells on a worksheet range, you need to specify which worksheet cells you do not want users to edit.

2. Click on the **Review** tab.
3. Choose **Allow Users to Edit Ranges** from the **Protect** group.
4. Select the range to protect from editing—in this example, **G2:O145**.
5. Note that the **Permissions...** icon is available, should you wish to specify specific users who are allowed to edit a range without a password. Click on **Apply** at the bottom of the dialog box.

Refer to the following screenshot to view the preceding information:

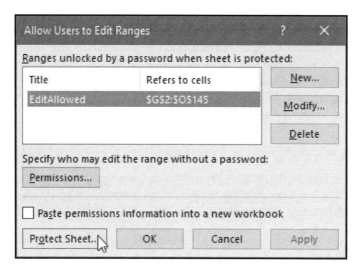

6. Click on the **Protect Sheet**... icon at the bottom of the dialog box, then enter a password, and enter it again to confirm.

7. Click on **OK** to commit to the changes.

8. If a user tries to delete or edit contents in a protected range, they will be greeted with the following error:

9. To remove protection from the worksheet, click on the **Unprotect Worksheet** icon on the **Protect** group, then enter the password to unprotect the worksheet. Save the workbook.

Comparing and combining documents

In this topic, you will learn how to compare different versions of a document and combine revisions from multiple authors.

If two reviewers receive the exact copy of a document with changes made to both, the documents can be compared using the **Compare Documents** utility. This feature takes two documents that have gone through the editing process and combines only what has changed between them into a new third document. The two original documents are not changed.

Please note that if you are working with edited documents from more than two reviewers, then **Combine revisions from multiple authors into a single document** is the option to use.

1. Open the first document to be used to compare with another. Here, we will open Resume1Furkidds.docx.

2. Select **Review | Compare**, as illustrated in the following screenshot:

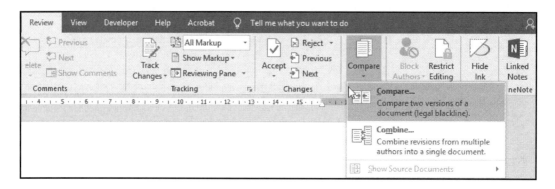

3. You will be offered the following two options:

- **Compare two versions of a document (legal blackline).**
- **Combine revisions from multiple authors into a single document.**

4. Click **Compare...**

5. A dialog box will present itself and will allow you to choose the two documents to compare, as illustrated in the following screenshot:

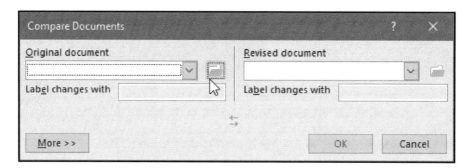

6. Choose the original document from the drop-down list or browse to locate it on your computer, and click the revised document from the drop-down list or browse to locate it on your computer, as illustrated in the following screenshot:

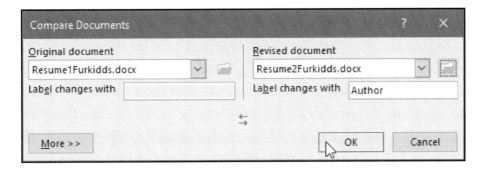

7. There are more settings that can be changed by using the **More >>** icon on the dialog box and selecting desired options, which are illustrated in the following screenshot:

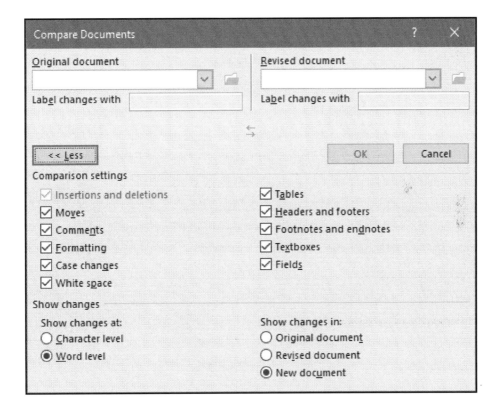

8. By default, the changes will appear in a new document (a third document).

9. Click on **OK** to compare the documents.

10. Your Word screen will now change to a new document called `Compare Result 4`. The screen is split into four parts, as follows:

    - The original document, called `Resume1Furkidds.docx`
    - The revised document, called `Resume2Furkidds.docx`
    - The compared document, which shows both revisions
    - A summary of changes highlighted and explained on the left of the screen, as illustrated in the following screenshot:

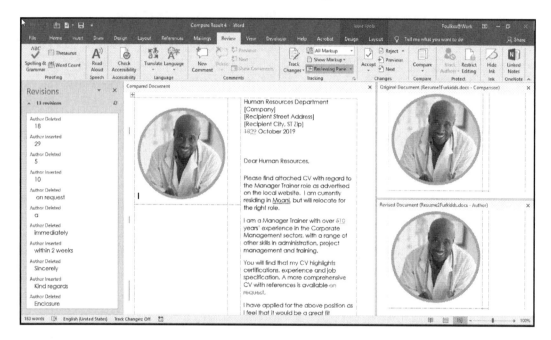

11. The next step is to accept or reject the changes in the compared document, to reach a combined final document, as illustrated in the following screenshot:

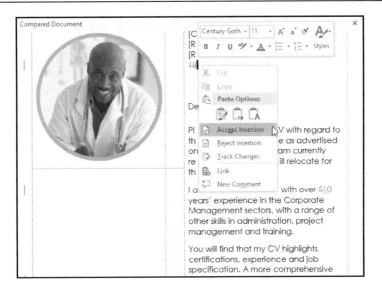

12. Right-click on the changes highlighted in the compared document and decide whether to reject or accept them, or go to the ribbon and locate the **Accept Insertion** and **Reject Insertion** options.

 All the text highlighted by a strikethrough indicates removed text, and underlined text is anything that is added in its place.

13. Once the revisions are complete, you will notice the **Revisions** pane will display **0 revisions**, as illustrated in the following screenshot:

14. Save the compared document as `ResumeFinal.docx`, and close all other windows to see the final document.

You have now learned how to compare two documents and combine the changes into one document.

Summary

This chapter has equipped you with the skills to share, collaborate upon, inspect, and protect documents in Word 2019. You have mastered the task of comparing different versions of documents, thereby combining revisions, and are able to use many methods of sharing documents with others.

In the next chapter, you will be introduced to the PowerPoint 2019 interface and presentation options. You will learn how to set application options, set up slides, and work with files and print options, and will be confident navigating around the interface.

Section 2: PowerPoint 2

PowerPoint 2019, being part of the latest desktop productivity suite, provides a rich set of tools for creating presentations. During this part of the book, we will introduce end users to this presentation software, identifying its new features and demonstrating how to use it to create and work with attractive, highly professional presentations. These chapters cover everything you need to know to start using PowerPoint 2019 productively in the workplace, at home, and for certification purposes.

In this section, we will cover the following chapters:

- Chapter 5, *The PowerPoint Interface and Presentation Options*
- Chapter 6, *Formatting Slides, Tables, Charts, and Graphic Elements*
- Chapter 7, *Photo Albums, Sections, and Show Tools*

5
The PowerPoint Interface and Presentation Options

In this chapter, you will be shown how to personalize the Backstage view and set various options. You will navigate the interface and perform basic tasks, including creating, saving, printing, and viewing presentations in PowerPoint 2019.

The following topics are covered in this chapter:

- Introduction and new features
- Saving presentations in different formats
- Setting print options and layouts
- Using the view and zoom options

Technical requirements

You should understand basic presentation terminologies such as slides, presentation, animation, and transitions. The examples used in this chapter are accessible from GitHub at: `https://github.com/PacktPublishing/Learn-Microsoft-Office-2019`.

Introduction and new features

It is important to note that a presentation is a collection of slides around a specific topic, generally delivered to an audience by a speaker. PowerPoint offers the user various slide views and printed formats (such as overhead slides, speaker notes, audience handouts, or outlines). The user makes the presentation professional, visually attractive, and understandable by adding elements such as special effects, sound, animation, and transitional effects to view on the screen. Slides are the separate pages of the presentation to which elements such as graphs, tables, shapes, WordArt, SmartArt, clip art, and other objects are added.

We will not cover all the interface skills here as you have been through these in the previous chapters, and these are identical across Office 2019.

There are a few new enhancements in PowerPoint 2019 that we will address practically throughout this part of the book, but we will highlight the following list as an introduction:

- **Morph effect**: The **Morph** tool helps you create smooth transitions by moving items around at the same time, and is illustrated in the following screenshot:

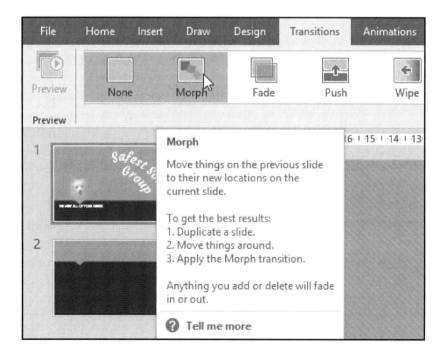

- **Zoom**: This allows the presenter to jump to a certain slide during a presentation with ease. The **Zoom** tool is illustrated in the following screenshot:

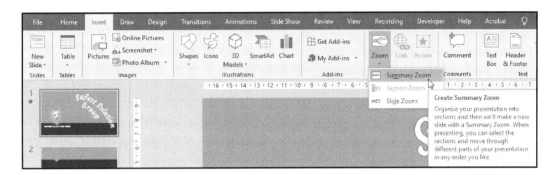

- **Text highlighter**: This tool allows you to apply highlight colors to text within a presentation to create emphasis, just as in Word 2019! It is illustrated in the following screenshot:

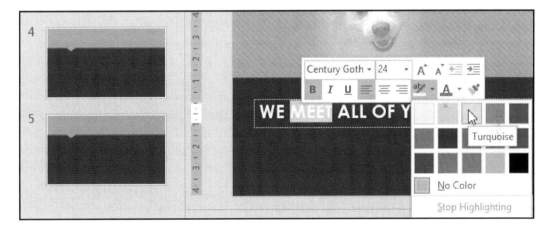

- **Scalable Vector Graphics (SVG) and other graphic properties**: SVG files can have color changes, can be disassembled and reassembled, and do not lose any quality when the size of the image changes. SVG files can also be converted to shapes in PowerPoint 2019, and 3D models can be inserted so that rotation can be utilized. Image background removal is also enhanced, as you no longer need to be restricted to highlighting areas to be removed via straight lines.

- **4K resolution for video**: You can record video, audio, and inking and export video at 4K resolution, all available from the **Recording** tab, as illustrated in the following screenshot:

- **Inking**: Highlighter pens are available in all the Office apps, which can be customized and are portable—this includes the new **Effects** option and a segment eraser when drawing. There is also support for touchscreens when placing objects on straight lines using the **Ruler**. These features can be seen in the following screenshot:

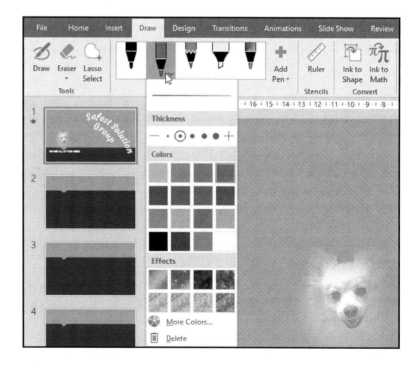

- **Digital pen to navigate a slide show**: You can advance slides using a Bluetooth pen in PowerPoint 2019.

- **Charts**: There are new charts available, such as **Map** and **Funnel** charts, as illustrated in the following screenshot:

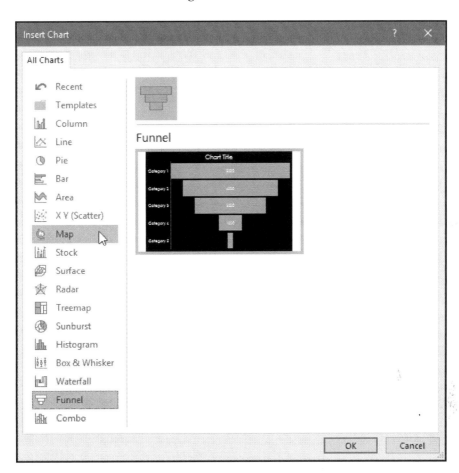

These are some of the stunning new features available in the PowerPoint 2019 application.

Creating presentation templates

A template is a presentation with a predefined look and contains default text, layouts, and even animations. Templates are often used as a basis for presentations, especially in the 2019 version, as there are many professional animated effects available. They are created to suit the needs of the user and are often a quick way to get things done!

Office 2019 has a huge range of templates within the PowerPoint environment, as well as the ability to search and download templates online from within the application. Categories are available just below the search bar and guide the user when searching online.

To search for templates online, you must first have an internet connection. Then, proceed as follows:

1. Click on **File** | **New** and search for a template by inputting a keyword into the text area provided, or select a template from the **Featured** list provided, as illustrated in the following screenshot:

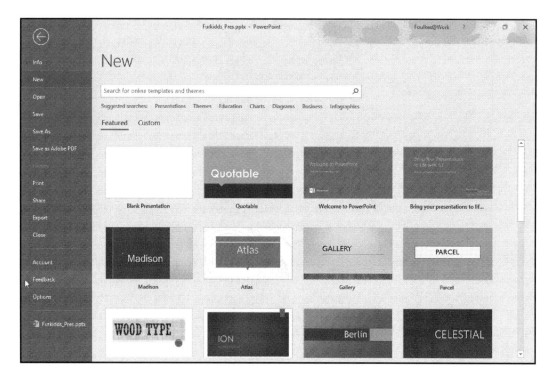

2. Once you have decided on a template, click on the template to view details about it. You are able to scroll through all the templates using this method as a preview, using the arrow to the right of the preview, as illustrated in the following screenshot:

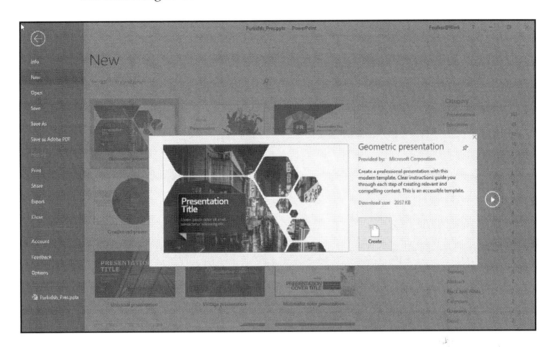

3. Click on **Create** to open the template in PowerPoint and add content.

Setting up slides and working with files

In this section, you will master slide size and orientation options, use Compatibility Mode, add tags to a presentation, embed fonts so that you do not lose formats when presenting on different devices, and learn how to save a presentation in the required format.

Setting slide size

Access the **Page Setup** dialog box to change the size of the slide presentation to a custom format. This dialog box contains a range of different sizes (**Slide Show**; **Banner**; **35 mm slides**; **Overhead**, to name but a few). Proceed as follows:

1. Click on **Design** | **Customize** | **Slide Size**.
2. You will be presented with two default slide sizes, **Standard** and **Widescreen**, as illustrated in the following screenshot:

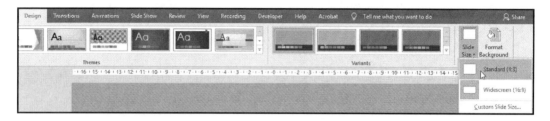

3. Click on **Custom Slide Size...**, and once the dialog box has opened, choose a slide size from the **Slides sized for:** drop-down list. Some options will ask if you would like to maximize the size of the content or to fit the content.
4. You can select **Custom** if you wish to enter your own measurements in terms of width and height of the slides in the presentation, as illustrated in the following screenshot:

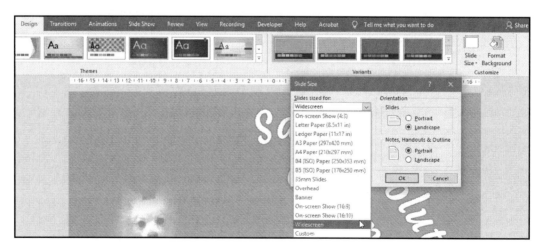

We will now learn how to change the slide orientation in the next topic.

Changing the slide orientation

Slide layouts are landscape by default in PowerPoint and are always the same throughout the presentation. You cannot have some slides in portrait format and others in landscape format. When the orientation is changed, the entire presentation will update to the new orientation. To change the orientation, follow these steps:

1. Click on **Design** | **Customize** | **Orientation**, and the following options will appear:

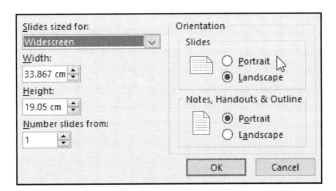

2. Choose **Portrait** from the **Orientation** options, after which you will be asked to select a scaling option, as illustrated in the following screenshot:

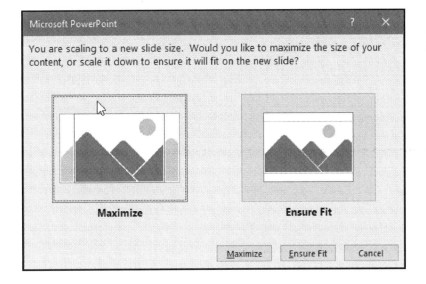

3. If you have graphical objects on the slide and you change the slide orientation, you may find that the objects shift around. Try switching between **Maximize** and **Ensure Fit** to alleviate too much change, but it may be necessary to reposition objects after changing the orientation. The following screenshot shows an example of this:

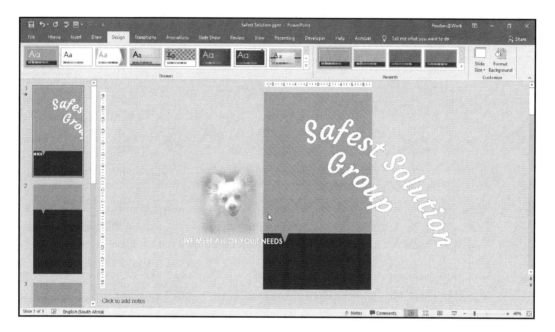

Note that it is possible to link two presentations together (one portrait and one landscape). To change the orientation of notes, handouts, and outlines, visit the relevant icon on the **Slide Size** dialog box.

Adding tags to a presentation

When you create presentations, you can add metadata such as tags to allow files to be sorted and located. Tags are used to categorize presentations. To add tags to a presentation, proceed as follows:

1. Open the presentation you wish to tag. Click on **File | Info | Properties** (on the right-hand side of the window).

2. Look for **Tags**. Enter a tag into the space provided, such as `Safest` or `Furkiddz`, in this instance.

3. Save the presentation to update it.

Searching using tags

Tags are very useful when searching and locating specific presentations on your computer. Click to open the Explorer window on the desktop, then proceed as follows:

1. Navigate to a folder of your choice or, alternatively, select the `Documents` folder, as illustrated in the following screenshot:

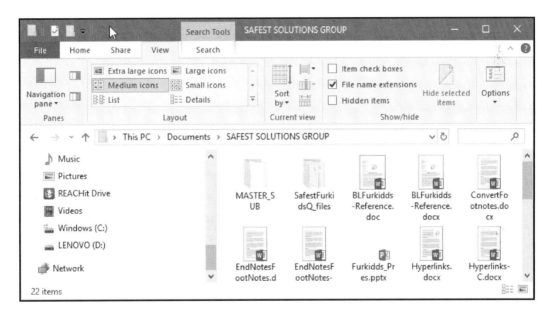

2. Choose the **Search** tab directly under the **Search Tools** contextual tab.

3. Select **Tags** from the **Other properties** drop-down list, as illustrated in the following screenshot:

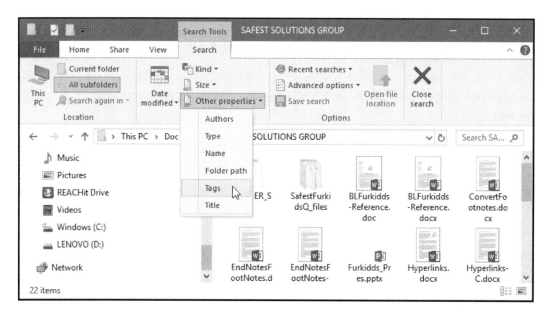

4. The `tags:` search is inserted into the search box at the end of the toolbar, as illustrated in the following screenshot:

5. Type the tags you would like to search for through the presentations. As you type the tags, the search is activated and the presentations containing those tags become visible in the window, as illustrated in the following screenshot:

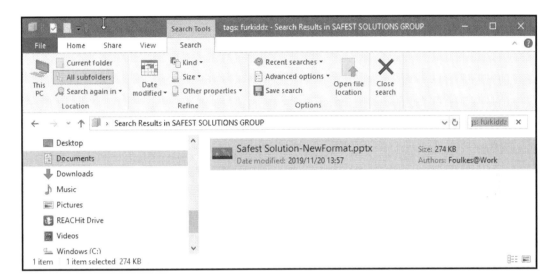

6. When you are done searching and have located the presentation according to the tag search, open the presentation to see its contents.

Embedding fonts

When customizing presentations, adding specific fonts to a presentation aids the look of the design, and also enhances diagrams and custom drawings. The only problem is that when sharing the presentation with others or presenting it at a specific location, you might find that the fonts are converted automatically, which will drastically change your presentation design. This is because fonts that are *not default* application fonts are not necessarily available at another location or computer.

Let's fix this, as follows:

1. Click on the **File | Save As...** option.
2. Navigate to the location where you wish to save the presentation. Click on **Browse** to populate the **Save As** dialog box. Look for the **Tools** option at the bottom of the dialog box, as illustrated in the following screenshot:

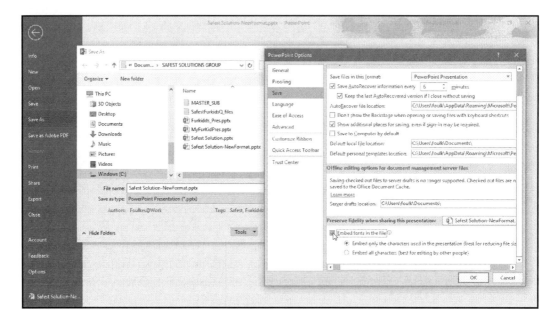

3. Choose **Save Options...** from the **Tools** drop-down list. The **PowerPoint Options** dialog box will populate. You will notice that the **Save** option is highlighted, and options related to **Save** are presented on the right-hand side of the dialog box.
4. Navigate to **Preserve fidelity when sharing this presentation**.
5. Click the checkbox to the left of **Embed fonts in the file**.
6. Then, choose **Embed only the characters used in the presentation** or **Embed all characters**.
7. Click **OK** to commit the change. Save the presentation and then share it with others.

Saving presentations in different formats

We will now look at the different ways in which we can save PowerPoint 2019 presentations such as saving the presentation slides as separate images and saving the presentation in the **Portable Document File (PDF)** format.

Saving presentation slides as pictures

Follow these steps to save every slide separately as a picture from a completed presentation—a great way to alleviate any font issues when presenting. Although you will lose any animation or transitions as the files will become static files, this is a great way to use slides as images within other design or print media. Proceed as follows:

1. Open the presentation that contains slides you wish to save as pictures. For this exercise, we will use the presentation called `SafestSolution_Benefits.pptx`.
2. Select **File** | **Save As…**.
3. In the **Save As…** dialog box, choose a location to save your presentation as pictures.
4. Change the **Save as type:** option to save in a picture format such as **Graphics Interchange Format (GIF)** or **Portable Network Graphic (PNG)** format.
5. Change the name of the file (if you prefer).

6. The name you specify in the **File name:** text area will become the folder in which all the slide pictures will save individually, as illustrated in the following screenshot:

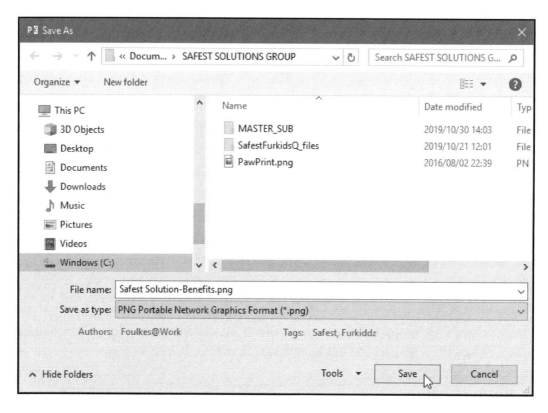

7. Click on **Save**.

8. A dialog box will appear in the presentation, asking whether you would like to save every slide or just the current selected slide in the presentation, as illustrated in the following screenshot:

9. Choose **All Slides** for this example.

10. When the presentation has completed saving the pictures, a dialog box will pop up, indicating the location the pictures have been saved to. Click on **OK** to return to the presentation. Your screen should now look like this:

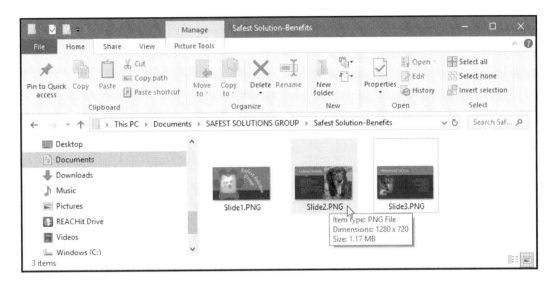

11. Use **This PC** to view the results of the save, and navigate to the folder, as shown in the preceding screenshot.

We can also save a presentation in a PDF format, which prohibits editing and has a smaller file size, but is still able to be shared and viewable. The **Save as PDF** option is perfect for this purpose. You don't need additional software to achieve this with the new Office 2019 applications, and the document format is retained when viewing online or in printed form. It is also useful to save presentations in this format when you need to visit a printing company as it is a widely used format and compatibility is not an issue. Once you save as a PDF document, you cannot reverse this unless you use additional software. To view a PDF file, you must have a reader installed on your computer. A typical example of this is Acrobat Reader, which is available free from `http://www.adobe.com/products/acrobat/`.

The **Save to PDF** option is also available on the Backstage view. Use the **File** tab to access the Backstage view, choose **Save as Adobe PDF**, as well as the **Export** facility located on the **File** tab options.

Saving as a template

A presentation template is a presentation you can create that can be used to produce frequently used types of presentations more quickly and easily. You could format, for instance, a training presentation, budget report, or photo album with the corporate fonts, company information, and logos, and save the presentation as a template. As the presentation is a template, it allows new presentations to be created based on this template.

To save a presentation as a template, follow the steps as per the preceding example, but change the **Save as type:** option to **PowerPoint Template (*.potx)**. If you would like the presentation template to be available in the template folder and be accessible through the **File | New…** templates option, then saving to the correct location is very important. Once you click **PowerPoint Template (*.potx)** in the **Save As** dialog box, PowerPoint automatically changes the location to the default personal template folder. This will ensure that the template is available when clicking on the **File** tab and selecting the **New** option.

Saving a presentation as an outline

Saving as an outline in **Rich Text Format** (.rtf) removes all formatting and leaves only the text in the slide presentation. Follow the same steps as in the preceding section to save a presentation in another format, but choose the **Save as type:** outline option instead.

Saving as a presentation show

This option exports your presentation so that it opens in slideshow view, rather than in normal view. This is a popular option when sending presentations via email, as the presentation is attached to an email message in the Presentation Show format so that the recipient only launches the show, not the application and the presentation.

1. Open a presentation to save as a PowerPoint show. For this example, we will use the SSGreenGroup.pptx presentation.
2. Choose the **Change File Type** option from the **Export** list, then click on the **PowerPoint Show (*.ppsx)** option:

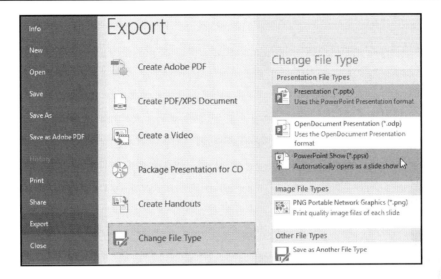

3. In the **Save As...** dialog box, choose a location to save the file to, as well as a filename, if applicable.

4. Click on **Save**. The PowerPoint show is saved to the specified location. Note the difference in the presentation icon when you save it as a presentation show.

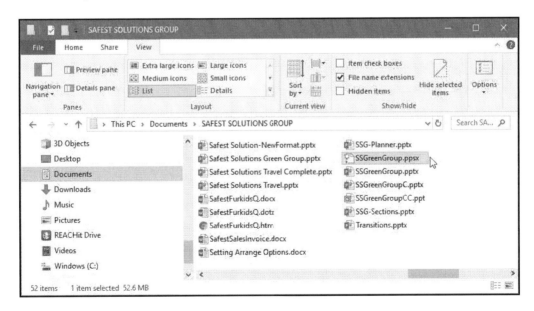

5. Double-click on the file to launch the presentation in slideshow view.

The PowerPoint presentation opens in slideshow view, which allows the user to click through the presentation to view the next slide. Press the Esc key on your keyboard to exit the presentation when done.

Exporting file types

In addition to the various methods of saving presentations as different file types, there is an **Export** option on the **File** tab that is also useful when saving presentations in different file formats. These are covered in detail in Chapter 11, *Exporting and Optimizing Files and the Browser View*. To use the Export feature, click on the **File** | **Export** | **Change File Type** option, as illustrated in the following screenshot:

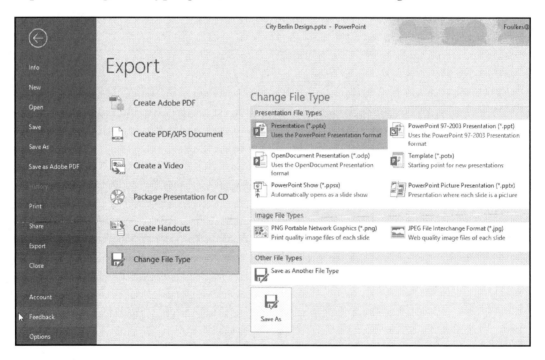

Choose a file type from the list provided to save the presentation as either a presentation type, image type, or another type.

Setting print options and layouts

In this topic, you will learn how to set print options and layouts, change settings, and preview presentations. Although it is not often that you would want to print an entire presentation, there may be a need to print handouts for an audience to refer to while you are going through an onscreen presentation.

Adjusting print settings

Let's have a look at the presentation print and slide options available in PowerPoint 2019, as follows:

1. To access the **Print Settings**, click on the **File** tab to access the Backstage view and select **Print** from the menu, as illustrated in the following screenshot:

2. Under the **Settings** heading, click to choose a printer from the drop-down list provided. Printer properties are accessible just underneath the **Printer** list, and options therein will differ depending on the printer type selected. The list can be seen in the following screenshot:

3. Just to the right of the **Print** icon, you will notice the **Copies:** spin button, which allows the user to specify the number of sets of slides to print, as illustrated in the following screenshot:

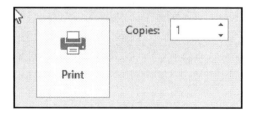

4. Often, you would use the **Collate** option with the **Copies:** option. If printing multiple copies of the same presentation, you might want to collate them so that the printout is in sets or prints the number of copies of *slide 1*, then the number of copies of *slide 2*, and so on. This option is illustrated in the following screenshot:

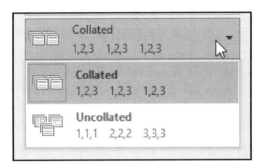

5. From the **Settings** option, you can choose the following printing options. The default is set to the **Print All Slides** option for the presentation, as illustrated in the following screenshot:

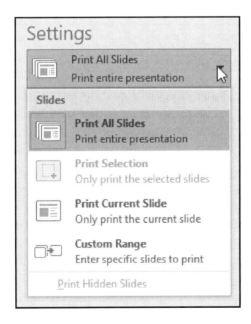

6. If you click on the **Full Page Slides** option, you get will access to other options allowing the printing of **Notes Pages**, **Outline**, and **Handouts**. The **Handouts** option offers many methods of placing slides onto a page. At the bottom of the list, you will find options to add a frame around each slide, scale the slides to fit the paper, print in high quality, print comments, or print ink drawings, as illustrated in the following screenshot:

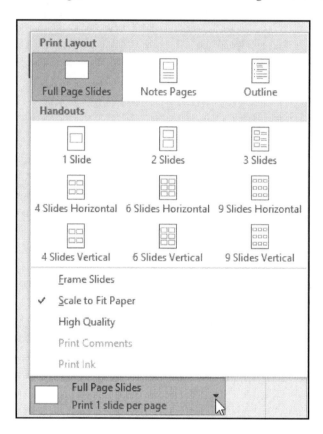

7. To print back to back (both sides of the paper), click on the **Print One Sided** drop-down list, and select **Print on Both Sides**. There are also options relating to flipping the page the long or short edge of the paper, as illustrated in the following screenshot:

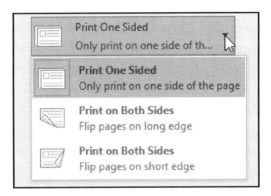

8. To print the slides in **Grayscale**, click to choose the **Color** drop-down list, as illustrated in the following screenshot:

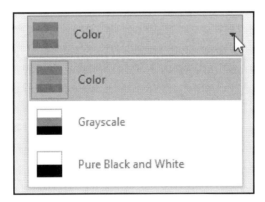

9. Click on the **Header and Footer** option to make final changes to these areas before you print the presentation, as illustrated in the following screenshot:

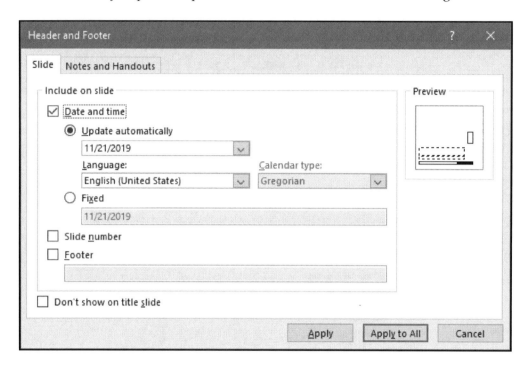

10. Click on **Apply** to add the changes to the current slide or **Apply to All** to make the changes to the entire presentation.

Previewing presentations

The **Print Preview** mode is available, along with the presentation printing options.

1. Click on **File** | **Print**.

2. In the following screenshot, you will see the presentation now in **Print Preview** mode to the right, and the options to the left. The first slide is enlarged to fill the landscape page with various options along the bottom of the window, from which you can customize the view and navigate from one slide to the next, as illustrated in the following screenshot:

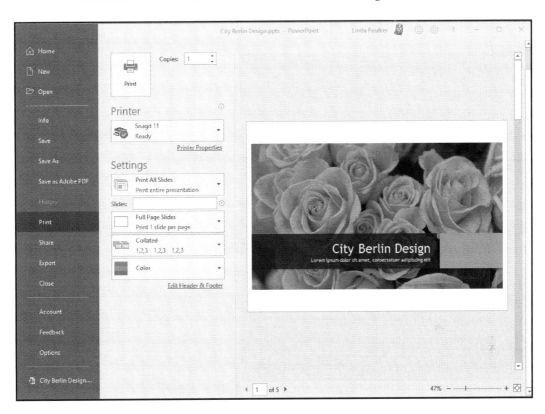

3. Navigate using the left- and right-hand arrows at the bottom of the slide to move from one slide to another.

4. Please note that you will not be able to see animations or transitions in this view.

5. To see the full presentation for presenting purposes, use the **From Beginning** icon on the **Slide Show** tab, as shown in the following screenshot:

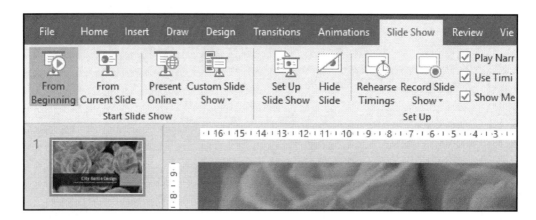

Using view and zoom options

By the end of this topic, you will understand the function of the various presentation views in PowerPoint 2019 and how to set up presentation zoom options, as well as use the **Window** tab to switch between multiple presentations.

Presentation Views using the ribbon

There are five **Presentation Views** in PowerPoint 2019, as well as three **Master Views**. Two additional views are available. The first, called the **Presenter View**, is located on the **Slide Show** tab. This view allows the presentation to be viewed on two monitors. The audience display will show the presentation without notes, while the speaker can enjoy having access to the slides and notes as well as other great features while presenting. Setting up **Presenter View** is addressed under its own topic in this book. The other view is the **Slide Show View**, which is used to show the presentation to the audience. The **Slide Show View** takes up the whole screen, hiding the program tabs, ribbon, and menu. Use this view to see how your presentation will display to an audience when presenting.

Click on the **View** tab on the ribbon to access the **Presentation Views** group, as illustrated in the following screenshot:

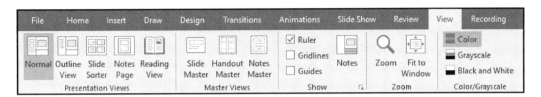

We'll get to see the following types of view:

- **Normal View**: This allows the user to work on all features of the presentation in one place. This is the main view, where all editing and formatting takes place. It consists of the Slide pane and Notes pane (if active), as illustrated in the following screenshot:

- **Outline View**: Use this view to paste a Word outline into a presentation with ease. It is also a really easy way to edit text on presentation slides, as illustrated in the following screenshot:

- **Slide Sorter View**: This shows slides in thumbnail view. In this view, you can copy and move slides with ease, reorder slides, and play animations and transitions per slide. A great feature in this view is the ability to organize your presentation into sections (categories), which will be discussed under a separate topic in this book. This view is illustrated in the following screenshot:

- **Notes Page View**: This view consists of Notes pane contents, as well as the slide the notes refer to. These notes can be printed out as handouts for the audience. This view is illustrated in the following screenshot:

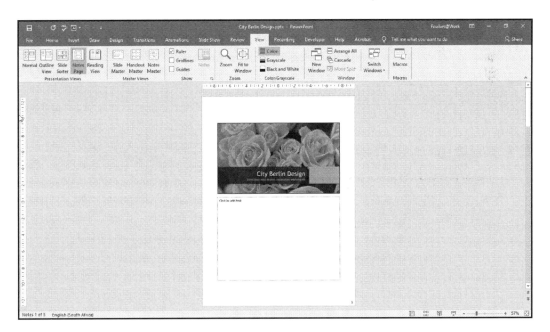

- **Reading View**: This view is not used to present to an audience on a big screen, but rather to someone viewing the presentation on a computer. When using **Reading View** the screen will display as a window on the screen, with similar controls as viewing the presentation in Slide Show view when presenting to an audience. To exit this view, simply press the *Esc* key on your keyboard. This view can be seen in the following screenshot:

We will now look at the different options presented to us on the status bar.

Using the status bar commands

Changing the presentation view is also possible via the view icons located on the status bar, but a more comprehensive list is available along the **View** tab, as illustrated in the following screenshot

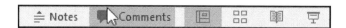

Setting presentation zoom options

The default slide zoom is set at 66% when opening or creating new presentations. To change this setting, use one of the following options:

1. Use the status bar zoom slider to increase or decrease the presentation slide size within the PowerPoint environment or, alternatively, click on the minus (-) and plus (+) signs to adjust, as illustrated in the following screenshot:

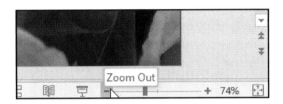

2. Click on the zoom percentage indicator on the status bar to access the zoom options, which you can adjust according to your requirements, as illustrated in the following screenshot:

3. The **Percent** text area enables you to type a custom value to zoom, as illustrated in the following screenshot:

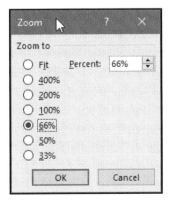

4. Or, use the **View** tab to access the **Zoom** group on the ribbon. Click on the **Zoom** icon to launch the **Zoom** dialog box, which can be seen in the following screenshot:

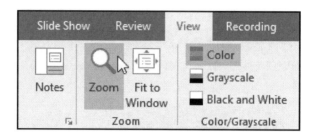

5. The **Fit to Window** option allows the user to zoom the slide quickly to fit the Slide pane. Click on the **Fit to Window** icon at the bottom right-hand corner of the presentation, as illustrated in the following screenshot:

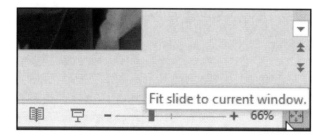

6. You can also visit the **View** tab and select **Fit to Window** from the **Zoom** group, as illustrated in the following screenshot:

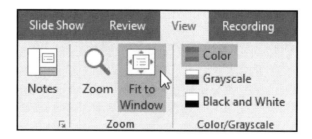

You have learned to navigate and apply different view options in PowerPoint 2019. Let's now look at how to navigate between open presentations in the next topic.

Switching between multiple presentations

1. Click to select **File | Open**.
2. Click to select the first presentation file.
3. Hold down the *Ctrl* key on your keyboard and click on the second file, and then on the next, and then release the *Ctrl* key.
4. Click on **Open**, whereafter all selected files will open in Microsoft PowerPoint—one on top of the other, as illustrated in the following screenshot:

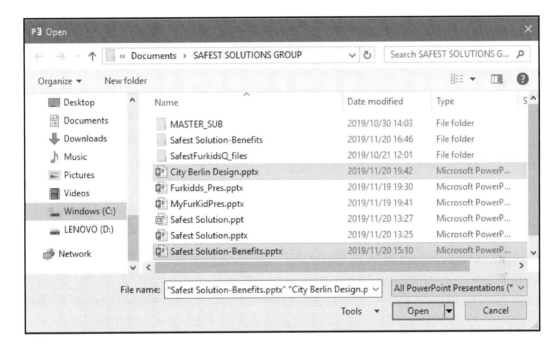

5. Click on the **View** tab on the ribbon.

6. Navigate to the **Switch Windows** drop-down option and click on the arrow, as illustrated in the following screenshot:

7. A list of open presentations will appear as a drop-down list.
8. Click on the presentation you wish to make the active presentation.

Alternatively, you can follow these steps:

1. Take a look at the Windows taskbar, shown in the following screenshot:

2. If you position your mouse over the PowerPoint application icon, a list of open PowerPoint presentations (in tiny windows) will be displayed just above the taskbar.

Summary

Now that you have finished this chapter, you have the skills to personalize the PowerPoint 2019 Backstage view and set various options. You have also acquired the skills to navigate the interface and perform basic tasks, which included the creation, saving, printing, and viewing of presentations in PowerPoint 2019.

In the next chapter, we will use predefined options to give slides a particular *look and feel*. In addition to covering how to set up a basic presentation, you will be able to order a sequence of slides, apply a presentation theme and slide layout, and reuse slides. You will also learn how to work with tables and charts that make data much easier to present and explain, adding to the impact of a presentation.

6

Formatting Slides, Tables, Charts, and Graphic Elements

In Microsoft PowerPoint 2019, you can easily add slides to a presentation and use predefined options to give the slides a particular *look and feel*. In this chapter, you'll learn how to set up a basic presentation, order a sequence of slides, apply a presentation theme and slide layout, and reuse slides. You will also learn how to work with tables and charts, which make data much easier to present and explain, thus adding to the impact of a presentation.

The following topics will be covered in this chapter:

- Setting up slides and applying layouts
- Working with themes and text manipulation
- Formatting text boxes
- Arranging and manipulating objects
- Constructing and modifying tables and charts
- Inserting audio and video

Let's get started!

Technical requirements

After reading the previous chapter, you will now be confident with moving around the PowerPoint 2019 interface, adding slides to a presentation, being able to use the **Info** tab, and being able to set basic application options. In addition, you will be proficient in working with the presentation print options.

The examples that will be used in this chapter can be accessed from the following GitHub URL: `https://github.com/PacktPublishing/Learn-Microsoft-Office-2019`.

Setting up slides and applying layouts

In this section, you will learn how to add, remove, and duplicate slides; insert an outline; reuse saved slides; and apply layouts.

Adding new slides

Follow these steps to learn how to add new slides:

1. We will use the presentation called `City Berlin Design.pptx` for this example.
2. Position the mouse pointer in-between two slides within the presentation:

3. Use *one* of the following methods to insert a new slide into the presentation:

- Press *Enter* on the keyboard to create a new slide. The new title and content slide type are inserted by default between slides 1 and 3 in this example.
- Click on **Insert** | **New Slide** from the **Slides** group, which will populate a list of available slide layouts to choose from:

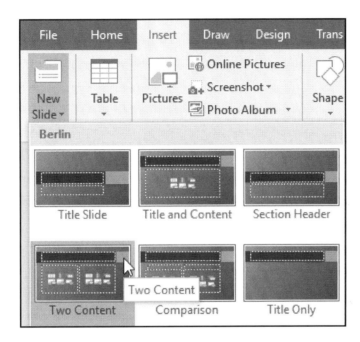

Now that you have the skills to insert new slides, we will learn how to duplicate slides.

Duplicating selected slides

The difference between duplicating slides and using the **copy** command is that the duplication method does not send the item into the clipboard memory, whereas the **copy** command does send the slide to the clipboard, ready to be inserted elsewhere. Follow these steps to learn how to duplicate selected slides:

1. Select a slide on the left-hand side of the presentation to copy.

2. **Go to Home | New Slide | Duplicate Selected Slides** (at the bottom of the menu). An exact duplicate of the slide will appear:

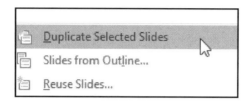

3. Select a slide to duplicate, then right-click on the slide and choose **Duplicate** from the shortcut menu. Alternatively, use the *Ctrl + D* shortcut to duplicate a slide.

Deleting multiple slides simultaneously

To delete a single slide, simply select the slide and press the *Delete* key on the keyboard. To select slides in a presentation to delete, use your *Ctrl* key to select slides beneath each other using the mouse pointer, or slides that are non-contiguous. Right-click on one of the selected slides and choose **Delete** from the shortcut menu.

If you delete slides by mistake, you can bring them back by using the **Undo Delete Slide** (or *Ctrl + Z*) icon from the Quick Access Toolbar:

Copying non-contiguous slides to other presentations

Copying slides that are not next to each other is possible by using *Ctrl + C*, as follows:

1. Select your slides using the *Ctrl* + click method, then right-click the slide and choose **Copy**.
2. Move to the destination slide presentation or create a new presentation, then place your mouse pointer where you would like to paste the slides.
3. Then, right-click and choose **Paste** to insert them into the new presentation.

Inserting an outline

In this section, we will learn how to insert an outline from a previously-typed Word document. Follow these steps:

 Please note that you will not able to insert images, shapes, or any artistic features in the Outline view.

1. Open the `Safest Solution-Benefits.pptx` presentation for this example.
2. Go to **Home** | **New Slide** | **Slides from Outline...**:

3. Browse to locate the outline (`Outline.docx`) to insert it into the presentation. The file extension can be `.rtf` (**Rich Text Format**); `.docx` (**Microsoft Word document**); or `.txt` (**text file format**).
4. Click **Insert**.

5. The outline will be inserted into PowerPoint, thus splitting the information across multiple slides.

6. Format the information as required.

Reusing presentation slides

Using slides from an already created presentation saves a lot of time, especially if the presentation you are creating is going to consist of numerous slides that you can reuse from another presentation:

1. Open a new presentation called `Safest Solution-Benefits.pptx`.

2. Go to **Home | New Slide | Reuse Slides...** (at the bottom of the menu).

3. A **Reuse Slides** pane will open to the right of the PowerPoint environment:

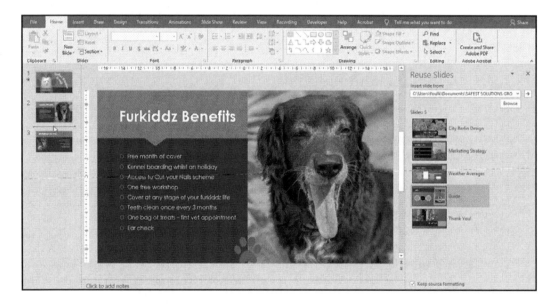

4. Click on the **Browse** button to access the folders on your computer.

5. Choose **Browse File...** to open another presentation in the **Reuse Slides** pane – use the `City Berlin Design.pptx` presentation to follow this example. Once selected, the file will open on the right-hand side of the PowerPoint screen as a **Reuse Slides Task** pane.

6. Before we insert a slide from the browsed presentation, we must *click* on a slide in the existing presentation to indicate where we would like to insert the new slide.

7. To insert a slide beneath the selected slide, click to select a slide from the **Reuse Slides** pane. The slide will be inserted into the existing presentation, beneath the selected slide:

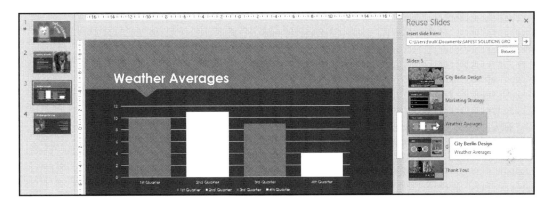

8. Notice that the inserted slide takes on the theme from the existing presentation.

9. Should you wish to keep the formatting of the selected slide and not merge it with the existing slide presentation theme, click on the **Keep source formatting** checkbox at the bottom of the **Reuse Slides** pane:

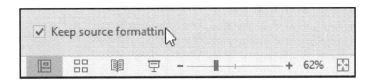

With that, you have learned how to combine slides from other presentations into an existing or new presentation, as well as how to access the option to keep the formatting of the inserted slides as-is. Now, we will look at the different types of layouts available within PowerPoint 2019.

Applying slide layouts

A slide layout is a predefined slide that contains formatting (font, paragraph, styles, and so on) and placeholders (these are the text boxes that you type text on a slide into) that are positioned for you on the slide as a default. In addition, a slide layout could contain placeholders for images, charts, SmartArt, and header and footer placeholders. These layouts make it easier and faster to construct a presentation without the hassle of you having to build a blank slide from scratch. You are able to create custom layouts or choose from the 12 different slide layouts in PowerPoint 2019.

When creating a new presentation in PowerPoint, the first slide is based on the **Title Slide** layout. Click on **File** | **New** | **Blank Presentation**. To add a new slide, simply press the *Enter* key on the keyboard, or right-click and choose **New Slide...** from the shortcut menu. Every new slide that's inserted is based on the **Title and Content Slide** layout.

If you continue to click on **New Slide** or press *Enter* on the keyboard, new slides will insert based on the **Title and Content** slide.

Changing slide layouts

Often, when you insert a slide, a certain layout is applied automatically. You can change the layout before you add content or after content is inserted into the slide. The **Layout** option is also very useful when copying slides from other presentations into a new or existing presentation as it refreshes the layout and fixes common slide design, background, or font issues. Follow these steps:

1. To change a slide layout, click on the slide you wish to change the layout of in the presentation. Continue to use the presentation from the previous example.
2. Click on the **Home** tab and locate the **Layout** icon.
3. Click the **Layout** icon and select a layout from the list provided.
4. Note that the slide layout from the inserted slide (*slide 3*) is also an option in the **Layout** drop-down list.
5. For this example, we will change the layout of *slide 2* to the **Content with Caption** layout:

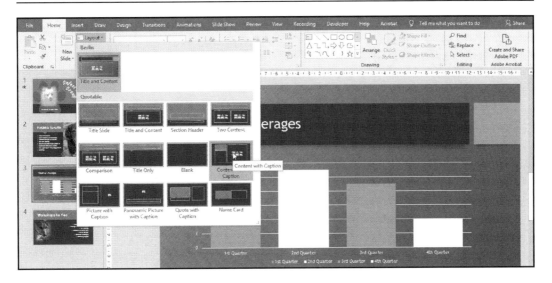

6. After you've selected a layout from the list, the selected slide will be updated with the new layout.

Working with themes and text manipulation

After working through this section, you will be able to copy, move, and paste text; insert and format lists; and add headers and footers to a presentation. In addition, you will also know how to apply and modify a theme.

Duplicating, moving, and pasting text

You can duplicate, move, and paste text using the keyboard shortcut keys. This skill has been addressed in the previous chapters of this book. The keyboard shortcut keys are the quickest way to achieve the move and copy actions; use *Ctrl + C* for copy, *Ctrl + X* for cut, and *Ctrl + V* for paste. You can also use the right-click method – click on an object or select some text to copy or cut (move), right-click it, and choose the option you desire, that is, either **Copy** or **Cut.** Then, right-click in the presentation where you would like to position the object or text and select **Paste**.

Note that there are numerous paste options in Office 2019, depending on the object you have cut or copied. To paste without formatting, select the **Text-only** option.

Inserting and formatting lists

It is a personal preference as to how you would like to insert and format lists on slides in PowerPoint. Either insert the text first and then apply the list or apply the list and then enter the text:

1. Open the presentation called `ProductGrpSSG.pptx`
2. Locate the slide that contains the text you wish to apply a bullet or numbered list to.
3. Choose the desired option from the **Paragraph** group by clicking on either the bullet or numbers icon.
4. To change the bullet or number type, click on the drop-down arrow next to the bullet or numbering icon.
5. Select **Bullets and Numbering** from the bottom of the list.
6. A dialog box will open, offering options that you can use to customize the numbered or bulleted list:

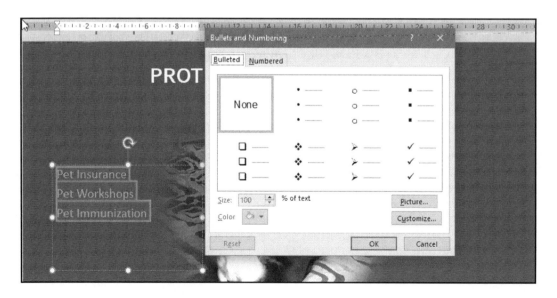

7. You can change the color of the bullet or number using the **Color** fill bucket.

8. The **Customize**... icon is available, should you need to browse for a different symbol from the huge range available.

9. Adjust the spin controls of the % of the text area (**Size:**). If you are using symbols as a bullet, then this option works really well to maximize the symbol.

10. Change the bullet to a picture of your choice by clicking on the **Picture...** button and browsing your the computer for an image to insert as a bullet. For example, we will insert the `PawPrint.png` image.

11. Click on **Insert** to add the picture as a bullet type. The numbering option works in exactly the same way as the bullets icon.

12. Should you wish to number items from a specific starting number point, use the **Start At:** position to control this.

13. To change the distance between the number or bullet and the text, select the text first, then use the *indent markers* along the ribbon to increase (or decrease) the distance between the two:

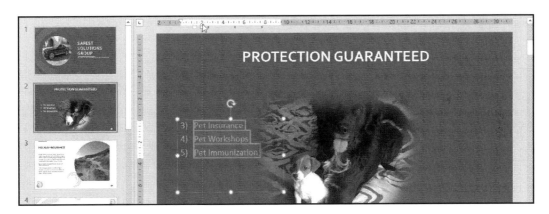

With that, we have inserted bullet and numbered lists and learned how to customize them. Now, we will learn how to set up slide headers and footers.

Add headers and footers to slides

The footer is the area at the bottom of the slide, constructed by way of placeholders that contain information that's repeated on every slide in the presentation. The header or footer accepts information such as custom text, dates and times, and the slide number. Headers and footers can be applied to **Notes and Handouts**. The **Notes and Handouts** tab can be seen in the following screenshot, just to the right of the **Slide** tab.

1. Open an existing presentation. For this example, we will use the `Safest Solutions-Benefit.pptx` presentation.
2. Click on the **Insert** tab and select **Header & Footer** from the **Text** group.
3. In the **Header and Footer** dialog box, select the option that best suits your presentation:

4. Select the **Slide** tab at the top of the dialog box to view the options to include on slides.
5. Click on the **Date and time** checkbox and choose whether to add a static fixed date or whether this will **Update automatically** (this option will update the date to the current date every time the presentation is opened).
6. You can include a **Slide number** and also a static **Footer**. This option is located just under the **Fixed** date option.
7. Sometimes, we may want to exclude a header from the title slide of the presentation. Select this option by clicking in the checkbox provided to activate it.

8. Please note that at the bottom of the dialog box, you can choose whether to **Apply** changes to the current slide or choose to **Apply to All** to commit the changes to the entire presentation. Also, note that there is no header section on the **Slides** tab.

9. The **Notes and Handouts** tab contains many of the same options as the **Slide** tab but includes a **Header** section so that you can create a static custom header for notes and handouts only.

Applying and modifying themes

A **theme** is a collection of fonts, colors, and effects that are saved as a name in the Theme Gallery. Pre-defined themes are available from the **Themes** group on the **Design** tab. Should you wish to customize your own theme, use the **Fonts**, **Colors**, and **Effects** icons to the right of the Themes Gallery. In my experience, it is always easier to decide on a theme prior to adding all of your content to it. Applying a completely new theme design or changing a design theme once your presentation is complete can cause a few complications, with you having to redo certain formatting elements. Follow these steps:

1. Open the presentation called `Safest Solutions-Themes.pptx`.
2. Click **Design** | **Themes** | **More...**:

3. Select a theme to apply to the presentation.
4. Notice that themes also have **Variants**, which are displayed just to the right of the chosen design theme on the ribbon.

5. We are also able to format the background of a slide using the **Customize** group (alternatively, right-click on a slide background and select **Format Background...** to change the background properties).

6. Once you have chosen a design theme and a variant (if applicable), the existing presentation will update all the elements on the slides with the new theme.

7. In this particular design theme example, notice that applying the new design theme has caused the first slide's main title to distort somewhat as the elements are now trying to fit into the new design theme that's been applied. Change the formatting of the title of this slide so that it looks more presentable.

8. Save the presentation to keep the design changes.

Applying a theme to selected slides

Follow these steps to learn how to apply a theme to selected slides:

1. Select the slides in the presentation that will be updated with a new theme.

2. Click on **Design** | **Themes**.

3. Locate a theme to apply to the selected presentation slides.

4. Right-click on the selected theme and choose **Apply to Selected Slides** from the shortcut menu:

Now, let's learn how to create a customized theme.

Creating your own custom theme

Follow these steps to learn how to create a custom theme:

1. We will use a new presentation for this example.
2. Apply a theme to the presentation, then customize its elements using the **Variants** options.
3. To save the customized theme as your new theme, click on **Save Current Theme...** from the drop-down themes list. By default, themes are saved to the `Templates` folder on your local hard drive:

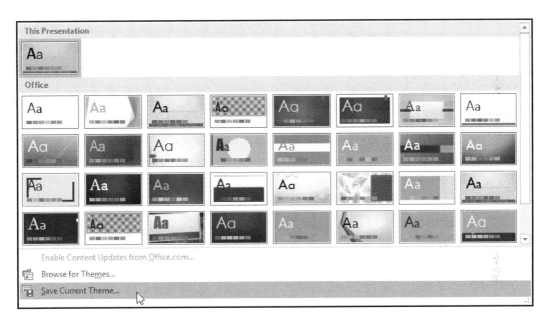

4. Enter a filename into the text area provided (note that the filename extension for themes is `.thmx` and is saved to the `Templates\Document Themes` folder automatically).
5. Click on **Save**. The new theme, called `SafestSolTheme`, will be added to the **Custom** list in the Theme Gallery.

> Themes that you do not need anymore can be removed from the Theme Gallery. To delete a theme, click on **Design**, select the theme, and then right-click and delete.

Working with text boxes

In this section, you will learn how to format text boxes by adding, manipulating, and applying styles and effects to them.

A **text box** is a shape that is drawn onto a presentation slide that you can type text into. The **Text Box** feature is located on the **Insert** tab, under the **Text** group:

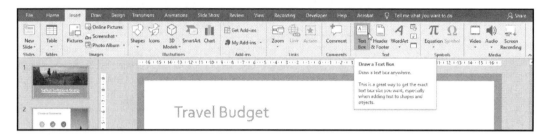

Draw a text box onto the slide by holding down the left mouse button and dragging to the desired size, or simply by clicking on the slide's background.

Formatting text boxes

Once a text box has been inserted onto a slide, use the Drawing Tools **Format** tab to apply shapes, styles, text styles, text effects, and text alignment options.

Applying a theme fill color

Follow these steps to learn how to apply a theme fill color:

1. Click on the text box to apply a fill color.
2. Click on **Format** | **Shape Styles** and select a theme to apply to the shape:

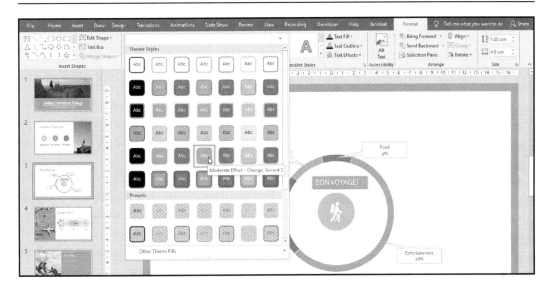

3. Click on **Shape Fill** to access the different colors available:

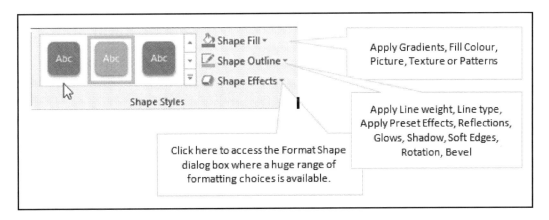

4. Now, click on a color or visit the **More Fill Colors...** option to access the color wheel or custom color area.

5. To remove a fill color from a text box, click on the shape and then select **No Fill** from the **Shape Fill** drop-down list.

The Eyedropper tool is fantastic for picking up a color from a specific theme on a particular slide and using that specific color by applying it to the background of the text box. To use the Eyedropper, select the text box, visit the **Shape Fill** drop-down list, and select **Eyedropper**. Use the dropper to click on a specific color you want to use for the background of the text box.

Applying a gradient

Follow these steps to apply a gradient:

1. Click on the shape to apply the gradient color.
2. Choose **Gradient** from the **Shape Fill** drop-down list on the **Drawing Tools** contextual menu.
3. Click on **More Gradients...** at the bottom of the submenu to access the **Format Shape** pane to the right of the PowerPoint window. Here, you are able to choose your own gradient blends.

Applying a picture

Follow these steps to apply a picture:

1. Right-click on the text box or shape to apply a picture background.
2. From the shortcut menu, choose **Format Shape.**
3. The **Format Shape** *pane* will populate to the right of the slide. Select **Picture** or **Texture Fill**.
4. Choose **Insert Picture from File**. Note that you can also insert it from the clipboard or from an online location.
5. Browse to locate a picture on the computer. For this example, we will insert the picture called IMG_3066.jpg.
6. Double-click to select the picture and place it into the text box or shape. Alternatively, single-click the picture and choose **Insert** at the bottom of the dialog box.
7. Select the relevant options from the pane to make any additional picture adjustments to the picture:

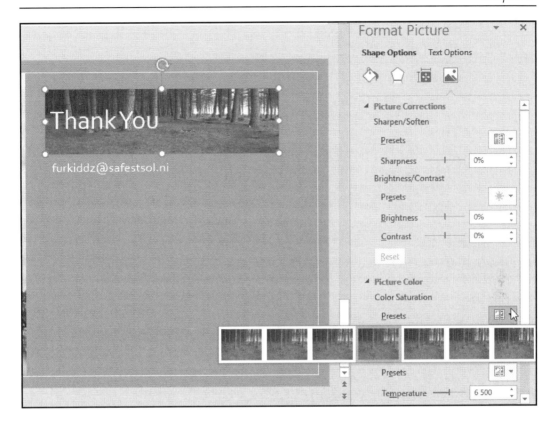

8. When we insert a shape, a **Format** tab appears at the top of the PowerPoint environment, just under the **Drawing Tools** contextual tab, allowing you to make formatting changes to the shape or text box. Since we have inserted a picture into the shape, note that you now have a second **Format** tab, just to the right of the existing **Format** tab, which contains **Format Picture** options. This opens up further picture customization options, such as **Color**, **Artistic Effects**, and **Corrections** (experiment with these options as you wish).

Changing the outline color and weight

Follow these steps to change the outline color and weight:

1. Select the text box, locate the **Drawing Tools** contextual menu, and click on the **Format** tab.
2. Click on **Shape Style | Shape Outline** in order to select a line color.

3. If the theme or standard colors are not what you are looking for, select **More Outline Colors...** to choose a custom color or select one from the color wheel.

4. If the default weight of the line is not thick enough, use the **Weight** option from the **Shape Outline** drop-down list to change it.

5. Click on the **Dashes** option to display different line styles to apply to the text box.

6. To remove an outline from a shape, select the shape and click on the **No Outline** option from the **Shape Outline** drop-down list.

Arranging and manipulating objects

By the end of this section, you will be confident with arranging, grouping, and rotating objects, as well as being able to use the **Selection and visibility** pane to locate hidden objects. We will also teach you how to resize and reset objects.

Arranging objects

There are numerous **Arrange** options available from the **Picture Tools** context menu. To access these options, follow these steps:

1. Select a picture on a slide in your presentation. We will use the `Safest Solution-Objects.pptx` presentation for this example.

2. There are many **Arrange** options you can use to order, group, and position objects on slides. You are able to access the **Arrange** options using any one of the following methods:

   - The first is accessible via the **Drawing** group on the **Home** tab.
   - The second is accessible via the **Format** tab of the **Picture Tools** contextual menu, at the very top of the PowerPoint ribbon once an object has been selected.
   - The third is accessible via right-clicking on an object, after which the shortcut menu will appear for you to choose from the **Arrange** options.

Sending an object forward or backward

Follow these steps:

1. Click on the picture you wish to bring to the front of the text box.
2. From the **Arrange** group of the **Drawing Tools** menu, select the **Bring Forward** option to access the drop-down menu. Alternatively, right-click on the shape and choose **Bring to Front** from the shortcut menu:

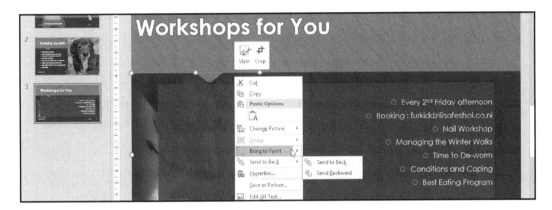

3. The picture will move to the front and the text box shape will move to the back:

4. Experiment with the other options available in this menu.

When working with pictures, you will access the **Arrange** group from the **Picture Tools Format** tab and with shapes, the **Drawing Tools Format** tab.

Flipping an object

Follow these steps to flip an object:

1. Click on the picture to flip.
2. Find the **Arrange** group and click on **Rotate** | **Flip Horizontal**:

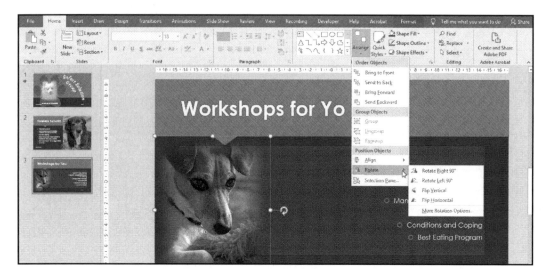

3. The picture will be flipped horizontally.
4. Experiment with the other rotations or click on **More Rotation Options...** to access the dialog box.

Rotating an object

Follow these steps to rotate an object:

1. Click on the picture you wish to rotate.
2. The rotate icon will appear at the top center of the object and is identified by a circular arrow:

3. Place the mouse pointer on the circular arrow and, while holding the left mouse button down, drag the position to rotate the object.

Another method would be to locate the **Arrange** group on the **Picture Tools Format** tab, as follows:

1. Click on the **Rotate** drop-down arrow.
2. Select the rotation option or access **More Rotation Options....**
3. The layout dialog box is very useful if a specific degree of rotation is required. Simply type the required degree of rotation into the text area provided next to the **Rotation:** heading, as shown in the following screenshot:

Aligning objects

It is difficult to align objects at a specific position using the mouse. The align feature is available for this purpose and allows the user to create professional-looking documents. There is nothing worse than looking at objects on a slide presentation that are uneven and slightly off in terms of position.

Aligning objects to the top

Follow these steps to align objects to the top:

1. Open the presentation called `Safest Solution-Align.pptx`.
2. Select the objects to align while holding down the *Shift* or *Ctrl* key. You can also use the **Select Objects** option, located in the **Home** tab, located on the **Editing** group.
3. Click on the **Align** drop-down list, which is located in the **Arrange** group:

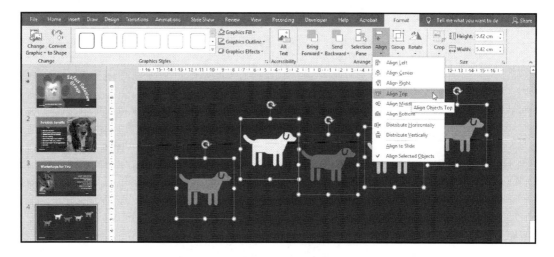

4. For this example, we will align the objects to the top.

5. Once the objects have been aligned to the top, you will notice that the gaps between each object are of different sizes. The **Distribute Horizontally** icon from the **Align** drop-down list is perfect for fixing this:

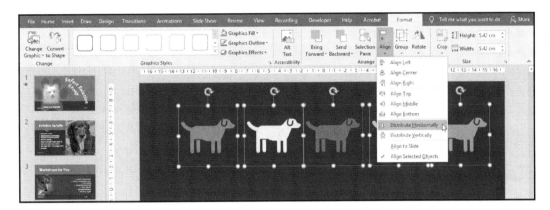

6. Note the change in the distribution of the shapes. If you are having problems lining up objects, use the **View Gridlines** icon to guide you.

Using the selection and visibility pane

This feature is absolutely brilliant when working with numerous objects that are overlapping. Sometimes, you won't be able to see all the elements on a slide and often, elements are hidden from view. I use this extensively when working with Microsoft PowerPoint animations as it allows me to move elements up and down in order, to rename elements so that the order and element make more sense when working with the diagram, and to hide or unhide elements from view. Follow these steps:

1. We will use the presentation called `Safest Solution-Selection.pptx`.

2. Select an object and click on the **Drawing Tools Format** tab on the ribbon to access the **Selection Pane** option. Alternatively, without selecting an object first, visit the **Arrange** option of the **Drawing** group and locate the **Selection Pane...** option at the bottom of the drop-down list.

3. Note that the **Selection** pane is now visible on the right of the PowerPoint environment:

4. Each object is an item in the pane. To use the pane, click on an object listed in the pane – the object will be selected on the slide.

To rename an object listed on the pane, simply click twice on the name of the object and type the new name into the text box provided by replacing the current name. To hide an object, use the eye icon on the right-hand side of the pane.

5. Click again to make the object visible. This feature is great for objects that overlap so that you don't have to move your whole document around to access the shape and make a change!

6. The **Selection** pane can also be used to select objects.

7. Use the **Selection** pane to rename the dogs in order from **DOG1** to **DOG5**.

8. Hold down the *Ctrl* key on the keyboard while selecting **DOG1** through **DOG5**:

 To close the **Selection** pane, click on the **Selection Pane** icon from the ribbon or the close icon on the right of the pane.

Grouping objects

Grouping objects together creates one object. This might be the way to go if you are moving objects or working with multiple objects on one slide. Instead of formatting each object separately, you can group them and then apply formatting. In the instance or designing manuals, when objects relevant to each other are grouped together, they can be moved together from one position in the document to another without repeating the step for each part of the drawing. An example would be to group labels on a picture so that they stay intact when moving to another location in the presentation:

1. Use the **Selection** pane, as per the previous example, to select the objects on a slide. Alternatively, select the objects that you wish to combine into one object. To do this, click on the first object and hold down the *Shift* or *Ctrl* key on the keyboard. Move your mouse pointer to the second object, making sure that the *Shift* key (or *Ctrl* key) is still depressed, and click on each object to add it to the group.
2. To form a group, click on the **Drawing Tools Format** tab and select the **Group** icon drop-down list.
3. Alternatively, right-click the selected objects and choose the **Group** option.
4. The object will become one movable object.

5. To ungroup objects, simply navigate to the **Group** options and select **Ungroup**.

Resizing objects

Follow these steps to learn how to resize objects:

1. Select the object to resize by clicking on it.

2. Place your left mouse pointer on the sizing handle. Hold down the left mouse button and drag toward the center of the image to make it smaller and to keep the proportion of the image intact. Alternatively, drag outward to make the object bigger. The ribbon is another method that can be used if you wish to enter specific widths and heights for objects.

3. Select the object by clicking on it.

4. Notice that the **Drawing Tools** or **Picture Tools Format** tab is now visible, depending on the object type (picture, shape, or chart) that you are resizing.

5. Locate the **Size** group and enter the width and height measurements as desired. The object will adjust on the slide as you enter the new measurements.

6. To access even further **Layout** options, click on the **Size** dialog box launcher on the **Format** tab of the ribbon. The dialog box will present itself:

Take note of the **Lock aspect ratio** checkbox. This is very important if the objects height and width settings must change in relation to one another and not separately.

Resetting objects

The reset option removes all changes with regard to size, effects, rotation, and scaling and brings the object back to its original size. Follow these steps:

1. Select the object to reset.
2. On the **Picture Tools Format** tab, select the **Reset Picture** option (when dealing with pictures):

3. Click on **Reset Picture** to remove all formatting changes and **Reset Picture & Size** to remove any formatting and size changes.

In the next section, you will learn how to create new tables using a range of methods and apply table styles. You will also master chart creation by entering data and applying a quick layout. With this, you will be able to master chart modifications by switching elements; editing elements such as data labels, data tables, legends and chart titles; and adding objects.

Constructing and modifying tables

Tables can be inserted into PowerPoint in many ways. They can be created in PowerPoint directly using a table placeholder or via the **Insert table** options, can be copied from Microsoft Word or Microsoft Excel and placed into PowerPoint, or drawn directly into PowerPoint. It is easier if you copy data from Excel and paste it into a PowerPoint slide than using the **Insert spreadsheet** options.

Inserting a table

Follow these steps to learn how to insert a table:

1. Click on a slide to add a table.
2. Select **Insert | Table** and then select the number of rows and columns you would like to insert by dragging over the diagram to select rows and columns. Alternatively, you can click on the **Table** icon in the center of the slide (if the slide layout type contains the table placeholder) or choose **Insert Table....**
3. Click and drag the table size with the mouse pointer.
4. Once you release the mouse, the **Table Tools** contextual menu will appear, along with the relevant tabs you can use to format the table:

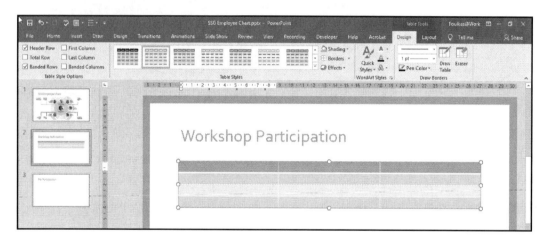

5. Click on the **Layout** tab to insert rows and columns into the table. You can use the *Tab* key on your keyboard to insert more rows. Formatting and constructing the table is the same concept as using the Word program.

Inserting an Excel spreadsheet

Follow these steps to learn how to insert an Excel spreadsheet:

1. From the **Table** icon, select **Excel spreadsheet**. The Excel environment will open. This is where you will type your data onto the worksheet. Note that the options on the ribbon will have changed to offer the Excel formatting options while you're working with the spreadsheet in PowerPoint. This table option is not a popular option as it is quite cumbersome – it's much better to copy and paste data from Excel directly!

2. Type and format your table as required.

3. Click on the background of the slide to view the table within PowerPoint.

4. Double-click to edit the table or resize it using the resize handles around the edge of the table.

5. Note that if you use this method of inserting a table, any themes that were applied to the slide will not be applied to the spreadsheet table.

6. The options for editing the table within PowerPoint are also not available.

Setting table style options

Follow these steps to learn how to set table style options:

1. Insert a table with three columns and three rows onto a new slide in the presentation.

2. Fill in the following data:

	Workshop 1	Workshop 2
October	43	88
November	23	6
December	67	109

3. If you do not have time to format your table with colors, shading, borders, and fonts, use the **Preset Table Styles** option to format the table quickly.

4. Select the table and click on the Table Tools **Design** tab.

5. Click to choose a **Table Styles** by using the select more arrow. By doing this, you will be able to access more styles. This can be seen in the following screenshot:

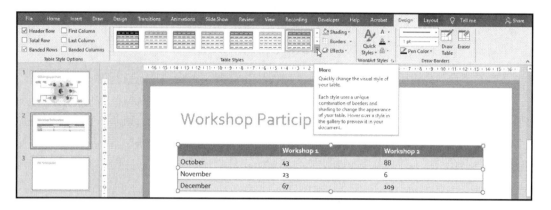

6. Your table should now reflect these changes.
7. Should you wish to do more in the way of formatting your table (merging, alignment, distributing, inserting or deleting rows or columns, adding borders, shading, and so on) use the ribbon once the table is selected or consult `Chapter 2`, *Creating Lists and Constructing Advanced Tables*, in the *Word* section.

 Applying a table style will replace any existing styles in a table!

Inserting and modifying charts

We use charts to make information more appealing, as well as clearer and easier to read. A **chart** is a graphical representation of worksheet information. It is a good idea to become familiar with the names of different elements of a chart so that you know which part you are changing from the options you will be presented with on the chart ribbon and the chart edit icons. The best way to become familiar with the different parts of a chart is to create a default chart and then spend some time hovering over the chart elements. When you do this, you will be presented with a popup specifying the name of the element:

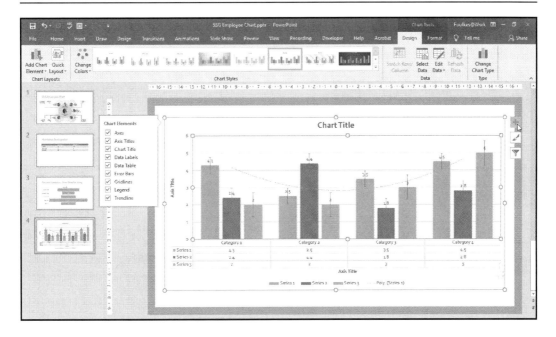

When we create a chart in PowerPoint, the chart is automatically linked to a worksheet that will open when we edit data. When we make changes to the information on our worksheet, the chart is updated automatically. We can edit this data directly within PowerPoint or Excel.

Selecting a chart type

Follow these steps to learn how to select a chart type:

1. Open a presentation called `SSG Employee Chart.pptx`.
2. Choose a slide to create a chart on.
3. Select the **Insert** tab.
4. Select **Chart** (or use the chart icon, which is located on the relevant slide layout).
5. The **Chart Type** dialog box will present itself on the slide – choose a chart type from the list provided. Note that the Funnel chart is a new chart that was added in Office 2019.
6. Once you have selected a chart, click on **OK** to create the chart on the slide.

7. The chart will be available on the PowerPoint slide and offers a datasheet that you can type or paste data into in order to update the chart:

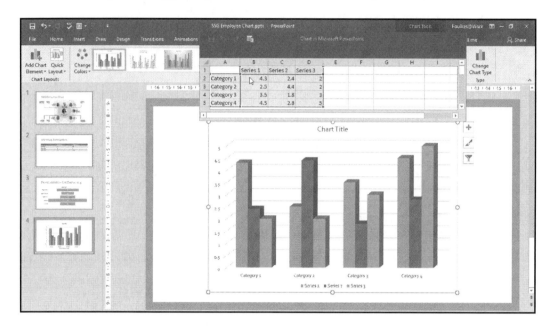

Now, we will learn how to enter data into a chart.

Entering chart data

Follow these steps to learn how to enter chart data:

1. Enter the chart data into the datasheet provided or select the **Edit Data in Microsoft Excel** icon from the top of the datasheet (if you use this option, you will be working in Excel and will have access to all of Excel's functionality):

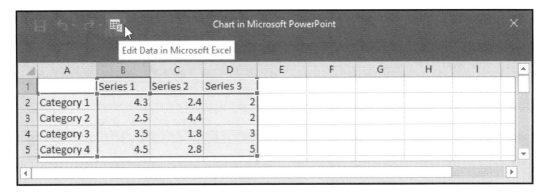

2. Please note that the ribbon will change to reflect all the chart icons and tabs that you can use to formulate the chart.

3. The datasheet gives you a very clear example of which part of the data is category data and which data is called a series, which makes editing or inserting chart data much simpler for the user.

4. To add or remove the rows and columns of the chart, simply click and drag the blue border at the bottom-right-hand corner of the range, as indicated on the datasheet.

5. If you prefer to use Excel to enter the data, don't forget to close Microsoft Excel if you have finished entering the relevant data.

6. The chart will update in PowerPoint as you continue adding and formatting data.

7. If you close the datasheet by mistake and need to revisit it to edit or add data, click on the **Edit Data** icon, located near the end of the **Design** ribbon, to access the **Edit Data** (PowerPoint) or **Edit Data in Excel** datasheet options:

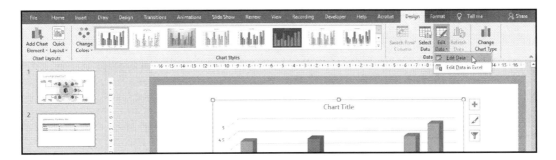

8. Enter some data into your chart datasheet.

Changing chart style

Follow these steps to learn how to change the style of your chart:

1. Firstly, select the chart that you want to change the style of.
2. Locate **Chart Styles** on the **Design** tab.
3. Use the **More...** option to view all available chart styles. Alternatively, click on the **Chart Styles** icon, which is located directly to the right-hand border of the selected chart.
4. The **Chart Style and Color** options will open to the left of the chart. This is where you can make the desired changes. Alternatively, use the ribbon method.
5. Select another chart type by clicking on it.
6. The chart will update immediately on the slide.

Changing the chart's quick layout

On the **Design** tab of the Chart Tools contextual menu, you will find all the tools you can use to manipulate charts. Using a style from the **Quick Layout** icon will save the user a huge amount of time. Each option in the list will change the overall layout of the chart as each includes multiple chart elements. Click on them to investigate them and how they will be applied to your chart.

If you prefer to edit the entire chart type and options, you will use the **Change Chart Type** icon at the end of the **Design** tab ribbon:

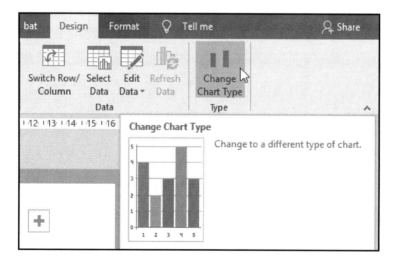

Switch Row/Column is also available via the **Select Data** icon (located on the **Design** tab). This feature allows you to switch the x and y chart axes. It is important to note that this is not active by default (grayed out) and this doesn't mean that it is not working or that there is a problem:

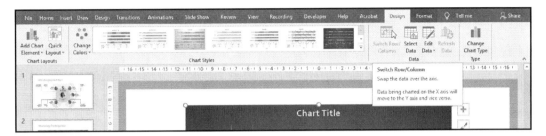

1. To switch the x and y axes around, select the chart.
2. Click on **Design | Switch Row/Column** from the **Data** group. If the icon is not active and appears grayed out, then you must click on the **Edit Data** icon to locate the correct option (using the datasheet within PowerPoint will not make the feature active):

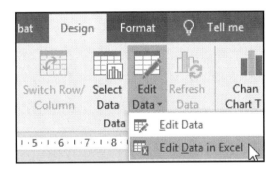

3. Click on **Edit Data in Excel**.
4. Microsoft Excel will launch and display the chart data.
5. The **Switch Row/Column** icon still won't be active and will remain inactive until you physically select the data range (even if the data is selected when Excel opens, you'll need to reselect the range).
6. Click back on the chart in PowerPoint.
7. The **Switch Row/Column** icon will now be active.

8. Click on the **Switch Row/Column** icon to update the data on the
   PowerPoint slide:

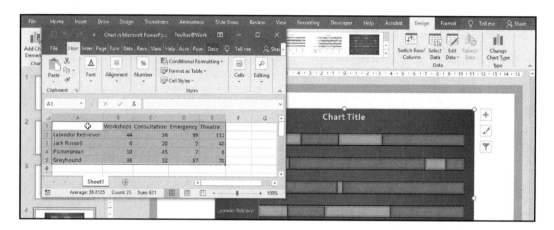

9. If you are happy with the visual change, then close the Excel application.

Working with chart elements

There are many elements you can add, remove, and customize when working with
charts in the Microsoft Office 2019 suite, and just as many methods can be accessed
via the ribbon, the right-click shortcut menu, from the chart panes to the right of the
PowerPoint window, and from the quick access icons to the top right of a chart. Let's
learn how to add chart labels.

Data labels

To make a chart more understandable and easier to read for the user, we need to add
data labels. Use the data shown in the following screenshot to construct a 3D pie chart
on a new blank slide in PowerPoint 2019:

	A	B
1		EMERGENCIES - SEPTEMBER 2019
2	Labrador Retriever	99
3	Jack Russell	2
4	Pomeranian	7
5	Greyhound	37
6	Beagle	24

To apply data labels to the preceding chart, follows these steps:

1. Select the chart.
2. From the **Chart Elements** icon to the right of the chart, select **Data Labels**. Alternatively, use the **Design** ribbon to locate **Add Chart Element** (the first icon on the ribbon):

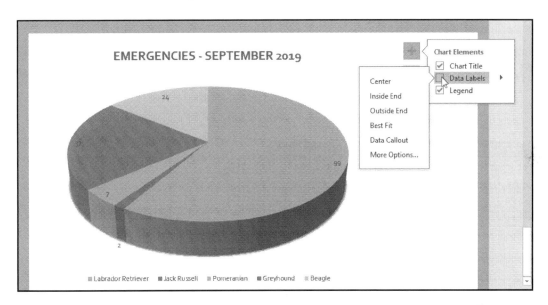

3. Click on the small black arrow to open further options to add the data label. For this example, we will use the **Best Fit** option (**More Options...** will open the **Format Data Labels** pane, where you will find many more options you can use to customize your chart).
4. The chart will be updated.
5. Click on one of the data labels once (this will select all the data labels).
6. To make formatting changes to the labels, visit the **Home** tab and apply the formatting options as required.

Adding a data table

A **data table** is how the data is represented in the worksheet cells that were used to create the chart. The data table, once inserted, forms part of the chart so that it is visually more appealing when printed or displayed onscreen. Remember that there are lots of quick layout chart options, including data tables. Follow these steps:

1. Select the chart to add data labels.
2. Click on the **Add Chart Element** icon on the **Design** tab ribbon:

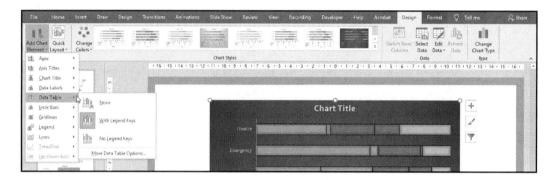

3. Locate **Data Table** from the list provided.
4. From the drop-down list, choose an option to apply to the chart.

Displaying the chart legend

Displaying the position of the legend or removing it completely from the chart background is possible via the **Design** tab ribbon:

1. Select the chart.
2. Decide whether you wish to change the legend placement or remove the legend altogether.
3. Locate the **Legend** option by clicking on the **Add Chart Element** icon. Alternatively, use the **Chart Elements** icon to the top right of the selected chart.
4. Once the legend appears on the chart, choose where to position the chart on the chart background.

Adding objects to a chart

Objects such as images and illustrations (shapes, pictures, icons, WordArt, text, and so on) can be added to the chart's background using the **Insert** tab, after which they can be formatted using the same methods as if we were editing in Word or Excel 2019. These elements can also be animated to create focus when presenting them:

1. To add an object to the chart, locate the **Insert** group on the **Layout** tab.
2. Click to add a **Picture**, **Shape**, or **Text Box** to the chart.
3. Click on the background of the chart.
4. The object will be inserted – resize, format, or position the object as required:

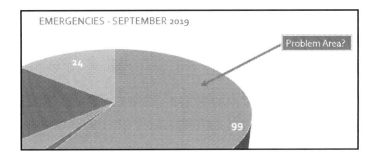

Changing the chart's title

PowerPoint automatically assigns titles to the chart if it finds relevant data it can use from the selected data source range. The chart title tells you about the data and makes a chart easier to read. To edit the chart title or axis title, simply click into the text box provided. Then, edit and format the text using the ribbon or the format titles pane to the right of the chart. If you do not need a chart axis, simply click on it and press *Delete* on the keyboard to remove it:

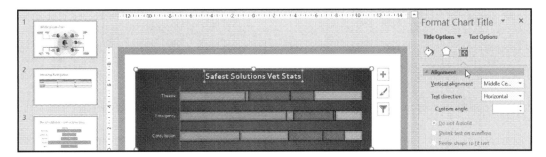

Inserting audio and video

In this section, you will become proficient with adding video and audio content to a presentation and learn how to modify the content and playback options to suit your presentation's requirements.

Before we look at editing video and audio content, we will learn how to insert a video clip.

Inserting a video clip

Follow these steps to learn how to insert a video clip:

1. Open the presentation called `VideoAudioContent.pptx`.
2. We will insert a video on *Slide 3*.
3. Click on **Insert** | **Video** from the **Media** group at the end of the ribbon.
4. You can insert a video from an online source or from a location on your computer.
5. Locate the video called `AUS1.AVI` and double-click to insert it onto the slide.
6. The video will appear on the slide. Note that a range of options are now available so that you can edit and play back video content:

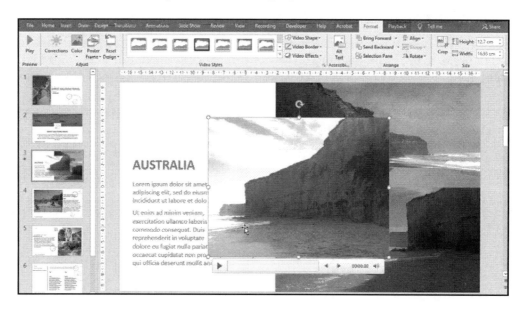

Applying styles to video content

Follow these steps to learn how to apply styles to video content:

1. Make sure the video is selected on *Slide 3*.
2. Locate the **Video Styles** group on the **Video Tools Format** tab.
3. Click on the **More...** icon to see all the styles available.
4. Select a style to apply to the video.
5. Let's insert another video into the presentation; click on *Slide 7*.
6. Insert the video called KANGAROO-KOALA.mp4.

Resizing and positioning video content

Changing the size of a video is exactly the same as resizing any object within PowerPoint. Simply select the video and use the resizing arrows on any corner of the video to drag it so that it becomes bigger or smaller. Alternatively, use the width and height option on the **Format** ribbon to resize the video.

Experiment with the video on *Slide 3* and then position the video, as per the following screenshot:

Applying a style to an audio clip

Follow these steps to learn how to apply a style to an audio clip:

1. Using the presentation from the previous example, click on *Slide 2.*
2. Click on the **Insert** tab and choose the **Audio** icon from the **Media** group.
3. Select **Record Audio**, as you do not have an audio recording:

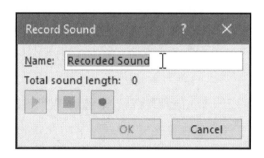

4. Name the recording and click on the **Record** icon to begin recording (the red dot icon).
5. Click on the **Stop recording** icon when complete (the blue square).
6. Click on the **OK** icon to insert the audio onto the slide:

7. Notice that formatting audio is the same as it was for formatting videos.

8. The audio icon can be resized and repositioned using the same methods we discussed previously.

9. On the **Playback** tab, you will see the **Audio Styles** icons. Here, you can choose to remove a style or play the audio in the background while presenting the slide show.

Adjusting playback options

Video playback options are located on the **Playback** tab. Make sure you have clicked on the video on *Slide 3* before you do any of the following tasks:

1. To start the video with a mouse click when clicking on the video icon, select **When Clicked On** from the **Start:** option:

2. To start the video automatically when the slide is displayed on the screen, click on **Automatically**.

3. **In Click Sequence** means that the video will play in the order it appears among all the other animated elements on the slide.

4. To hide the video icon so that it does not show on the slide show while you're waiting for the video to play, click on **Hide While Not Playing**:

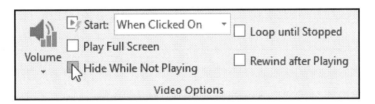

5. Be careful of this option if you have the **Start:** option set to **On Click**. This is because you won't see the icon and be able to click on it to play the video. Only use this option for automatic playback.

6. To play a video continuously in a presentation, click the **Loop until Stopped** checkbox. This is great to use if you're presenting at a show and the presentation must keep on playing for many visitors walking by a marketing stand, for instance.

7. The **Rewind after Playing** options will set the video to the start position once it's finished playing.

8. The **Play Full Screen** checkbox will play the video over the entire slide when it's playing.

9. The **Volume** setting allows you to adjust the sound level, as well as mute the video.

10. The audio playback options are very similar to the video playback options.

Summary

This chapter has equipped you with the necessary skills to manipulate PowerPoint 2019 slides and apply themes, as well as work with text boxes, tables, and charts. You are now proficient in applying styles, arranging and manipulating objects, and adding and customizing video and audio content on slides within a presentation.

In the next chapter, you will learn how to create stunning photo albums and work with sections and motion effects. The chapter will finish with you creating a presentation and adding animations, transitions, and slide timings to it.

7
Photo Albums, Sections, and Show Tools

In this chapter, we will cover how to add photos and captions to an album and customize their order and appearance. You will also get to know how to navigate a presentation easily using sections and will learn how to rename and remove sections in a PowerPoint 2019 presentation.

Slide show presentation tools allow you to control all aspects of a slide show, ensuring that you can show your audience just the right content at the right time. In this chapter, you'll also learn how to set up and manage slide shows, including how to control slide timing and the playback of audio narration. This chapter also includes a section on master slides, where we check the consistency throughout a presentation and options for hiding or showing specific slides when you're delivering a presentation.

The following list of topics are covered in this chapter:

- Creating and modifying photo albums
- Working with presentation sections
- Applying animations and transitions
- Using hyperlinks, actions, and comments
- Exploring slide show options and custom shows
- Using master slides and hiding slides

Technical requirements

Prior knowledge to aid you in mastering this chapter would be the ability to work with different slide layouts; create and format elements such as textboxes, charts, and tables; and insert video and audio content. The examples used in this chapter are accessible from the following GitHub URL: `https://github.com/PacktPublishing/Learn-Microsoft-Office-2019`.

Creating and modifying photo albums

In this section, you will learn how to create, organize, and format a photo album using PowerPoint 2019. The ability to create a photo album was introduced as a new feature within Office 2010. This allows you to add a collection of photographs to a presentation, and set format options all in one go. It is a really efficient process that is perfect when creating presentations predominantly based on images, or for personal online photo album memories to which video, animations, transitions, audio, and other PowerPoint 2019 elements can be added to enhance the end product:

1. Open PowerPoint 2019 and create a new blank presentation.
2. To construct a photo album, click on the **Insert | Images** option.
3. Then, click on **Photo Album** and choose **New Photo Album...**, as illustrated in the following screenshot:

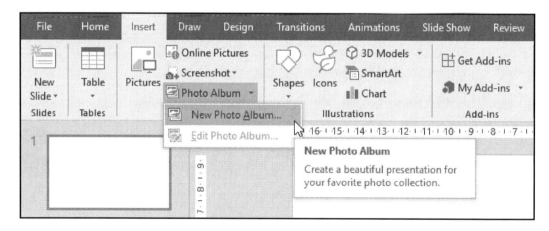

4. In the **Photo Album** dialog box that populates, locate the content you would like to insert as a photo album.

5. Click on the **File/Disk...** icon to browse and locate pictures on your computer. It is important to note that storing pictures in one single location/folder would be an advantage prior to creating the album, as well as having a descriptive filename for each picture so that locating, rearranging, and formatting pictures is trouble-free. The following screenshot illustrates how you can do this:

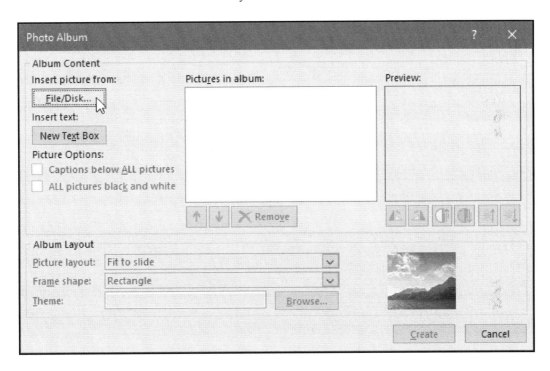

6. Select the pictures using either the *Ctrl* + click method to select individual pictures, or select multiple files in one go using the *Shift* + click method; or, use *Ctrl* and the *A* key to select all the files in the folder. You will use the images within the PHOTOALBUM folder in the following screenshot example:

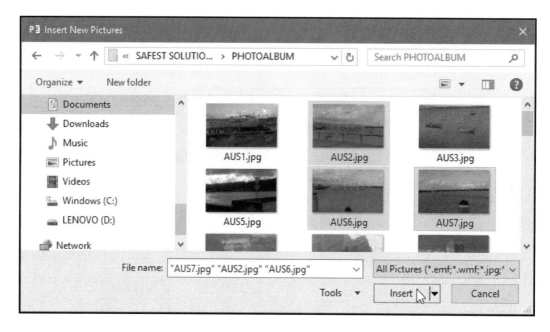

7. The pictures are added to the **Pictures in album:** window, located to the center of the dialog box. You will see from the following screenshot that the pictures are numbered and the picture names are displayed in the window for ease of use:

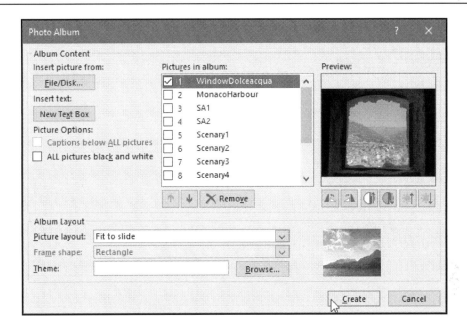

8. There are numerous formatting options to consider before you click on the **Create** icon at the bottom of the dialog box. In this instance, we will go ahead and create the album, and then revisit each individual formatting option so that you are familiar with the options and become comfortable working with photo albums in PowerPoint. An example photo album can be seen in the following screenshot:

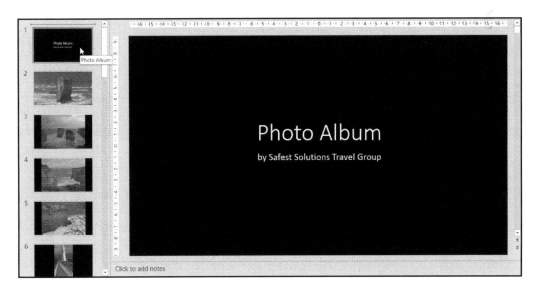

9. Each picture is displayed on an individual slide as the default layout was set to **Fit to slide**.

10. Notice that the **photo album** is created as an entirely new presentation and is not part of the existing blank new presentation you started off with.

11. Save the photo album as `SSG-PhotoAlbum.pptx`.

Adding picture captions

1. Make sure you have the `SSG-PhotoAlbum.pptx` photo album open from the previous example.

2. To add picture captions, you would need to be in **Edit** mode. Click on **Insert | Photo Album | Edit Photo Album...** .

3. When editing a photo album, captions cannot be inserted below pictures in the presentation if the **Picture layout** heading is set to **Fit to Slide**. The **Fit to Slide** option covers the slide with the picture and therefore does not accommodate a caption, and the option will be grayed out.

4. Firstly, change the **Picture layout:** heading to any option other than **Fit to Slide**.

5. Then, click on the checkbox to select the **Captions below ALL pictures** option, as illustrated in the following screenshot:

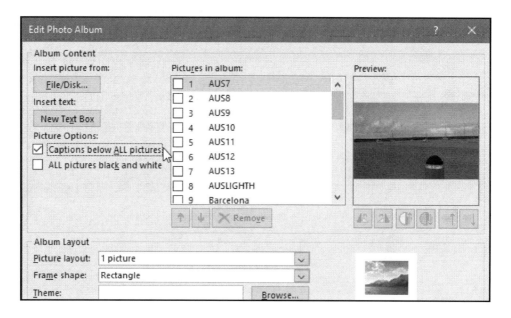

6. Click on **Update** at the bottom of the dialog box.

7. The album is updated and will look like the screenshot shown in the next step, with a default caption (the picture filename) under each picture on the slide.

8. Click on the caption text to select the placeholder and rename the caption for each slide, as illustrated in the following screenshot:

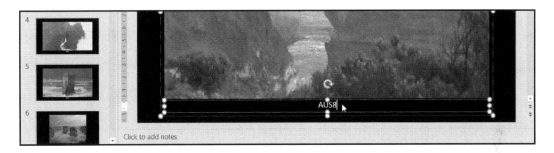

9. Don't forget to save the presentation to update it.

Inserting text

At times, you may wish to insert a text slide in between the photographs you have included in the album. To do this, follow these steps:

1. Make sure you are in the **Edit Photo Album** dialog box.

2. Click on a picture to select it.

3. Locate the **Insert text:** heading and click on the **New Text Box** button to insert the text slide.

4. The text slide is inserted after the currently selected picture.

    The following screenshot shows how to do this:

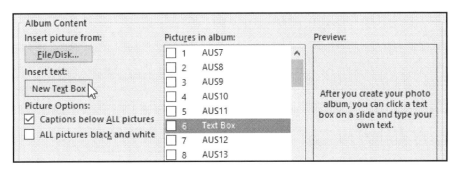

5. Click on the **Update** icon at the bottom of the dialog box to make the change to the photo album.

Removing images

1. If you insert an image or textbox by mistake, click on the image or textbox in the **Pictures in album:** list.
2. Be sure to click on the checkbox so that the picture is selected, otherwise the **Remove** icon will not be active.
3. Click on the **Remove** icon.
4. Click on the **Update** icon at the bottom of the dialog box.
5. Save the presentation.

Inserting pictures in black and white

To display all pictures in the photo album as black and white, simply select the checkbox next to **ALL pictures black and white**, under the **Picture Options:** heading, as illustrated in the following screenshot:

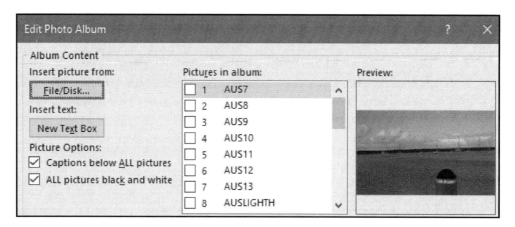

In the next topic, we will look at changing image order in the **Edit Photo Album** dialog box.

Reordering pictures

Moving pictures up and down in order is a very simple process. This option will determine where you would like the pictures placed in the photo album. Moving images around manually from slide to slide in a presentation could be extremely time-consuming and cumbersome, so being able to edit the photo album order within the **Edit Photo Album** dialog box before or after creating a photo album is a great feature:

1. Make sure you have opened the **Edit Photo Album** dialog box.
2. Click on a picture you would like to move up or down in the list of pictures. For this example, we will navigate to and select the last picture on the list.
3. Note that the move up and move down arrows will only become active if you have selected the checkbox to the left of a picture (selecting just the picture name to highlight the picture will not activate the options).
4. Use the move up or move down arrows to position the picture. For this example, move the last picture in the list to become the first picture in the list, as illustrated in the following screenshot:

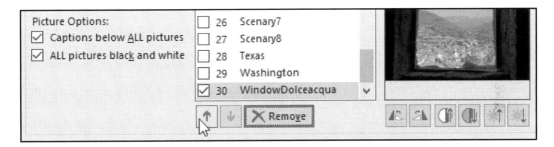

5. Lastly, click on the **Update** icon at the bottom of the dialog box.

Adjusting image rotation, brightness, and contrast

If an image included in the album is in portrait instead of landscape orientation, you can rotate the image using the vertical and horizontal rotation icons. These icons should be familiar as you would have already visited them in the other Office 2019 applications. In addition to the rotation feature, the brightness and contrast icons are also available if these require adjusting. The icons can be seen at the bottom of the following screenshot:

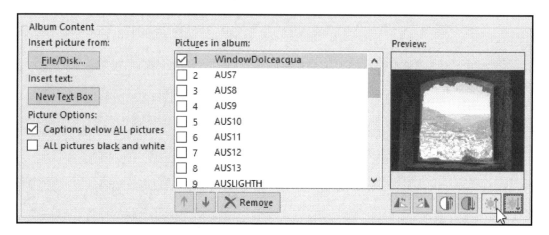

Changing album layout

We can change the number of pictures displayed on each slide, the picture frame shapes, and also the overall album theme of the presentation, using the options at the bottom of the **Edit Photo Album** dialog box.

Picture layout

1. Open an existing photo album or create a new photo album.
2. Click on the **Insert** tab and locate the **Images** group, where you will find the **Photo Album** icon.
3. From the **Photo Album** drop-down list, select **Edit Photo Album...** .

4. Locate **Picture layout:**, and then select the drop-down arrow to the right of the default **1 picture** option.
5. Choose a layout from the list provided (note the change to the picture list in the **Edit Photo Album** dialog box).
6. Click on the **Update** icon to view the changes to your album.

Frame shape

1. Visit the **Edit Photo Album** dialog box.
2. Locate **Frame shape:** and select an option from the drop-down list provided.
3. Click on **Update** to view the changes to the photo album.

Theme

1. Visit the **Edit Photo Album** dialog box.
2. From the **Theme:** option, click on **Browse...** to display the list of themes available, as illustrated in the following screenshot:

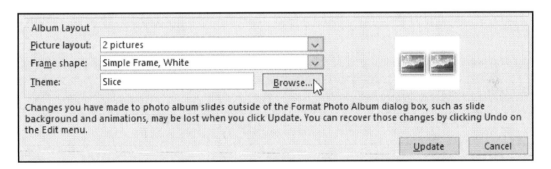

3. Click on a theme to select it, and then click on **Select**. If you are not able to view the themes as image thumbnails, change the display view by visiting the option at the top right of the window.
4. Select the **Update** icon to apply the theme to the photo album.

Working with presentation sections

In this topic, you will understand why we would use sections in PowerPoint; learn to create and rename sections; then, expand, collapse, and remove sections in a presentation.

Formatting sections

If you are scrolling through a huge presentation or applying finishing touches, it can be extremely frustrating to find slides to format or edit. The **Sections** feature allows you to organize your presentation into categories so that finding slides (for example, the introduction, sport, financials, charts) on a particular topic or category is simple.

In addition, if working on a presentation with multiple contributors, you can assign sections to different people. Reordering slides or viewing a presentation in **Slide Sorter** view with sections applied is a breeze!

1. To add a section, you can be in **Normal** view or **Slide Sorter** view. For this example, we will be using the `SSG-Sections.pptx` presentation.
2. The feature is accessible by right-clicking on a slide or in between two slides, or from the **Slides** group on the **Home** tab.
3. Once you have inserted a section, an arrow will appear just above the slide entitled `Untitled Section`, and the **Rename Section** dialog box will populate, as illustrated in the following screenshot:

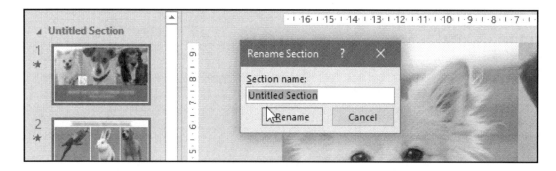

4. Type a new name for the section into the **Section name:** text placeholder. For this example, we will use the text `Introduction` and click on **Rename**, as illustrated in the following screenshot:

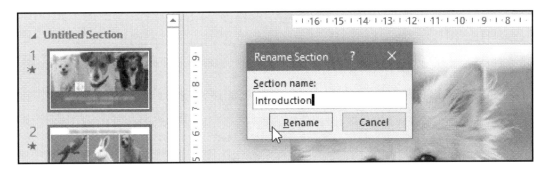

5. We will now create a section for dogs, rabbits, and birds.
6. Don't forget to save the presentation when complete.
7. The created sections are displayed in the **Slide Pane**, but can also be viewed much more clearly in the **Slide Sorter** view due to the sections showing the slide thumbnails, as can be seen in the following screenshot:

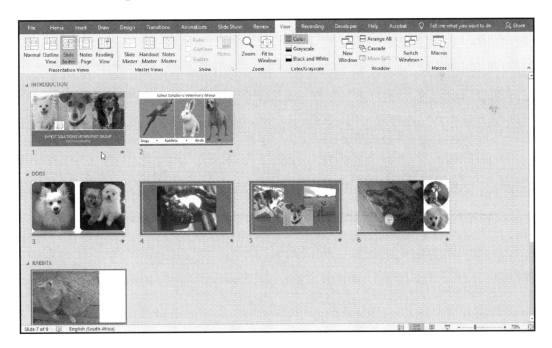

8. Sections can be collapsed or expanded using either the collapse or expand arrow to the left of a section name. To collapse or expand all sections in a presentation, click on the **Sections** icon located on the **Slides** group, and select **Collapse All** or **Expand All**, as illustrated in the following screenshot:

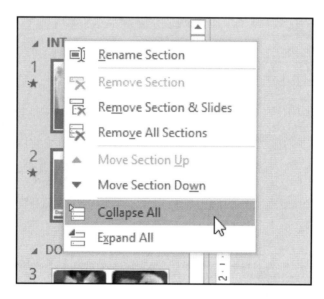

9. To rename a section, right-click on the section name, and then choose **Rename Section** from the shortcut list provided.

10. To move sections within a presentation, right-click on the section name, and then choose **Move Section Up** or **Move Section Down.**

11. If you want to remove a section, simply right-click on the section name and choose the applicable option from the shortcut menu. Be really careful with this option as at times, you may want to remove just the section category and not the slides underneath the section!

Applying animations and transitions

In this topic, we will learn to add different types of built-in animations to a slide and customize these animations to add effects. We will use the **Animation pane** to configure, set triggers, and modify transitions, and look at the new features called **Zoom** and **Morph**.

Animations are found on the **Animations** tab on the PowerPoint 2019 ribbon. Animations can be applied to pictures, charts, tables, SmartArt graphics, shapes, clip art, and many other objects in PowerPoint.

Adding animation effects

1. Open the `Animations.pptx` presentation.
2. Select an object on the slide to apply a custom animation. For this example, we will select a single petal on the first slide.
3. Click on the **Animation** tab and locate the **Animation** group. Then, select an animation type or click on **More** to gain access to further category options, such as **Entrance**, **Emphasis**, and **Exit** animations, as illustrated in the following screenshot:

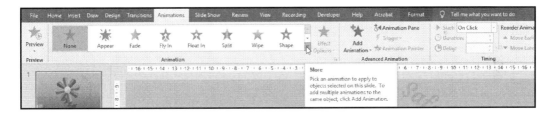

4. Notice in the preceding screenshot that the first animation type is the **None** option, which allows you to remove an animation.
5. You will not see a preview of the animation type unless you exit the **More** option and return to the ribbon, where you can click on the **Preview** icon to view the animation effect on the object on the slide.

6. If you don't find what you are looking for under the animation effects provided, then access the **More Entrance Effects...** options at the bottom of the drop-down list. A further dialog box will open, offering more effects of this type, as illustrated in the following screenshot:

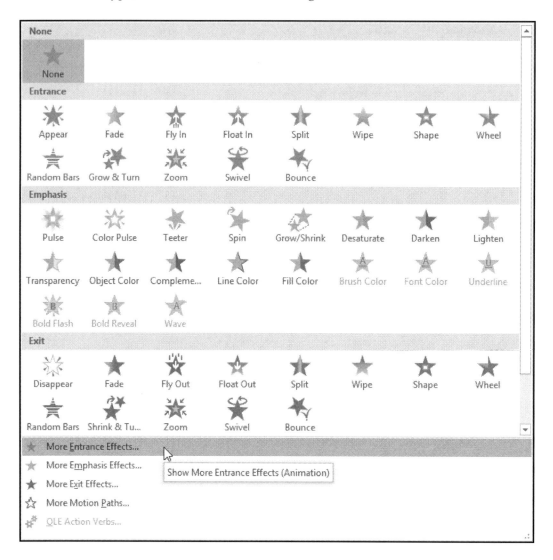

7. As you click on an effect, a preview of the effect will display on the object on the slide. Notice that the **Preview Effect** checkbox is present at the bottom of the dialog box, as illustrated in the following screenshot:

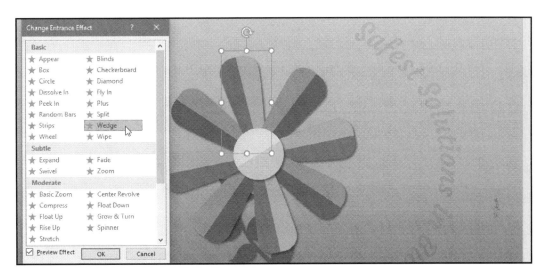

8. After an animation effect is applied, a rectangle with a number **1** in it will appear next to the object on the slide, indicating that it is the first animation on the slide and will always be the first animation to play when presenting the slide show, as illustrated in the following screenshot:

Now that you are comfortable inserting animations onto slide elements, we will learn how to apply further effect options in the next topic.

Applying effect options

You can set further options once an animation is applied to an object. Effect options will vary depending on the type of animation applied to an object on the slide, and not all animations have additional options:

1. Select an object that has an animation applied, or click on the animation indicator (the animation rectangle with the number applied) next to the object on the slide, as illustrated in the following screenshot:

2. Click on the **Effect Options** icon to access the drop-down list that appears.
3. Choose from the options available to enhance your animation effect.

Previewing animations automatically

To preview animations automatically, click on the **Preview** icon to the very left of the **Animation** ribbon, and then select **AutoPreview**. Every time you apply an animation or animation effect option, the preview will automatically play the changes without having to click on the **Preview** icon each time.

Applying an animation effect to multiple objects

The only difference in applying the same animation effect to multiple objects is in the selection of the objects:

1. Select each petal of the image on *slide 1*. To achieve this, hold down the *Ctrl* or the *Shift* key on the keyboard; and then, while keeping the *Ctrl* or *Shift* key depressed, click on each individual petal, as illustrated in the following screenshot:

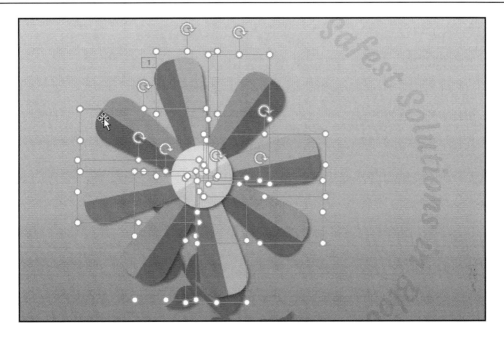

2. Keeping the petals selected, click on the **Animation** tab on the ribbon, and then select an animation effect to apply to the selected objects. In this example, we have chosen the **Zoom** animation effect.

3. Notice that after the animation is applied, all the animation rectangle icons display the number **1**, indicating that the animations all happen at the same time due to the fact that they were all selected prior to applying the animation effect.

4. Preview the animation.

Using the Animation Pane

The **Animation Pane** provides access to animation start options, timing, and effect options, as well as the ability to remove animations from objects. These options are explained throughout this chapter using other methods, so we will concentrate on these individually, and in more detail, in those sections.

Setting up advanced animations

You can apply more than one animation to a single object on a slide, as follows:

1. Select an object on a slide that already has an animation applied.
2. Click on the **Add Animation** icon located on the **Advanced Animation** group. Note that applying another animation to an already animated object using the normal animation effect options will replace the animation.
3. Select an animation from the drop-down list provided.
4. The animation is applied to the object and becomes the second animation applied, as illustrated in the following screenshot:

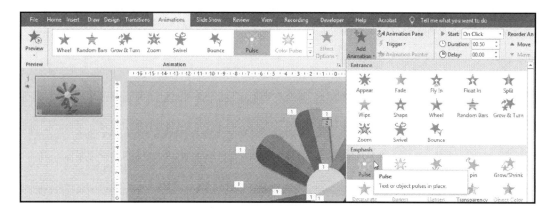

5. Preview the animation. The first animation will play, followed by the second animation.

Removing animations

To delete an effect using the **Animation** ribbon, you can do any of the following:

- Click on the animation indicator alongside an object (or select the object that has an animation applied). Then, select the **None** option from the **More** drop-down list.
- Click on the animation indicator alongside an object, and then press the *Delete* key on the keyboard.
- Using the **Animation Pane**, select an animation, and then visit the drop-down list and select **Remove**, as illustrated in the following screenshot:

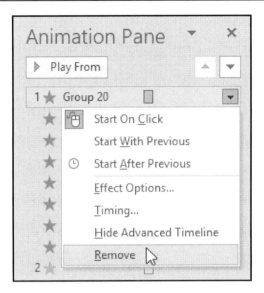

Setting animation timing

Animation timing can be set by using either the **Animation Pane** or the **Timing** group. The **Animation Pane** is a great way to visualize changes to these options.

Setting start options

1. Select an object to set when you would like an animation effect to start. In the petal example that we have been working with, the petals have the same animation effect applied and, when previewed, the animations all happen at the same time. We will now change the start options so that each petal plays after the previous petal, and so on. Let's get started by selecting the first petal on *slide 1*.

2. Locate the **Timing** group on the **Animation** tab.

3. Use the **Start:** drop-down list to set how the animation should begin.

4. For this example, we will set the petals to start after each other, using the **After Previous** start option.

5. Continue to do the same to each petal of the flower, this time using the **Animation Pane**.

6. Select the next petal, and then click on the **Animation Pane** option from the **Advanced Animation** group.

7. Click on the arrow to the right of a group and select **Start After Previous**. Notice that the visual representation here is easier to follow due to the *green thumbnails* that appear next to each animated group, as can be seen in the following screenshot:

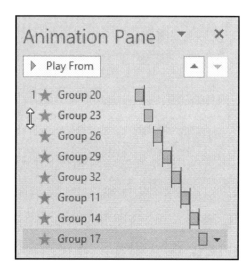

8. Repeat this process until all the petals have been set with the **Start After Previous** option.
9. Preview the animation when complete.

Selecting delay or duration options

Setting a delay on an animation effect means that you will essentially pause an animation for a period of time before it should start playing. If you would like an animation to play for a certain amount of time, then you need to set the duration of the animation. You can do this in the following way:

1. Select an object on a slide that has an animation effect applied. For this example, we will select the center of the flower and apply the **Grow & Turn** animation effect, and then set a delay.
2. Locate the **Timing** group on the **Animation** tab.
3. Use the **Duration:** text area to set the animation duration, or the **Delay:** text area for the number of seconds the animation must wait until it starts.

4. Launch the **Animation Pane** by selecting the appropriate icon from the **Advanced Animation** group.

5. Click on the arrow to the right of the animated object in the **Animation Pane**.

6. From the drop-down list, select **Timing...**, as illustrated in the following screenshot:

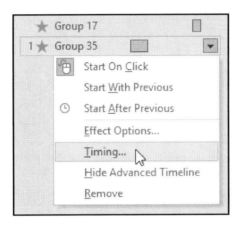

7. Set the delay options in the **Effect** dialog box.

8. Click on the **OK** command when complete and commit to the changes made, and then play the animation. The center of the flower should play **3** seconds after the previous animation has ended, as illustrated in the following screenshot:

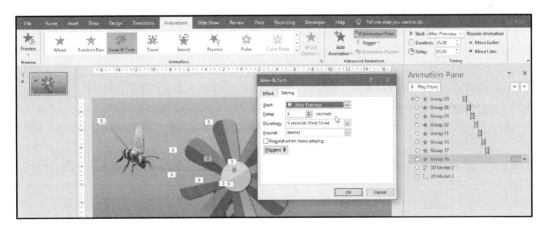

9. Let's set the duration of the animation to **5** seconds. The **Animation Pane** should still be resident to the right of the slide.
10. Click on the drop-down arrow to the right of the **Group 35** animation.
11. Choose **Timing...** from the list provided.
12. In the **Grow & Turn Timing** dialog box, set the duration to **5** seconds.
13. Click on **OK** to commit the change.
14. Play the animation. The center of the flower should take 5 seconds to play from start to finish.

Working with 3D models and cube animations

There are a couple of new features included with PowerPoint 2019. 3D models allow the insertion of objects from online and offline sources that can be viewed in 3D (by rotating to view all angles of the object). Cube animations are animations solely for any 3D model you insert into PowerPoint 2019, and will only be accessible after inserting and selecting a 3D object on a PowerPoint slide.

Inserting a 3D model

1. Click on the **Insert** tab.
2. Locate the **3D Models** icon from the **Illustrations** group.
3. Click on the **3D Models** icon, or choose an option from the drop-down list provided after selecting the bottom section of the **3D Model** icon.
4. Click to select **From Online Sources...** .
5. Type a search keyword—for instance, **bee**—into the area provided, or select from the comprehensive list of categories displayed.
6. Click on the 3D model to select it, and then choose **Insert (1)** at the bottom of the search box, as illustrated in the following screenshot:

7. The 3D model is placed directly onto the slide, and you are then given the opportunity to explore the **3D Model Tools** contextual format tab, as well as its ribbon options. Note that there are numerous model positions available under the **3D Model Views** group, as can be seen in the following screenshot:

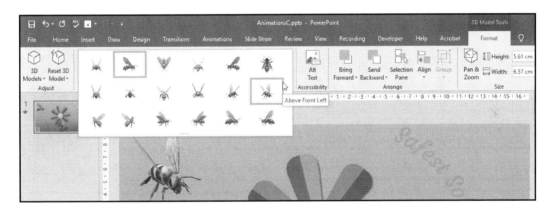

8. Select an appropriate view for your slide.

Animating a 3D model

Once a 3D model element has been added to a slide, you can animate the model using the default animations available, or select from the 3D cube animation options:

1. Make sure the 3D model is selected.
2. Click on the **Animations** tab.

3. Notice that the **Animation** group now offers five new 3D model animation types, as highlighted by the notification in the following screenshot:

4. These new types are in addition to the standard animations. Included for each new 3D model animation type is the new **Effect Options** feature for each animation type, which you can certainly have a lot of fun with!

5. Experiment with these new animation types, and apply any timing or effect options.

6. Let's finish this off with a *Motion Effect* animation—click on the 3D model of the bee, then visit the **Animation** group and select **More Motion Paths.**

7. Select a motion path of your choice to apply to the bee as a second animation, so as to create movement. Experiment with moving the endpoint of the animation to land in the center of the flower. This process can be seen in the following screenshot:

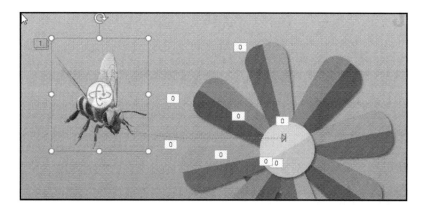

8. Preview the animation and save the presentation when complete.

Attaching sound to an animation

1. Select an object on a slide to add sound to. In this case, we will use the bee.
2. To add an enhancement such as sound, click on the **Effect Options...** icon from the drop-down arrow next to the animation effect of the selected object in the **Animation Pane**.
3. From the **Effect Options** dialog box, locate the **Sound:** text area, directly below the **Enhancements** heading.
4. Click the drop-down arrow to view and select from the sounds available.
5. Alternatively, choose **Other Sound...** at the bottom of the list to collect a sound saved on your computer.
6. Click on **OK** to confirm.
7. Play the animation to test it.

Using the Animation Painter features

The **Animation Painter** feature in PowerPoint 2019 is much like the **Format Painter** icon from within the Office programs. It allows you to copy animations from one object and apply them to another object. Single-clicking on the **Animation Painter** icon enables you to copy the animation from one object to another object. Double-clicking on the **Animation Painter** icon enables you to copy the animation from one object to multiple objects.

1. We will use the SSG-Planner.pptx presentation to demonstrate this example.
2. Select an object on the slide and apply an animation to it. For this example, select the textbox on slide 1 and apply the following attributes:

Select the **Float In** animation effect. Set the animation to **Dim** to another blue color after the animation, and then choose the **By word** option from the **Animate text:** drop-down list, applying a **20%** delay between words. This process can be seen in the following screenshot:

3. Make sure the textbox is selected on slide 1, and then single-click on the **Animation Painter** icon located on the **Animations** tab (in the **Advanced Animation** group) to copy once to another object, or double-click to copy multiple objects.

4. The painter icon will appear as the mouse pointer.

5. Click on another object to paste the animation to it—we will copy the animation to all the textboxes throughout the presentation slides.

6. The object that now contains the animation will indicate this by displaying the animation number positioned in the top-left corner of the object, and the **Animation Pane** will update to reflect the new object animation.

7. Press the **Animation Painter** icon to stop pasting the animation, or press the *Esc* key on the keyboard.

Reordering animations

Often, you may need to reorder animations, especially if you have a number of objects with multiple animations and effect options. At times, this could get a bit confusing, and a little editing would need to take place before you arrive at the perfect set of animation orders:

1. Locate the **Animation Pane**.
2. Click on the animation whose order you wish to change. We will use the previous topic example here. You will notice that there are two animations on slide 6 of the presentation shown in the following screenshot:

3. A **Float In** animation effect is applied to the textbox, and a **Split** animation applied to the picture. There is a **0** in the animation box for the first animation and a **1** in the animation box for the second animation.
4. To reorder the animations, follow these steps:
   1. On the **Animation** tab, locate the **Timing** group.
   2. From the **Reorder Animation** heading, select either **Move Earlier** or **Move Later**; or click on the reorder arrows at the bottom of the **Animation Pane**.

Working with transitions

A **transition** is a motion effect that happens when the presentation moves from one slide to another. Remember that *less is more* and that too many animations and effects lead to a distracting presentation for an audience. Try to focus on the point of each slide.

Just like animations, transitions also have further effects and settings to customize after a transition has been selected. Transitions fall under the following categories: **Subtle, Exciting,** and **Dynamic Content.** There is a new transition called **Morph** that allows the smooth transition of objects from one slide to another.

Modifying the transition effect

1. Click on a slide to add a transition effect.
2. Click on **Transition | Transition to This Slide | More** to access further transition effects.
3. The **Effect Options** icon is shown, where further criteria for the chosen transition can be set. For instance, if the **Shape** transition were applied, you could choose the shape type that the transition must use.
4. To apply the same transition to all slides in the presentation, click on the **Apply To All** icon on the **Timing** group; otherwise, a transition will only apply to the currently selected slide.
5. You can identify whether a transition has been applied to a slide by looking to the far left of the **Slide Pane.** If there is a star symbol under the slide number, a transition exists on the slide.

To remove a transition effect, select the slide that has the effect applied. Click on the **None** icon from the **Transition to This Slide** group on the ribbon.

Adding a transition sound

1. Select a slide that has a transition effect applied.
2. To add sound to the effect, click on the **Sound:** drop-down arrow on the **Timing** group, as illustrated in the following screenshot:

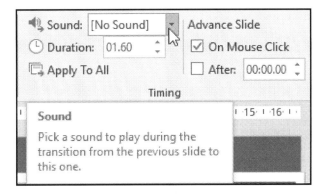

3. Choose a sound from the list or click on **Other Sound...** at the bottom of the list to browse for a sound from a location on the computer.

Modifying transition duration

1. Select a slide that contains a transition effect.
2. Locate the **Timing** group on the **Transition** tab.
3. Type the duration in seconds into the **Duration:** area provided, or use the spin arrows to increase or decrease the amount of time of the transition.
4. Entering a value will determine the time in seconds that the transition should last before moving to the next slide.

Setting manual or automatic time advance options

Advancing slides manually (that is, on a mouse click) is set by default in a presentation. The slide will advance on the mouse click and play for the duration of the timing set (if any). You would then need to mouse-click again for the next slide to advance on screen, and so on. The **Advance** option is set under the **Advanced Slide** heading of the **Timing** group.

To change this option to automatically advance after a set number of seconds, do the following:

1. Select the slide that contains the transition effect.
2. From the **Timing** group, remove the tick next to the **On Mouse Click** option.

3. Click on the checkbox next to the **After:** heading, as illustrated in the following screenshot:

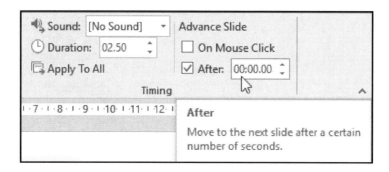

4. In the **After:** text area, enter (in seconds) the time the slide should take to advance to the next slide. If you do not want to add additional seconds, leave the timing at **0** but ensure that the **After:** setting is active.

Using the Morph transition

The **Morph** transition can be applied to WordArt, SmartArt, text, graphics, and shapes, but not charts. After you have applied the **Morph** transition, you can set various effects for objects, characters, or words. The **Morph** transition transforms an object across slides.

1. We will use the MorphTransition.pptx presentation to demonstrate the **Morph** transition. Note that this is a simple example of the **Morph** transition, as you can get quite creative with this feature!
2. Click on the first slide in the presentation.
3. Go to **Insert | Icon** and search for a ring icon.
4. Insert the ring icon onto slide 1, and then position and resize the icon to suit your presentation.
5. Format the ring color to any color of your choice.
6. Select the slide 1 thumbnail and apply the **Morph** transition (don't forget that you can choose between **Object**, **Character**, or **Words Morph** effects after applying the transition), as illustrated in the following screenshot:

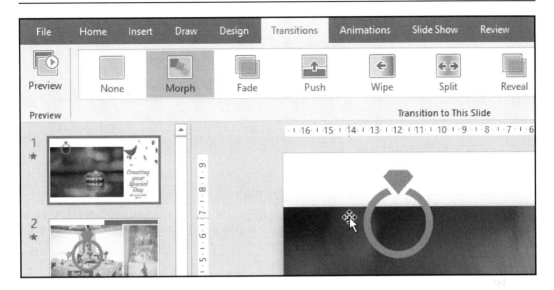

7. Copy the icon from slide 1 onto slide 2, and then resize and format the icon as per your requirements, as illustrated in the following screenshot:

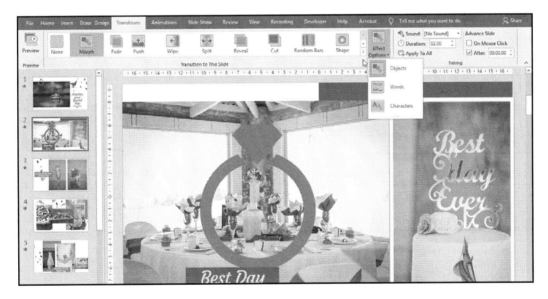

8. Click on the slide 2 thumbnail and apply the **Morph** transition.
9. Preview the slide show to see the changes, and then save the presentation.

Using hyperlinks, actions, and comments

In this topic, we will learn how to insert and edit hyperlinks and actions, and work with comments. The new inking feature in PowerPoint 2019 will also be included here.

Adding hyperlinks

A hyperlink is a piece of text, graphic, picture, chart, or shape in a presentation that, when clicked upon, will take you somewhere else! Sometimes, you might want to insert a hyperlink to a website or file in your presentation. Hyperlinks are used also to link to other files, external documents, a place in the same presentation, and web pages or graphics. We will look at numerous options in this section, including the new **Zoom** feature:

1. Open an existing presentation or create a new presentation.
2. Insert or select an object on which to create a hyperlink.
3. Right-click with your mouse and choose **Hyperlink...** or click on the picture, and then click on the **Insert** tab. Choose the **Hyperlink** icon from the **Links** group. The **Insert Hyperlink** dialog box will be displayed, as illustrated in the following screenshot:

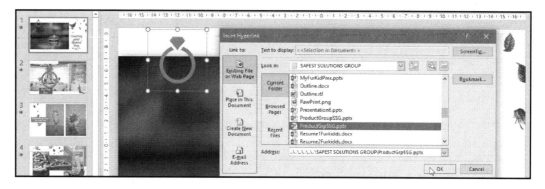

4. Type the hyperlink address into the space provided to the right of the **Address:** field at the bottom of the dialog box, or navigate to a folder on the computer and select a file to link to.
5. Click on **OK** to complete the hyperlink.

Launching a hyperlink

1. To launch the hyperlink, make sure you are in **Slide Show** view (select the **Slide Show** tab, and then choose **From Current Slide**).

2. Click on the graphic to which the hyperlink is applied, and the file will open up within PowerPoint (if you linked to a PowerPoint Show file, it will open the **Slide Show** view automatically). Alternatively, the linked website will open in the default browser.

3. When a hyperlinked object is selected in the **Slide Show** view, the linked presentation will open. Please note, however, that the presentation you are linking to should reside within the same folder as the source presentation. Failure to do this will be very embarrassing when presenting to an audience, as the link could be broken!

4. Place the mouse pointer over the hyperlinked object, where you will see the hyperlink pop up. Hold down the *Ctrl* key on the keyboard and, while keeping it depressed, click with the mouse pointer on the object, as illustrated in the following screenshot:

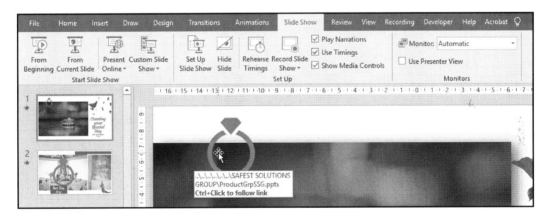

You can also right-click on an existing hyperlink, and then launch the content from the **Open Link...** option from the shortcut menu provided.

Hyperlinking to a slide in the same presentation

1. Position the mouse pointer on an object in the presentation, or select a portion of text.
2. Click on the **Insert** tab and choose the **Hyperlink** icon.
3. In the **Insert Hyperlink** dialog box, click on **Place in this Document** under the **Link to:** heading.
4. Slide titles appear in the dialog box as a **place** in the document, and a preview of each slide is present to the right of the dialog box.
5. Click on the **Custom Cake Design** heading.
6. Click on **OK** to create the link.
7. You can also hyperlink to a new document, as well as to an email address that would populate the Outlook new email template with the email address of the recipient.

Easy linking

Easy linking is such a great tool when working with sections in PowerPoint. It allows you to drag a section heading onto another slide, which in turn creates a thumbnail of the first slide of the section with a link to that slide:

1. Open the Zoom.pptx presentation.
2. Note that there is an **OUR PRODUCTS** section heading just above slide 3.
3. Click on slide 2 (we will create the link on this slide to demonstrate).
4. Position the mouse pointer over the **OUR PRODUCTS** section heading, and while keeping the mouse depressed, drag the heading to slide 2, as illustrated in the following screenshot:

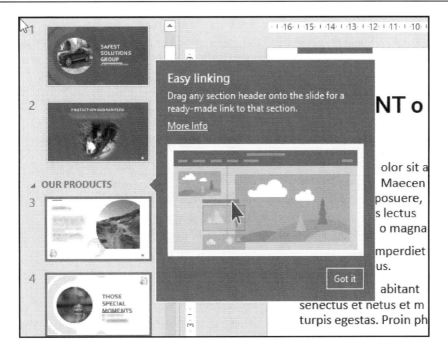

5. The link is created on slide 2 along with the thumbnail of slide 3.

6. Resize or reposition the thumbnail on the slide as required, as illustrated in the following screenshot:

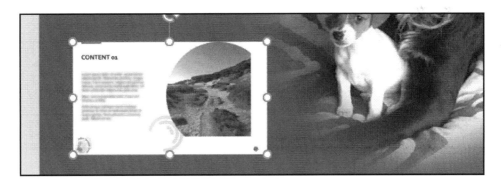

7. Click on **Slide Show** and select **From Current Slide** to test the link.

 To remove a hyperlink, select the object or text that has a hyperlink applied, and right-click and choose **Remove Hyperlink** from the shortcut menu.

Editing a hyperlink

1. Select the text or object that contains a hyperlink.
2. Right-click and choose **Edit Hyperlink...** from the shortcut menu.
3. The **Edit Hyperlink** dialog box appears. Make the change to the hyperlink.
4. Click on **OK** to apply changes to the hyperlink.

Adding actions

You might be asking yourself what the difference is between hyperlinks and actions in PowerPoint. Hyperlinks are mainly used for navigation only. Actions can do the same things as hyperlinks but have many more options, and can be set up by hovering the mouse over an object, or by means of a mouse click:

1. Click on an object to select it (we will use the `Actions.pptx` presentation for this example).
2. Go to **Insert | Links | Action**.
3. Select the **Mouse Over** tab.
4. Choose the option that best suits your presentation. You will notice that you can hyperlink to **Custom Shows** and many more options from the **Action Settings** dialog box.
5. Click on **OK** at the bottom of the dialog box to commit the changes.
6. To remove an action, visit the **Action Settings** dialog box and select the **None** radio button at the top of the dialog box.

Using Zoom

The **Zoom** feature allows the creation of interactive links to a section summary, a section zoom, or a slide zoom. It is a quick way to insert links, essentially to move efficiently from one part of the presentation to another really quickly:

1. Open a presentation or create a new one (we will use the `Zoom.pptx` presentation for this example), as illustrated in the following screenshot:
2. Create sections through the presentation, where necessary.
3. Go to **Insert | Links | Zoom**.

4. You have a choice of three **Zoom** options (**Summary Zoom, Section Zoom,** or **Slide Zoom**).

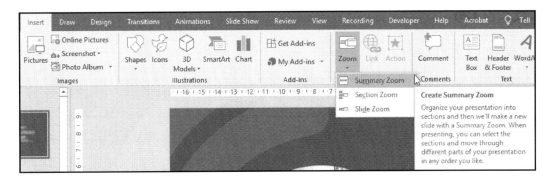

5. Let's investigate the **Summary Zoom** option. For this feature to work, you will need to select the beginning slide for each of the sections you created, and then click on the **Insert** icon at the bottom of the dialog box to create the **Summary Zoom** slide with section links, as illustrated in the following screenshot:

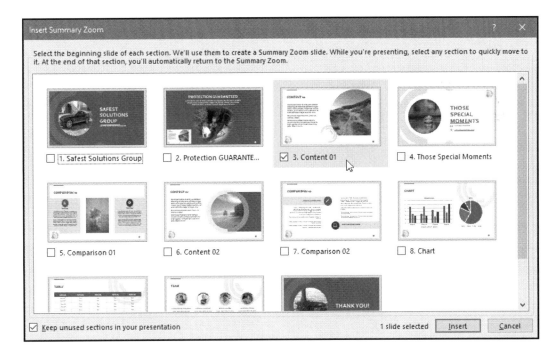

The **Summary** section slide is created with linked thumbnails to the first slide of each section. The **Section Zoom** option inserts a link to a section or sections on a thumbnail that, when presenting, will zoom to the corresponding section. The **Slide Zoom** option is very similar to the **Easy linking** option. Simply choose slides to insert as thumbnails with links onto an existing slide. When presenting, you simply click on the thumbnail to advance to that slide in the presentation.

Inserting and editing comments

Comments are useful when collaborating with others online in real time, or for sharing a presentation with others for comment at a later time. You can add comments to any part of a presentation. Note that comments are not displayed while presenting a slide show.

1. Open the presentation to which to add comments—we will work on the `Comments.pptx` presentation as an example.
2. Select an object (text, picture, textbox, chart, table, shape, clip art object, SmartArt object, or slide) to insert into the presentation.
3. Comments can be inserted using the **Insert** tab, the **Review** tab, or from the Comment icon on the status bar.
4. Click to select the **Insert** tab.
5. From the **Comments** group, select the **New Comment** icon.
6. The **Comments Pane** will open to the right of the application—notice that the comment is inserted ready for input in the **Comments Pane**, and the Comment icon marker is displayed in the top-left corner of the slide.
7. Enter a comment in the comment text area provided in the **Comments Pane**, as illustrated in the following screenshot:

8. The comment is inserted and awaits a reply. If the presentation is created in a shared location, users will be able to reply to comments and collaborate.

9. To receive comments from people outside of your organization, share the presentation with others, who would then be able to reply to comments in real time.

Editing comments

1. Locate the comment you wish to edit from the **Comment Pane** in the presentation.
2. Double-click on the existing comment.
3. The comment text area will open up, allowing you to make the desired changes.
4. Click off the comment area onto the background of your slide to close the comment.

Showing or hiding markup

Use the **Show Markup** option to show or hide comments and annotations on slides in a presentation.

1. Click to select **Review** I **Show Comments** I **Show Markup**, as illustrated in the following screenshot:

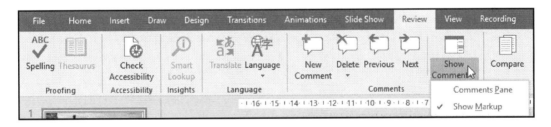

2. If a checkmark appears to the left of **Show Markup**, this means that the option is already on and comments are displayed throughout the presentation.

Deleting comments

Click on the comment marker for the comment you wish to delete, and then press the *Delete* key on the keyboard or, on the **Review** tab, select the **Delete** icon to display the options. You are able to delete a single comment, delete all comments on a slide, or delete all comments within a presentation. You can also delete comments using the mouse right-click on a comment icon indicator on the slide, and then clicking on **Delete Comment**; or use the **Delete** icon to the right of the comment in the **Comment Pane** to remove the comment.

Inking feature

If you draw with a pen, mouse pointer, or your finger on a touch-enabled device, PowerPoint will convert the drawing to shape automatically with the *inking* feature. Simply draw onto the slide background and watch the magic happen. When writing any math problems with a pen, mouse pointer, or finger, the writing will be converted to math symbols and will subsequently open up the **Math Tools**, **Structures**, and **Symbols** groups. Note that you can use different **Pens** to draw with ink on slides within the presentation:

1. Click on the **Draw** tab on the ribbon, and then select **Ink to Shape** from the **Content** group, as illustrated in the following screenshot:

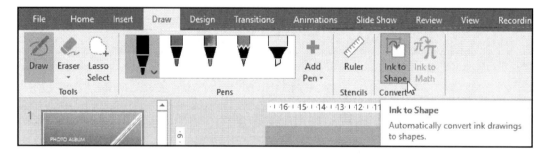

2. Draw onto the slide using the mouse pointer, or use a touch pen or your finger to draw a shape if you have a touch-enabled device. The drawing is immediately converted to a shape. After drawing text, select the text, and click **Ink to Shape**.

Exploring slide show options and custom shows

In this topic, you will learn how to set up a slide show using various options. The **Loop continuously** option is perfect for those conference marketing scenarios when you would like the show to run continuously on a monitor, and the **Presenter View** is great as you can view your speaker notes on your device while presenting to an audience.

You will be shown how to show all or specific slides in a presentation, as well as adjust slide timings and set slides to use these timings when presenting. The benefits of custom slide shows will be explained here.

Setting up a slide show

1. Click on the **Slide Show** tab along the ribbon.
2. Select the **Set Up Slide Show** icon.
3. In the dialog box, select the **Show type** as **Presented by a speaker (full screen)**, as illustrated in the screenshot after the following information box:

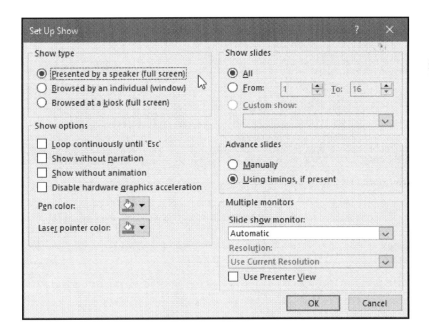

This is normally full screen, but there are other options, including **Browsed at a kiosk**, which is used when running business presentations without the presenter being in attendance, and without the option to skip slides. Once you have set up kiosk mode, rehearse slide timings by advancing to the next slide to set a time limit, in order to cover the slide content for viewing. This is to make sure that the audience walking by are able to digest all the content on each slide.

4. Under the **Show options** heading, select the **Loop continuously until 'Esc'** option if you are going to be repeating your slide show repetitively for a *walk-by* audience.

5. From the **Show slides** heading, select which slides will need to be in the slide show while presenting the **Slide Show** to an audience.
   If any **Custom Shows** are available in this presentation, they would display in the **Custom Show:** drop-down list.

6. The **Advance slides** category is very important—make sure that you select **Using timings, if present** so that you do not have to click your way through a presentation when presenting to an audience.

7. Set **Advance slides** to **Manually** if you need to pause (or be in control) throughout the presentation while presenting to an audience.

Playing narrations

If you have used narrations and recorded them using the **Record Slide Show** option from the **Recording** tab options, you would need to make sure that when playing back to an audience, the relevant options are selected. These are located on the **Slide Show** tab ribbon, as illustrated in the following screenshot:

1. From the **Slide Show** tab (under the **Set Up** group), make sure that the **Play Narrations** checkbox is selected.

2. Also, make sure that the option under the **Set Up Show** dialog box for **Show without narration** is not selected, as illustrated in the following screenshot:

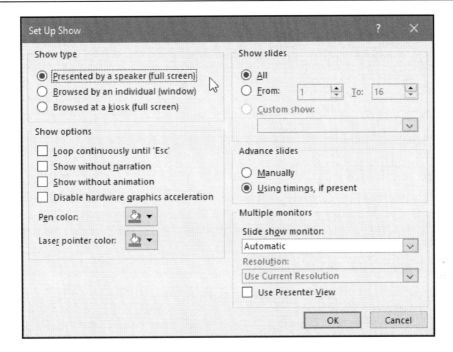

Let's see how we would set up the **Presenter View** on the next topic.

Setting up the presenter view

The presenter view enables you to view speaker notes while presenting to an audience. The audience views the presentation on the main monitor, and the presenter views the presentation with access to speaker notes on another monitor. The presenter view enables the presentation to be viewed on multiple monitors. In the presenter view, you can also decide to darken or lighten the screen for the audience—for example, during a break or when a question-and-answer-type session is in progress:

1. Open the presentation to set up viewing on multiple monitors. We will continue with the presentation from the previous topic.
2. Insert speaker notes to help you with presenting to the audience. To help you, click on a slide to add speaker notes, and then click on the **Notes** icon on the status bar to activate the **Notes** section below the slide. Type the following note: **Welcome to our presentation on Safest Solutions Group Travels. We hope to entice you to explore more of our wonderful trips on offer, including the appropriate cover for your journey.**

3. From the **Slide Show** tab, locate the **Set Up** group.

4. Click on the **Setup Slide Show** icon.

5. Locate the **Use Presenter View** checkbox, and then click to select it. If you have multiple monitors connected, the feature will automatically detect the primary and secondary monitor. Note that the **Use Presenter View** option is also present from the **Monitors** group on the **Slide Show** ribbon.

Using timings

You can rehearse your presentation in PowerPoint 2019 to accommodate your slide advance timings. We will learn how to set the timings and set up the environment to use the timings. Make sure that the **Using timings, if present** option is selected if the presentation you are setting up has advanced slide timings selected throughout the presentation:

1. Firstly, set the slide timings using the **Advance Slide** option on the **Transitions** tab, or use the **Record Slide Timings** icon on the **Recording** tab to play the presentation and set the slide timings. The first option is illustrated in the following screenshot:

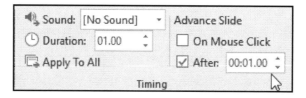

2. Go to the **Slide Show** tab and select the **Set Up Show** icon to launch the dialog box.

3. Under the **Advance slides** heading, make sure that **Using timings, if present** is selected, as illustrated in the following screenshot:

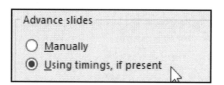

4. Click on **OK** to commit the changes.

Showing media controls

The media controls are the icons that appear below the audio or video content inserted into the presentation.

1. Click on the **Slide Show** tab on the ribbon.
2. Locate the **Set Up** group.
3. Make sure that the checkbox for **Show Media Controls** is selected—otherwise, the control buttons will not show when the presentation is being shown to an audience.

Creating a custom slide show

The **Custom Slide Show** feature in PowerPoint is extremely useful when you need to create several different shows within one PowerPoint presentation. Not all slides apply to all audiences, so different categories of slides can be sent to a custom show and named as such so that you can present just the right content for a particular audience, without having different presentations for different audiences/content:

1. To create a custom show, click on the **Slide Show** tab on the ribbon.
2. Click on the **Custom Slide Show** icon.
3. Choose **Custom Shows…**, as illustrated in the following screenshot:

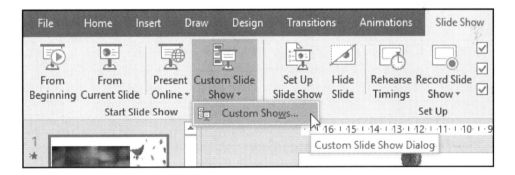

4. Click on the **New…** icon.
5. Name the slide show by typing text into the **Define Custom Show** dialog box.
6. Click to select slides to add to the custom show.

7. Use the **Add>>** icon to move the slides to the right side of the dialog box, to be included in the new custom show. Click on **OK** when done. Note: it's very important to make sure that slides are included in a specific order (especially if preparing for an international computer examination).
8. The new custom show will appear in the **Custom Shows** dialog box.
9. To make changes, click on the **Edit...** icon.
10. To delete the custom show, click on the **Remove** icon.
11. To display the show, click on the **Show** icon.
12. Click on **Close** when done.
13. The new custom show will be visible when clicking on the **Custom Slide Show** icon on the **Slide Show** tab.

Using master slides and hiding slides

In this topic, you will learn to create, modify, and format a master slide, and be able to hide or show certain slides when delivering a presentation.

Creating master slides

The slide master stores information such as logos, styles, and fonts, which the user can set as a default for all slides in the presentation. For instance, a company logo could be set in a certain position on the slide with certain attributes. When placed on the Slide Master, all slides within the presentation—and any new slide inserted in the presentation—will display the logo in the same position with the same attributes. Any elements placed onto the slide master will not be editable when creating the presentation unless the user is familiar with editing master slides or has been given permission to do so. Editing master slides for different presentation slide layouts is extremely popular when companies wish to lock down branding for all stationery within a business:

1. For this example, we will create a new presentation based on the **Quotable** theme.
2. Click to select the **View** tab.
3. From the **Master Views** group, select **Slide Master**.
4. The slide master view is now displayed on the screen.

5. Depending on the theme and the slides you have within the presentation, you will be presented with different slide layouts and masters, but you should see a slide master and then different layout masters beneath that in the **Slide Pane**.

6. Note that you can also create master slides for handouts and notes, as well as many other master slide layout types.

7. Once you have activated the slide master, the **Slide Master** ribbon will open up, with a lot of different options for you to use to customize your master slides, as can be seen in the following screenshot:

8. We will insert a picture onto the slide background. Make sure that the picture is visible on all masters—if not, copy and paste to the various slide masters visible in the **Slide Pane**.

9. Click on the **Insert** tab, and then choose **Pictures**.

10. Locate the picture on your computer and insert it onto the slide masters, where appropriate. For this example, we will use SafestSolutionsLogo.png.

11. Switch back to **Slide** view to see whether the master has updated the slides in the presentation—notice that you are unable to select the picture, and all picture editing will need to happen in the **Slide Master** view.

12. Click on the **View** tab and choose **Normal.**

13. Click on the **View** tab and select **Slide Master** to return to master editing mode.

14. Adjust the fonts, styles, colors, and effects, and add any text—such as footers—that you would like to appear on all slides as a master. We will update the font for the main titles to the **Courgette** font.

15. Click on the **Close Master View** icon at the end of the ribbon to view the changes to the presentation.

16. Experiment with the options available on the **Slide Master** tab to create the perfect presentation master for your requirements.

Hiding slides

At times, certain slides in the final presentation might not be suitable for the presentation audience. It is possible to hide slides in the **Slides Pane** or in the **Slide Sorter View**:

1. Right-click on a slide to hide it.
2. From the shortcut menu choose **Hide Slide**, or click on the **Slide Show** tab and choose **Hide Slide,** or use the **Slide Sorter view** to hide a slide. The former option is illustrated in the following screenshot:

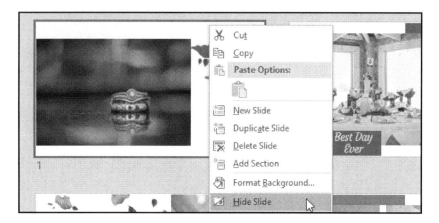

3. An icon identifies hidden slides; this is located in the top-left corner of the slide (in **Slide Sorter** and **Slide view**).
4. To unhide a slide, simply click on the **Hide Slide** icon again.

Summary

We have learned an abundance of skills in this detailed chapter, enabling the creation and modification of photo albums and the ability to set up sections to create a presentation order and to hide slides, when appropriate. You have mastered the relevant presentation motions, effects, timing, transitions, and animations, and how they work with the final presentation output with the Slide Show options. Driving consistency with the use of slide masters to conserve company branding and productivity when creating presentations has been another important achievement in this chapter.

In the next chapter, you will learn about another application—Excel.

3
Section 3: Excel

Excel 2019 is a very powerful application with most audiences only using a small fraction of its capability. In this part of the book, you will learn how to navigate around the interface, creating, formatting, and manipulating data. The heart of Excel 2019 is the ability to calculate and analyze data, which you will master through this part of the book. You will be introduced to new and improved functions, namely CONCAT, IFS, MAXIFS, MINIFS, SWITCH, and TEXTJOIN; and learn how to visualize and analyze data and create data models.

In this section, we will cover the following chapters:

- Chapter 8, *Formatting, Manipulating, and Presenting Data Visually*
- Chapter 9, *Applying Formulas and Functions*
- Chapter 10, *Analyzing and Organizing Data*

8
Formatting, Manipulating, and Presenting Data Visually

In this chapter, you will be shown how to personalize the Backstage view, set various spreadsheet options, and also distinguish between spreadsheet elements. You will be taken on a journey, through formatting elements to manipulating data, and will also learn to print elements and set print options.

You can enhance Excel 2019 with decorative, professional-looking charts such as Sunburst and Funnel charts. You will gain all the skills you need to format, print, and present data professionally.

The following list of topics will be covered in this chapter:

- Introducing the interface and setting options
- Constructing and formatting an Excel worksheet
- Working with worksheets and sheet tabs
- Sorting and filtering data
- Setting print options
- Creating charts based on worksheet data

Technical requirements

Prior to working through this chapter, you should have an understanding of the purpose of spreadsheets and be proficient at locating and launching Excel 2019. If you have worked through previous chapters of this book, you will already be familiar with some of the interface elements.

The examples used in this chapter are accessible from the following GitHub URL: `https://github.com/PacktPublishing/Learn-Microsoft-Office-2019`

Introducing the interface and setting options

This topic will highlight the important elements that make up the Excel 2019 visual environment. You will be able to identify parts of the Excel 2019 application as a whole, set view zoom options, and explore the **View** tab. We will explore the help facility and some **Review** elements (such as **Accessibility**, **Translate**, and **Smart Lookup**), as well as set customization options.

Microsoft Excel is an example of a spreadsheet program. Other types of spreadsheets are available—for example, Calc from OpenOffice, and Sheets from Google Docs. A spreadsheet is used to perform mathematical calculations and financial decision making—for example, for budgets, company reports, wage sheets, cash flows—to analyze data, and for graphical representation of data. You can process, summarize, sort, extract, analyze, and store information using a spreadsheet.

Identifying rows, columns, and cells

You work with rows and columns when using a spreadsheet program. The maximum number of rows and columns offered in a single worksheet in Excel 2019 is the following:

	MAXIMUM ROWS	MAXIMUM COLUMNS	MAXIMUM COLUMNS AND ROWS BY LETTER
EXCEL 2019	1,048,576	16,384	XFD1048576

The Excel document window consists of the following:

- Rows that are numbered vertically from **1** to **1,048,576** on each sheet
- Columns marked horizontally from A-Z, AA-ZZ, up to XFD—16,384 columns on each sheet

An example of a row and a column is provided in the following screenshot:

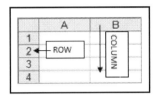

The number of columns displayed when viewing a worksheet on the screen depends on the column widths and computer screen size. You may need to scroll either to left or right to see anything that cannot fit into the screen display.

To view the number of columns and rows resident on a worksheet, proceed as follows:

Click on the **Select All** icon with the left mouse button and hold the mouse depressed to see the column and row indicators in the **Name Box** area, as illustrated in the following screenshot:

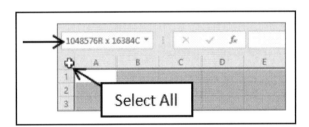

Or click on the **Home** tab, visit the **Find & Select** group, and then click on **Go To....** In the **Go To** dialog box, type XFD1048576 (this is the last column and last row of the workbook).

 To move from the very last row and column on a worksheet without having to scroll for ages, hold down the *Ctrl* key and then press the *Home* key to move instantly to cell A1. To go back to the active cell, we use the *Ctrl* key and the Backspace key.

A **cell** is a position on the worksheet where the rows and columns cross (intersect). The **cell address** is the position at which the column letter and row number intersect. An *active cell* contains a thick border. The border indicates the place on the worksheet where the mouse pointer currently resides and is ready for data input. Text aligns to the left, and values are aligned to the right when entered.

Once data is typed into a cell, press the *Enter* key on the keyboard to confirm the entry, and the cursor will move down one cell. Alternatively, click on another cell using the mouse pointer, directly after typing the data, or press an arrow key on the keyboard to move the cursor, as illustrated in the following screenshot:

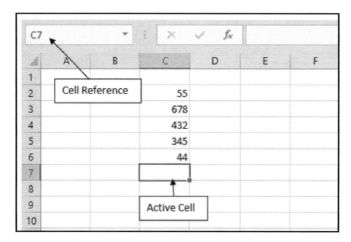

Workbooks and worksheets

Another name for an Excel document is a **workbook**. A workbook consists of a number of **sheets**, called **worksheets**. The default number of worksheets visible when you open Excel is 1 (**Sheet1**). You can add a new sheet at any time or set the default option to display more sheets upon opening each workbook. A sheet is similar to a page in a book. A workbook consists of a collection of worksheets. Another name for a worksheet is a spreadsheet. Please note that one worksheet consists of many pages, as can be seen in the following screenshot:

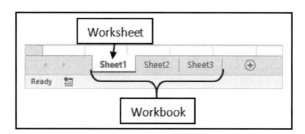

To move from sheet to sheet, you would either use the sheet tab scrolls, click on the sheet tabs individually, use the **...** navigation icon to move to the right or left one sheet at a time, or right-click over the sheet tab scrolls and select the sheet name to navigate to, as illustrated in the following screenshot:

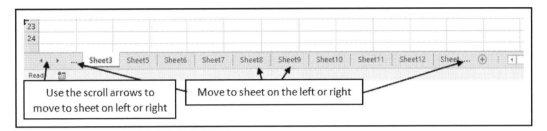

You can also use the *Ctrl + click* method to move to the very first or very last worksheet in the workbook (skipping all the sheets in between), as illustrated in the following screenshot:

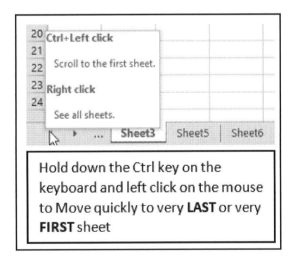

When working with a large worksheet, you will not always able to see all of the sheet tabs at once. If you cannot locate a sheet, right-click over the tab scroll buttons to obtain a list of available sheets in the workbook. This will populate the **Activate** dialog box, where you can select a sheet name, and then click on the **OK** command to move directly to that sheet in the workbook.

The title bar in Excel displays the name of the workbook that is currently open. `Book1.xlsx` would represent the first open unsaved workbook. We can collapse the ribbon in exactly the same way as the other Office 2019 applications. These generic sections (hot keys, tool tips, tabs, groups, dialog box launcher, **Quick Access Toolbar (QAT)**, and the ribbon) are all covered in the first chapter of this book, so we will not cover these again here.

In the next topic, we will investigate the function of the Name Box.

Name Box and Formula Bar

The Name Box is located under the ribbon on the left side of the workbook area. Use the Name Box to locate cells quickly or navigate to named ranges in the workbook. The Name Box can be seen in the following screenshot:

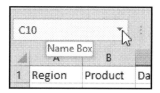

The Formula Bar is located next to the Name Box. This is where formulas are typed and or viewed. The *fx* item located on the left of the formula area is the Insert Function icon. There are many ways to construct formulas in a workbook, and this is one of the methods to gain access to all the available functions in Excel. The Formula Bar can be seen in the following screenshot:

Status bar

The status bar resides at the very bottom of the Excel environment. It is a gray bar that displays information about the current workbook and provides quick access to some tasks. The status bar resides on all Office applications and has information relevant to the specific application that appears along it. You will notice a **Ready** indicator at the start of the bar (refer the next screenshot for the position of the status bar). Right-clicking on the status bar will provide you with a shortcut menu to make changes to the status bar. You can add or remove items from the status bar. A tick to the left of the text identifies items that are already active. Active means already selected, visible, or selected. To add or remove an item from the status bar, simply click on the desired text option on the shortcut menu.

AVERAGE, **COUNT** and **SUM** are the default functions that provide a result to selected values on a worksheet along the status bar. To change how these values are calculated, right-click, and select another function to perform. If you highlight a range of numerical values on a worksheet, Excel will display the count, sum, and average of those values on the status bar.

The position of the status bar can be seen in the following screenshot:

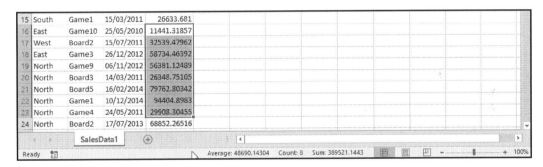

We will now look at the different zoom magnification options available in Excel 2019.

Setting view options

Various zoom magnification percentages are available in Excel. This is to give the user the opportunity to reduce the size of the percentage zoom when working with large amounts of data so that all information can be viewed on screen while working.

The zoom options are located on the **View** menu and at the end of the status bar. Click on the **100% zoom** option to access the **Zoom** dialog box and change to **Magnification**, or enter a custom percentage. Once complete, click on the **OK** command to confirm and commit to the change. Please note that changes apply to the current worksheet only. The other sheets in the workbook are not affected, unless selected.

The **View** tab contains more options relating to zooming in or out on a worksheet. To access the zoom options via the ribbon, click on the **Zoom** icon on the **View** tab, or click on the **100% zoom** indicator on the status bar to access the options.

Select a **Magnification** option from the dialog box, or type your own custom percentage into the **Custom** text area.

A great tool in Excel 2019 is the **Zoom to Selection** icon. Select a range of cells on the worksheet and click on the **Zoom to Selection** icon on the **View** tab. The selected area magnifies. Click on the **100% zoom** icon to return to the normal view mode.

Clicking on the **View** tab as well as accessing the **Zoom** icon from the **Zoom** group will allow you to customize the zoom level using the **Zoom** dialog box, as illustrated in the following screenshot:

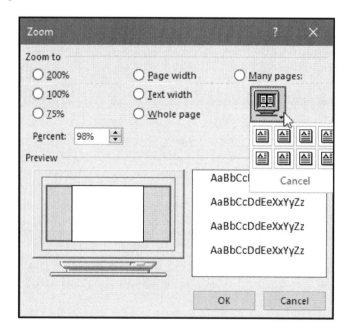

Using the help facility

Office 2019's help function is available, as usual, by pressing the *F1* keyboard key, which will open the **Help** pane to the right of the worksheet. You will then be able to select a topic of interest from the list provided, which will offer further sub-topics until you find what you are looking for.

Alternatively, you can search using the **Tell me what you want to do** feature, located at the end of the tabs along the top of the ribbon. Be careful of this tool as, although it is very efficient, taking you directly to the help menu and performs the action for you from within the help facility.

To use the help function, proceed as follows:

1. Simply click to the right of the light bulb icon, which will open the text placeholder.
2. Start typing a question to get help, and the feature will offer suggestions as you type, as illustrated in the following screenshot:

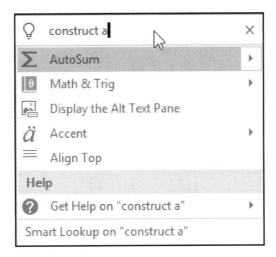

3. Select a topic in the drop-down list to obtain the help topic you require.

Proofing tools

When visiting the **Review** tab, you will notice the **Proofing** group, along with other very useful reviewing tools, as can be seen in the following screenshot:

Use the **Spelling** icon to spellcheck an Excel worksheet. You also have access to the **Thesaurus**, where alternate words to the current word you are using can be searched for and replaced.

Checking **Accessibility** is an extremely useful tool as it checks accessibility best practices. This means that it will offer suggestions such as changing a font if it seems unreadable due to hard-to-read text contrast, as well as a section on the reason why it should be altered in the workbook, as can be seen in the following screenshot:

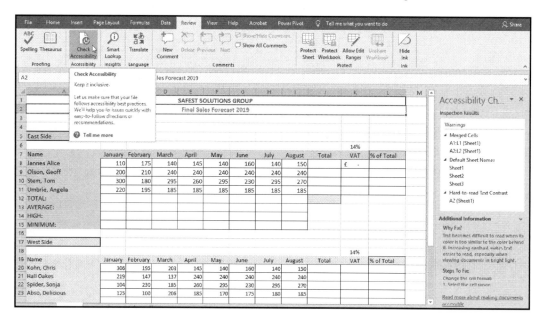

The **Smart Lookup** feature will open a pane to the right of the worksheet after selecting text on the worksheet—this is more popular when using Microsoft Word 2019 as it will offer information such as images, definitions, and more from online sources.

The **Translate** feature will convert text into any other language via the pane to the right of the worksheet. The remainder of the **Review** tab icons refers to commenting, protecting, and inking, which will be visited later in this book.

Changing default options

The **File** tab allows access to the Backstage view, where default options in Microsoft Excel can be set. This view is where workbooks are managed by creating, sending, saving, sharing, inspecting, and setting options. We will look at some of the most important user options next, including changing the number of workbooks on the recently used file list and setting the default location of files.

Note that when changing default options within Excel 2019, the options are set globally for the whole of Excel and not just the current workbook. The **Options** dialog box is full of custom settings that will make use of Excel 2019 in a more streamlined way, for daily use.

Changing the default username

The username in Office 2019 is located under **General**. It is an important element when collaborating with others as it identifies the user when commenting or reviewing workbooks using **Track Changes**, and is also included as part of the workbook properties. When Office 2019 is installed, you are usually prompted to enter a username, but you can also edit that as follows:

1. Click to select **File** | **Options** | **General** | **Personalize your copy of Microsoft Office** | **User name:**.

2. Type the desired username into the text area provided, as illustrated in the following screenshot:

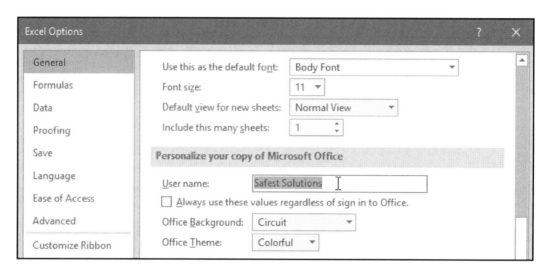

Changing the default document location

When a workbook is saved or opened in Microsoft Excel, the default file location is displayed in the dialog box by default. By this, we mean the drive and folder you are presented with when clicking on **File** | **Open** or by clicking on **File** | **Save**. Then, locate the **Save workbooks** heading.

In the **Default local file location** text area, change the location that you would like files to be saved to and opened from by default, and then click **OK**.

Changing the default number of workbooks

A single new worksheet is visible—by default—when you create a new workbook in Excel 2019. If you prefer to have Excel automatically show a set number of worksheets in a single workbook each time you create a new blank workbook, complete the following steps:

1. Click on **File** | **Options** | **General**.
2. Locate the **When creating new workbooks** heading.

3. Use the spin arrows to increase or decrease the number of sheets you wish to include in a single workbook, as illustrated in the following screenshot:

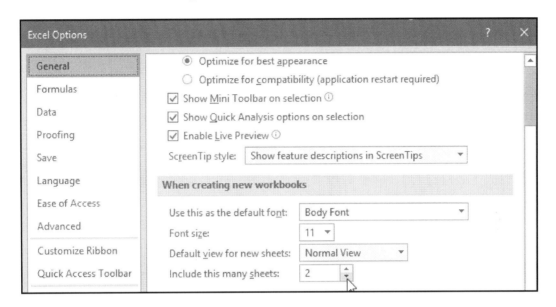

4. Click on the **OK** command to commit to the changes. Open a new workbook to see the change.

Saving automatically

Saving automatically in the background while working on Excel workbooks is very important, as you would like to ensure that you are able to recover any work if the system crashes. Excel offers the capability to set an automatic save feature for some minutes and also to keep the last auto recovered version, should the workbook be closed without saving. To make use of this feature, follow these steps:

1. Click on **File** | **Options** | **Save**.
2. Make sure that the **Save AutoRecover information every __ minutes** option is active, and set the minutes using the spin arrows provided.

3. Also, check that the **Keep the last AutoRecovered version if I close without saving** option is active, as illustrated in the following screenshot, and click on **OK**:

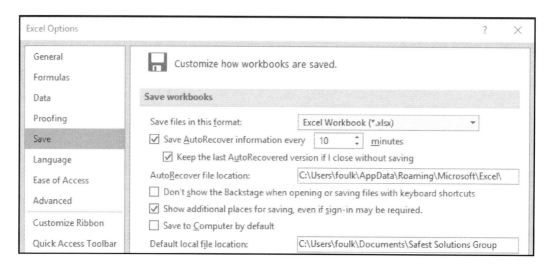

Constructing and formatting an Excel worksheet

In this chapter, you will learn methods to quickly input and work with Excel data, and then apply and modify cell formats. You will enhance these skills by merging or splitting cells, and learning how to hide and show rows and columns. You will also apply cell styles, insert and delete rows and columns, set column and row widths/heights, and work with worksheets, workbooks, and sheet tabs.

Inputting data efficiently

To input data into Excel, simply click on a cell and start typing. When you are done, press the *Enter* key on the keyboard. Values are always aligned to the right, and text aligned to the left of the cell. You can use the Formula Bar to enter data into a cell, although this could be more time-consuming than typing the data directly into the cell. When we select cells from one point to another, it is called a **range**. There are numerous efficient ways to enter data into a worksheet—some of the most important ones are discussed in the next subsections.

Entering data into a set range

If you know the extent of the range you are needing to enter in a worksheet, then the best way is to select a range of cells and type up the data. This method is fantastic when entering university marks into a spreadsheet, as you can concentrate on the paperwork and not on the screen when entering the values.

1. Select a range on the worksheet.
2. Type the first value and press the *Enter* key to confirm.
3. The cursor will move to the next cell, as illustrated in the following screenshot:

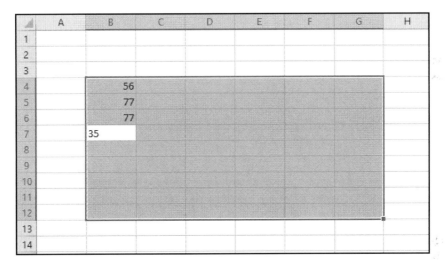

4. Type the next value, and so on...

Entering data in non-contiguous ranges

A non-contiguous range means cells not next to each other. We will learn how to select non-contiguous cells and then enter data into this range. Selecting using this method is also very useful when needing to apply formatting to selected cells at once.

1. Click on a cell in the worksheet.
2. While holding down the *Ctrl* keyboard key, select other cells in the worksheet.
3. Let go of the *Ctrl* key and start typing values or text into the selected cells.

To enter exactly the same cell content into non-contiguous cells (meaning cells not next to each other), this is possible using the *Ctrl + Enter* key combination.

1. Select a number of cells not next to each other by using the *Ctrl + click* method.
2. Notice that one of the cells is lighter in selection than the others—this is due to the lighter-shaded cell being the active cell.
3. Enter data into the active cell, and before pressing the *Enter* key as you would normally do, hold down the *Ctrl* keyboard key and press *Enter* on the keyboard. The result can be seen in the following screenshot:

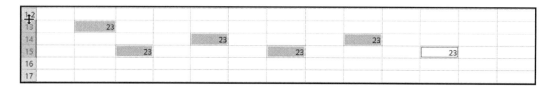

4. The value is copied into each selected cell automatically.

Using fill down

Often, you will need to copy a cell from the range above it, using the exact data and formatting. The fill down facility is the quickest way to do this by using the *Ctrl* key on the keyboard and the *D* keyboard letter.

1. Open the `EfficientDataEntry.xlsx` workbook.
2. Cell **B9** contains the text **Marketing**, which has formats applied.
3. To copy the cell content and the cell formatting, click to select cell **B10**, and then press and hold down the *Ctrl* keyboard key and press the *D* keyboard key.
4. The content and formatting are duplicated into the next cell.

Using a data entry form

To restrict users while entering data into cells on the worksheet, a data form is used. This will control the navigation on the worksheet and ensure data is placed into the correct cell. To set up the form, you will need to add the **Form...** icon to the QAT first.

1. We will continue using the `EfficientDataEntry.xlsx` workbook.
2. Click to select **Sheet2** at the bottom of the workbook.
3. Notice that **Sheet2** contains headings at the top of the worksheet without any data entered—in order for the form to work, we will need to have entered column headings prior to adding the **Form...** icon to the QAT.
4. Select the drop-down arrow at the end of the QAT.
5. Click to select **More Commands...** .
6. From the **Popular Commands** drop-down list, select **Commands Not in the Ribbon** option.
7. Scroll to locate the **Form...** icon.
8. Click on the **Add>>** icon in the middle of the dialog box to add it to the QAT. Click on **OK**.
9. The **Form...** icon is now visible on the QAT, as illustrated in the following screenshot:

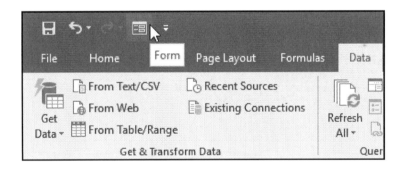

10. Click to select cell A1 on the worksheet to indicate where the form column headings are.
11. Click on the **Form** icon at the end of the QAT to populate the form (you will receive an error dialog box to help guide you to select the correct column headings before entering data; click on **OK** to close this error), and then start typing the first record (row). Click on **New** to enter the record into the worksheet and start the new record, as illustrated in the following screenshot:

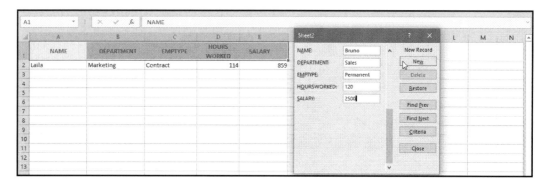

12. Continue until all records have been entered into the worksheet.
13. Click on the **Close** icon on the form dialog box to return to the worksheet.

Using Alt + down arrow

When entering data—such as a status or departments within an organization—into a worksheet repetitively down the column, Excel will offer a suggestion after typing the first letter of the word into the cell above. If the choice offered is correct, you can save time by pressing the *Enter* key to accept the choice offered. If you prefer to choose from a populated list, use the Alt key on the keyboard and press the down arrow. The result can be seen in the following screenshot:

	A	B	C	D	E	F
1	NAME	DEPARTMENT	EMPTYPE	HOURS WORKED	SALARY	
2		Marketing				
3		Sales				
4		Sales				
5		Marketing				
6		Human Resources				
7		Admin				
8		Catering				
9		Information Technology				
10						
11		Admin				
12		Catering				
13		Human Resources				
14		Information Techn				
15		Marketing				
		Sales				

Entering dates and times

You will find steps to add the current date and time into a worksheet cell. Note that neither of these entries will update should the workbook be closed and opened at another date or time:

1. To enter the current date into the worksheet, press down the *Ctrl* keyboard key and press the (;) semicolon key.
2. To enter the current time into the worksheet, press down the *Ctrl* and *Shift* keyboard keys and press the (:) colon key.

To insert a date and time that updates automatically every time the workbook is opened, do the following:

1. Insert =today() into a cell to return the current date.
2. Insert =now() into a cell to return the current date and time format.

Copying data using AutoFill

The AutoFill handle allows you to copy information to an adjacent range of cells. When you place your mouse pointer over the fill handle (the little black square located at the bottom right-hand corner of a cell), your mouse changes to a small black cross.

While holding down your left mouse button, drag to a new position on the worksheet. Any text typed into a cell with a number before or after it will be incremented when using AutoFill, as illustrated in the following screenshot:

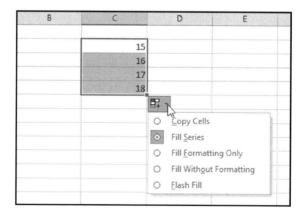

 AutoFill is not only used for text and values but also to copy formatting. Instead of left-clicking on the crosshair and dragging, right-click to view the AutoFill options available. These will appear once you release the mouse after dragging to the destination location.

Incrementing values

Entering a number— for example, 15—into a cell, and then holding down the *Ctrl* key while dragging the fill handle will create an incremented series. Notice that when holding down the *Ctrl* key, a second **+** is shown above the existing **+** fill handle. This indicates that you will increment values as you drag using the mouse. Instead of typing 1, 2, 3... into separate cells, simply type 1 into a cell, then hold down the *Ctrl* key and drag the AutoFill icon to increment the values, as illustrated in the following screenshot:

Once the values are entered into the cells, the AutoFill options icon is displayed, where further data customization can be selected.

Modifying cell formatting

It is possible to position or align text vertically and horizontally in a cell. When inserting text into a cell on the worksheet, this automatically aligns to the left of the cell by default. Numbers (values) are aligned to the right of the cell. The formatting of both these elements can be altered using the formatting tools provided.

Remember that formatting cell content is a cosmetic change only, and although values can be aligned to the left of the cell, Excel still identifies the difference between values and text when constructing formulas and functions.

Aligning text

There are two types of alignment—vertical and horizontal. To align text horizontally, follow these steps:

1. Open the `SafestSolutionsSales.xlxs` workbook.
2. Select the cell that contains the text to align. Locate the **Alignment** group on the **Home** tab.
3. Select the left, center, or right horizontal alignment icon.
4. The text moves to a new position in the cell.

The process can be seen in the following screenshot:

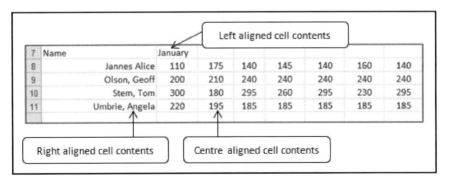

To make the cell contents more presentable, vertical alignment is possible, as follows:

1. Select the cell that contains the text. Click on the **Alignment** group on the **Home** tab.
2. Select the left, center, or right vertical alignment icon.
3. The cell contents move to the new vertical position, as illustrated in the following screenshot:

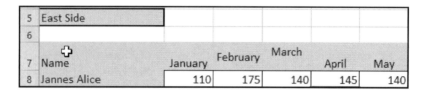

5	East Side					
6						
7	Name	January	February	March	April	May
8	Jannes Alice	110	175	140	145	140

Changing text orientation

It is possible to rotate or reposition data in a cell on a worksheet. This option will not apply to merge cells. Text orientation is a great tool to rotate text vertically in a cell or cells so that it provides more space on the worksheet when working with a huge number of columns. By changing the angle of text in the cell, information can fit onto a specific area of the worksheet.

1. Select or highlight the cells you wish to rotate.
2. Go to **Home** | **Alignment**.
3. Click on the drop-down arrow of the Orientation icon.
4. Select the alignment type from the list, as illustrated in the following screenshot:

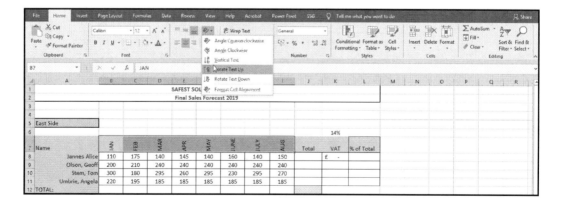

5. At the bottom of the drop-down list, click on the **Format Cell Alignment** option to access further alignment options. In this dialog box, you will be able to specify custom rotation degrees and other format cell changes.

6. If you need to align data to a specific angle size (for example, 42^0), then you would need to access the **Format Cell Alignment** dialog box. In the **Format Cells** dialog box, make sure you are on the **Alignment** tab.

7. Type the angle size into the textbox provided, or use the slider to drag to the orientation position of your choice. Click on the **OK** command at the bottom of the dialog box to confirm the changes.

Wrapping text

Data can appear on multiple lines within a single cell. Text wrapping is set using more than one method. Use the **Wrap Text** icon on the **Home** tab, the **Format Cells** dialog box, or by inserting a line break manually.

Using a line break to wrap text manually gives the user more control over where the text should wrap:

1. Click on an empty cell on the worksheet, and then type the text `Safest Solutions` into the cell.

2. Directly after the typed words, press *Alt + Enter* on the keyboard, which will insert the line break and move the cursor down to the next line in the cell.

3. Type the word `Group`.

4. Press *Enter* on your keyboard to accept the text or click on another cell to exit. The result can be seen in the following screenshot:

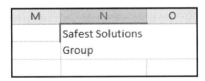

5. To use the ribbon to wrap text, click on the **Home** tab, and then locate the **Alignment** group.

6. Click on the **Wrap Text** icon, and the text is wrapped.

Indenting text:
Indentation means to move data toward the left or right within the cell. You can indent your data by going to the **Home | Alignment** group and selecting either the **Increase Indent** icon or the **Decrease Indent** icon.

Merging cells

Merging cells means combining a number of cells. The Excel merge tool is often used to combine and center the contents of cells across parts of the worksheet. It is not possible to split cells in Excel, but you are able to merge two cells above two columns to make it appear as if the cells were split.

Follow these steps to merge cells as well as place the text into the center of the merged cells using a single action:

1. Select the cells you would like to merge across—continue to use the example from the previous topic. We will select cells A5:L5.
2. From the **Home** tab, locate the **Alignment** group, and then click on the **Merge & Center** icon.
3. The text centers across the merged cells.
4. This option will not work with multiple headings—to demonstrate this, we will learn how to unmerge cells first so that we can use the top two headings of the worksheet as an example.
5. Select cells A1 and A2.
6. Locate the **Alignment** group on the **Home** tab.
7. Click on the arrow alongside **Merge & Center**, and then select **Unmerge Cells** from the drop-down list.
8. The cells are now unmerged and are located to the left of the worksheet.
9. Let's now center cells A1 and A2 across cells A1:L2.
10. Select the range A1:L2.
11. Click on the **Merge & Center** icon, after which an error will appear, notifying you that merging these cells will only keep the upper-leftmost value and discard the other values.
    If you choose to continue by clicking on the **OK** command, the first heading will center across the selected range, but the second heading will be deleted in the process.

12. To correct this, we will need to use the **Merge Across** option. This will keep all headings in separate rows and merge across the range in separate rows.

13. Click on the undo feature to remove the last action performed on the worksheet (alternatively, use the shortcut key *Ctrl + Z*).

14. Select the range A1:L2 once again.

15. Click on the drop-down arrow alongside **Merge & Center**, and then choose **Merge Across**, as illustrated in the following screenshot:

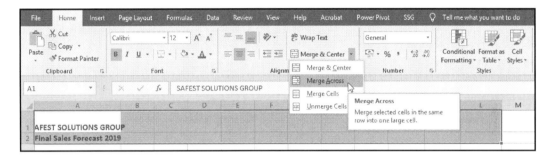

16. The problem is fixed, as the rows are merged and centered individually.

Hiding and showing rows and columns

You have the option to hide columns and rows should you wish to print your worksheet without them showing, or if another person needs to view the workbook and you do not want them to see a particular column of data. To select a column or row, simply click on the column letter or row number. To select multiple columns and rows, hold down the mouse and keep it depressed until all the columns or rows have been highlighted.

1. For this example, we will open the `SafestSolutions-Law.xlsx` workbook.

2. Select the column to hide by clicking on the column header. To do this, place the mouse pointer over the column letter, and click to select it.

3. Locate the **Cells** group on the **Home** tab.

4. Click on the **Format** drop-down list and locate the **Visibility** heading.

5. Click on **Hide & Unhide** and choose **Hide Columns** from the shortcut menu provided.

6. The column is now hidden from view. Notice that the image has shifted to the next column and is not hidden with the column. This is because it is an object that hovers over the column, and not actually part of the column contents. There is also a double line separating columns **D** and **F**—this indicates that a column is hidden. When placing the mouse pointer over the double line between columns **D** and **F**, the mouse pointer changes to double-lined arrows—double-click to show the hidden column, or drag with the mouse pointer to the right to display column **E**, as demonstrated in the following screenshot:

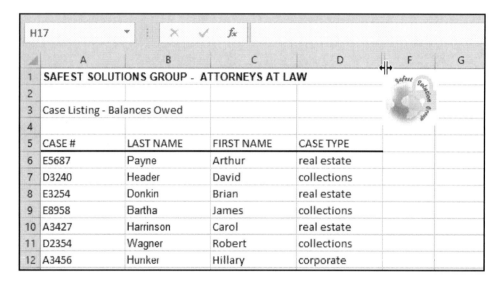

7. Sometimes, it may be difficult to grab hold of the hidden column's double arrow to show it again. If this happens, select the column before and the column after, and then right-click and choose **Unhide** from the shortcut menu provided.

Right-click on a column or row to access the **Hide** option if you prefer a shortcut.

Inserting and deleting rows and columns

1. Click on row **9** to select it. We are using the example from the previous topic.
2. Make sure that the mouse pointer is positioned on the **9** when you select it.
3. Click to select the **Insert** drop-down list from the **Cells** group.
4. Click to select **Insert Sheet Rows**, as illustrated in the following screenshot:

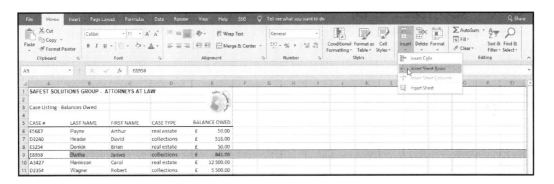

5. A new row (empty row) appears above row **9**.
6. Other methods are also available in order to insert a new row. You can right-click on a row, and then choose **Insert** from the shortcut menu provided; or select a row, and while holding down the *Ctrl* key on the keyboard, press the + sign. Hint: keep pressing + to insert more than one row.
7. To delete rows, click to select the row to delete, and then while holding down the *Ctrl* key on the keyboard, press the - sign. You can also use the right-click method on a row to delete the row, as well as choosing the **Delete Sheet Rows** option from the **Delete** icon, located on the **Cells** group.

 Note that the preceding instructions apply to columns, except that you would choose the **Insert Sheet Columns** and **Delete Sheet Columns** options from the **Cells** group.

Setting column widths and row heights

Column widths are set to 8.43 (64 pixels) and rows are set to 15 (20 pixels) by default. Select the column or columns you wish to resize. Use one of the following methods to change the column width:

1. Right-click over the highlighted column or columns and choose **Column Width**, as illustrated in the following screenshot:

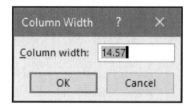

2. Enter a value to resize the column or columns into the dialog box provided, and then click on **OK** to confirm.

   Or

1. Locate the **Cells group**, and then select the **Format** option.
2. Choose **Column Width** from the drop-down list provided.
3. Enter a value to resize the columns/s in the dialog box provided.
4. Click on **OK** to confirm.

Alternatively, use the **AutoFit Column Width** and **AutoFit Row Height** feature to automatically size rows and columns to fit the contents within them. Either double-click on the column or row separator line between a column or a row to resize automatically or select a row and/or column, and then visit the **Format** tab of the **Cells** group, from which you will choose **AutoFit Row Height** or **AutoFit Column Width**.

If you see ###### displayed in a column instead of the actual cell content, this often means that the column is not wide enough to show the content within it. Simply use one of the preceding methods to widen the column to correct this.

Using the Format Painter

The **Format Painter** icon allows formats to be copied (not the cell contents, but the formatting applied to the cell contents) from one cell to another:

1. Format a cell in the worksheet using font, size, and attributes.
2. Select the formatted cells you wish to copy.
3. Click on the **Format Painter** icon on the **Clipboard** group of the **Home** tab once to copy the format to one other cell.
   To copy the format more than once, double-click on the **Format Painter** icon, as illustrated in the following screenshot:

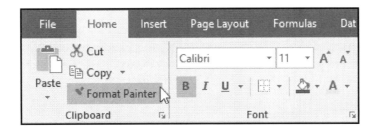

4. You will notice a white plus (+) sign as the mouse pointer with a little paintbrush to the right of it—this means that the **Format Painter** icon is active and is waiting for you to select cells to apply the formats.
5. Select the cells to apply the format to by clicking on them, or use the drag method for more than one cell. The formats copy over to the new cells.

Creating and applying cell styles

A style is a collection of formats that can be applied to cell contents. In Excel, you will find predefined cell styles to use that will save you time and give you a professional finish to your workbook. You may also create your own style and save it for use in any workbook. General formatting of font, size, attributes, and text color has been addressed in previous chapters of this book, and the procedure is exactly the same in all Office applications. We will cover some of these within this section, but not as a separate topic:

1. Click on the cell or select the cells to which you wish to apply a style.
2. Click on the **Home** | **Styles** group.

3. Click to choose the **Cell Styles** icon, after which a drop-down list will appear with style options.
4. Choose a style to suit your cell and its content.
5. The style applies to the selected text. To remove a style, make sure the text is selected, and then select **Normal** from the **Cell Styles** drop-down list.

Applying number formats

It is possible to change the appearance of values in a cell without affecting the actual value itself. Number formats are applied to values after the number has been entered into the cell. For instance, if I enter an amount of £4500.00 into a cell, I will not include the £ symbol to indicate Pound Sterling.

The £ currency number format is applied to the cells afterward. This is extremely important if you are going to be calculating in Excel or constructing any formula, as Excel will not know how to calculate values if a letter is included in front of the value. If you are unsure at any time, look in the Formula Bar below the ribbon, as this will display the actual cell content.

There are numerous options available to format data in Excel, some of which are located on the **Number** group of the **Home** tab. For more options, use the dialog box launcher to visit the **Number Format** dialog box.

1. Select the cells to apply a number format.
2. Locate the **Number** group on the **Home** tab.
3. Click on the drop-down list to the right of **General**.
4. Choose a format such as **Currency**. A preview of each type is displayed under each format. For access to more options, click on **More Number Formats...** at the bottom of the list to launch the dialog box.
5. Once the number format has been applied, you may notice ##### instead of values in a cell—this is because the column is not wide enough to accommodate the values. This can be seen in the following screenshot:

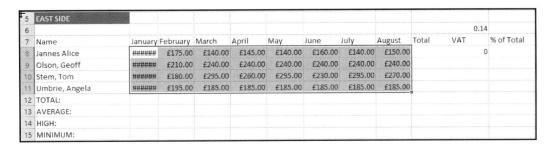

	EAST SIDE											0.14	
7	Name	January	February	March	April	May	June	July	August	Total	VAT		% of Total
8	Jannes Alice	######	£175.00	£140.00	£145.00	£140.00	£160.00	£140.00	£150.00		0	
9	Olson, Geoff	######	£210.00	£240.00	£240.00	£240.00	£240.00	£240.00	£240.00			
10	Stem, Tom	######	£180.00	£295.00	£260.00	£295.00	£230.00	£295.00	£270.00			
11	Umbrie, Angela	######	£195.00	£185.00	£185.00	£185.00	£185.00	£185.00	£185.00			
12	TOTAL:											
13	AVERAGE:											
14	HIGH:											
15	MINIMUM:											

6. To fix this, simply widen the column to display the values.

Working with worksheets and sheet tabs

By default, Excel 2019 opens a new workbook with one worksheet. The steps to insert more than one worksheet, by default, are mentioned in a previous topic—this is set in the Excel **Options** dialog box, by accessing the **Options** icon on the Backstage view.

A new workbook can consist of 255 sheets as a limit, but you can add as many sheets after creating the new workbook, dependent upon the computer's memory.

Inserting worksheets

There are numerous methods to insert worksheets in Excel, as outlined next, but the most efficient way is to click on the New sheet icon at the bottom of the workbook, located to the right of any existing worksheets in the workbook, as illustrated in the following screenshot:

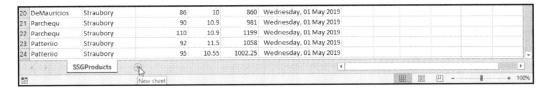

20	DeMauricios	Straubory		86	10	860	Wednesday, 01 May 2019
21	Parchequ	Straubory		90	10.9	981	Wednesday, 01 May 2019
22	Parchequ	Straubory		110	10.9	1199	Wednesday, 01 May 2019
23	Patteriio	Straubory		92	11.5	1058	Wednesday, 01 May 2019
24	Patteriio	Straubory		95	10.55	1002.25	Wednesday, 01 May 2019

Note that this option is the only method that inserts a worksheet *after* any existing worksheets.

Let's look at the other methods to insert new worksheets, as follows:

1. Open the `SSGProductSales.xlsx` workbook.
2. On the **Home** tab, locate the **Cells** group.
3. Click on the drop-down arrow below the **Insert** icon.
4. Click to select **Insert Sheet.**
5. Depending on which sheet you were working on when you chose the **Insert Sheet** icon, the new sheet will always appear before the sheet you were working on. In this case, the sheet inserts before the **SSGProducts** sheet in the workbook, as this was the only sheet in the workbook. The new sheet is provided with a name according to the worksheet number sequence. The last sheet in the workbook was **SSGProducts**, which is not understood by Excel as it is a custom worksheet name, so the new sheet is named **Sheet1.**

Or

1. Right-click on a worksheet tab to access the shortcut menu.
2. Click on the **Insert...** shortcut menu item.
3. From the **Insert** dialog box, choose **Worksheet**.
4. Click on **OK**, and the new worksheet is inserted into the workbook.

 The benefit of using this longer method to insert a worksheet is that you will have access to create different templates from the **General**, **Spreadsheet Solutions**, and **1033** tabs. You will also be able to access online templates from the icon at the bottom of the dialog box.

Deleting worksheets

Note that when deleting worksheets, make sure the correct sheet is selected. You cannot undo the operation once a worksheet is deleted.

1. On the **Home** tab, locate the **Cells** group.
2. Click on the drop-down arrow below the **Delete** icon.

3. Click to select **Delete Sheet**, as illustrated in the following screenshot:

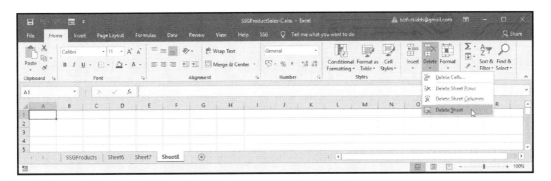

4. A dialog box will appear, asking if you are absolutely sure you wish to delete the sheet. Click on **Delete** to remove the sheet from the workbook. (Please note that this operation cannot be undone, unless you close and open the workbook without saving after deleting the worksheet.)

Or

1. Right-click on the tab of the sheet you no longer need.
2. From the shortcut menu that appears, click on **Delete**.
3. A dialog box will appear, asking if you are absolutely sure you want to delete the sheet.

Moving or copying worksheets

There are a few ways to arrange worksheets in a workbook. Often when inserting worksheets, they land up in the wrong position (order), and you need to move them to another location in the workbook.

1. Click on the **Sheet** tab of the worksheet you wish to move.

2. Hold down the left mouse button on the **Sheet** tab and drag it to another location. A page icon will appear above the mouse pointer, and, as you drag, a little black pointed-down arrow will guide you as you move along the sheets. Let go of the mouse at the location you would like to place the worksheet, as illustrated in the following screenshot:

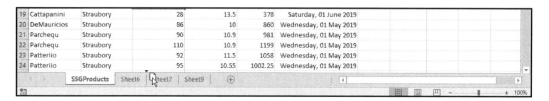

3. Click on the **Sheet** tab of the worksheet you wish to move.
4. Click on the **Format** drop-down list from the **Cells** group of the **Home** tab.
5. Choose **Move** or **Copy Sheet...** .
6. Click on a worksheet name to place your sheet before it.
7. Click on **OK** to confirm. The sheet moves to the new location.

Or

1. Right-click on the **Sheet** tab of the worksheet you would like to move.
2. Click on **Move** or **Copy...** from the shortcut menu. Click on a sheet name to place your sheet before it.
3. Click on **OK** to confirm. The sheet moves to the new location.

To copy worksheets, follow these steps:

1. Click on the **Sheet** tab of the worksheet you wish to copy and move to another location within the worksheet.
2. Hold down the *Ctrl* key on your keyboard.
3. Click on the **Sheet** tab and, while keeping the left mouse button depressed, drag the sheet to another location.
4. A page icon will appear above the mouse pointer with a + sign while you are dragging—this indicates that you are copying the sheet.
5. As you drag, a little black pointed-down arrow will guide you as you move along the sheets, as illustrated in the following screenshot:

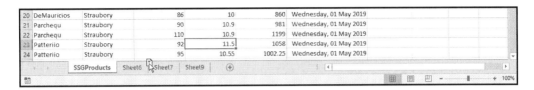

20	DeMauricios	Straubory	86	10	860	Wednesday, 01 May 2019
21	Parchequ	Straubory	90	10.9	981	Wednesday, 01 May 2019
22	Parchequ	Straubory	110	10.9	1199	Wednesday, 01 May 2019
23	Patteriio	Straubory	92	11.5	1058	Wednesday, 01 May 2019
24	Patteriio	Straubory	95	10.55	1002.25	Wednesday, 01 May 2019

SSGProducts   Sheet6   Sheet7   Sheet9

6. Let go of the mouse at the location you would like to place the worksheet.
7. You will notice that the worksheet name is the same as the sheet you have copied, except that it has a bracket enclosing the number 2, indicating that it is the worksheet copy.

To move or copy a worksheet to another workbook, follow these steps:

1. To move or copy a sheet from an existing workbook to a different workbook, right-click on the **Sheet** tab and select **Move** or **Copy**.
2. The **Move or Copy** dialog box opens.
3. At the top of the dialog box, choose **(new book)** from the drop-down list.
4. Click to select **Create a Copy** at the bottom of the dialog box, should you wish to send a copy to the new workbook, or leave this unchecked to move the worksheet from the current workbook to a new workbook.
5. Click on **OK** to confirm. The sheet remains in the current workbook and is also copied to the location you selected.

Renaming worksheets

Worksheets are named **Sheet1**, **Sheet2**, **Sheet3**, and so on, by default. To make the workbook more meaningful (especially if you are collaborating with others), it is a good idea to give your sheets a name appropriate to the data contained within them.

1. Open the SSGRegions.xlsx workbook to use for this example.
2. Double-click on the sheet tab you wish to rename.
3. The existing name will be highlighted (selected), as illustrated in the following screenshot:

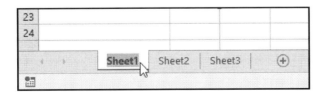

4. While the sheet name is selected, start typing a new name for the sheet, using the keyboard.

5. Click off the sheet tab onto a cell in the worksheet; alternatively, right-click on the sheet tab you wish to rename.

6. Choose **Rename**. The existing sheet name becomes highlighted (is selected).

7. Type a new name for the sheet, and then click off the sheet tab onto a cell in the worksheet; alternatively, click on the sheet you would like to rename.

8. From the **Editing** group of the **Home** tab, select the **Format** icon drop-down arrow from the **Cells** group.

9. Select **Rename Sheet** from the **Organize Sheets** heading.

10. The existing sheet name becomes highlighted (is selected).

11. Type a new name for the sheet, and then click off the sheet tab onto a cell in the worksheet.

Applying coloring to worksheet tabs

Adding color to sheet tabs is great fun and gives the user an opportunity to color the same sheet categories with the same color tab. It also makes the sheet name stand out when collaborating with others.

1. Click on the tab of the worksheet you would like to apply a color to.

2. Visit the **Editing** group of the **Home** tab and locate the **Format** icon.

3. Click on the drop-down arrow of the **Format** icon to access the **Organize Sheets** heading.

4. Select the **Tab Color** menu item and select a color from the sub-menu; alternatively, right-click on the tab of the worksheet to apply color.

5. Choose **Tab Color** from the shortcut menu and select a color from the sub-menu, as illustrated in the following screenshot:

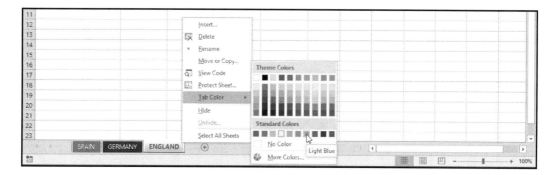

Now that you are able to work with worksheets and sheet tabs, let's learn to filter and sort data on a worksheet.

Sorting and filtering data

This topic deals with finding, replacing, and sorting data. We will learn to use the sort, filter, and auto filter features, as well as conditional formatting options, and to apply icon sets, data bars, and color scales.

Finding and replacing data

The **Find & Select** tool is valuable in order to locate data in a worksheet or workbook. Although it does not filter the data for you, it is a very useful tool in order to locate and replace data throughout the worksheet or workbook. In addition to finding and replacing text, you can also find and replace specific formatting only within a worksheet or workbook. The **Find & Select** feature is located on the **Editing** group of the **Home** tab ribbon.

When locating data on a worksheet, you are able to search using wildcard characters. For instance, once a range is highlighted, the user is able to search for all employees with first names that start with the letter **B**. The criteria to use in the **Find what:** text area would be **B***. To locate one instance, click on **Find Next**. To locate all the instances in the worksheet or workbook, click on **Find All**. The references and values are shown at the bottom of the dialog box.

1. We will use the SSGProductSort.xlsx workbook for this example.
2. Click on a cell within the range you wish to search.
3. Visit the **Editing** group on the **Home** tab, and then select **Find & Select**.
4. Select the **Find...** option from the drop-down list.
5. In the **Find what:** placeholder, enter **Smouthy**.
6. Click on **Find All** to see all the instances of the searched word, or **Find Next** to scroll to the next instance of the word individually.

7. To replace the word **Smouthy** with **Smoathly**, simply click on the **Replace** tab and type the word into the placeholder, as illustrated in the following screenshot:

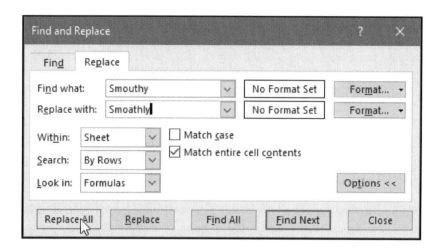

8. Click to select **Replace All** at the bottom of the dialog box.

Sorting ascending or descending

1. Click into the column you would like to sort. For this example, we will use the **Price/Unit** column.
2. Click on the **Sort & Filter** icon from the **Editing** group.
3. From the drop-down list, choose **Sort Largest to Smallest**, as illustrated in the following screenshot:

4. The data is sorted on the worksheet.

Filtering data

Filtering data in Excel allows you to locate data very quickly, as well as to filter so that you eliminate certain choices (text or values) from a list's results, or specify categories of data to get the result you need. Filters can also search by specifying the format (color) of a cell. The filter will search a column and hide the rows that do not fit the search criteria, thereby refining a search.

Defining a filter

1. Open the `SSGFilter.xlsx` workbook.
2. Place the mouse pointer within the range you would like to filter.
3. Locate the **Sort & Filter** group on the **Data** tab.
4. Click on the **Filter** icon.
5. Arrows will appear to the right of each heading of the selected area, as illustrated in the following screenshot:

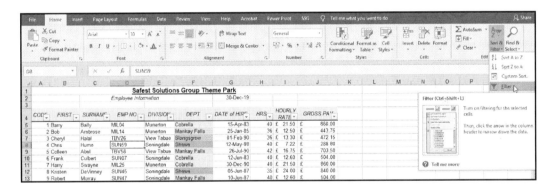

6. Once a filter is applied, an arrow will appear on the **Filter** icon to indicate that it was the last filter applied to the list, as illustrated in the following screenshot:

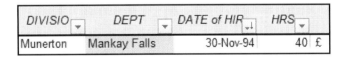

7. To turn off the filter, simply click on the **Filter** icon again from the **Sort & Filter** drop-down list.

Applying a filter

1. Click on the drop-down arrow next to the **DIVISION** heading.
2. Choose to sort from **Ascending to Descending**.
3. Click on **OK** to confirm. The data sorts alphabetically.
4. Let's try another example, where we will apply a filter to the **DIVISION** column to show only the **Parklands** data.
5. Click on the drop-down filter arrow to the right of the **DIVISION** column heading, and then click on the **(Select All)** checkbox to remove the checkmark.
6. Select the **Parklands** division by clicking on it, and then confirm by clicking on the **OK** command to return to the worksheet, as illustrated in the following screenshot:

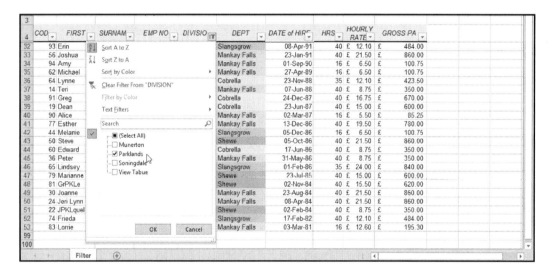

7. Please note that the icon on the **DIVISION** drop-down arrow has now changed to a **Filter** icon to reflect that a filter is applied. If you place your mouse pointer over the icon, it will give you information about the filter type, as illustrated in the following screenshot:

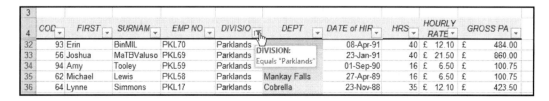

8. Also, note that the row numbers have changed to a blue font, indicating that a filter is applied and not all the records (rows) are displayed on the worksheet.

Removing a filter

1. Click on the icon to the right of **DIVISION**.

2. Select **Clear Filter from "DIVISION"** from the drop-down list, and make sure that **Select All** is ticked to display all the **DIVISION** column and not just **Parklands**, as illustrated in the following screenshot:

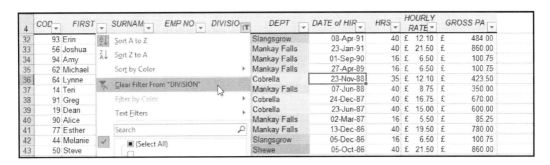

3. Click on the **Clear** icon located on the drop-down list of the **Sort & Filter** group. This option will remove all filters, and sorts from the selected list.

Applying conditional formatting

Conditional formatting is a format, such as a cell shading or font color automatically applied to cells if a specific condition is met (true). When the condition is met, a specific cell format is applied to the cells to answer any queries you may have about your data. Finding duplicates is another great use for this tool:

1. Open the SSGStudentMarks.xlsx workbook.

2. Select the cells to which you would like to apply conditional formatting.

3. On the **Home** tab, locate the **Styles** group. Click on the **Conditional Formatting** icon.

4. Choose **Highlight Cell Rules** from the drop-down list.

5. In the sub-menu, look for **Less Than…** (in this particular example, I need to locate values less than 40%).

6. Type the value of **40%** into the text area provided on the left, as illustrated in the following screenshot:

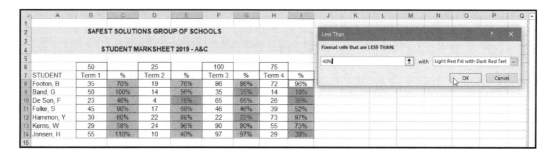

7. Choose the font color from the drop-down list on the right. I have chosen the red text color, but other formats are available by clicking on **Custom Format…** at the bottom of the list, which will take you to the **Format Cells** dialog box.

8. Note that the cells change color on the worksheet as you are making choices from the **Less Than** dialog box.

9. If I alter the % in cell **E10** to **41%** after applying the conditional formatting, the condition will not be met anymore and the format will be removed from the cell.

Icon sets, data bars, and color scales

Icon sets, data bars, and color scales were first introduced in Excel 2007 and are now even more enhanced with a wider range of icon sets to choose from, to enhance data by adding a visual effect. You can mix and match icon sets, and choose to show only for high and low values in the range.

The following example shows the arrow icon set applied to a cell range. If we edit the rule applied by default to this arrow set, we will notice that it has applied its own conditions to the data. The green arrow reflects any value greater than or equal to 67%; the yellow arrow reflects less than 67% and greater than or equal to 33%; and, lastly, the red arrow reflects less than 33%, as illustrated in the following screenshot:

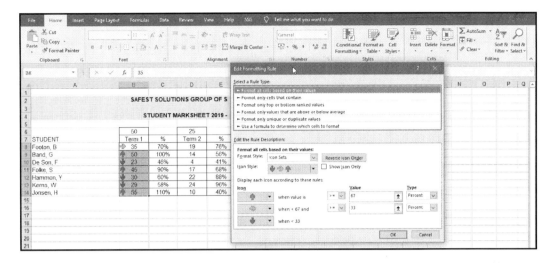

The following table shows an example of all types of icons and bars—namely, icon sets, data bars, and color scales. Application and editing of rules is exactly the same procedure in each of these sets of visual effects, which can be seen in the following screenshot:

6		50		25		100		75	
7	STUDENT	Term 1	%	Term 2	%	Term 3	%	Term 4	%
8	Footon, B	35	70%	19	76%	86	86%	72	96%
9	Band, G	50	100%	14	56%	35	35%	14	19%
10	De Son, F	23	46%	4	41%	65	65%	26	35%
11	Folke, S	45	90%	17	68%	46	46%	39	52%
12	Hammon, Y	30	60%	22	88%	22	22%	73	97%
13	Kerns, W	29	58%	24	96%	90	90%	55	73%
14	Jonsen, H	55	110%	10	40%	97	97%	29	39%

1. Open the SSGStudentMarks.xlsx workbook.
2. Select the range **B8:B14**.
3. From the **Conditional Formatting** drop-down list, select **Icon Sets**.
4. On the sub-menu, click to choose the **3-arrow icon set**.
5. Click on **OK** to apply the arrows to the selected range.
6. To edit the icon sets, return to **Manage Rules...**, and then select **Edit Rule** to experiment with the options available.

7. To remove a rule, click on **Clear Rules** from the **Conditional Formatting** drop-down list.
8. Select to remove rules either from selected worksheet cells or from the entire sheet.

Setting print options

In this section, you will learn how to print a single worksheet, selected worksheets, and a workbook; how to add and modify header and footer content and other options.

Before we delve into the actual printing of worksheets and workbooks, let's learn about the views that exist in Excel 2019, and other important tasks we need to know before looking at the printing aspects, as follows:

- **Normal view**: This is the default view you see when opening a workbook in the Excel environment. This is the view in which you would create your data. The different views are displayed on the **View** tab, or accessible via the status bar, as illustrated in the following screenshot:

- **Page Layout view**: Viewing your worksheet in **Page Layout** view displays the worksheet, as it would look when printed. It also displays all headers and footers in the document. Headers and footers are editable in this view. When changing a view from **Normal** view to any other view and then back to **Normal** view again, you will notice a slight change in the worksheet. Vertical and horizontal dashed lines appear on your worksheet, and these indicate the page breaks in the worksheet. Page breaks are also visible on all the other views to guide you when customizing the layout prior to printing. An example of **Normal** view can be seen in the following screenshot:

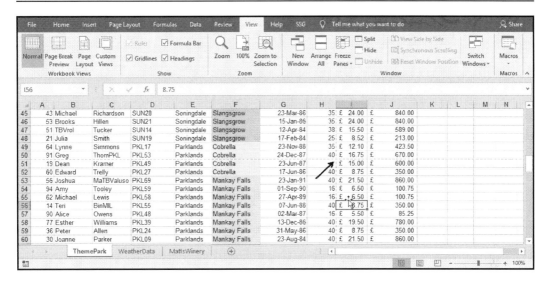

- **Page Break view**: This view gives you the opportunity to view horizontal and vertical page breaks in the document, and allows you to adjust these page breaks to fit information onto a worksheet. It also identifies each page number by placing a watermark on each page in the workbook to guide you, as illustrated in the following screenshot:

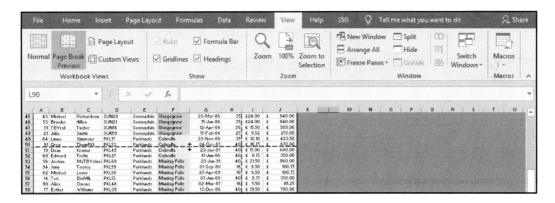

Now that you have had an introduction to the different workbook views, let's learn to insert page breaks on a worksheet in the next topic.

Adjusting breaks in the worksheet

1. Make sure you are viewing the worksheet in **Page Break** view by clicking on the **View** tab.
2. Choose **Page Break Preview** from the **Workbook Views** group.
3. Place the mouse pointer on the blue dashed lines that appear horizontally or vertically in the worksheet—the blue dashed lines indicate the automatic page breaks in the worksheet.
4. Drag the blue dashed line to a new position on the worksheet.
5. Once you have moved the dashed line, it will change to a solid blue line, indicating that you have forced a break in the worksheet—this is a manual page break, and can be seen in the following screenshot:

	A	B	C	D	E	F	G	H	I	J
45	43	Michael	Richardson	SUN28	Soningdale	Slangsgrow	23-Mar-86	35	£24.00	£ 840.00
46	53	Brooks	Hillen	SUN21	Soningdale	Slangsgrow	15-Jan-86	35	£24.00	£ 840.00
47	51	TBVrol	Tucker	SUN14	Soningdale	Slangsgrow	12-Apr-84	38	£ 15.50	£ 589.00
48	21	Julia	Smith	SUN19	Soningdale	Slangsgrow	17-Feb-84	25	£ 8.52	£ 213.00
49	64	Lynne	Simmons	PKL17	Parklands	Cobrella	23-Nov-88	35	£ 12.10	£ 423.50
50	31	Greg	ThomPKL	PKL53	Parklands	Cobrella	24-Dec-87	40	£ 16.75	£ 670.00
51	19	Dean	Kramer	PKL43	Parklands	Cobrella	23-Jun-87	40	£ 15.00	£ 600.00
52	60	Edward	Trelly	PKL27	Parklands	Cobrella	17-Jun-86	40	£ 8.75	£ 350.00
53	56	Joshua	MaTBValue	PKL63	Parklands	Mankay Falls	23-Jan-91	40	£ 21.50	£ 860.00
54	34	Amy	Tooley	PKL53	Parklands	Mankay Falls	01-Sep-90	16	£ 6.50	£ 100.75

Now that you know how to view and adjust page breaks on a worksheet, let's learn how to manually insert and reset them in the next topic.

 To reset all page breaks, make sure you are in **Normal** view or **Page Break Preview**. Go to **Page Layout** | **Page Setup** | **Breaks** | **Reset All Page Breaks**.

Inserting manual breaks into the worksheet

1. Make sure you are in **Page Break** view by clicking on the **View** tab.
2. Choose **Page Break Preview** from the **Workbook Views** group.
3. Select a cell to insert the page break above it, and then click to select the **Page Layout** tab.
4. From the **Page Setup** group, select the **Breaks** icon to access the drop-down list menu.

5. Select **Insert Page Break**. A solid line appears on the worksheet, indicating a manual page break.

TIP

To remove a page break, click on the **Page Layout** tab. Click on the **Breaks** icon and select the **Remove Page Break** option from the drop-down list.

Constructing headers and footers

Headers and footers reside at the top (header) or at the bottom (footer) of worksheets in Excel. The content of headers and footers usually consists of page numbers, worksheet or workbook titles, author names, the creation date of the workbook, the date the workbook was updated, or text a user enters to describe the workbook.

Headers and footers do not display in **Normal** view. **Normal** view is the default view of the Excel environment and is what you see when you open a workbook in Excel. Headers and footers are displayed in **Page Layout** view and on Preview pages (visible in Backstage view after clicking on the **File** tab, and choosing **Print**). Once in the **Header and Footer** dialog box, you can choose to add predefined headers or footers, or input text of your choice. There are numerous methods to insert headers and footers into a workbook. We will learn about some of these methods, as follows:

1. Open the workbook to which you would like to add headers and or footers. We will continue using the same workbook as the preceding example.
2. Select the **Page Layout** tab to access the **Page Setup** group.
3. Click on the **Page Setup** dialog box launcher, located to the right of the **Page Setup** group, as illustrated in the following screenshot:

4. Alternatively, locate the **Text** group using the **Insert** tab, and then select the **Header & Footer** icon.

Or

Click on **File** | **Print** from the drop-down menu, locate the **Settings** heading, and click on **Page Setup**.

Or

Click on the **View** tab to change the view of the workbook to **Page Layout**, and then click to access the **Header** or **Footer** section of the worksheet. Notice the **Header & Footer** tools provided on the ribbon. The worksheet displays in **Page Layout** view when selecting the **Insert** | **Header & Footer** option. At the top of the worksheet, you will see three separate areas (rectangles) above the worksheet—this is the **Header** area.

5. Click to select one of the rectangles to input text to the left, center, or right of the **Header** area. The same applies to the **Footer** area. Scroll down to the bottom of the first page of the worksheet using the mouse, or alternatively, click on the **Go to Footer** icon along the ribbon.

6. The **Header & Footer Tools** contextual menu is visible and includes a **Design** tab where you will format, type, and/or select predefined layouts. The **Header** and **Footer** drop-down options to the left of the ribbon offer predefined headers and footers to format the document quickly. Header and footer elements are also available along the ribbon, should you wish to insert page numbers, dates, the worksheet name, sheet name, or document location. You can also use this ribbon to navigate between **Header** and **Footer** areas or set further options, as illustrated in the following screenshot:

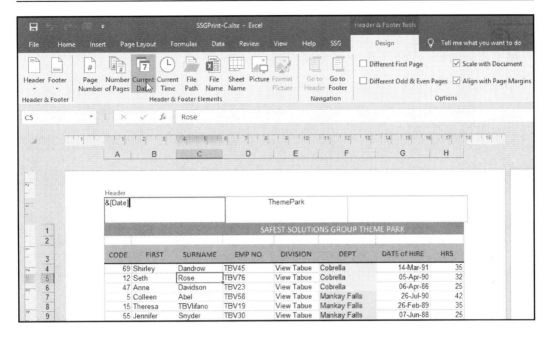

7. Once the header is inserted using the header elements or predefined header styles, the user can view the result by clicking off the **Header** area onto the worksheet.

8. To edit the header, simply click on the **Header** area to change information.

9. Once you have clicked into the **Header** or **Footer** area, the **Header & Footer Design** tab will appear, reflecting the header and footer elements along the ribbon.

10. To format header and footer text, use the relevant format icons on the **Home** tab (remember to select text before making any changes).

11. Please note that you will only have access to certain basic icons for formatting—some icons will appear grayed out (not available) when in this view.

12. To apply **Different First Page** or **Different Odd & Even Pages** headers or footers, select the relevant icon option from the **Design** tab, as illustrated in the following screenshot:

13. To apply the same header and/or footer to the workbook or a selected number of worksheets, make sure that they are selected (grouped) before you insert a header or footer.

14. To remove a header or footer from a worksheet, click in the relevant **Header** or **Footer** area and delete the item displayed, or select **None** from the **Header** or **Footer** icon on the **Header & Footer** group of the **Design** tab.

Note that if you click into the **Header** or **Footer** area of a worksheet, the worksheet views will be grayed out and you would need to click on the worksheet data to gain access to change the view, as illustrated in the following screenshot:

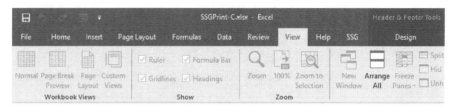

Setting the header and footer distance

Often, you need just a little more space at the top of the printed worksheet to either fit data onto a page or to separate the header a little further from the worksheet data. The distance between the header and the top of the page, as well as the distance between the footer and the bottom of the page, can be set using the **Page Setup** dialog box, as illustrated in the following screenshot:

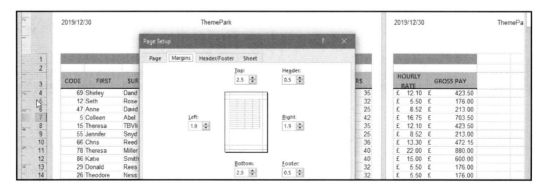

1. Open a workbook and change the view to **Page Layout** so that you can visibly see the **Header** area at the top of the worksheet view.

2. Select the **Page Setup** dialog box launcher from the end of the **Page Setup** group on the **Page Layout** tab.

3. In the **Page Setup** dialog box, select the **Margins** tab.

4. Alter the **Header:** and **Footer:** values by using the increase or decrease spin arrows, or type a value into the placeholder provided.

5. Click on **OK** to confirm, when complete. View the change at the top of the worksheet.

Setting the worksheet orientation

Microsoft Excel prints worksheets in portrait orientation by default. Portrait orientation means that the page is more tall than wide. Landscape (as the name suggests) is when the width is considerably wider than the height of the page, as can be seen in the following screenshot:

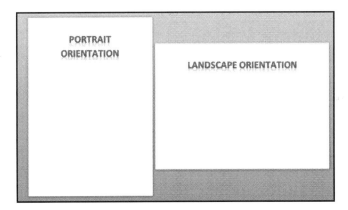

You are able to change the orientation before, during, or after the worksheet is completed. If the worksheet contains more columns than rows, it would be best to use landscape orientation to present your data. Orientation options are located on the **Page Layout** tab on the ribbon or from **File | Print** settings.

Setting the worksheet scale

At times, you might need to scale a worksheet to fit it onto one page. The options available in 2019 are so effortless to use. Scaling is located on the **Page Setup** dialog box, as usual, but a visit to the **File** tab is the better option, especially if you are printing the worksheet right away:

1. Open the workbook to scale to size—we will use the `MattsWinery` worksheet for this example.
2. Click on **File** | **Print** from the menu provided.
3. Notice that the **Sales** column is not showing on the first page of the worksheet.
4. From the **Settings** heading, locate the **No Scaling** drop-down menu item.
5. Select **Fit All Columns on One Page**. The **Sales** column is now included in the preview.
6. You can also fit an entire worksheet on one page using the **Scale to Fit** option, available by clicking on the **Page Layout** tab under the **Scale to Fit** group (notice that in the preview, the worksheet consists of four pages currently), as illustrated in the following screenshot:

7. Click to change the **Width:** to **1 page** and the **Height:** to **2 pages**.
8. Click on the **File** tab, and then choose **Print** to preview the worksheet.

Checking the paper size

The paper size will depend on the type of document created, as well as its purpose. The most common paper size for most printers and users would be A4 (210 x 297 mm). Documents sent to a printer using the incorrect printer size could result in the document not printing, or holding up the print queue.

To choose a paper size, click on the **File** tab, and then click to choose **Print** from the menu. Under the **Settings** heading, you will find a drop-down list item titled **A4**. Click on the arrow to choose a different paper size, if required. Alternatively, visit the **Page Layout** tab, and locate the **Size** drop-down list to select a paper size.

Setting page margins

If you are unable to fit information onto a worksheet, the first thing you should try to change is the document margins. Achieve this by clicking on the **File** tab, and choose **Print** to access the **Settings** or via the **Page Layout** tab on the worksheet ribbon. Click to select the **Margins** icon to select a custom margin, or visit the **Custom Margins...** option to launch the **Page Setup** dialog box in which to set your own margins. The **Page Layout** tab option is illustrated in the following screenshot:

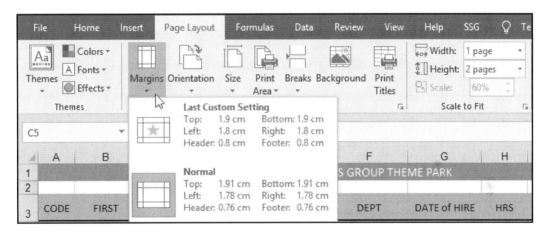

The **Custom Margins...** dialog box is easier to use when requiring a certain custom setting for different parts (left, right, top, bottom, **Header** area, **Footer** area) of the worksheet.

Aligning data horizontally and vertically

Information, by default, positions itself at the top-left corner of the worksheet. If you would like to center information horizontally and vertically on a worksheet, make sure the **Center on page** option (located on the **Margins** tab) is set to **Horizontal** and **Vertical** alignment.

Printing a single worksheet

1. We will open the `SSGPrint.xlsx` workbook to work through this example.
2. Make sure that you have clicked on the sheet tab of the relevant worksheet you wish to print.
3. In this case, we are printing the **ThemePark** sheet.
4. Click to select **File | Print**.
5. Locate the **Settings** heading. Ensure that the first option in the list is set to **Print Active Sheets**.
6. Click to choose a printer, and modify the printer properties if necessary.
7. Click on the **Print** icon to send the worksheet to the printer.

Printing selected worksheets

Select the worksheets to be printed as per the following instructions:

1. Click on the first worksheet tab (in this example, **ThemePark**).
2. Hold down the *Shift* key on the keyboard to select sheets that are next to each other, or hold down the *Ctrl* key on the keyboard should you wish to select sheets not next to each other (non-adjacent), as illustrated in the following screenshot:

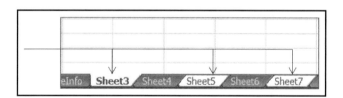

3. Click on the second worksheet tab (in this example, **WeatherData**).
4. Notice that the worksheets appear white in color—this indicates sheets selected using the *Ctrl* key.
5. Notice on the title bar of the Excel environment that the name of the workbook has changed to reflect the text (group) at the end of the filename.
6. Remember to ungroup the sheets once you have finished printing them. There are two ways to do this: click on another sheet in the workbook to take the focus off the selected sheets, or right-click on the selected sheet tabs and choose **Ungroup Sheets**.

7. Click to select **File | Print**.
8. Locate the **Settings** heading, and then ensure that the first option is set to **Print Active Sheets**.
9. Click to choose a printer and modify the printer properties, if necessary.
10. Click on the **Print** icon to send the worksheets to the printer.
11. If you are unsure that the correct sheets will print, visit the **Next Page** and **Previous Page** navigation arrows at the bottom of the **Preview** area.
12. Click on the **Print** icon to send the worksheet to the printer.
13. To print an entire workbook, select **Print Entire Workbook** from the **Print Settings** option.

Creating charts based on worksheet data

In this section, we will learn how to create a chart from worksheet data; plot non-contiguous data; select, resize, delete, and change chart options and layouts; view the Sunburst and Funnel charts; look at how to change chart placement. You will also be shown how to change the chart titles, add a series, and change chart elements manually.

We use charts to make information more appealing, clearer, and easier to read. A chart is a graphical representation of worksheet information. It is important to get used to the names of the different elements of a chart so that you know which part you are changing when presented with options while editing. An example chart and its elements are shown in the following screenshot:

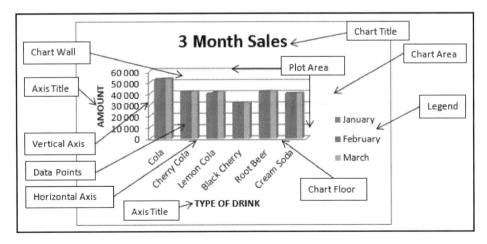

Charts automatically link to data on the worksheet. When we make changes to the information on the worksheet, the chart automatically updates:

1. Open the SSGCharts.xlsx workbook.
2. Select the data on the worksheet from which you would like to create a chart.
3. Click on the **Insert** tab, and then locate the **Chart** group.
4. You will notice a **Recommended Charts** icon that offers charts appropriate to the selected data on the worksheet.
5. Alongside the **Recommended Chart** icon, you will be able to select from specific chart categories that house further examples of chart types of the same chart category, as well as Maps, PivotCharts, 3D Maps, Sparklines, and Filters.
6. If you choose the **Recommended Chart** icon, you will also have access to all the charts available by clicking on the **All Charts** tab at the top of the dialog box—this is the most comprehensive list of charts, with subcategories and even previews of row-/column-switched charts.
7. After selecting worksheet data and browsing chart types, you will notice that Excel displays a preview of the chart applied to the worksheet data within the dialog box (or directly on the worksheet, should you have selected any of the char-type, drop-down categories on the **Chart** group).
8. Click on the **OK** command to place the selected chart on the worksheet alongside your data, as illustrated in the following screenshot:

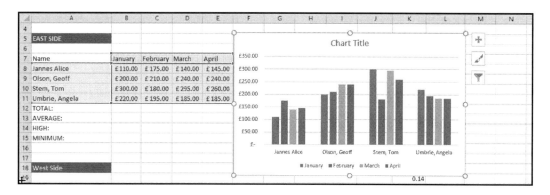

9. Notice that the **Chart Tools** contextual menu is now visible, as the chart is selected on the worksheet, and that the **Design** and **Format** tabs are accessible in order to customize the chart further.

10. Once clicking off the chart back onto the worksheet, the **Chart Tools** contextual menu will disappear.

Double-clicking on a chart element will open the **Format Chart** pane to the right of the worksheet, with the icons applicable to the element you have clicked on in order to format them quickly, as illustrated in the following screenshot:

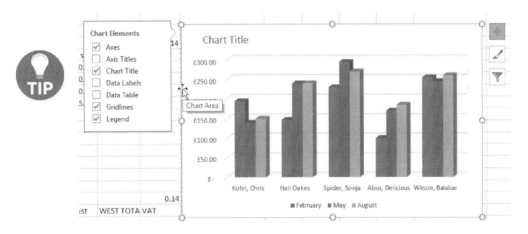

Plotting non-contiguous data

When we select data on the worksheet to create a chart, there may be instances when we need to select non-contiguous data (data that is not next to other data). If you do not want to make a graph out of all your information, you would need to select only the information you require. We call this selecting non-contiguous information:

1. Highlight (select) the first range of data to include in the chart.
2. Hold down the *Ctrl* key on the keyboard while dragging (selecting) the next range with your mouse.
3. Release the *Ctrl* key once you have selected the data.
4. Continue to the **Insert** tab to create the chart as usual.

5. Once you have finished creating the chart, click off the chart onto the worksheet, and then select the chart again by clicking on it, as illustrated in the following screenshot:

6. Notice that the worksheet data does not select when selecting the chart as the first chart does—this is because the chart has a non-contiguous selection. So, to view the worksheet data, click on a data series to display the connected worksheet data, as shown in the following screenshot:

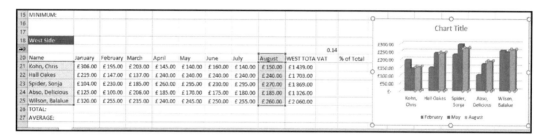

Let's continue to learn more about editing charts in the next topic.

Selecting a chart

Once the chart exists on the worksheet, you may deselect the chart (click off the chart onto the worksheet) to continue working on the worksheet data. If you need to make changes to the chart, you will need to click on the chart first. When selecting a chart, the ribbon changes and gives one option to edit the chart. This context menu that appears is called **Chart Tools** and consists of two tabs (**Design** and **Format**) from which you will make the majority of chart edits. A frame exists around the current chart when selected. Once the focus moves back to the worksheet data, the ribbon will disappear.

Clicking on a chart will display three icons to the top right of the chart. These icons are quick tools to customize chart elements. When selecting the first crosshair icon, it will display a list of **Chart Elements** to the left of the chart, where you can display certain elements or hide certain elements on the chart. The second icon, the paintbrush, will display style and color options, and the third—funnel—icon will enable you to customize the values and names of selected series. The icons can be seen in the following screenshot:

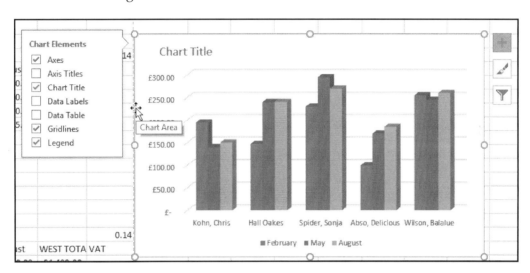

When visiting the **Print Preview** tab on the Backstage view, you will notice that only the chart is displayed for printing. This is because the chart is currently selected on the worksheet. Clicking off the chart onto the worksheet data will show the data and the chart on the same sheet if you return to the **Print Preview** by selecting **File | Print**.

Resizing a chart

1. Place your mouse pointer on the chart frame that surrounds the chart (preferably on one of the corners to resize the chart in proportion); alternatively, click on the chart background.
2. Move the mouse pointer to one of the corners of the chart (one of the white circles).
3. The mouse pointer will change to an arrow pointer.

4. Hold down the mouse pointer, and the mouse pointer will change to a black crosshair pointer.
5. Drag toward the center of the chart to make it smaller, or drag outward to enlarge it, as illustrated in the following screenshot:

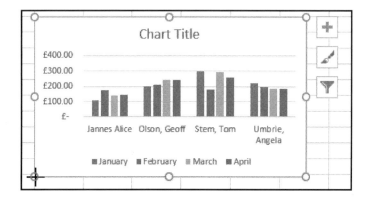

6. If a certain part of a chart is clicked on, it will become active (selected).
7. It is possible to resize or move some chart elements, such as the legend of the title, to improve your chart appearance.

To delete a chart, select the chart and press the *Delete* key.

Changing chart placement

1. To move a chart, click to select it.
2. Use one of the methods from the **Clipboard** group (you have learned this skill in all previous chapters of this book) to move or copy the chart, either to another location on the same worksheet or to a different worksheet or workbook.
   Or
3. Right-click on the selected chart, and then use the cut, copy, and paste icons from the shortcut menu provided (these were also explained in previous chapters of this book).

Or

4. Select the chart, and then visit the **Design** tab of the **Chart Tools** contextual menu, where you will see the **Move Chart** icon at the very end of the ribbon. Note that this method creates a completely new sheet named **Chart1** when choosing the **Move to New Sheet** option from the dialog box, with the chart taking up the entire worksheet), as illustrated in the following screenshot:

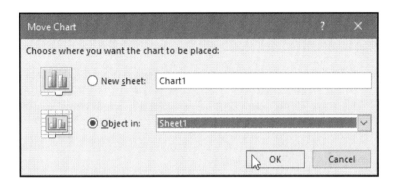

5. Choose to send the selected chart to a new worksheet or as an object on an existing worksheet. Click on the **OK** command when done. If you chose the **New** worksheet option, the chart will appear as a separate chart sheet to the left of **Sheet1** in the workbook—the actual chart will take up the entire worksheet, as illustrated in the following screenshot:

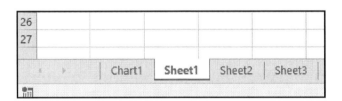

Changing the chart type

1. Select the chart to edit.
2. From the **Chart Tools** menu, select the **Design** tab.
3. Click on the **Change Chart Type** icon.
4. The **Chart Types** dialog box will open on the worksheet.

5. Select the chart category and choose a subcategory to apply to the existing chart.

6. Click on **OK** to confirm, and update the chart type.

Changing the chart style

Excel 2019 has some great chart styles to choose from that make your chart more professional and appealing to others. This is so much easier than editing existing elements or adding and customizing new elements to the chart to suit your needs. Once you have applied a chart style, you are able to manually edit the chart elements:

1. Select the chart to change the style.

2. Click on the launch more arrow to the right of the **Chart Styles** group, located on the **Design** tab. Alternatively, use the **Format** icon located to the right of the selected chart.

3. All the available styles will display—note from the following screenshot that each style has a style number:

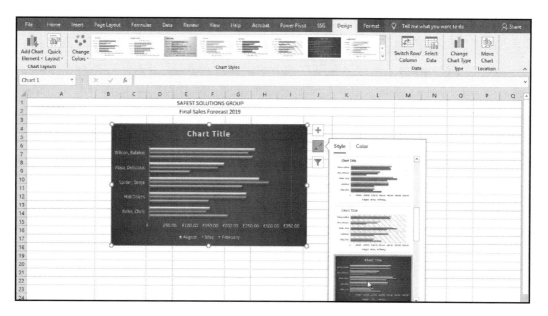

4. Click on a style to apply to the existing chart, and the chart will update.

Changing the Quick Layout

1. Select the chart to adapt to a new layout style—the **Quick Layout** option changes the overall layout of the chart.
2. Click on the **Design** tab and locate the **Quick Layout** icon to the left of the ribbon.
3. To see all the layouts, click on the drop-down arrow to the right of the **Quick Layout** icon.
4. Choose a layout from the list provided, as illustrated in the following screenshot:

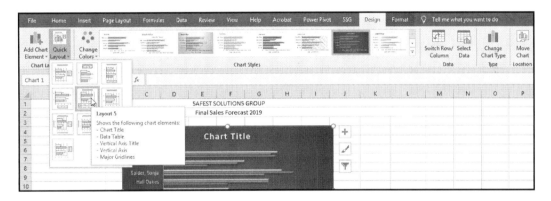

5. The chart updates with the new layout.

Changing chart elements manually

It is necessary to be able to change chart elements manually, as for each element you will notice that there is a multitude of options available. Each of the following methods will take you to the **Chart** pane, where you can locate options applicable to the selected chart element, as follows:

1. Double-click on an element within the chart area, which will open the **Chart** pane to the right of the worksheet, where further options that apply to the chart element selected can be altered.
   Or
2. Right-click on an element and choose the relevant **Format** option from the shortcut menu.
   Or

3. Select the chart, and then click on the **Format** tab of the **Chart Tools** contextual menu. Select **Format Selection** from the **Current Selection** group to the left of the ribbon, as illustrated in the following screenshot:

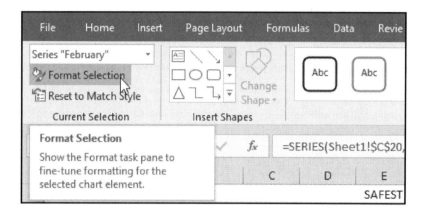

4. The relevant options will populate in the pane to the right of the worksheet, where further customization can take place.

Changing the chart and axis titles

Excel automatically assigns titles to the chart if it finds relevant data it can use from the selected area. A chart title tells you about the data and makes a chart easier to read:

1. We will use the SSGProductChart.xlsx workbook for this example.
2. Select the chart to add a title.
3. From the **Design** tab, click on the **Add Chart Element** icon.
4. From the drop-down list provided, choose **Chart Title**, and then select where to place the title on the selected chart—note that the **More Title Options**... feature is available at the bottom of the list.
5. Type the title text into the chart title placeholder.
6. Click on the **Axis Titles** icon to add a horizontal or vertical axis title.

Displaying gridlines

Choose whether you would like to display more gridlines behind the chart on the x or y axis. You will see from the following screenshot example that I have chosen the **Primary Minor** gridlines on the x axis, which has now placed lines closer together on the chart background:

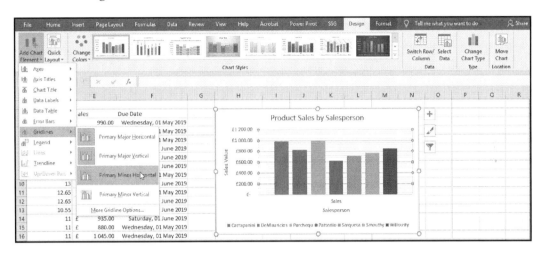

Displaying the legend

A legend describes each part of the chart in a separate textbox on the chart background. The legend can be displayed on different areas of the chart background or can be removed from the background, as follows:

1. Click to select the chart to change the legend placement or to remove the legend altogether.
2. From the **Design** tab, click on the **Add Chart Element** icon.
3. Locate the **Legend** category, and then select an option from the drop-down list.

Adding data labels

To make a chart more understandable and easily readable for the user, data labels are necessary. In the following example, a pie chart exists without data labels:

1. Select the pie chart in the workbook.
2. From the **Design** tab, click on the **Add Chart Element** icon.

3. Locate the **Data Labels** category, and then select an option from the drop-down list.

4. Choose the label type, after which the chart updates.

5. Click on a data label (this will select all data labels).

6. To make formatting changes to the labels, use the formatting icons on the **Format** tab, located on the **Chart Tools** contextual menu.

Adding a data table

A data table is the representation of the data in the worksheet cells, used to create the chart. The data table information forms part of the chart so that it is visually more appealing when printed or displays on screen:

1. Open the Win-Loss.xlsx workbook to use for this example.

2. Locate the chart beneath the data in cell A26.

3. Click to select the **Add Chart Element** icon located on the **Design** tab ribbon.

4. Locate the **Data Table** icon.

5. From the drop-down list, choose an option to apply to the chart.

Deleting a data series

To remove data from your chart is easy. As you will see from the following chart, the user selected the **January** data series. If this data is no longer required, delete it, as follows:

1. Make sure the series is selected (tiny light blue circles will appear if clicking once on the **January** series).

2. Press **Delete** on your keyboard.

3. You will notice that **January** will disappear from the legend, the chart, and from the selected chart data on the worksheet. There are other methods to delete a data series, such as right-clicking on a series and choosing **Delete** from the shortcut menu provided; or selecting the chart from which you would like to remove a series and then clicking on the **Select Data** icon located on the **Design** tab.

4. The **Select Data Source** dialog box will appear, as illustrated in the following screenshot:

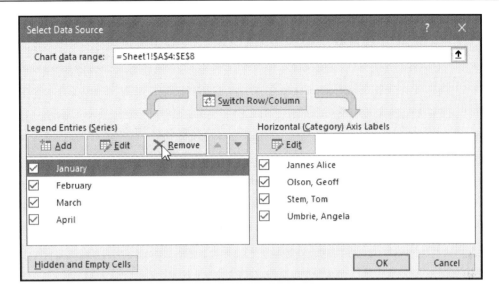

5. Click to select the **January** data series to remove this from the chart.

6. Click on the **Remove** icon to delete the series from the chart, and then click on the **OK** command to update the chart. The data selection is then removed from the worksheet data and the chart, as follows:

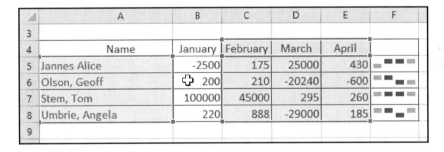

	A	B	C	D	E	F
3						
4	Name	January	February	March	April	
5	Jannes Alice	-2500	175	25000	430	
6	Olson, Geoff	200	210	-20240	-600	
7	Stem, Tom	100000	45000	295	260	
8	Umbrie, Angela	220	888	-29000	185	
9						

Let's learn how to add a data series now that you have been through the steps to delete a series.

Adding a data series

Let's add the **January** series back to the chart located in cell A26, as follows:

1. Select the chart to which you need to add a series.

2. Click on the **Select Data** icon located on the **Design** tab.

3. The **Select Data Source** dialog box will appear, as illustrated in the following screenshot:

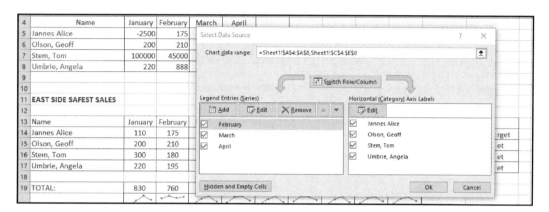

4. Click to select the **Add** icon from the **Select Data Source** dialog box.
5. Click on the fly-out arrow located on the right of the **Series name:** text area and select the **January** heading.
6. Click on the fly-in arrow to return to the **Edit Series** dialog box, as illustrated in the following screenshot:

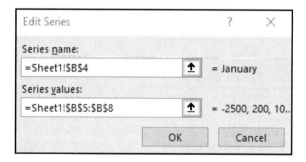

7. Click on the fly-out arrow under the **Series values:** text area and select the B5:B8 **January** sales figures.
8. Click on the fly-in arrow to return to the **Edit Series** dialog box.
9. Click to select **OK** to confirm the series to be added to the chart.
10. The data is updated in the chart, and **January** is now included.

Changing the chart scale

Microsoft Excel always determines the scale of the axis by default from the data on the worksheet. Sometimes, the minimum to maximum scale range determined by the application is a bit too large and could impact the visual appearance of the chart. The vertical value axis (also known as the *y* axis) can be altered by visiting the **Format Axis** pane to the right of the worksheet data:

1. Click on the chart to edit.
2. Double click the **Vertical (Value) Axis** on the chart to open the Format Axis pane, or
   Select the chart, then select the **Vertical (Value) Axis** option from the **Format** tab ribbon.
3. From the **Current Selection** group, choose the **Format Selection** icon.
4. This will open the **Format Axis** pane to the right of the worksheet.
5. Click to edit the scale of minimum or maximum axis—for this example, we have altered the **Minimum** value to read **-30000.0** and the **Maximum** value to read **10000.0**, as can be seen in the following screenshot:

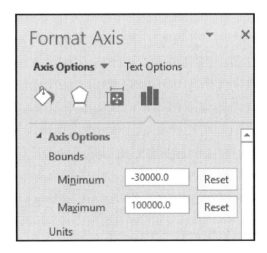

6. The chart is updated immediately with the new axis values.

Formatting the chart background

1. Select the chart to change the background.
2. Various options exist on the **Format** tab to color the chart background. Alternatively, you could right-click on the chart background or element and select a **Fill** option from the **Format Chart Area** pane to the right of the worksheet.
3. These options include **Shape Fill** (colors and textures), **Shape Styles**, and **Shape Effects**—apply these in the same way as the format options in Microsoft Word and Microsoft PowerPoint.
4. To change the **Chart Wall** or **Chart Floor** background color, click on the **Layout** tab, and select **Chart Wall** or **Chart Floor.**

Adding objects to a chart

1. On the **Format** tab of the **Chart Tools** contextual menu, you will find the **Insert Shapes**, **Shape Styles**, **WordArt Shapes**, **Arrange**, and **Size** groups—use these tools to draw arrows and shapes onto the chart background.
2. You can also use the **Insert** tab along the Excel ribbon to add illustrations, just as you would do when using Microsoft Word or PowerPoint.
3. Once inserted onto the worksheet, the object can be moved and placed onto the chart—edit and format it as you would when using Microsoft Word.

Using the sunburst chart type

The sunburst chart type in Excel 2019 is definitely an enhancement over the normal pie charts and doughnut charts. When creating a Pie chart, only one data series can be plotted per Pie chart. When doughnut charts were added to the **Chart Type** list, it solved the problem by being able to add more than one data series to a chart, but only presented data in circles and is quite a messy read. With the sunburst chart type, hierarchical data can be plotted. Let's have a look at this stunning chart type!

When selecting data for this chart type, do not include the column headings. An example of a sunburst chart can be seen in the following screenshot:

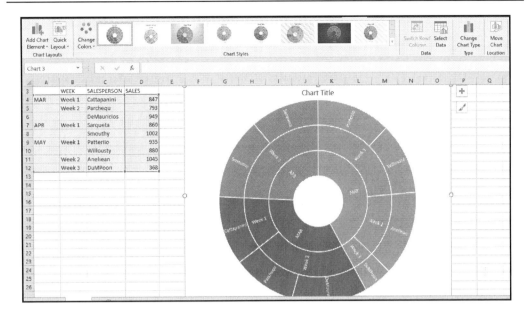

Using funnel charts

Funnel charts are new to Office 2019, along with map charts (these will be discussed in a later chapter). Funnel charts show stages in a process as values—for example, a sales progression. An example of a funnel chart can be seen in the following screenshot:

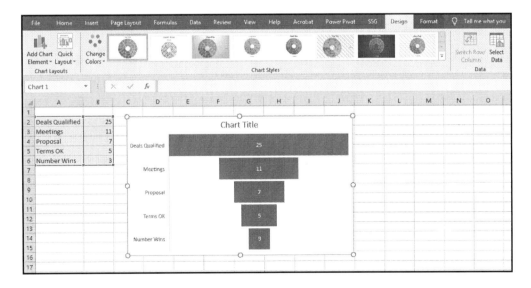

Summary

You have certainly learned an abundance of skills throughout this chapter. Now, you can confidently use the Excel 2019 interface, having a thorough knowledge of all parts of the work area, and are able to set customization options and fine-tune the QAT and the ribbon. You are able to input data and understand the various formatting options with regard to rows, columns, cells, worksheets, and workbooks.

Importing and exporting data should now be a simple task, and manipulating data using sort and filter capabilities will be a skill to take to new heights. You have also learned all about printing and the options available to set up a worksheet or workbook for the printing process, and should now be able to create and format professional-looking charts.

In the next chapter, you will learn all about the heart of the Excel 2019 application. You will learn to create basic formulas and functions, understanding the differences between them. You will construct formulas, use named ranges, and peruse the function library, and then make sure your formulas are error-free.

9
Applying Formulas and Functions

Microsoft Excel 2019 houses an enormous number of functions. During this part of the book, you will learn how to create a formula and investigate the difference between a formula and function, and learn about operators and formula construction, using the correct order of evaluation. After learning the different methods of constructing a formula, you will be introduced to a number of functions from different categories located in the **Function Library**.

The following list of topics are covered in this chapter:

- Learning basic formula operations
- Constructing a formula
- Using the **Function Library**
- Error checking in formulas
- Applying named ranges in a formula

At the end of the chapter, we will highlight common formula errors and learn how to use named ranges in a formula.

Technical requirements

As you have learned how to navigate workbooks, work with rows and columns, and format elements, we will assume you are equipped with these prerequisite skills.

The examples used in this chapter are accessible from the following GitHub URL: https://github.com/PacktPublishing/Learn-Microsoft-Office-2019.

Learning basic formula operations

Here, we will look at formula theory and the order of operations so that you have a good understanding of how calculations are constructed within Excel 2019.

When you enter a formula into a cell, it always starts with an = sign. Once the = sign is typed into a cell on a worksheet, the Formula Bar will become active, with the formula icons changing color and becoming ready for input.

The Formula Bar is located just above the worksheet column headers and consists of three parts. To the left of the Formula Bar, you will see a list of commonly used functions and access to the **More Functions...** icon to locate more functions. Note that this part is active while the Formula Bar is active, after which it is referred to as the Name Box.

The middle section of the Formula Bar is where you will find the icon to cancel formula input, to enter a formula, and to access the Insert Function dialog box to search for more functions. The main part of the Formula Bar is the formula entry area where you will enter, copy, or edit calculations created in Excel. It can be expanded or collapsed, which is really useful when dealing with lengthy calculations consisting of multiple functions and operators, and can be seen in the following screenshot:

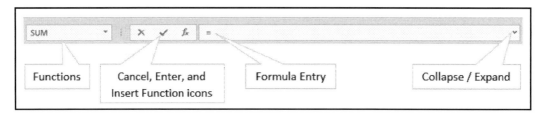

A formula is a cell entry that performs a calculation and returns a result. To enter a formula, we use cell references and seldom enter a calculation, as we would do on a calculator. This is because the power of performing calculations using references is that the data within the cell reference is often altered by the user, which in turn updates the calculation and produces different results, depending on data input and workflow.

In the following example, the formula is using the addition operator (+) to sum the **January** sales for all four sales reps. The answer to the formula will be placed in cell C12, and therefore the calculation is performed in that cell in order to return the result (the answer once the calculation is performed). Although this is the longer method of adding up in Excel, it shows how cell references are collected on the worksheet to construct the formula.

After entering the = sign, you would then select the cell reference on the worksheet for the first sales rep by clicking on cell C8, followed by the + operator, then the second sales rep cell reference C9, and so on. Once all cell references are selected, the formula is entered into the cell by pressing the *Enter* key on the keyboard or the green tick on the Formula Bar. To follow any examples in this topic, please use the `SSGRegions.xlsx` workbook. Refer to the following screenshot to view the formula in action:

C11		✕ ✓ *fx*	=C8+C9+C10+C11		
	A	B	C	D	E
5	EAST SIDE				
6					
7	Name	SalesCode	January	February	March
8	Jannes Alice		£ 110.00	£ 175.00	£ 140.00
9	Olson, Geoff		£ 200.00	£ 210.00	£ 240.00
10	Stem, Tom		£ 300.00	£ 180.00	£ 295.00
11	Umbrie, Angela		£ 220.00	£ 195.00	£ 185.00
12	TOTAL:		=C8+C9+C10+C11		
13	AVERAGE:				
14	HIGH:				

Note that we never leave an operator at the end of a formula. This will result in a formula error, as Excel will assume you have not finished the formula. We also never use the mouse to click off of a formula to enter it into a cell, as it will assume that you want to include further cell references and collect these as you click around the worksheet area. The only way to confirm a formula is complete is to *Enter* using the keyboard key or to click on the *green tick* on the Formula Bar to indicate you are finished constructing the formula and would like to view the result.

In the preceding screenshot, you will see that Excel uses color-coding to help you manage your cell references. Just at a glance, you can see which cells are matched with the cell references in the formula.

The following screenshot shows some examples of basic formula construction using operators:

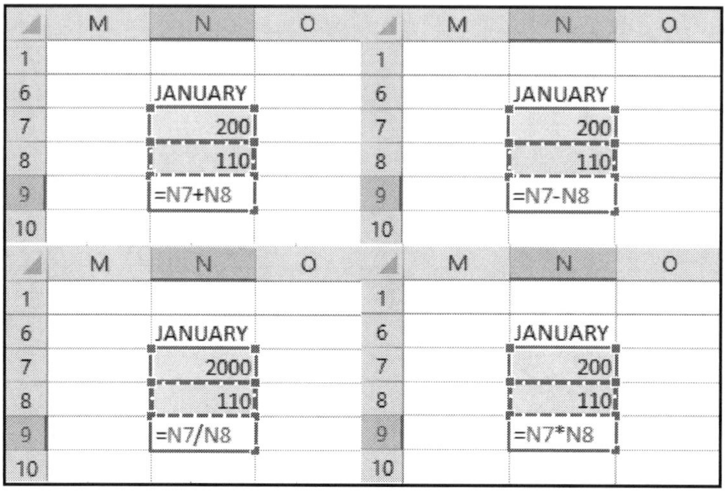

The operators are listed as follows:

- **Add**: Type =N7+N8 and then press *Enter*
- **Subtract**: Type =N7–N8 and then press *Enter*
- **Multiply**: Type =N7*N8 and then press *Enter*
- **Divide**: Type = N7/N8 and then press *Enter*

Order of evaluation

There is a strict order of operation to be adhered to when constructing formulas and functions. The basic order is as follows:

1. **Brackets ()**
2. **Percentage (%)**
3. **Exponent (^)**
4. **Division (/)**
5. **Multiplication (*)**
6. **Addition (+)**
7. **Subtraction (-)**

This order is termed **BODMAS**, which stands for **brackets, orders, division, multiplication, addition, subtraction**. If you do not specify which part of the formula Excel must do first, Excel will decide for you based on BODMAS. Next, we will see an example of a formula that includes the brackets, indicating that this part of the formula needs to be calculated first.

Operator precedence is applied when you have different operators in a formula—the order is applied by the order of operation using BODMAS. Here, the formula result is calculated by Excel performing the multiplication, then the addition, and finally the subtraction of values to arrive at an answer of 41: $=5 * 9 + 3 - 7$.

Use the formula = C7 * E7 + G7 – F22 in the cell on the basic calculation worksheet to test this formula.

Parenthesis or **brackets**, ( ), are used to define the order of the operations. **Enforce precedence** means to add the brackets around certain parts of the formula to indicate that those calculations need to be done first. So, to calculate the addition part of the formula first, we would need to place a bracket before and after the calculation to indicate that we would like to complete this part of the formula first. We now have an entirely different result from the first calculation we performed, so be careful when you are constructing formulas in Excel and make sure you are getting the result you require!

Once you put $=5 * (9 + 3) - 7$ as the formula, Excel gives you the answer: 53. So, we use this formula in the cell on the basic calculation worksheet to test this formula: $= C7 * (E7 + G7) - F22$.

The difference between a formula and a function:
Any cell that includes a calculation is a formula. An example of a formula is A22-A45. A function is a named calculation that performs a specific action such as average, sum, min, max, and so on. An example of a formula comprising multiple functions is
$=(sum(A22:B44)+(average(C98:C115)))$.

Constructing a formula

In this topic, we will look at how to type formulas using various methods. Continue using the `SSGRegions.xlsx` workbook for the following examples:

1. Click on a cell in the worksheet into which you would like to place the answer to a calculation. For this example, we will select B12. Press the = key on the keyboard to start the formula.

2. Start typing the formula you wish to use. In this case, we are adding up, so we will use the SUM function. Type sum directly after the = sign. When entering an s for sum, Excel will offer all the formulas that start with the letter *s*. Just to the right of the formula, you will see a tooltip with information about the formula you have chosen. Continue to type the formula you require or select one from the list, as illustrated in the following screenshot:

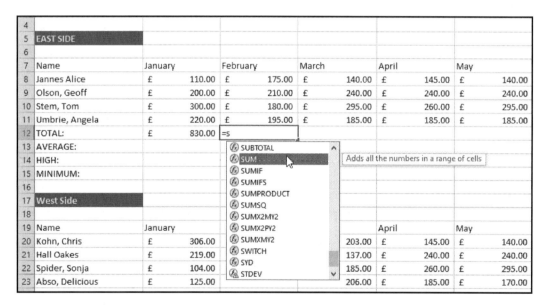

4										
5	EAST SIDE									
6										
7	Name	January		February		March		April		May
8	Jannes Alice	£	110.00	£	175.00	£	140.00	£	145.00	£ 140.00
9	Olson, Geoff	£	200.00	£	210.00	£	240.00	£	240.00	£ 240.00
10	Stem, Tom	£	300.00	£	180.00	£	295.00	£	260.00	£ 295.00
11	Umbrie, Angela	£	220.00	£	195.00	£	185.00	£	185.00	£ 185.00
12	TOTAL:	£	830.00	=s						
13	AVERAGE:			*SUBTOTAL*						
14	HIGH:			*SUM*		Adds all the numbers in a range of cells				
15	MINIMUM:			*SUMIF*						
16				*SUMIFS*						
17	West Side			*SUMPRODUCT*						
18				*SUMSQ*						
19	Name	January		*SUMX2MY2*				April		May
20	Kohn, Chris	£	306.00	*SUMX2PY2*		203.00	£	145.00	£	140.00
21	Hall Oakes	£	219.00	*SUMXMY2*		137.00	£	240.00	£	240.00
22	Spider, Sonja	£	104.00	*SWITCH*		185.00	£	260.00	£	295.00
23	Abso, Delicious	£	125.00	*SYD* *STDEV*		206.00	£	185.00	£	170.00

3. Open a bracket to separate the formula from the range of cells you would like to add up: `=sum(`.

4. Select the cells (range) you would like to add up. You can achieve this in three ways, as follows:
   - Drag the range B8 to B11 to select it, or type `B8:B11` to identify the range. As you type this formula, you will notice that Excel is selecting the range for you.
   - Or click on cell B8, then hold down the *Shift* key on your keyboard, and while keeping it depressed, use the down arrow keyboard key to move down one cell at a time to reach cell B11.

5. Press *Enter* to finish your formula. You do not need to close the bracket, as Excel will do this for you.

6. The Formula Bar displays the completed formula and allows you to edit it here simply by clicking into the Formula Bar. Alternatively, you can press the *F2* function key on the keyboard directly into the cell on the worksheet to edit the formula. Excel automatically highlights the selected range used in the formula by way of an outlined colored border when you are in **Edit** mode. The formula will display in the answer cell by double-clicking on the formula result.

7. We can also use the **AutoSum** icon to add up values. This is quicker but is not the most effective, error-free way of adding information. Click on the cell in which you would like to place your total—in this case, cell D12**.**

Click on the **AutoSum** icon in the **Editing** group of the **Home** tab, illustrated in the following screenshot:

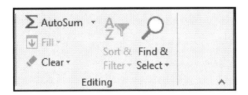

Note you will also find this icon in the **Function Library** group on the **Formulas** tab, as can be seen in the following screenshot:

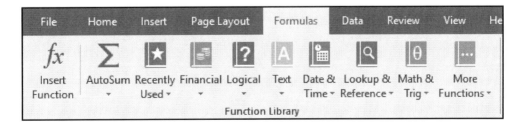

8. Excel automatically inserts the range to sum (always check that it has assumed the range correctly!). Press *Enter* to complete the formula.

So, you have learned how to enter the SUM function and understand the order in which the formula is constructed using a function. You are now ready to use the *quickest method* to enter the SUM function in a workbook—click into a cell on the worksheet; press the *Alt* key on the keyboard, and, while keeping the *Alt* key depressed, press the = key.

In the next topic, we will learn about a few more of the many functions that exist in Excel 2019.

Learning Excel functions

Excel 2019 has 479 functions, of which the following are new functions: IFS; SWITCH; CONCAT; TEXTJOIN; MAXIFS; MINIFS.

Let's look at a few of the commonly used functions in Excel, shown in the following table:

Type of function	Function	Description
Sum function	= sum(range)	Adds all values in a selected range
Average function	= average(range)	To find the arithmetic mean
Minimum function	= min(range)	To find the lowest value in a list
Maximum function	= max(range)	To find the highest value in a list
Count function	= count(range)	To count the number of values in a list
CountA function	= counta(range)	To count the number of names (text) in a list
CountBlank function	= countblank(range)	To count the number of blank cells in a range

We will continue with the SSGRegions.xlsx workbook for this example, to work out the average, minimum, and maximum values of a range of cells, as follows:

1. Click on cell B13.
2. Click the drop-down arrow on the **AutoSum** icon.
3. Choose the **Average** function from the list provided, as illustrated in the following screenshot:

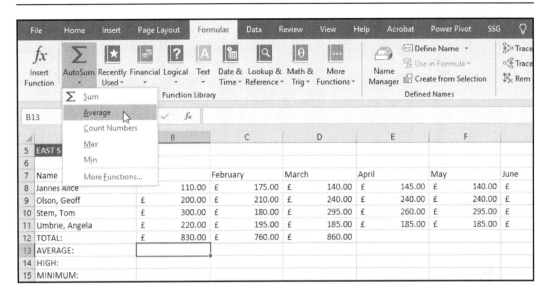

4. The **Average** function is inserted into cell B13, and Excel automatically assumes the range by selecting the range B8:B12. This is incorrect, and is one of those instances where you need to be very careful when using these quick methods of inserting functions.

5. Edit the formula to reflect the correct cell reference range B8:B12 by replacing B12 with B11.

6. Press *Enter* when done to view the formula result.

7. Let's do the **Max** and the **Min** calculations. This time try the type method and the ribbon method to work out the maximum and the minimum values.

8. Click on cell B14, then type the following: =MAX(B8:B11. Then, press *Enter* on the keyboard.

9. Click on cell C14, then select the **Max** function from the drop-down list from the **AutoSum** icon **Formulas** ribbon. Check that the formula cell reference range is correct and edit if necessary, then press *Enter* to see the result in the cell.

10. Click on cell B15, then type the following: =MIN(B8:B11. Then, press *Enter* on the keyboard.

11. Click on cell C15, then select the **Min** function from the drop-down list from the **AutoSum** icon **Formulas** ribbon. Check that the formula cell reference range is correct and edit if necessary, then press *Enter* to see the result in the cell.

12. If you are typing a formula and made a mistake, or realize you are entering the formula into the incorrect cell and need to exit the formula, simply press the *Esc* key on your keyboard.

Using the Show Formulas command

The **Show Formulas** command is a valuable feature to use when working on large complicated workbooks that were compiled by another department or person. Often, you see the result of a formula, but do not know how the person arrived at that answer, especially if it contains connections to other workbooks or worksheets. To display formulas instead of the formula result in cells on the worksheet, use the *Ctrl* key and the ~ key on your keyboard, or use the **Show Formulas** icon on the **Formulas** tab. To turn this feature off, simply toggle by repeating the steps. Press *Ctrl* and the ~ key on the keyboard again to return and display the cell content, as illustrated in the following screenshot:

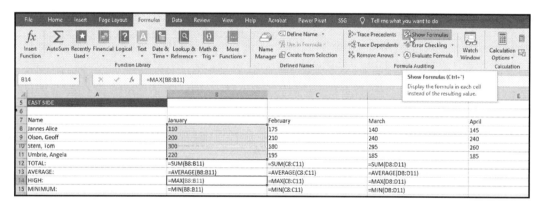

The next topic concentrates on converting values to calculate percentages.

Converting values and percentage increase

We will go through the steps to convert college marks to arrive at a percentage. Make sure you have the ConvertingValues.xlsx workbook open.

Look at cell C6; the first student has achieved 89 marks out of a total of 140. We need to convert the student mark to a mark out of 125 instead of 140 and place the answer in D6, as follows:

1. Click on cell D6.
2. Press =.
3. Click on the student mark in cell C6.
4. Press /.
5. Click on the **Test Total** cell, C5.
6. Press *.
7. Click on cell D5.
8. Press *Enter* to see the formula result, which is illustrated in the following screenshot:

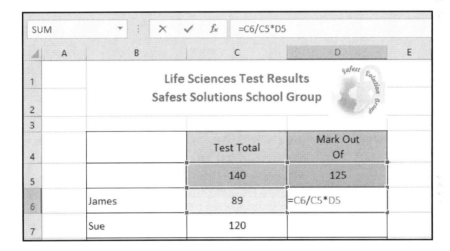

9. To copy a formula, we use the **AutoFill** feature—this skill was addressed in `Chapter 8`, *Formatting, Manipulating, and Presenting Data Visually*. Position the mouse pointer on the + in the bottom right-hand corner of the cell. Hold the mouse down and drag the + sign to fill the formula to the remaining cells to see the converted mark out of 125 for the remaining students.

10. To check that the formula has copied down correctly, double-click on one of the answer cells—for instance, D8. You will notice that the formula has copied down relative to the row and column from one cell to the next. Although the formula is displaying no errors in this case, even though it is using the incorrect **Test Total** and **Mark Out Of**, you will find this a problem when working out the % for each of the students. Let's investigate this!

11. Click on cell E4, and enter the % heading.

12. Click on cell E6 to work out the first student's %.

13. Type the following formula: =D6/D5.

14. Press *Enter*.

15. The first student's percentage is now visible in cell E6. Now, autofill cell E6 to E7:E11.

16. Notice that the formula is now producing errors. Double-click on cell E9 to see the problem. We will need to ensure that each student's **Mark Out Of** is divided by cell D5 and that the cell reference is made *absolute* so that it cannot move when copying down a formula, as illustrated in the following screenshot:

SUM	▾	⋮ × ✓ ƒx	=D9/D8		
	A	B	C	D	E	F
1			Life Sciences Test Results			
2			Safest Solutions School Group			
3						
4			Test Total	Mark Out Of	%	
5			140	125		
6		James	89	79	64%	
7		Sue	120	107	135%	
8		Elena	87	78	73%	
9		Genine	111	99	=D9/D8	
10		Nicole	138	123	124%	
11		Brent	75	67	54%	
12						

17. Let's fix the error and make cell D5 absolute. Double-click on cell E6 to view the formula. Select D5 by highlighting it, then press the *F4* function key on the keyboard. Note that if you are using a laptop, you will need to press the *Fn* key and then press the *F4* function key. The result can be seen in the following screenshot:

		Test Total	Mark Out Of	%
3				
4				
5		140	125	
6	James	89	79	=D6/$D$5

18. Press *Enter* to update the formula in cell E6.
19. Place the mouse pointer at the bottom right-hand corner of cell E6, then double-click on the **AutoFill** handle (the + sign at the bottom right-hand corner of the cell—this basic skill was explained in the previous Excel chapter) to update the formula in the following cells, thereby fixing the error.

Working out the percentage change

Formulas are very important when working as a financial analyst, as you need to make sure you are using the correct formula construction. There are many methods to construct a formula for a particular outcome, so understanding is very important when calculating to ensure you arrive at the correct answer. In addition, the simplest method is always the best, rather than typing a long, complicated formula to arrive at the same result. Choose to use the most efficient method.

Let's have a look at how we would calculate the percentage change. We have **ACTUAL SALES** figures for our products in cells C16:C20 of the worksheet, and **BUDGET SALES PROJECTION** in cells D16:D20. We would like to work out the percentage change in cells E16:E20. You can work this out in two ways, as follows:

1. Actual sales minus budget divided by budget
2. Actual sales divided by budget minus budget divided by budget

So, to elaborate, you would use this formula in this particular example: `=C16/D16-D16/D16`, which can be simplified to *actual sales divided by budget - 1*, **=C16/D16-1**, as shown in the following screenshot:

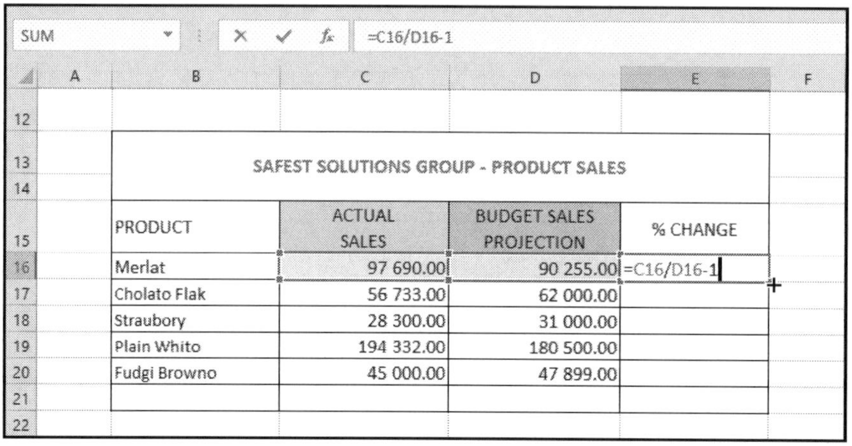
SUM =C16/D16-1

	A	B	C	D	E	F
12						
13		SAFEST SOLUTIONS GROUP - PRODUCT SALES				
14						
15		PRODUCT	ACTUAL SALES	BUDGET SALES PROJECTION	% CHANGE	
16		Merlat	97 690.00	90 255.00	=C16/D16-1	
17		Cholato Flak	56 733.00	62 000.00		
18		Straubory	28 300.00	31 000.00		
19		Plain Whito	194 332.00	180 500.00		
20		Fudgi Browno	45 000.00	47 899.00		
21						
22						

We will continue using the `ConvertingValues.xlsx` workbook for this example. Proceed as follows:

1. Click on cell E16.
2. Type the following formula, clicking on the relevant cell references as you formulate it: `=C16/D16-1`.
3. Place the mouse pointer at the bottom right-hand corner of the cell.
4. The **AutoFill** handle (the + crosshair pointer) will appear; then, double-click to fill the formula down to the rest of the cells. The result can be seen in the following screenshot:

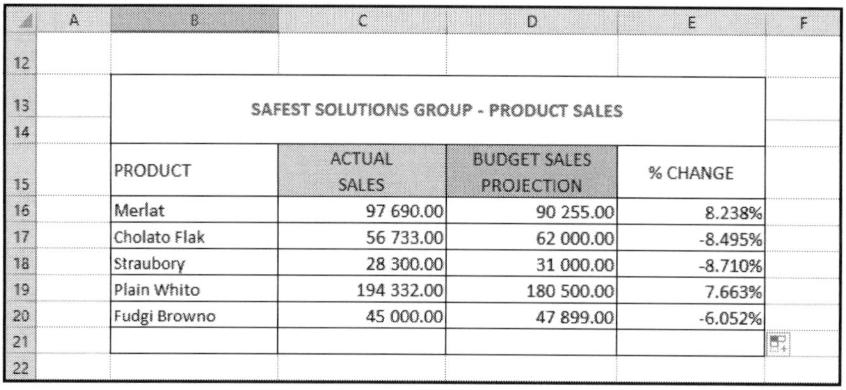

	A	B	C	D	E	F
12						
13		SAFEST SOLUTIONS GROUP - PRODUCT SALES				
14						
15		PRODUCT	ACTUAL SALES	BUDGET SALES PROJECTION	% CHANGE	
16		Merlat	97 690.00	90 255.00	8.238%	
17		Cholato Flak	56 733.00	62 000.00	-8.495%	
18		Straubory	28 300.00	31 000.00	-8.710%	
19		Plain Whito	194 332.00	180 500.00	7.663%	
20		Fudgi Browno	45 000.00	47 899.00	-6.052%	
21						
22						

5. You are now able to view the percentage change in cells E16:E20 and can adjust actual and budget projections where necessary, and the change will be reflected in the **% CHANGE** column. If we adjust cell C17 to read 65,000.00 as the **ACTUAL SALES** figure, then **% CHANGE** will update to a positive 4.839%.

In the next topic, we will concentrate on working out the percentage increase or decrease.

Working out a percentage increase or decrease

Before we look at the percentage calculations, it is important to highlight how to format cells as a % at this point. If you change a cell number from **General** to **Percentage** format after typing a value into a cell, you are going to get the *incorrect* percentage displayed (1500%). So, follow the basic percentage format rules listed here:

- Click on a cell in the workbook and type 15% (include the % sign to force the number format to change to %), then press *Enter*.
- Click on a cell in the workbook and format the cell as a %, then type the percentage value into the cell (for instance 15) and then press *Enter*.

Percentage increase

For this example, make sure you have clicked into cell J5 of the worksheet used in the preceding example. Our task is to work out the percentage increase for product prices in-store and add this to the current product price. We are also having a store sale and would like to reduce our prices by a certain percentage and arrive at the new sale price.

To work out this formula, we would need to take the **Product Price** and add it to the **New Product Price**, then multiply by the **Price Increase** we would like. We can write this formula in another way, for example, **Product Price** multiplied by 1 plus the percentage increase. That is a much easier formula to construct and would be typed up as follows, according to our =H5*(1+I5) example:

	SAFEST SOLUTIONS CLOTHING GROUP		
	Product Price	Price Increase	New Product Price
	100	7%	=H5*(1+I5)

Type the formula =H5*(1+I5) into the cell J5 and use the **AutoFill** handle to copy the formula down to the rest of the cells. Note that you can adjust **Price Increase** by entering another percentage into a cell in that column, after which **New Product Price** will adjust accordingly.

Percentage decrease

We are working in cell J10 of the first worksheet of the ConvertingValues.xlsx workbook to calculate the product price decrease as we are having a store sale. This calculation is the same as the preceding percentage increase formula, except we will use a minus sign instead of an addition sign in the last part of the formula, as we are wanting a decrease in **Product Price**. Type =H10*(1-I10) into cell J10 of **Sheet1**, as illustrated in the following screenshot:

Product Price	Price Decrease	New Sale Price
132	30%	=H10*(1-I10)
56	15%	47.60
45	20%	36.00

Now, we will learn how to customize the status bar in the next topic to obtain a quick peek at various calculations on the worksheet.

Getting results using the status bar

As you are busy highlighting cells on the worksheet, Excel displays information on the status bar. This information can be customized to suit your requirements. If you highlight values on the worksheet, the sum of those values will appear on the status bar, as well as the count and the average. This function is great to use if you, at a glance, just want to get an indication of—for instance—the sum of highlighted cells, as illustrated in the following screenshot:

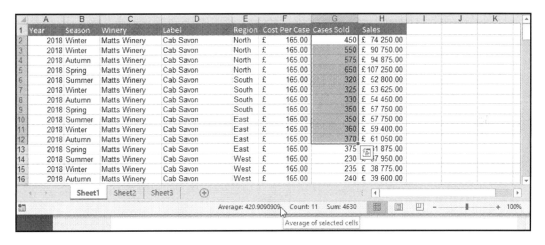

To customize the information along the status bar, simply right-click anywhere along the status bar. In the shortcut list that appears, click to select or deselect items to view on the status bar, as demonstrated in the following screenshot:

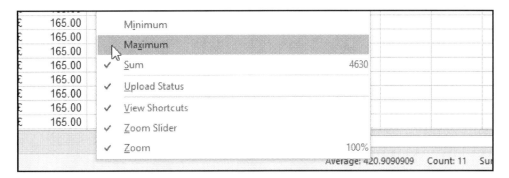

Using the Function Library

The Excel functions are continuously being updated and improved in the **Function Library** group on the **Formulas** tab. Each book along the ribbon houses functions in categories, which makes it much easier for the user to locate functions and understand the purpose of using them. We will be looking at some functions from the various books available in the **Function Library** group. The first example we will use is the **COUNTA** function, which can easily be typed into the cell directly, but we will take the long-method route for the purpose of demonstrating the process of using the **Function Library**. The **Function Library** group can be seen in the following screenshot:

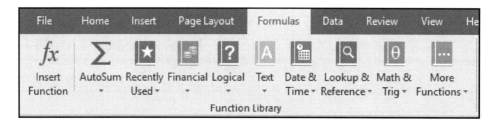

1. Open the SSGRegions.xlsx workbook.
2. Click on the cell in which to apply a function—in the case of this example, we will use cell B30 to work out the count of the employees. From the **Function Library**, select the function book you desire. We are using a statistical function, so will need to visit the **Statistical** book under the **More Functions** drop-down list.
3. Once you click on the **More Functions** book, choose the **Statistical** category, after which a drop-down list will appear with all the available functions from that category, as illustrated in the following screenshot:

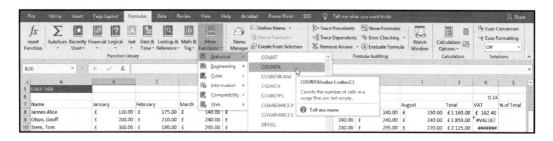

4. If you click on the **COUNTA** function to select it, Excel will automatically place an = sign into the cell at the start of the formula, and then insert the function directly after the equals (=) sign.

5. The **Function Arguments** dialog box will appear, where the user is able to enter values as cell references to construct the formula. Excel automatically assumes the range to use, which you need to remove as you would like to select your own range of cells from the worksheet. Select range **A8:A11** for **Value1** and **A20:A24** for **Value2**, as illustrated in the following screenshot:

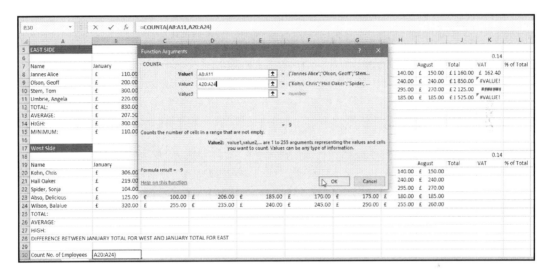

6. Notice that the formula description is displayed at the bottom of the **Function Arguments** dialog box as well as the *result* of the formula.

7. Click on **OK** when complete to view the result.

Using the formula composer (Insert Function icon)

The **fx** icon is located as the first icon on the **Formulas** tab, and well as at the bottom of all the function books in the **Function Library**, and along the **Formula Bar**. You can use the **fx** option to search for a function and follow steps in order to complete the formula. Another name for this option is the **Insert Function** icon. We will use the same function example we used in the preceding section.

The **Insert Function** icon can be seen in the following screenshot:

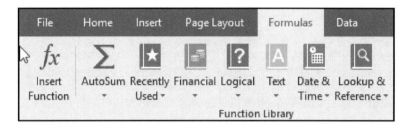

1. Click on the cell in which you would like the formula answer to reside. Click on the **Insert Function** icon, using one of the methods listed. The **Insert Function** dialog box will populate on your screen. Select a function to use or type a function to search for at the top in the **Search for a function:** text area. Click on **Go** to search for a function, as illustrated in the following screenshot:

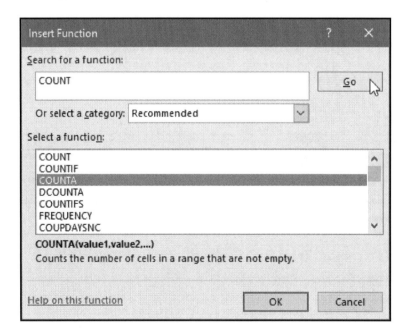

2. Excel will open the **Function Arguments** dialog box, and automatically identify cells from the work area to use in the formula. Remove any cell references from the **Function Arguments** dialog box, and select cells on the worksheet to use.

3. Click on **OK** to accept the suggested formula.

Editing formulas

If you need to edit the formula and make changes to its parts, such as to the range or fixing an error, you can achieve this using more than one method, as follows:

- Double-click on the cell that contains the formula to edit. The formula displays and the cells are highlighted on the worksheet. Note that if you have used functions in your formula, the function tip pops up under the function used. Edit the formula, then press *Enter* to update it.
- Click on the cell that contains the formula to edit. The formula displays in the Formula Bar. Click in the **Formula Bar** to make changes to the formula. Edit the formula, then press *Enter* to update it.
- Click on the cell that contains the formula to edit. Press the *F2* function key on the keyboard. The cell will display the formula to edit. Edit the formula, then press *Enter* to update it.

Understanding relative versus absolute

When you refer to cell references when constructing formula, you have two options. You can refer to cells using relative references or you can use absolute references. The type of reference used is only relevant when you copy the formulas to other cells.

As the name suggests, *r*elative references will change—so, they refer to cells relative to the cell containing the formula. In other words, when you copy a formula down a column, the cell references used in the formula move down the column too.

Absolute references will always refer to the same cells. Sometimes, cell references need to remain the same when copied or when you use the **AutoFill** command. I always refer to *absolute* as cementing the cell reference so that it cannot be moved when calculating. You can press the *F4* function key to make a cell *absolute* (fixed /constant), or add dollar signs ($) to cell references to make a column and/or a row constant (fixed).

Naming a cell and using it in a formula is another way of using *absolute* cell referencing. If you use this method, you do not have to press *F4* to make the cell *absolute*. We will learn about defining a name range in the next topic.

Let's look at an example using the `SSGRegions.xlsx` workbook, as follows:

1. In cell K8, we have entered the formula to calculate **VAT** on **Total** sales. We have entered the formula as =J8*K6, as can be seen in the following screenshot:

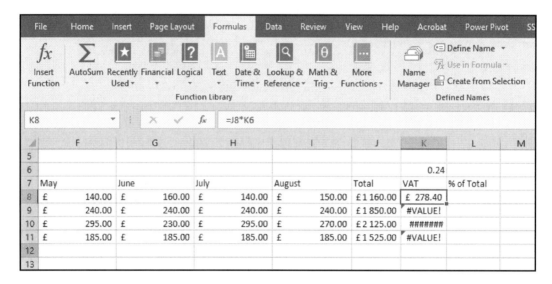

2. K6 is the cell that contains the percentage **VAT** (entered as a decimal). This is the cell in which all the Product Totals will be multiplied.

3. After entering the formula, we copied the formula using the **AutoFill** handle down to fill the formula to the rest of the cells in the **VAT** column. When we had finished copying the formula, the errors appeared in column **K**.

4. On investigation, we noticed that the formula in cell K8 is correct, but the other cells are incorrect due to the formula referencing cell K6 as relative. This means that when copied down the column, K6 moves too! The formula in cell K9 has a #**VALUE!** error. This means that text has been included in the formula in error. If we look at the formula in K9, we will see that the formula is referencing cell K7, which contains the text **VAT**, which is what is causing the error in the cell.

5. To fix all these errors, we simply need to change the formula in cell K8. Double-click on cell K8.

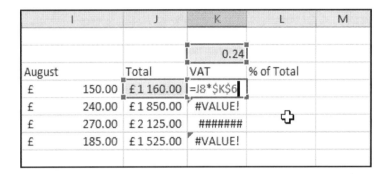

	I	J	K	L	M
			0.24		
	August	Total	VAT	% of Total	
	£ 150.00	£ 1 160.00	=J8*K6		
	£ 240.00	£ 1 850.00	#VALUE!		
	£ 270.00	£ 2 125.00	#######		
	£ 185.00	£ 1 525.00	#VALUE!		

6. Select K6 by highlighting it with the mouse, then press the *F4* function key on the keyboard to make the cell reference absolute. Note in the following screenshot that dollar signs are added before and after the **K**:

	I	J	K	L	M
			0.24		
	August	Total	VAT	% of Total	
	£ 150.00	£ 1 160.00	=J8*$K$6		
	£ 240.00	£ 1 850.00	#VALUE!		
	£ 270.00	£ 2 125.00	#######		
	£ 185.00	£ 1 525.00	#VALUE!		

7. Press *Enter*, and then copy the formula down the column using the **AutoFill** handle. Your formulas are now all correct.

Applying dates in calculations

When entering dates into a cell, make sure that the slash (/) or hyphen (–) is used between the day, month, and year. Excel will then recognize the cell contents as a date, and calculations will be possible. To follow the explanations that come next, we will use the `DateFunctions.xlsx` workbook.

To insert the current date

1. Click on cell A1 to enter the system date. Type the formula =TODAY() in the cell. Press *Enter* on the keyboard.
2. The date displays in the current cell and will update each time you open the workbook.
3. To enter the current date without updating, use the keyboard shortcut *Ctrl* and *;*.

> To enter the current time, use the keyboard shortcut *Ctrl + Shift + ;* .

To insert the current date and time

1. Click on cell A2 to enter the system date and time. Make sure you are on the **Formulas** tab, and then locate the **Function Library** group.
2. Locate and click on the **Date & Time** book. Choose **NOW** from the list of functions. A dialog box will appear, giving you information about the function. Click on the **OK** command to enter the date and time into the cell.

To separate the day from a date

1. Click on a cell in the worksheet to return the day from a date value. For this example, select cell H2. Enter =day(into the cell. Click on the date cell you are retrieving the day from. Select cell B8.
2. Press *Enter* on the keyboard to display the day as the result. Experiment with the year and month functions on the worksheet using =month(G6) and =year(G6).

To calculate the number of days, years, and months between two dates

1. Click on a cell in the worksheet that must return the number of days between two dates, and select cell B14.

2. Enter the following formula into the cell: `=day(cell that contains the first date)-day(cell that contains the second date)`. In this example, the formula will be `=day(C8)-day(B8)`.

3. Press *Enter* on the keyboard. If cell B8 was used as the first date in the calculation, the formula result would have been negative (that is, *-11* in the first instance). To fix this, edit the formula to add the absolute function at the start of the formula, as follows: `=ABS(day(E8)-day(D8))`.

4. You can also just minus the cells from each other to get the same result, but if any other criteria are required—such as month or year—then you would need to use the appropriate function instead.

To work out the **February** working days, proceed as follows:

1. Enter the formula `=ABS(day(E8)-day(D8))` into cell C14.

2. Press *Enter* on the keyboard. The result can be seen in the following screenshot:

AND		✕ ✓ f_x	=ABS(DAY(D8)-DAY(E8))					
	A	B	C	D	E	F	G	H
2	2020/05/14 07:40						Day Function	5
3							Month Function	1
4	SAFEST SOLUTIONS GROUP CASINO : DAYS WORKED & EARNINGS RECORD						Year Function	2019
5								
6	Name	January		February				
7		FROM	TO	FROM	TO			
8	Jannes Alice	2019-01-05	2019-01-16	2019-02-09	2019-02-20			
9	Olson, Geoff	2019-01-19	2019-01-25	2019-02-21	2019-02-26			
10	Stem, Tom	2019-01-01	2019-01-22	2019-02-05	2019-02-12			
11	Umbrie, Angela	2019-01-06	2019-01-17	2019-02-01	2019-02-04			
12								
13	No. of Days worked per Staff member	January	February					
14	Jannes Alice	11	=ABS(DAY(D8)-DAY(E8))					
15	Olson, Geoff	6	5					
16	Stem, Tom	21	7					
17	Umbrie, Angela	11	3					
18								

3. The **February** column is displaying the full date and not the day. This has happened in this example as the cell format set to date format prior to entering the formula. To correct this, simply change the cell format to **General**.

Using mathematical functions

In this topic, we will learn how to create more advanced functions that allow you to create calculations based on multiple inputs.

The INT and ROUND functions

The INT function rounds a number down to the nearest integer. The INT function does not round off to the nearest whole number; only the decimals are removed, and the number without the decimals is used in calculations. For example, =INT(95.77) is displayed and stored in memory as **95**. To follow each of these examples explained in this topic, open the Round.xlsx workbook (to try the formulas yourself), or alternatively, the completed workbook, Round-C.xlsx.

It is also possible to insert the INT function before a formula so that the formula answer is an integer. An example of this type of formula would be =INT(sum(C45:C55)).

In the workbook, look at the data to the right of the worksheet. The first table shows the SUM formula result without INT, and the second table displays the SUM formula with the INT function applied: =INT(SUM(N11:N13)). Double-click on cell N14 to see the INT formula.

The ROUND function is also a mathematical function that rounds the value off to a certain number of decimal places. The ROUND function rounds up or down, depending on whether the digit is greater than or less than 5. Numbers, by default, have 15 decimal places in Excel.

Formulate the ROUND function as =ROUND(76.677897,2). It will round the number to **76.68** (the remainder of the decimals are removed).

It is also possible to insert the ROUND function in front of a formula to round it off at the same time as completing the calculation—for example, =ROUND((C7*F9+D3),2).

The ROUNDUP and ROUNDDOWN functions

The ROUNDDOWN function rounds the number down to a specified number of digits and always rounds down towards 0 (the lowest number). Open the file called `Round-C.xlsx` to see the formula results, or try the formulas out using the `Round.xlsx` workbook.

Type the formula, either ROUNDUP or ROUNDDOWN, directly into the answer cell. Or you can access the formula from the **Math & Trig** book located in the **Function Library**.

The ROUNDUP function returns a number rounded up to the next highest number.

The SUMIF function

The SUMIF function calculates the total of a range of cells where certain conditions are met. Using the example in the `SSGProductSUMIF.xlsx` workbook, we will demonstrate how the syntax of the formula is constructed.

In column *B*, we have a list of products. In the list, the product name **Fudgi Browno** occurs more than once. The SUMIF function will quickly add up all the sales values if the range B3:B44 contains the text **Fudgi Browno** to obtain the product total sales. If the amounts in the list change for **Fudgi Browno** after the formula is constructed, the formula will automatically update to include the new sales values in the cell containing the SUMIF function.

The syntax of the SUMIF function is shown in the following diagram:

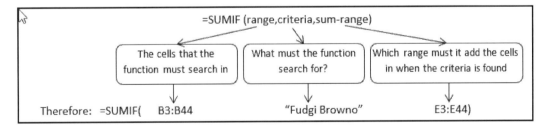

When typing in formula criteria, enter any text used for the criteria between *inverted commas* (not the single but the double kind). Enter the SUMIF function directly into the cell, or choose from the list of **Math & Trig** functions in the **Function Library**. Then, proceed as follows:

1. Open the SSGProductSUMIF.xlsx workbook.

2. Click on cell J4 on the worksheet to construct the formula to work out the total sales for the product named **Straubory**.

3. We can use the type directly in a cell method to construct the formula if you feel confident (the formula you need to enter would be **=SUMIF(B3:B44,"Straubory",E3:E44)**, or locate the function from the **Math & Trig** book, located in the **Function Library**. Click to choose the **SUMIF** function from the **Maths & Trig** drop-down list, as illustrated in the following screenshot:

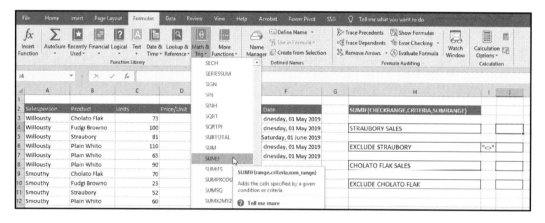

4. The **Function Arguments** dialog box is populated over the worksheet area, and the formula has started to build in the answer cell automatically.

5. Make sure you click into the **Range** placeholder, then move to the workbook and select the range **B3:B44**.

6. Once you have the range selected, click back into the **Function Arguments** dialog box and click into the **Criteria** placeholder and type Straubory. Excel will fill in the inverted commas for you automatically.

7. Click into the **Sum_range placeholder** area, and then drag the cell range **E3:E44** on the worksheet to add up all the sales values, as illustrated in the following screenshot:

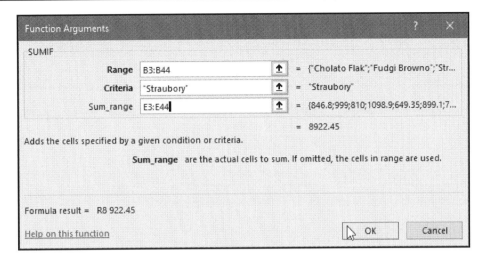

8. Return to the **Function Arguments** dialog box.

9. Click on **OK** to confirm the arguments and enter the formula into the cell.

10. This time, we will use the type in the cell method to find the total sales for all the products *excluding* **Straubory**.

11. Click on cell J6 to construct the formula as follows: **=SUMIF(B3:B44,"<>Straubory",E3:E44)**.

12. Press the *Enter* key to see the formula result.

Using the COUNTIF statistical function

The COUNTIF function counts the number of cells within a range that meet a condition you specify. Open the CountFunctions.xlsx workbook to follow this next example given here:

1. We will use the COUNTIF function to find out how many times **View Tabue** appears in the **Division** column.

2. The syntax of the formula is as follows: =COUNTIF(range,criteria).

3. Click into cell B13.

4. Type =COUNTIF(F3:F30,"View Tabue")

5. Press *Enter* to see the formula result.

6. Click into cell B15, then use the COUNTIF function to count all the *surnames* that start with the letter *A*. It is possible to use the wildcard characters such as * and ? for this purpose—type **=COUNTIF(D3:D30,"A*")**.

7. Press *Enter* to see the formula result.
8. Use the COUNTIF function to count all the hourly rates greater than 15. Note that when using text (or characters on the keyboard such as ?, *, <, > and <>), *inverted commas* must be used around the criteria.
9. Click into cell B17.
10. Type **=COUNTIF(J3:J30,">15")**.
11. Press *Enter* to see the formula result.

For the next example, make sure you are on the *second sheet* in the workbook named **COUNTIF2** (if you have been following in the workbook called CountFunctions.xlsx). We will then proceed as follows:

1. We will count how many students will achieve an award. Click into cell **P3**.
2. Enter the following formula: **=COUNTIF(M3:M17,"Y")**.
3. Press *Enter* to see the formula result.

For the next example, make sure you are on the third sheet of the CountFunctions.xlsx workbook. You can use the COUNTIF function to count more than one criterion within a single range. Proceed as follows:

1. Click into cell B19. To count how many times the *Soningdale* and *Munerton* entries appear in the **Divisions** range, use the following formula: **=COUNTIF(F3:F30,"Soningdale")+COUNTIF(F3:F30,"Munerton")**.
2. Press *Enter* to see the formula result.

Using financial functions - PMT

The PMT function calculates payments for a loan with constant interest rate and constant payments. You would like to purchase a second-hand car for about 30,000.00. Different dealers give you different rates and different payment plans. You know that you cannot afford more than 30,000.00 and the payment you want to make per month must not be more than 800.00. As you were saving for a car, you have about 5,500 in your savings account for a down payment but you would prefer not to use that cash. You would like to find out how to put down as little as possible on the deposit to pay the amount of 800.00 per month for the car. On investigation at a few car dealers, you now have an idea of the number of years you could pay for the car over, and also the interest rate you would qualify for.

The syntax for the PMT function is: =PMT(rate,nper,pv,fv,type).

- **Rate**: This is the annual interest rate for the loan.
- **Nper**: This is the total number of payments to be made for the loan.
- **Pv**: This is the present value of the investment (principal value).
- **Fv**: This is the amount you want the investment to be at the end of the last payment on the loan. Therefore, fv is 0.
- **Type**: Enter 0 for the end of the month or enter 1 for the beginning of the month when payments will be made.

Let's use the preceding information to work out the figures and see if you can afford the car, as follows:

1. To follow this example, make sure you have the PMT.xlsx workbook open.
2. Type the following information into the relevant cells in column **A** on the worksheet.
    1. Enter an interest rate of 0.005% in cell **C4**. This is one-twelfth of a 6% annual rate—this example interest rate is relating to a single repayment period and not an annual rate. Note that this is a simple example and that interest rates and the repayment period differ depending on various loan conditions, as well as credit scoring.
3. Enter the payment period in months that the loan will be over in cell **C5**. For this example, we will use *36 months*.
4. The amount of the loan is entered into cell **C6** as **30000**.
5. Only enter a future value if the loan will have a cash balance to be made when the last loan payment is paid; otherwise, enter a **0**.
6. The formula will be constructed in cell **C8** as follows: **=PMT(C4,C5,C6,0,0)** if using the typing method; alternatively, follow these next steps to access the **Function Library**.

7. Click on the **Financial book** located on the **Function Library**, then select the **PMT** function, as illustrated in the following screenshot:

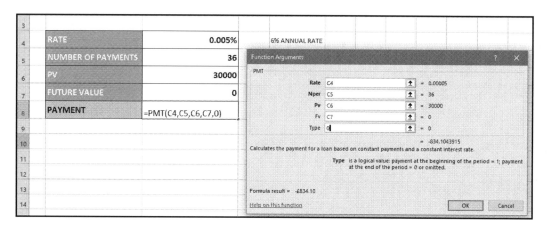

8. Add the function arguments as per the information given.
9. Click on the **OK** command to see the result and the payment per month based on the input.
10. Notice that there is a *negative payment value* now in cell *C8*. To make this a *positive value*, add a minus sign in front of the **PMT** function so that it returns a positive value and not a negative value, as follows =-**PMT(C4,C5,C6,0,0)**.

Now, you have a good idea of the PMT function and can change the payment period to 48 months to see if you can bring down the payment or ask the dealer for a better interest rate.

Applying conditional logic in a formula

In this section, we'll see how to apply conditional functions in a formula: IF, AND, and OR.

The IF function

The IF function is an example of a formula with values that match conditions. This formula means that if a specified condition or logical test is satisfied, the first action (if true) is performed; otherwise, the second action (if false) is taken.

Locate the IF function by visiting the **Function Library**, under the **Logical** category. This is how the IF formula is structured:

IF(logical_test,value_if_true,value_if_false), as illustrated in the following screenshot:

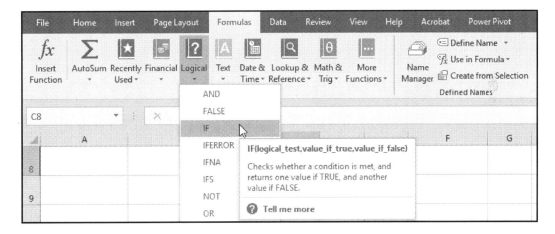

Let's try an example of the IF function, as follows:

1. Open the IF-Function.xlsx workbook.
2. There are two methods you can use to enter the IF function in a formula:
   - Using the typing method (which is the one I prefer) or
   - Using the **Logical** book from the **Function Library** group.
3. In cell C2, we will construct a formula that will display **Within budget** if the amount spent in the first month is less than or equal to the budget total in F2. If it is greater, the text will display **Over budget** in the cell. The formula will be typed as follows: **=IF(B2<=$F$2,"Within Budget","Over Budget")**.

4. Click to select cell C2. Type an = sign followed by **IF** in cell C2.
5. Type a **(** after the **IF**.
6. The autocomplete option will offer you help on how to construct the formula you are using. The process can be seen in the following screenshot:

	A	B	C	D	E	F	G
1	DEPARTMENT	FIRST QUARTER EXPENSES	WITHIN BUDGET?			BUDGET AMOUNT	
2	Sales	£ 4 520.00	=if(			£ 4 000.00	
3	Customer service	£ 3 576.00	IF(**logical_test**, [value_if_true], [value_if_false])				

7. The **logical_test** part of the formula appears **bold**. This means that this part of the formula must occur first. As we are working out whether the first month was *within budget*, we need to use cell B2 in our formula to test the result against the budget total in cell F2. Therefore, the first part of the formula should reflect this, as illustrated in the following screenshot:

	A	B	C	D	E	F
1	DEPARTMENT	FIRST QUARTER EXPENSES	WITHIN BUDGET?			BUDGET AMOUNT
2	Sales	£ 4 520.00	=if(B2<=F2			£ 4 000.00
3	Customer service	£ 3 576.00	IF(**logical_test**, [value_if_true], [value_if_false])			

8. The second part of the formula is to enter what must happen if the condition **is met** (true). Before we type this part of the formula, we need to place a comma after the F2 cell reference to indicate that we are moving on to the next phase of the formula. After the comma, we will type "**Within Budget**", as illustrated in the following screenshot. Note that you need to enter any text in a formula with double inverted commas, before and after the text. Failure to do so will result in a formula error:

	A	B	C	D	E	F
1	DEPARTMENT	FIRST QUARTER EXPENSES	WITHIN BUDGET?			BUDGET AMOUNT
2	Sales	£ 4 520.00	=if(B2<=F2,"Within Budget"			£ 4 000.00
3	Customer service	£ 3 576.00	IF(logical_test, [value_if_true], [value_if_false])			

9. The third part of the formula is to enter what will happen if the condition is **not met** (false). Before we type this formula, we need to place a comma after the words "**Within Budget**" to separate the second and third part of the formula. After the comma, we will type "**Over Budget**" and end with) to indicate that the formula is complete.

10. Press *Enter* on the keyboard to place the formula into the cell and preview the result.

11. If we use **AutoFill** to drag (copy) the formula to cells C3:C7, we will notice that all the cells reflect "**Over Budget**". This is *incorrect*. We need to make cell F2 *absolute* (it has to be fixed so that cells C3:C7 use the same formula as in C2). Refer to the section (*Understanding relative versus absolute*) on absolute cell references if you are stuck, but the easiest way is to double-click on cell C3 and investigate why the formula is not working correctly, and then go back to C2 and edit the formula.

12. Edit the formula in cell C2 so that when copying the formula to cells C3:C7, the correct absolute cell reference will be used.

13. Double-click on cell **C2** to edit the formula.

14. Highlight (select) the F2 cell reference. Press the *F4* function key on the keyboard to make cell F2 absolute.

15. Press *Enter* on the keyboard to update the formula. **AutoFill** cell C2 to cells C3:C7. The formula is working!

Let's look at a more complicated IF function, as follows:

1. Open the `SafestSolutions.xlsx` workbook.
2. Type an = sign in cell D5 (the answer cell) to start the formula.
3. Type the function you wish to use—in this case, the IF function.
4. Type a bracket to start formulating your arguments. Remember the IF function has three parts to it: **=IF(logical_test,value_if_true,value_if_false***)*.

5. We will structure our formula according to the information given. In this example, we are working out the bonus amount each salesperson should receive if their **Sales Made** figure is greater than their **Predicted Sales** figure. If their **Sales Made** figure is greater, then they will receive £500 plus 7% of the difference between **Predicted Sales** and **Sales Made**. If the salesperson's **Sales Made** figure is not higher than the **Predicted Sales** figure, they will receive only **£500**. Ask yourself the following questions:

Question	Answer
What are we testing?	If the Sales Made is bigger than the Predicted Sales
What must we do if the test is correct?	We must give the sales person £500 plus 7% of the difference between the Sales Made and the Predicted Sales
What must we do if the Sales Made is smaller than the Predicted Sales?	The sales person will only receive £500

6. Therefore, the formula will look like this (please note the following formula is expanded for viewing ... you do not put spaces in between formula arguments!):

```
=IF(C5>B5,500+(C5-B5)*7%,500)

=IF(logical_test,value_if_true,value_if_false)
```

7. Finish the formula to read as follows: **=IF(C5>B5,500+(C5-B5)*7%,500)**, as illustrated in the following screenshot:

	A	B	C	D	E
1					
2		BONUS CALCULATIONS SAFEST SOLUTIONS GROUP			
3					
4	Salesperson	Predicted Sales	Sales Made	Bonus	
5	James	55000	72000	=IF(C5>B5,500+(C5-B5)*7%,500)	
6	Sune	29000	21000	IF(logical_test, [value_if_true], [value_if_false])	
7	Emerentia	17000	22500	885	
8	Duayne	100000	150000	4000	
9					

8. Close the bracket to end your formula, and press *Enter*.
9. Use your **AutoFill** handle to drag the formula to the rest of your cells.

Take time to experiment with the following comparison operators to compare two values and produce the logical value of true or false—the IF function is a very powerful function! Have a look at the following table:

Operator	Meaning
=	equal to
<	less than
>	greater than
>=	greater than or equal to
NOT =>	not greater than or equal to
<=	less than or equal to
<>	not equal to
(OR (...)	where 1 or up to 30 conditions can be met
(AND (...)	where 1 to 30 conditions must be met

Here is an example of comparison operators used in a function:
=if(AND(A23>=100,A23<110),"True","False")).

Text values can also be used with the IF function. We will use the same example as previously, but adapt it slightly...If our **Sales Made** figure is greater than or equal to a certain amount, we will display the words **Bonus 25%** in the cell; otherwise, the bonus will only be **4%**.

Our logical test would be?	If Sales Made is greater than or equal to 69000
If it is true, what must we do?	Display the text - Bonus 25%
If it is false, what must we do?	Display the text - Bonus 4%

So ... enter the following into cell D5, then press *Enter* and **AutoFill** the results down the column: **=if(C5>=69000,"Bonus 25%","Bonus 4%")**.

The AND function

The AND function returns true in the cell if all conditions are met. It is a *logical* function and is used to involve more than one condition. Let's try a simple example before we look at more complicated arguments. Have a look at the following screenshot:

11		Test 1	Test 2	Result
12	Student 1	58	79	
13	Student 2	89	55	
14	Student 3	65	88	
15	Student 4	43	65	

We will work on the AND-Function.xlsx workbook for this example.

1. Make sure you are on the second sheet, then click in cell D12 to enter the AND function. We will use the AND function to return **TRUE** in cell D12 if the first test result is greater than or equal to 48 and the second test result is greater than or equal to 85; else, it will return **FALSE**.

2. Type **=AND(B12>=48,C12>=85)** into cell D12, then press *Enter* to see the results, which are shown in the following screenshot:

11		Test 1	Test 2	Result
12	Student 1	58	79	FALSE
13	Student 2	89	55	FALSE
14	Student 3	65	88	TRUE
15	Student 4	43	65	FALSE

You will see from the following examples that they are much more complicated in terms of the number of arguments that need to be met. Try out both of the following examples. The criteria for each part of the formula is listed to the right of the subject mark. The examples are located on the first sheet of the workbook, for reference. Have a look at the following screenshot:

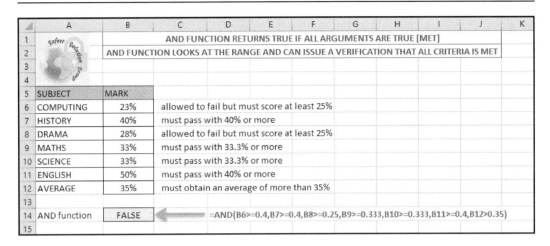

The following example displays **TRUE** when it is satisfied that all of the arguments in the AND formula are met:

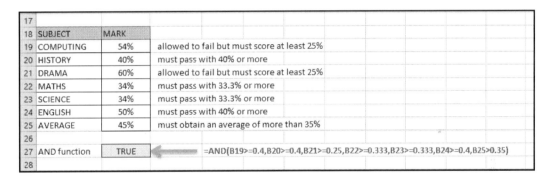

The OR function

The OR function returns **TRUE** if any argument is true and returns **FALSE** if all the arguments are false. In the following example, the student must pass at least one subject and with at least 60%. We will use the OR function to work this out, as follows:

1. We have the OR-Function.xlsx workbook open for this example.
2. Click on cell C8 and enter the following formula: **=OR(B8>=0.6,B9>=0.6,B10>=0.6)**.
3. Press *Enter* to see the formula result.
4. Try the OR function on the second set of results—this time, the arguments return **TRUE**.

Using text functions

Text functions in Excel are very useful when working with a lot of text data on a worksheet. You can access a huge range of text functions to extract, trim, or combine parts of a text string in Excel. We will investigate a few of these in the following topics.

The CONCAT function

This is a wonderful new function in Excel that replaced the CONCATENATE function in Excel 2016. It combines the contents of separate cells together into one cell. For instance, you have a list in Excel where first names are in column A and the surnames are in column B. You would like to combine these two into one cell, separating them with a space or possibly putting the surname first, separated by a comma, then the first name of the person. You can join up to 255 strings/texts together using CONCAT.

The CONCAT function allows you to join several text strings into one! Open the CONCAT.xlsx file and proceed as follows:

1. We will use the CONCAT function to *combine* the first names in column B with the surnames in column C.
2. The result will be collected in cell L5. Click into cell L5. Type **=CONCAT(B5,C5)**.
3. Press *Enter* to view the result. Note that the name and surname have combined into cell L5, but we need to use a *separator* to create distance between the two words.
4. Let's edit the formula. Double-click on cell L5. We will add a space in between the arguments referring to cells B5 and C5. The space would need to be enclosed by inverted commas, as you have learned previously. The new formula will read **=CONCAT(B5," ",C5)**, as illustrated in the following screenshot:

AND	▼	⋮	✕	✓	*fx*	=CONCAT(B5," ",C5)		

⩘	B	C	H	I	J	K	L	M
1								
2								
3								
4	FIRST	SURNAME	HRS	HOURLY RATE	GROSS PAY			
5	Barry	Bally	40	21.5	860		Barry Bally	=CONCAT(B5," ",C5)
6	Bob	Ambrose	35.5	12.5	443.75		Bob Ambrose	
7	Cheryl	Halal	35.5	13.3	472.15		Cheryl Halal	
8	Chris	Hume	40	7.22	288.8		Chris Hume	

5. Press *Enter* to view the new result. Copy the formula down using **AutoFill** so that all the names and surnames are combined with a space in between.

The TRIM function

The TRIM function removes unwanted spaces in a cell. It falls under the string/text category. This is very useful when you have imported data from another source and spaces exist at the end, middle, or beginning of data in a cell. To use this function, we will proceed as follows:

1. We will use the CONCAT.xlsx workbook for this example. The list of names and surnames on the sheet were imported from another source and have trailing spaces—actually, three spaces—at the start of the first name and at the end of the surname. We need to remove these spaces from the data.
2. Click on the TRIM worksheet. Select cell E3. Type the formula **=trim(B3)**. Press *Enter* to see the result.
3. The spaces are removed from the text in cell E3.
4. Let's do the surname. Click into cell F3 and type the formula **=trim(C3)**. Press *Enter* to see the result.
5. Use **Autofill** to copy the formula to cells E4:E7 and F4:F7, respectively.

Investigating formula errors

A few examples of the types of formula errors that could occur in Excel are shown next. For a more comprehensive list, please consult the **Help** facility within the Excel program. You can search for help by pressing the *F1* key on the keyboard, which will open the **Help** pane to the right of the workbook. In this pane, search for formula error, where you will find a huge range of categories with some very useful troubleshooting tips, as illustrated in the following screenshot:

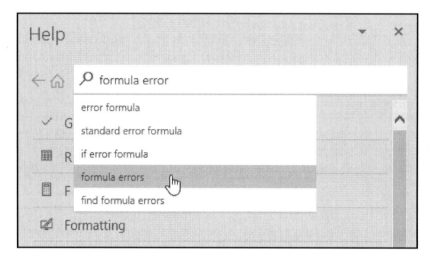

When entering a formula into a cell, various error messages display if there is something wrong. The calculations are therefore not able to work. Error messages normally always begin with #. Here are a few examples:

- Do not divide by 0. The #DIV/0 error will appear in the cell if you try to divide by 0.
- Enter values without formatting. For instance, do not enter the currency sign before a value in a cell, as the cell will be identified as text and not as a value. Apply formatting after the value is entered into the cell. This is a cosmetic change to the value in the cell.

- Enter the correct type of arguments. If you are working with a text function, then be sure to use `text` as the cell argument.
- Enter all arguments required for the function. The formula will not be complete if you do not do so.
- Use a colon to indicate a range—for example, **=sum(A4:E7)**.
- Use a parenthesis at both ends of the formula and make sure you have the correct number of brackets depending on the number of functions you use in a formula.
- Start every formula with an = sign.
- #### displayed in the cell means that the cell is not wide enough to display the result of the formula.
- **#ref!** indicates that an invalid cell reference is included in the formula.
- **#VALUE!** means an incorrect operator or text is included in the formula.
- **#NAME?** means a non-existing name range is included in the formula.
- **#NULL!** means a space is incorrectly included in the formula to separate cell references.
- **#NUM!** refers to a number incorrectly used in the formula.
- **#n/a** means that the value is not available.

When a formula refers back to its own cell, it creates a *circular reference*. You can tell if a workbook contains *circular references* in many different ways, illustrated here:

- By consulting the status bar, you will see the **Circular References** tab, along with the problem cell, as illustrated in the following screenshot:

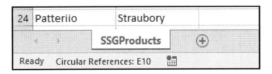

- This provides a notification to the user via a dialog box on opening the workbook, as illustrated in the following screenshot:

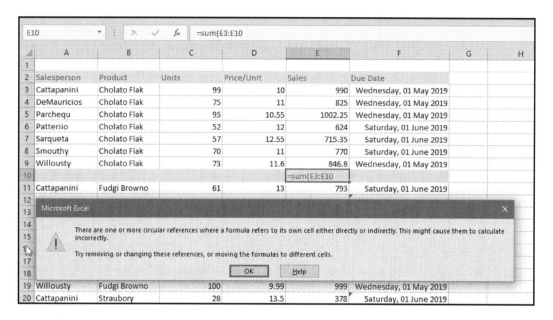

- When you press *Enter* to accept an incorrect formula, an error will appear at the top-left corner of the cell, then the **Error Checking** icon will appear to guide you to fix the error, as illustrated in the following screenshot:

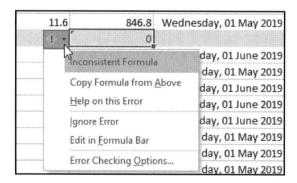

- You can visit the **Error Checking** icon in the **Formula Auditing** group, located on the **Formulas** tab. From the drop-down list, select **Circular References**. Here, you will see the location of the problem cell, or use the **Error Checking** icon to get some help. You can see the **Error Checking** and the **Circular References** icons in the following screenshot:

We will see a circular reference error next. We will use the `SSGProductSales.xlsx` workbook for this example.

A *circular reference* appears when the formula entered refers back to the source cell. The formula includes the cell in which the answer should appear. To correct this error, change the formula to reflect the correct cell references, as follows:

1. Double-click on cell **E10** on the `SSGProducts` worksheet.
2. With the formula now visible, look at the cell references to understand that the cell range is incorrect and refers back (includes) to the answer cell E10, which is incorrect. Alter the formula to read **=SUM(E3:E9)**, then press *Enter*.
3. The formula errors are removed from the workbook.

Note that, unfortunately, Excel **Help** will not be able to fix the error for you in this instance, and only human interaction will do the trick!

Applying named ranges in a formula

Named ranges are a great feature in Excel, allowing the user to refer to a cell name instead of a cell reference when constructing a formula, or to use a named set of cells to which you can navigate on the worksheet or workbook quickly. Let's investigate this feature.

Defining a named range

If you refer to a certain block of cells on a worksheet repeatedly, it may be necessary to name the cells so that you can move to that particular range with ease. Use name ranges when constructing formulas as well. For instance, if you need to check up on a certain range of cells or one cell regularly, such as budget figures, you could name the cell budget and use the Name Box to move to that cell quickly. In addition, when using cell references in a formula it can get complicated, and it would be much easier if you used the cell name instead. Don't you think that this makes more sense?

Have a look at the following:

=sum(A34:D56) OR *=sum(salesprofit)*

Please note that when naming a range, the following is **not accepted**:

- Using cell references as the range name
- Using the letters C, c, R, or r as a name range
- Using spaces

What is accepted? Have a look at the following list to find out:

- An underscore (_), backslash (\), or letter as the first character of a range name. The rest of the range name can contain full stops, letters, numbers, and underscore characters.
- Name ranges can be up to 255 characters in length.
- Uppercase and lowercase letters are allowed—Excel does not distinguish between them.

Naming a range of cells

1. Open the RangeNames.xlsx workbook.
2. Select the cells you wish to enter as a name range on the worksheet. For this example, we will name the Product and the Sales column data. Firstly, we will name the products.
3. Select cells B3:B44.
4. Click in the Name Box area, as illustrated in the following screenshot:

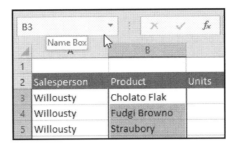

5. Type a name for the selected range into the Name Box area. For this example, we will use the name **PRODUCTS**.

6. Press *Enter* on your keyboard to confirm the range name. Alternatively, select the cells you wish to enter as a range name on the worksheet.

7. Select the **Formulas** tab, then locate the **Define Name** icon from the **Defined Names** group, as illustrated in the following screenshot:

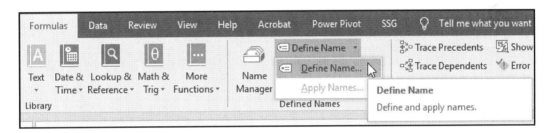

8. Click to select **Define Name...**.

9. In the **New Name** dialog box, enter a name for the selected range in the text area provided, or use the default name given, as illustrated in the following screenshot:

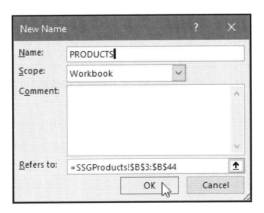

10. Click on **OK** when complete. Click on another cell far away from the range of cells you were just working with.
11. To move to this name range quickly and to highlight the selected cells, click on the drop-down arrow in the Name Box area, and then select **PRODUCTS**. The range highlights automatically on the worksheet.
12. Repeat the steps to name the **SALES** range of cells.

Editing a named range

1. Using the same workbook from the preceding example, we will edit the name range.
2. On the **Formulas** tab, locate the **Define Names** group. Click to select **Name Manager**.
3. Click to select the **PRODUCT** name to edit in the dialog box provided, as illustrated in the following screenshot:

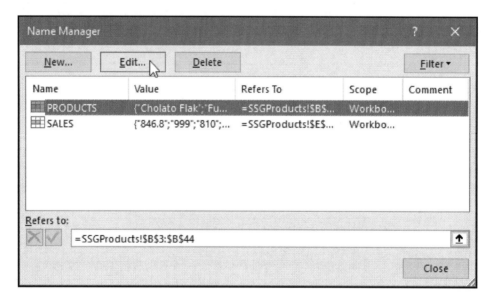

4. Click on the **Edit...** button.

5. When the **Edit Name** dialog box appears, edit the name of the range or location to which it refers.

6. Click in the **Refers to** placeholder at the end of the name range formula, after which you can move to the worksheet to correct the range or add to the range.

7. You can select cells directly from the worksheet, then return to the **Edit Name** dialog box, as illustrated in the following screenshot:

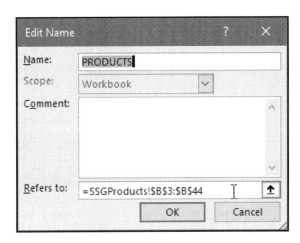

8. Click on **OK** to confirm. Click on **Close** to exit the **Name Manager** dialog box.

Creating a named range from selected cells

1. Continuing from the preceding example, highlight a range of cells that have headings to the top and left. Include the headings in your selection. We will select the range A2:F20.

2. On the **Formulas** tab, locate the **Define Names** group, and then click on **Create from Selection**, as illustrated in the following screenshot:

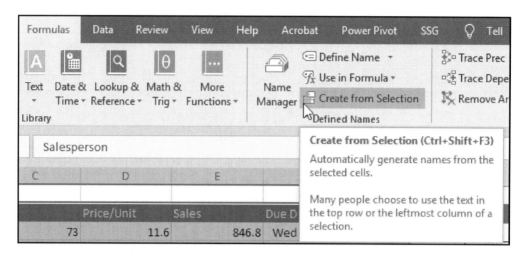

3. Excel automatically assesses the data and indicates how it will generate range names for the selected range. In this case, it has selected **Top row** and **Left column**. Remove the tick from **Left column** in the box shown in the following screenshot as we do not have headings in the first column on the worksheet and only want to include **Top row** for this example:

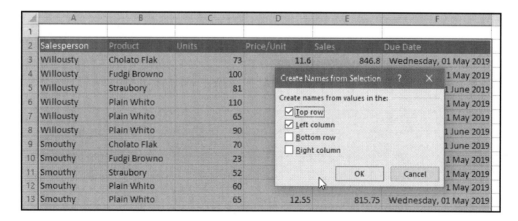

4. Click on **OK** to continue.

5. To see a list of existing or newly created range names in the worksheet, select the arrow on the Name Box to view the name ranges just created from the selected data, as illustrated in the following screenshot:

Using range names in a formula

When you use range names in a formula, the cell references insert as absolute references. This is great when you require a constant value. Let's see how we insert range names into a formula, and let's investigate the keyboard shortcut to insert a range name, as follows:

1. Open the `RangeName.xlsx` workbook.
2. We will be creating a formula to calculate the VAT amount on the total sales of each sales rep. The VAT % is entered into cell K6. In order to use this cell in the formula to work out the VAT amount, we would need to make the cell absolute (fixed) in the formula so that each item is multiplied by the VAT % in cell K6. We would not use the actual value in the formula but the cell reference—or, in this case, the range name, as the % VAT could change. This would mean that we would need to reconstruct the formula every time. Therefore, to save time, the best thing would be to name the range that contains the VAT %.
3. Make sure you click on cell K6.
4. Click in the Name Box area and type the word **VAT** to name the range K6.
5. Press *Enter* on the keyboard when done.
6. Alternatively, use one of the other methods mentioned previously to name the range.
7. Now that the cell has a name, we can use it in our formula. Before we do this, we will work out the total for each of the sales reps. Do this before moving on to the next step.
8. Click in cell K8 to construct the formula. Type the following: **=J8***.

9. Type the range name into the formula directly after the * sign (if you have forgotten the range name for cell K6, then press *F3* on your keyboard to obtain a list of all the name ranges for this workbook, then select **VAT** and press *Enter*), as illustrated in the following screenshot:

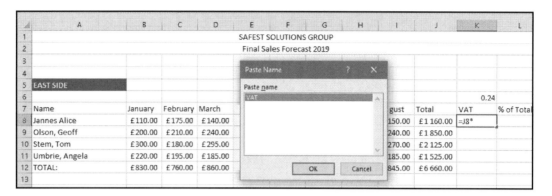

10. Press *Enter* to confirm the formula. **AutoFill** to cells K9:K11.

You now have the skills to work with range names in formulas, which will save you a huge amount of time and keep your formulas error-free when dealing with absolute references.

Summary

You now have theoretical knowledge about formula construction and should feel confident to perform basic calculations adhering to a basic order of operation. You are also able to construct and edit formulas and have mastered working out percentage change, increase, or decrease; use the **Function Library** to access more complex formulas from the formula composer; and finally, use relative and absolute cell references in formulas. During this chapter, you worked with dates in formulas; used mathematical, financial, and text functions; and finally, learned how to apply conditional logic in formulas. You should now be confident at locating and fixing formula errors and be able to apply named ranges for workbook navigation or within a formula.

Excel 2019 includes several features for sharing and collaborating on workbooks and worksheets. In the next chapter, we'll learn how to analyze and organize data with Excel.

10
Analyzing and Organizing Data

In this chapter, you will learn about the tools required to effectively analyze and organize data in Excel 2019. We will cover summarizing data using PivotTables and PivotCharts and you will learn how to access the Quick Analysis tools. We will also work with maps and the new **3D Maps** feature, use **Power Pivot** to effectively build and use relational data sources in an Excel workbook, consolidate workbook data by creating a summary sheet, build a relationship between datasets for easy reporting with Excel's data model, and take a look at macros.

The following topics are covered in this chapter:

- Consolidating data and investigating macros
- Creating and managing PivotTables and PivotCharts
- Working with the 3D Maps feature
- Using tools for analysis in Excel
- Understanding data models

Technical requirements

Before starting this chapter, you should have the adequate file management skills to be able to save workbooks and interact with the Excel 2019 environment comfortably. We assume that you are also able to construct a basic formula and manage worksheet data.

You should have explored charts and formatted data into tables in worksheets before and should be familiar with the Excel Options dialog box and the **Quick Access Toolbar (QAT)**. The examples used in this chapter can be accessed from `https://github.com/PacktPublishing/Learn-Microsoft-Office-2019`.

Consolidating data and investigating macros

In this section, you will learn how to build a summary sheet to consolidate workbook data and become an expert at creating macros to perform common tasks in workbooks. You will also master how to create macros and make them globally accessible within Excel, as well as how to display macros on the QAT or as a new tab on the Excel ribbon. Finally, you will learn how to remove macros from a personal macro workbook.

Creating a summary sheet

If you are a business analyst, you receive worksheets that calculate the same data each month, such as product sales for different areas and/or parts of the company. Once you receive these worksheets, you need to combine (consolidate) them by collecting data from various workbooks, creating a summary table in one workbook to perform analysis on the data.

Another example is consolidating budgets from different departments into the entire company budget. We can use PivotTables to achieve this, but the **Consolidate** feature allows us to automatically ensure that all the changes made to all of the worksheets show up in a consolidated worksheet. Let's work through the following steps to set up a summary sheet:

1. Open the workbook that contains the data you wish to consolidate. For this example, we will use the `SafestSolutionsSales.xlsx` workbook. This workbook contains four sheets—NORTH, SOUTH, EAST, and CONSOLIDATE—the data is constructed in all four sheets with identical formatting applied, including the same data labels (column headings). This is crucial for the consolidation to correctly compute. Note that all the data does not need to be in the same workbook, as you can browse for separate workbooks when consolidating.

2. Click on a cell in the worksheet you want the consolidation to be placed in. For this example, we will use the CONSOLIDATE worksheet. It is important to note that the data in all the worksheets is organized in a consistent manner. Data can be arranged in a different order but it would need to contain the same labels (column headings) in each worksheet. Notice that the sales reps' names in the NORTH and SOUTH worksheets are different, as well as a number of sales reps and the values.

3. Click on the CONSOLIDATE worksheet. For this example, we will place the consolidation in cell A4.

4. Click on the **Data** tab, then locate the **Data Tools** group. Select the **Consolidate** icon:

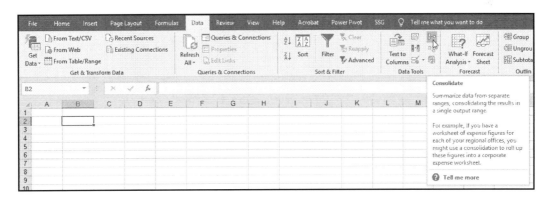

5. The **Consolidate** dialog box pops up. It is always a good idea to name the range you wish to consolidate in each of the workbooks, especially if you add new data to your source workbooks, as the data is included automatically.

6. Choose how you would like to aggregate the data by choosing an item from the drop-down list in the **Consolidate** dialog box. We will use **SUM** for this example as we want to find out the total sales for all the sales reps.

7. Click on the **Reference** placeholder, then navigate to the first worksheet (NORTH) to collect the range, A6:I10, then click on the **ADD** icon. Place the mouse pointer back on the **Reference** placeholder, then navigate to the second worksheet (SOUTH) to collect the range, A6:I11, then click on the **ADD** icon. Although the range is automatically assumed by Excel, there could be more data on other worksheets to collect. Be sure to check this before adding and moving on to the next range. Do the same again for the third worksheet, called EAST:

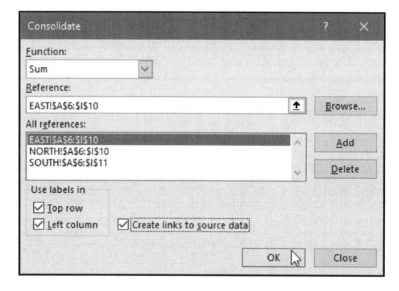

8. The final step is to choose whether you would like to use the labels in the top row and/or the left column to consolidate the data and whether to create links to the source data. Creating links to the source data allows data to be updated automatically (that is, refreshed to the consolidation sheet when any editing takes place in the source data). Select all three options for this example.

9. Click on the **OK** button to view the results on the CONSOLIDATE worksheet:

	A	C	D	E	F	G	H	I	J	K
1				SAFEST SOLUTIONS GROUP						
2				Final Sales Forecast 2019						
3										
4		January	February	March	April	May	June	July	August	
7	Jannes Alice	344	406	280	811	681	371	354	894	
10	Olson, Geoff	755	431	814	894	481	761	473	573	
13	Stem, Tom	411	692	517	402	883	588	1106	715	
16	Umbrie, Angela	261	410	499	596	870	370	602	417	
18	Kohn, Chris	306	195	203	145	140	160	140	150	
20	Hall Oakes	219	147	137	240	240	240	240	240	
22	Spider, Sonja	104	230	185	260	295	230	295	270	
24	Abso, Delicious	125	100	206	185	170	175	180	185	
26	Wilson, Balalue	320	255	235	240	245	250	255	260	
27										
28										

10. You will see expand icons to the left of the consolidated data. This allows you to see more detail about a particular sales rep or month. Format the consolidated data as you wish and add any further calculations, such as the sum of all sales reps by month and individual reps' sales to date. As you have created links to the source data, you will be able to edit the data in the source worksheets and see the change immediately in the consolidated data:

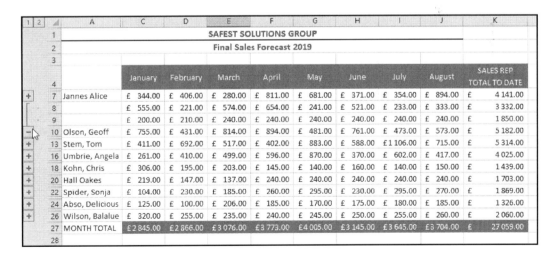

	A	C	D	E	F	G	H	I	J	K
1				SAFEST SOLUTIONS GROUP						
2				Final Sales Forecast 2019						
3										
4		January	February	March	April	May	June	July	August	SALES REP TOTAL TO DATE
7	Jannes Alice	£ 344.00	£ 406.00	£ 280.00	£ 811.00	£ 681.00	£ 371.00	£ 354.00	£ 894.00	£ 4 141.00
8		£ 555.00	£ 221.00	£ 574.00	£ 654.00	£ 241.00	£ 521.00	£ 233.00	£ 333.00	£ 3 332.00
9		£ 200.00	£ 210.00	£ 240.00	£ 240.00	£ 240.00	£ 240.00	£ 240.00	£ 240.00	£ 1 850.00
10	Olson, Geoff	£ 755.00	£ 431.00	£ 814.00	£ 894.00	£ 481.00	£ 761.00	£ 473.00	£ 573.00	£ 5 182.00
13	Stem, Tom	£ 411.00	£ 692.00	£ 517.00	£ 402.00	£ 883.00	£ 588.00	£1 106.00	£ 715.00	£ 5 314.00
16	Umbrie, Angela	£ 261.00	£ 410.00	£ 499.00	£ 596.00	£ 870.00	£ 370.00	£ 602.00	£ 417.00	£ 4 025.00
18	Kohn, Chris	£ 306.00	£ 195.00	£ 203.00	£ 145.00	£ 140.00	£ 160.00	£ 140.00	£ 150.00	£ 1 439.00
20	Hall Oakes	£ 219.00	£ 147.00	£ 137.00	£ 240.00	£ 240.00	£ 240.00	£ 240.00	£ 240.00	£ 1 703.00
22	Spider, Sonja	£ 104.00	£ 230.00	£ 185.00	£ 260.00	£ 295.00	£ 230.00	£ 295.00	£ 270.00	£ 1 869.00
24	Abso, Delicious	£ 125.00	£ 100.00	£ 206.00	£ 185.00	£ 170.00	£ 175.00	£ 180.00	£ 185.00	£ 1 326.00
26	Wilson, Balalue	£ 320.00	£ 255.00	£ 235.00	£ 240.00	£ 245.00	£ 250.00	£ 255.00	£ 260.00	£ 2 060.00
27	MONTH TOTAL	£2 845.00	£2 866.00	£3 076.00	£3 773.00	£4 005.00	£3 145.00	£3 645.00	£3 704.00	£ 27 059.00
28										

Now that you have learned how to create a consolidated workbook, we will look at how to create a macro to perform multiple steps in a workbook automatically.

Creating a macro

A macro is a recording of a series of steps that are performed regularly. You can compare this to a recorded voice that is played back over and over when required. An example of a simple macro is to record the steps to create a header and footer in a certain format for all your worksheets. A macro should be used to save the user time by automating a process.

Macros are usually assigned to buttons or icons and reside under the Excel ribbon. This way, they can be used with the click of a button to make changes to an existing worksheet. When recording macros, mouse actions and keystrokes are not recorded. So, any errors made when recording, such as fixing a typing mistake, will not show up in the macro when playing it back—only the corrected entry will.

As with any other actions on the Excel interface, there are multiple ways to perform tasks within the environment. Therefore, there is more than one method to record macros:

- The first method is to click on the macro indicator icon located on the leftmost side of the status bar:

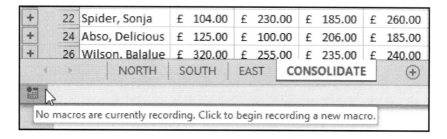

- The second method is via the **View** | **Macros** icon:

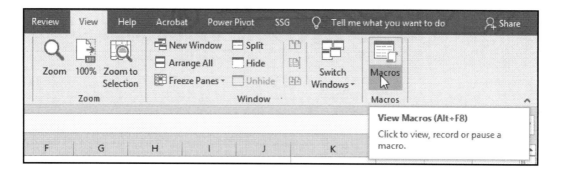

- The third method is via the **Macros** icon on the leftmost side of the **Developer** tab (note that this is only visible if you have added the **Developer** tab to the ribbon):

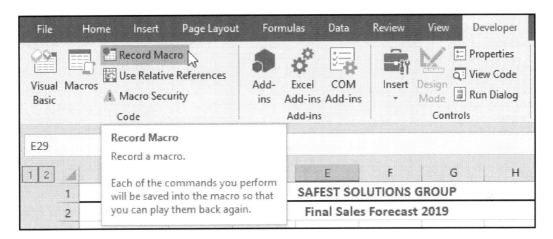

Macros are stored in the current workbook, a new workbook, or in the global personal macro workbook named `personal.xlsb` that is stored in a folder called `XLSTART` on your computer. The personal macro workbook opens up in the background every time you open Microsoft Excel. When macros are stored in the personal macro workbook, they can be run on any open workbook.

It is very important to plan the steps of the macro, as recording unnecessary steps could lead to having to use the undo key or typographic errors in the document. You only want to record what is required. Without taking this planning step, you will find that recording your macro takes longer than necessary.

We will record a macro to set the worksheet to **Landscape**, create a custom header with the date on the left and the filename on the right, insert a custom footer with the page number and the number of pages in the center, and center the data horizontally and vertically on the page:

1. Open up the workbook from the previous example to record the macro in.

2. Go to **View** | **Macros** | **Record Macro...** to start recording:

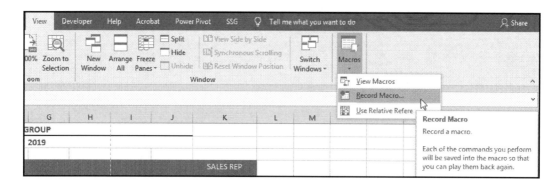

3. The **Record Macro...** dialog box appears, where you can enter a name for the macro. For this example, we will use `PrintSettings` as the macro name. You can also enter a shortcut key to run the macro after creating it.

4. Choose to store the macro in this workbook, to the personal macro workbook, or to a new workbook. For this example, we will store the macro in the personal macro workbook.

5. It is always important to enter a description of what the macro will do so that other users are aware of how it changes the workbook data before using it:

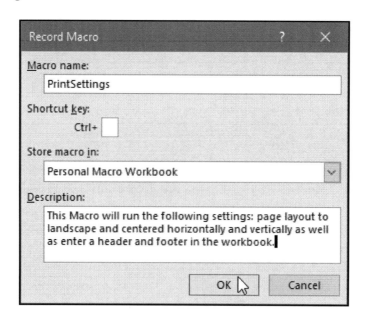

6. Click on **OK** to start recording.

7. Perform the previous steps, just as if you are working on the current workbook.

8. Notice that the **Ready** indicator on the status bar changes to recording mode. To stop the recording, either click on the stop recording icon alongside the **Ready** indicator on the status bar, go to **View | Macros | Stop Recording,** or use the **Stop Recording** icon under the **Developer** tab:

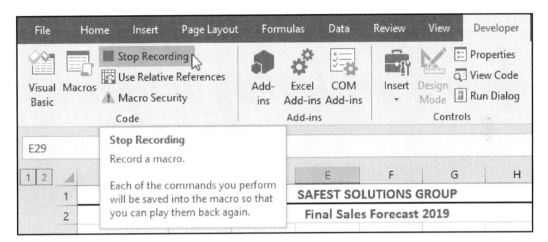

9. Close the workbook without saving it as we only used the workbook to create the macro and have not added any extra important information.

10. Open the workbook you just closed, then go to **File | Print** to get to the print preview pane. Notice that the workbook is set to **Portrait** with no header or footer. Go to **View | Macros** to see a list of the macros available.

11. Click to select the `PrintSettings` macro, then click **Run**:

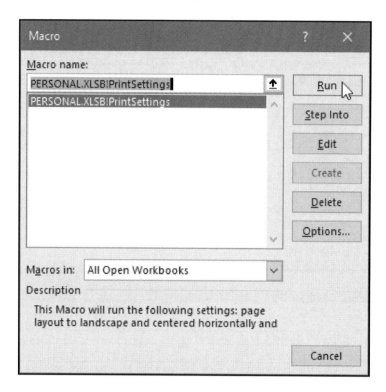

12. The macro is immediately applied to the workbook. It happens so quickly behind the scenes that you will not even notice all the changes made in a split second. Return to the print preview pane to see the changes made to the workbook by running the macro.

13. Save the workbook to keep the print settings applied to the workbook.

Adding a macro to the ribbon for easy access

The *Alt + F8* keyboard shortcut opens the **Macro** dialog box, where you can select from the list of macros to run on an Excel workbook. If you have a few macros that perform calculations on workbooks daily, weekly, or monthly, you may want to add these to a **Macro** tab on the Excel ribbon or to the QAT. Take the following steps to add the macro to either the QAT or the ribbon.

Adding a macro to the QAT

1. Click on the **Customize the Quick Access Toolbar** arrow at the end of the QAT.
2. Select **More Commands...** from the drop-down list:

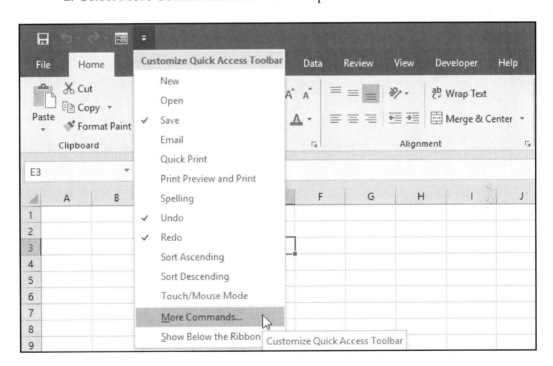

3. In the Excel options dialog box, click on the drop-down list to the right of **Popular Commands**.

4. Locate the `PrintSettings` macro from the list provided on the left, then click on **Add>>** to place the macro on the QAT:

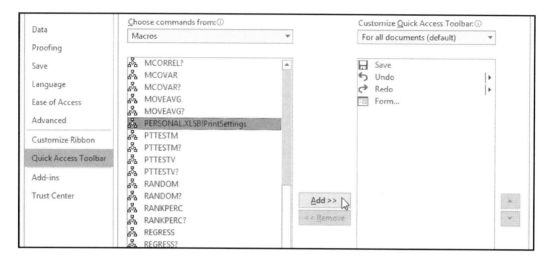

5. Click on **Modify...** at the bottom of the dialog box to edit the macro.

6. Change the macro's name and the icon so that it is easier to identify on the QAT. For this example, we will use the printer icon and a `PRINT MACRO` name:

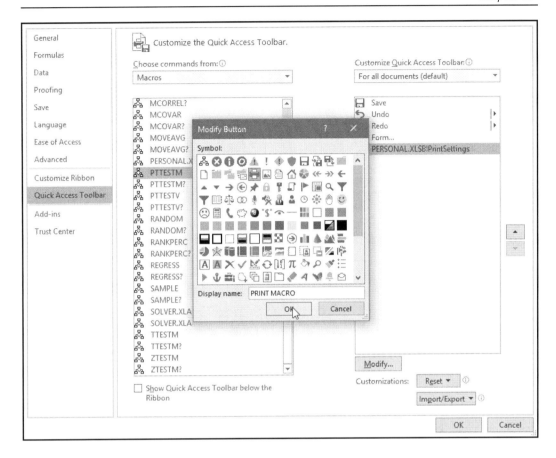

7. Click on **OK** to add the icon to the QAT:

We have learned how to add a recorded macro to the QAT for easy access. Now, we will go through the steps to create a new tab and then add the macro to the ribbon.

Adding the macro to the ribbon tab

Tabs and groups in Excel are full of exciting icons to format and manipulate features within workbooks. We will learn how to create a new tab called **Macros**, then add any recorded macros to this new tab.

You can create your own tabs and groups on the Excel 2019 interface. You may want to create a tab with groups of icons that are relevant to your business or specific calculations, or for formatting specific features—in this case, we are creating a new tab to house our macros. Existing tabs and groups cannot be edited and appear grayed out while working in the customize menu:

1. Go to **File | Options**.
2. Choose **Customize Ribbon** from the leftmost side of the tab.
3. Under the **Choose commands from:** heading, select **Macros** to see a list of the macros used in Excel. On the right, under the **Customize the Ribbon:** heading, select **All Tabs** from the drop-down list—this displays a list of all the default tabs that are already on the ribbon.
4. To add a new tab after the **View** tab on the ribbon, click on **View**.
5. Click on the **New Tab** icon and the new tab displays on the ribbon.
6. Click on the **Rename...** icon to give the tab a name. I used `Macros` as the new tab name.
7. Click on the **New Group (Custom)** text, located underneath **Macros**.
8. Click to select **Rename...**.
9. Give the group a name and choose a display icon (for this example, we used `Print` for the group name and a printer icon).
10. Now, all we need to do is add the icons we want to see on the **Print** group of **Macros**.
11. Click on the **Print** group to add commands.
12. To the left of the dialog box, select the macro called **Print Settings** to add to the **Print** group. Click **Add>>** to include the command to the **Print** group.
13. Click on **Rename...** to change the macro's name and icon, if applicable. We will call our macro `Print Settings` and add a printer as the icon:

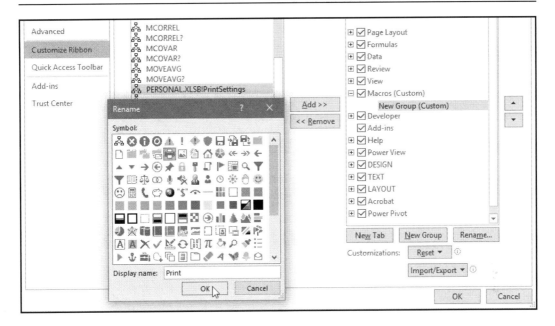

14. Click on **OK** to confirm your choices, then **OK** again to exit the Excel options dialog box.
15. Click on the **Macros** tab on the ribbon to make sure the commands update on the group. If, at any time, you need to remove a tab or group, simply click on the item on the **Customize the Ribbon** dialog and click on **<<Remove**.

The **Macros** tab is visible in the group and the **Print Settings** macro is assigned:

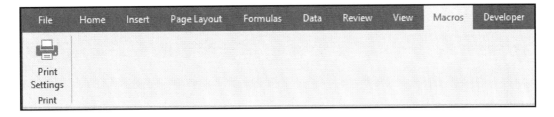

Removing a macro from the personal macro workbook

When storing macros in the personal macro workbook, you need to unhide the workbook in order to remove a macro:

1. Go to **View | Unhide** from the **Window** group.

2. In the **Unhide** dialog box, make sure that the PERSONAL.XLSB workbook is selected, then click on **OK**. The personal macro workbook will open:

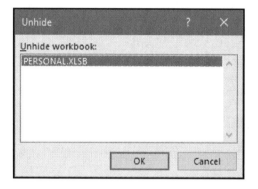

3. To remove the macro, click on **Developer | Macros**:

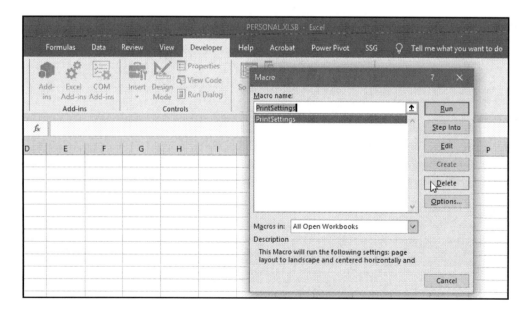

4. Make sure **PrintSettings** is selected, then press the **Delete** button.
5. You will be asked to confirm the deletion of the macro via an information dialog box. Click **OK** to confirm.
6. Close the workbook and click on **Yes** if prompted to save.

In this section, you learned about consolidating data, as well as creating macros to perform workbook tasks. In the next section, we will learn how to work with PivotTables and PivotCharts to reorganize and summarize data.

Creating and managing PivotTables and PivotCharts

In this section, you will learn how to create a PivotTable using cell data and how to modify it using the field options and selections, as well as how to organize, summarize, and report data. In addition, we will create slicers and timelines and learn how to group PivotTable data. PivotCharts are also covered in this section as they are used to create graphical representations of PivotTables.

Creating a PivotTable

When creating a PivotTable, the data used to create the table remains as it is in the workbook—unchanged. A separate table is produced after creation where the data is manipulated to make it more understandable to the reader. There are a few things you should know before creating a PivotTable to get the workbook data ready to get the most out of PivotTable reports.

The first point is that data needs to be organized vertically and contain column headings. The second point is to ensure that no blank rows are present in the data and that there are no additional descriptive notes or text in any of the cells or any additional formula to the side or underneath the data. Another recommendation is that you format the data as a table before creating the table. The only reason for this is that any new data rows added to the table are included automatically in the range, adding them to the dataset.

Let's get our data ready and create the PivotTable:

1. Open the `ChoklatoFlakSales.xlsx` workbook.

2. On the first sheet, `SSGProducts`, you will see data relating to product sales itemized by `Salesperson`. Before we create a PivotTable from this data, we will format the data as a table.

3. Click on the data on the worksheet, then go to **Home** | **Format as a Table** from the **Styles** group.

4. Select a table style from the list provided.

5. The **Format as a Table** dialog box pops up, asking you to confirm the range that was automatically selected. Although this is normally accurate, check the range to be sure that all the data is included in the selection. Ensure that you select the **My table has headers** option, too:

6. Click on the **OK** button to format the selection as a table.

7. To create the PivotTable, go to **Insert** | **PivotTable**:

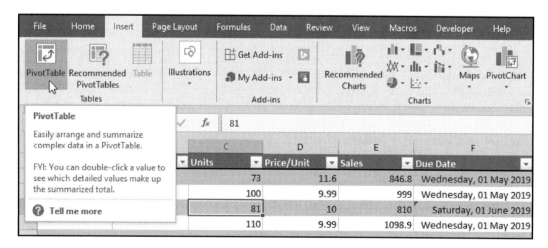

8. The **Create PivotTable** dialog box pops up, where you can specify the data range and where you would like to place the PivotTable in the workbook. Excel automatically assumes you are using the table and refers to it in the **Select a table or range** option at the top of the dialog box. Note that you can also use an external connection.

9. We will choose to place the PivotTable in the existing worksheet for this example and then define which cell to use as the location for the PivotTable. For this example, we will use cell H2:

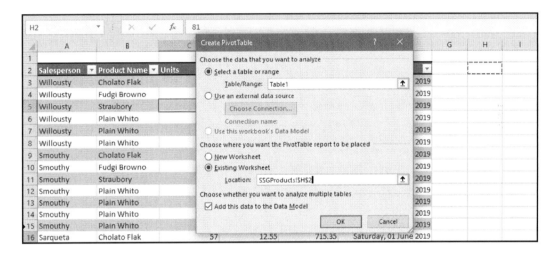

10. The last step is to decide whether to add this data to the data model so that you can analyze more than one table. We will add it to the data model for this example.

11. Click on **OK** to confirm.

12. Let's continue on to the next section by adding fields to build our PivotTable.

Adding PivotTable fields

In the previous section, you followed the steps to create a PivotTable from the worksheet data. Now, we will learn how to construct our PivotTable report by adding fields from the worksheet columns:

1. The blank PivotTable can be seen in cell H2 and to the right, you can find the **PivotTable Fields** pane. This is where you add and customize field placements to produce a report:

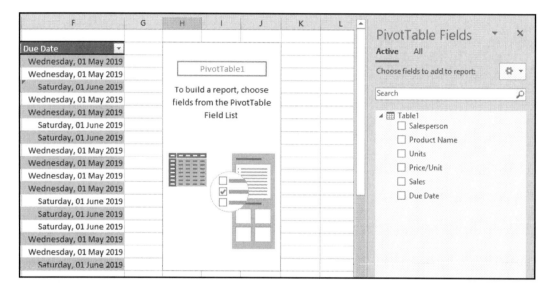

2. If you click on the tool icon to the right of the **Choose fields to add to report** text, you will see various options to change the layout of the **PivotTable Fields** pane. Let's change the view layout to **Fields Section** and **Areas Section Side-by-Side**.

3. Drag the field names from the left into the areas you require on the right. For this example, `Due Date` will serve as the filter, `Product Name` will move to **Rows**, `Salesperson` will move to **Columns**, and `Sales` will move to **Values**. Experiment with your table fields to see how you would like to present the data in the PivotTable by simply dragging and dropping fields into the relevant areas:

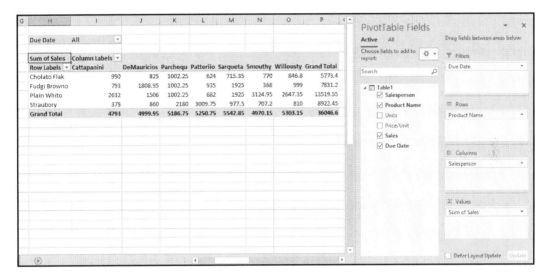

4. Drag `Due Date` from **Filters** to **Rows** to see the change apply to the PivotTable.

5. Now, remove the `Due Date` filter by dragging it off the **Filters** area to the **Table** area. Then, drag `Salesperson` from the **Table** area to the **Filters** area.

6. We can now filter by `Salesperson`. Click on the dropdown next to **All** at the top of the PivotTable. This is where you can select certain items to filter your PivotTable data.

7. To select certain `Salesperson` fields only, click on the **Select Multiple Items** checkbox at the bottom of the list. Notice that there is now a checkbox next to each `Salesperson` field in the list.

8. Click to deselect a `Salesperson` field to remove it from the PivotTable. Click on **OK** to save the changes and update the PivotTable:

9. Notice that when clicking on the PivotTable report, the **PivotTable Tools** contextual menu appears on the title bar and consists of two tabs (**Analyze** and **Design**). We will look at some of these tools in the next section:

10. That's it—you have constructed your own PivotTable! If you change the source data and need the PivotTable to update, simply click on the worksheet data, then navigate to **Analyze** | **Refresh** from the **Data** group.

Grouping with PivotTables

In the previous section, we created a PivotTable. We will now look at analyzing data even further by making changes so that the dates in our PivotTable are grouped by quarter and are, therefore, easier to use:

1. Open the `SSGThemePark.xlsx` workbook. We have already created a PivotTable in this workbook. The `DATE of HIRE` field was added to the **Row** area but the report looks very clumsy and hard to decipher. Let's fix this by learning how to use the *group* feature in PivotTables.

2. In the PivotTable report, right-click on a date. Choose **Group...** from the shortcut list provided:

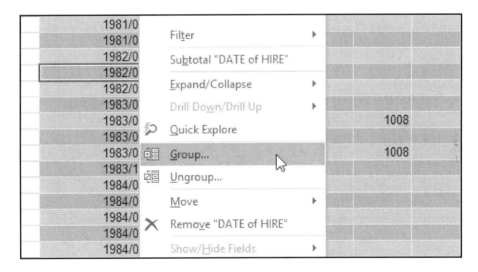

3. Click on the **Quarters** item to select it, then click on **Months** to remove it:

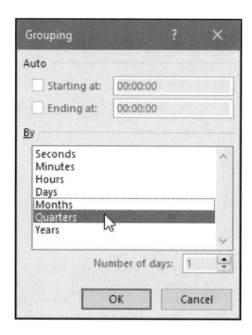

4. Click on **OK** at the bottom of the dialog box to apply the new grouping to the PivotTable:

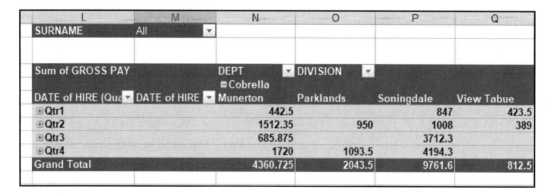

SURNAME	All				
Sum of GROSS PAY		DEPT	DIVISION		
		⊟ Cobrella			
DATE of HIRE (Qua	DATE of HIRE	Munerton	Parklands	Soningdale	View Tabue
⊞ Qtr1		442.5		847	423.5
⊞ Qtr2		1512.35	950	1008	389
⊞ Qtr3		685.875		3712.3	
⊞ Qtr4		1720	1093.5	4194.3	
Grand Total		4360.725	2043.5	9761.6	812.5

5. The report is updated and easier to read. To customize it further, you can add the Surname field to the rows so that you can expand or collapse the quarters according to Salesperson and Date.

Using slicers and timelines

Using slicers and timelines is an excellent way of filtering data in a PivotTable. The difference between filtering and using slicers is that slicers is more visually appealing and also allows you to quickly retrieve data:

1. Before we add slicers, let's reorganize our data fields. Use the following example to get the data ready for slicers. Use the same worksheet as in the previous example:

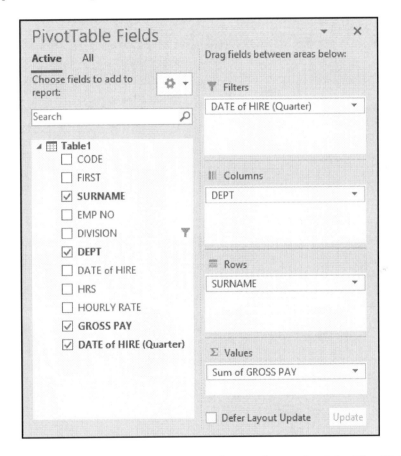

2. Click on the PivotTable, then go to the **Analyze** tab of the **PivotTable Tools** contextual menu.

3. Click on **Insert Slicer** under the **Filter** group:

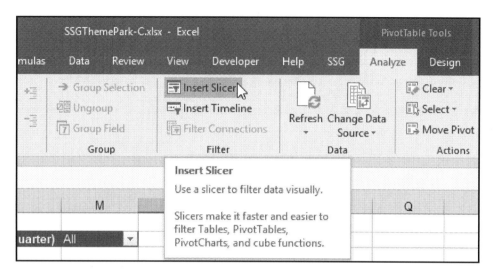

4. Select a field to use as the slicer. We will use DIVISION for this example. Click on **OK** to add the slicer.

5. The slicer is placed over the PivotTable and can be moved by dragging it to another location. Use the categories on the DIVISION slicer to filter the data in the PivotTable. The slicer has two icons at the top right. Click on the first icon to select multiple categories in the slicer or use the second icon to remove existing filters:

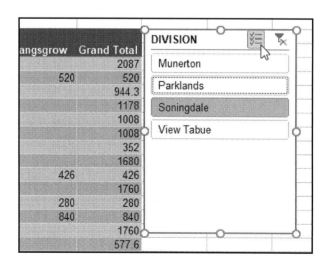

Now, we will look at the timeline feature:

1. We will first reorganize our data so that we create a focus on the **DATE of HIRE** field:

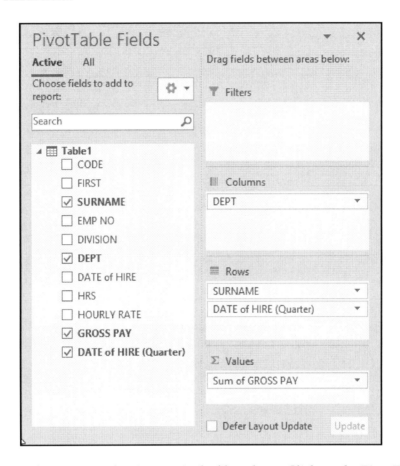

2. Timelines are used to interactively filter dates. Click on the PivotTable, then select **Insert Timelines** from the **Filter** group, located under the **Analyze** tab.

3. Select **DATE of HIRE** from the options listed in the dialog box.

4. The timeline is placed over the PivotTable and can be moved by dragging the title bar to a new location:

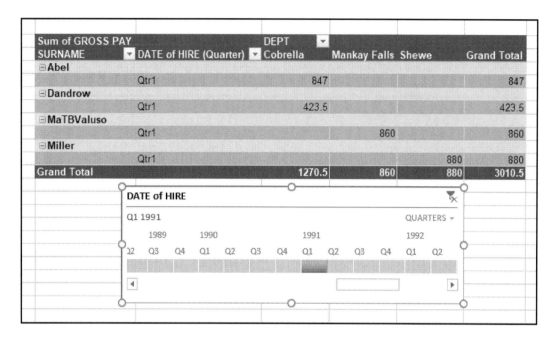

5. To filter the dates, simply click on the filter arrow to the right of the timeline to change **YEARS** to **QUARTERS**, then select items along the timeline to filter the PivotTable data.

We learned how to add PivotTables, slicers, and timelines, as well as how to group dates, in this section. We will now create a PivotChart.

Creating a PivotChart in Excel

Just like normal Excel charts, a PivotChart is a graphical representation of worksheet data and/or PivotTables. PivotTables and PivotCharts are connected and so it is very important to make sure that a PivotTable is analyzed and visualized correctly to ensure that the correct representation flows through the PivotChart:

1. Use the workbook from the previous topic to create a PivotChart. Click on the data on the worksheet, then go to **Insert** | **PivotChart**. Select **PivotChart** from the drop-down list:

Note that the other option allows you to create both the PivotChart and PivotTable at the same time. If you select the **PivotTable & PivotChart** option, you will simply drag fields into the different areas to organize your layout and both the PivotTable and PivotChart are updated. Let's continue to build our PivotChart.

2. Check that the selected range is correctly assumed by Excel and select the option to place the PivotChart onto a new worksheet.

3. Click on **OK** to continue to build the PivotChart.

4. Add fields from the left of the PivotChart **Fields** pane to the area on the right to create the PivotChart (use the following example as a guide, or try using your own field placements). Note that you can also add filters and slicers or insert a timeline on PivotCharts. When you click on the PivotChart, you will see that the PivotChart tool's contextual menu appears on the title bar. Just underneath the menu are three tabs to customize PivotCharts—namely, **Analyze**, **Design**, and **Format**:

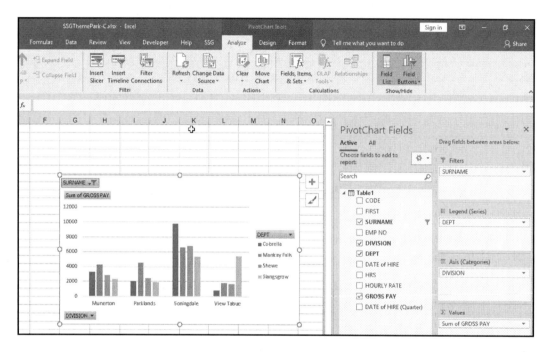

5. If you update the worksheet data at any point, you will need to refresh the PivotChart. Navigate to **Analyze | Refresh** from the **Data** group to do so.

In the next section, we will look at the wonderful three-dimensional visual analysis feature to create stunning maps.

Working with the 3D Maps feature

The **3D Maps** feature was available on Office 2016 but was called Power Map. In Office 2019, it is called 3D Maps and used to create animated three-dimensional map tours. It can plot financial, geographical, date, and time data model fields, as well as a range of other sources.

An example of the use of a three-dimensional map is to set up a virtual tour of galleries around the world to show artwork, its value, and the date it was created. You could also use the feature to plot product reviews according to country, region, or city. The use cases are endless for education and business analysis, so this feature is certainly not one to ignore!

Let's create a three-dimensional map:

1. For this example, we will use the `ProductReviews.xlsx` workbook. The workbook consists of a small table of reviews from clients and expert reviewers for our products over a specified time period. The data is formatted as a table so that any new data added at any point is included in the map range automatically.

2. Click on the table, then go to **Insert** | **3D Map** | **Open 3D Maps**:

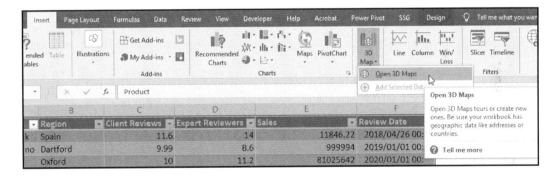

3. If you have any existing tours that use **3D Maps**, it opens the **Launch 3D Maps** pane and prompts you to choose which existing tour you want to open, or to select **New Tour** at the bottom of the pane. A separate window opens, where the **3D Maps** feature loads. Notice that there is a **File** and **Home** tab and the window is separated by a **Tour Editor** pane to the left and a **Layer** panel to the right. At the end of the **Home** ribbon, you will find the **View** options, which allow you to remove and show these panes, as well as the field list. The globe is positioned in the middle of the window. Themes can be applied to the globe by visiting the **Themes** options under the **Scenes** group. Try these out! When we add layers to our globe, we can plot on a flat map if we prefer this option to the globe. To zone in on a location, simply select the **Find Location** icon under the **Map** group:

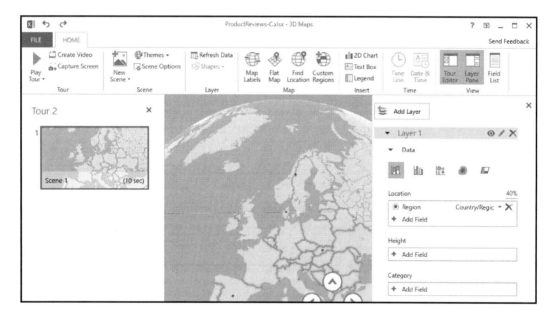

4. Let's drag items from the field list onto the pane. Click on the **Field List** icon to see a list of fields from our worksheet data. As a basic example, we will position the fields by dragging the Region field to the **Location** area, then changing the geographical type of the region to **City**. Then, drag Expert Reviews to **Height**, then drag Products to **Category**, and finally, drag Review Date to **Time**. Your map should change as you select the options:

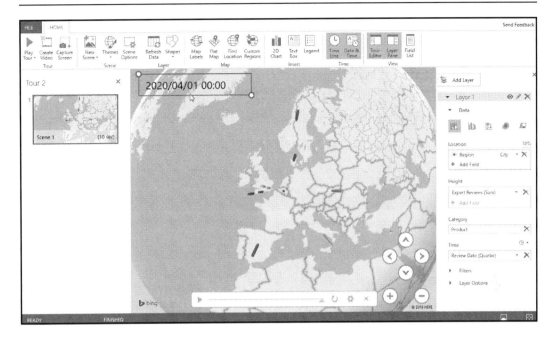

5. Notice how the date and time box now appears on the map, as well as the timeline at the bottom of the globe. Click on the **Play** arrow icon on the leftmost side of the timeline to play the date progression of product reviews over time on the map. Zoom into your map using the directional arrows, or use the **+** or **-** icons to zoom in or out. Hover over the region bars on the map to see detailed information for each plot point:

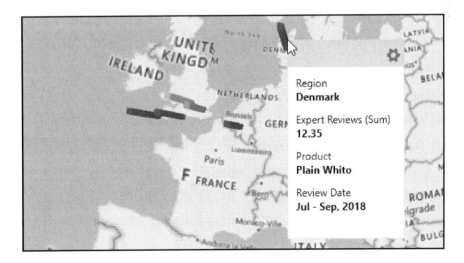

6. To display labels for the map, click on the **Map Labels** icon under the **Map** group:

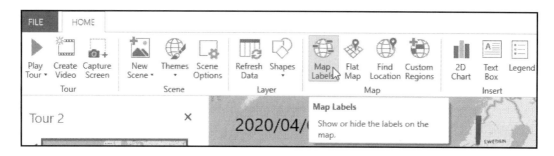

7. To play the tour in full-screen mode, click on the **Play tour from this scene** icon, or go to **Home | Play Tour** from the **Tour** group:

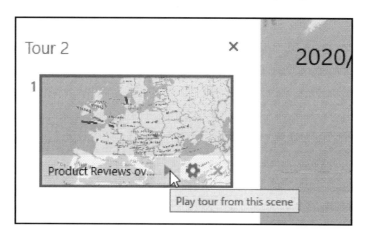

8. There are so many options to discover in 3D Maps, so be sure to check out the icons at the very bottom of the **3D Maps** window to view, zoom, or show/hide elements. Experiment by adding more than one layer or creating multiple scenes, export tours as a video or image, and change the scene options and effects, the visualization type, and the colors.

9. To change the visualization type, add a category, and edit the colors, go to the **Layer** pane and select the **Bubble** visualization icon. Notice how the data points on the chart are now huge bubbles. Navigate to the bottom of the **Layer** pane to **Layer Options** to edit the size of the bubbles by dragging the scale toward the left:

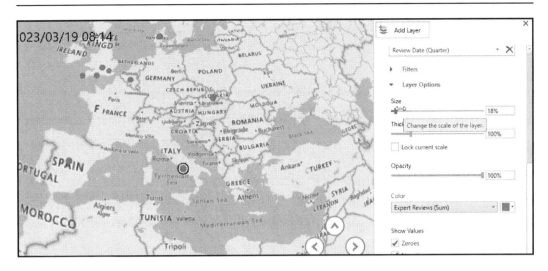

10. Edit the bubble color to red, or select individual plot points on the map and then edit the color for each one individually.

11. Add the `Sales` field by selecting it from the drop-down list under **Category**. Notice that the **Layer** legend alters to reflect the `Sales` figures and the bubbles alter to reflect the change:

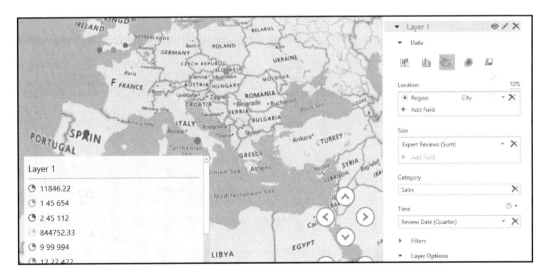

12. When you return to your Excel worksheet after closing **3D Maps**, you will see a text box over your worksheet data indicating that **3D Maps** tours are available for this workbook:

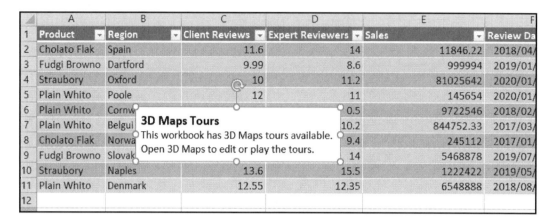

You have now learned how to display worksheet data in a three-dimensional map and can customize the map by adding fields, layers, and scenes, as well as change a range of options. There is so much more to editing visualizations to explore and so much you can experiment with using different datasets. In the next topic, we will experiment further by getting to grips with an overview of the different analysis tools in Excel 2019.

Using tools for analysis in Excel

You should be confident with accessing the Analysis ToolPak in Excel 2019, specifically for the quick analysis of financial, statistical, and engineering data. We will use the ToolPak to obtain the descriptive statistics of a range of weather data in a workbook and look at how to use the what-if analysis tools such as Goal Seek and Scenario Manager.

The tools in the Analysis ToolPak in Excel 2019 are used to gain more statistical scrutiny from your worksheet data. If you are not used to creating complex formulas in Excel, but you need to perform statistical t-tests or chi-square tests and/or correlations, then the Analysis ToolPak has the answers without having to waste valuable time trying to recreate these formulas.

Analysis ToolPak

To install the Analysis ToolPak, do the following:

1. Go to **File | Options | Add-ins**.
2. Locate the **Excel Add-ins** option at the bottom of the dialog box, then click on **Go...**:

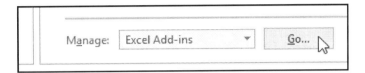

3. The **Add-ins** dialog box will pop up. Select the items to add to the Excel interface. Click to select the add-ins to install by ensuring there is a tick in each of the checkboxes. Click on **OK** to confirm your selection:

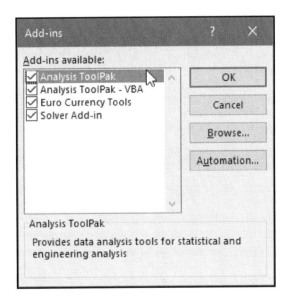

The tools are installed behind the scenes and you are now ready to use them on your workbook data.

4. We will now use the **Descriptive Statistics** tool to find the mean, median, variance, and standard deviation of our weather data.

5. Open the `WeatherData.xlsx` workbook. In this workbook, you will find a large amount of weather data spanning a number of columns. We are interested in finding the stats for the `Wind Speed` column. Select the `Wind Speed` column in the worksheet, then go to **Data | Data Analysis**.

6. The **Data Analysis** dialog box pops up. Select **Descriptive Statistics** for this example, then click on **OK**:

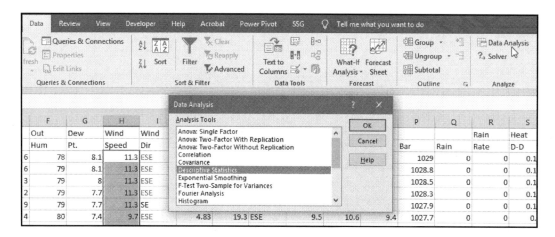

7. In the **Descriptive Statistics** dialog box, ensure that the correct values are inputted into the **Input Range** field (this needs to be the data under `Wind Speed` for this example) and that the data is grouped by **Columns**. In this case, we will leave the **Labels in first row** checkbox unchecked as we have not included this in our selected range. Choose the output options you require under the **Output options** heading (input cell `AD3` as the cell to place the stats once computed), then select **Summary statistics** for reporting:

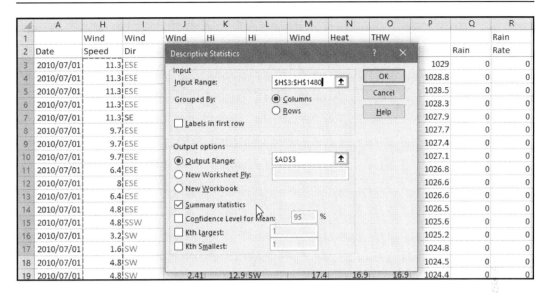

8. Click on the **OK** button to see the results:

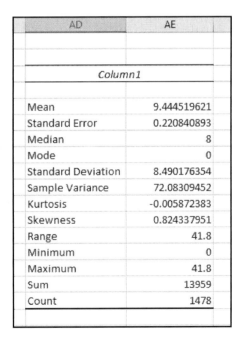

	AD	AE
	Column1	
	Mean	9.444519621
	Standard Error	0.220840893
	Median	8
	Mode	0
	Standard Deviation	8.490176354
	Sample Variance	72.08309452
	Kurtosis	-0.005872383
	Skewness	0.824337951
	Range	41.8
	Minimum	0
	Maximum	41.8
	Sum	13959
	Count	1478

9. Add a heading to the top of the stats to replace `Column1`, if preferred.

What-if analysis

We will now look at a set of analysis tools called what-if analysis in Excel 2019. This category consists of three tools—namely, **Goal Seek**, **Scenario**, and **Data Table**. In this book, we will only focus on **Goal Seek** and **Scenario**. Now, let's look at how to use the **Goal Seek** tool:

1. Open the `SSGSchoolA.xlsx` workbook and select the `BRITTON-FINAL` sheet.

   We will show you a really simple example of how to use **Goal Seek**. **Goal Seek** allows you to find out missing information based on the data you already have. For instance, take a situation where a student gets four results back from the exams they have already sat but still has one final exam to sit in order to pass the course. We can work out the average result of the five exams (the four received results and the missing result) and then use this average to work out the mark that the student needs to get in the final exam to achieve an overall grade of 60 to pass the course.

2. Click on cell `H7` and work out the average of all five results—this includes the empty `Final Exam` cell. You should receive a result of `57.2`. This is not enough to pass the course as the student needs to achieve at least `60` to pass. With this information, the student now knows how hard they need to work in the final exam to achieve the overall pass grade of `60`.

3. As we can see the average in cell `H7`, we can use that cell in **Goal Seek**. Go to **Data** | **What-If Analysis** | **Goal Seek...**:

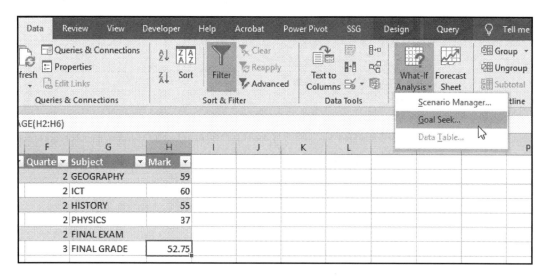

4. In the **Goal Seek** dialog box, enter 60 into the **To value:** placeholder, then click on cell H6 to place the reference into the **By changing cell:** placeholder. Click on the **OK** button to watch the magic happen:

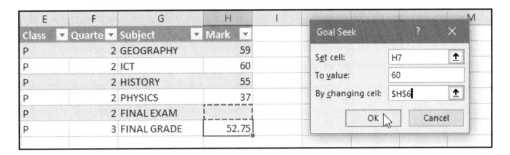

So, in order to achieve a final grade mark of 60, the student needs to get 89 in the final exam.

Let's now look at the financial modeling tool called **Scenario**. This tool is great to use to examine and evaluate future projections or estimations of possible effects on the value of a business in either a positive or negative way. It is used for business decision-making in order to find the best possible outcome (for example, profits) or worst-case scenarios, such as losses. When using this tool, you create the original scenario, the worse-case scenario, and the best-case scenario:

1. Open the ScenarioSolver.xlsx workbook. In cell A19, you will find the budget information that works out the operating income for a business. The values in the Gross Revenue, Cost of Goods Sold, Income, Rent, Utilities, and General Administrative cost cells are values that could change. We will use these cells to work out different scenarios for our business.
2. Go to **Data | What-If Analysis | Scenario....**

3. Type `Actual` into the **Scenario name:** placeholder, then select the actual cell values in the worksheet, as in the following screenshot, by pressing *Ctrl* and clicking your mouse:

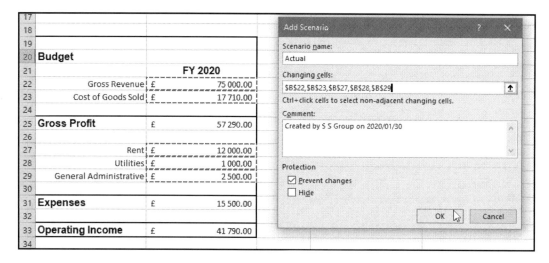

4. Type `Expenses` into the **Scenario name:** placeholder, edit the values as in the following screenshot, then click on **Add**:

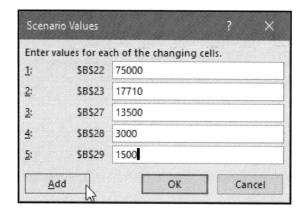

5. Type `Revenue` into the next **Scenario name:** placeholder, then click on **OK**. Edit the scenario values to alter the `Revenue` values, as shown, then click on **Add**:

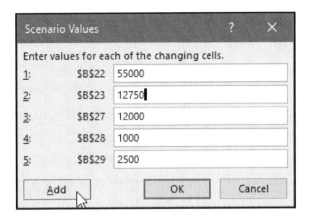

6. To see the different scenarios created, click on **Expenses** in the **Scenario** dialog box, then select **Show** at the bottom of the dialog box. Notice how the values update in the worksheet to project the future operating income. Click on the **Revenue** scenario to see those changes, too:

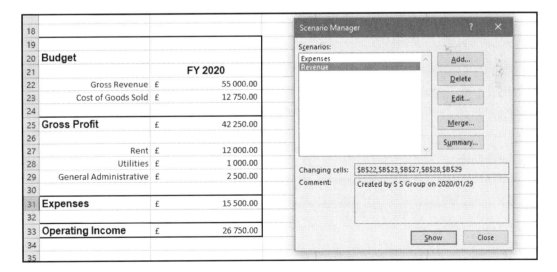

7. You can produce a summary from the different scenarios you created to visually see the changes next to each other. Click on **Summary...** in the **Scenario Manager** dialog box, then click on the result cells you wish to include in the summary:

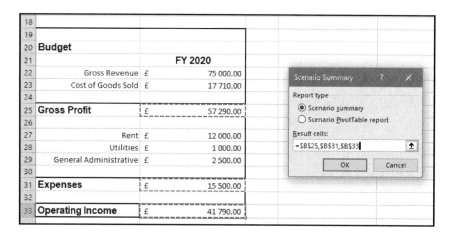

8. Click on **OK** to view the scenario summary; this is created on a separate sheet in the workbook:

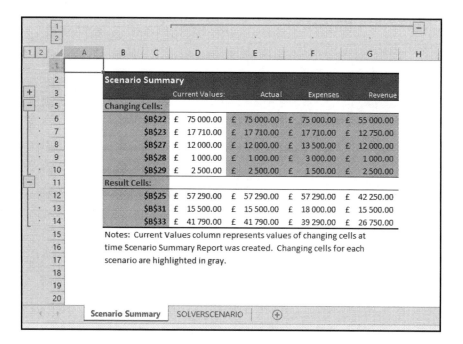

Notice that `Changing Cells` and `Result Cells` in column `B` and `C` are cell references. It would be easier to read if these were named range cells that reflect actual cell names, rather than references—consider this skill (shown in a previous topic) when you use data for analysis and reporting.

You have now learned about some of the analysis tools in Excel 2019 and know how to install the add-in Analysis ToolPak. In the next section, we will discuss data models and learn how to build relationships between datasets for easy reporting.

Understanding data models

In a nutshell, data modeling is when you combine data from multiple sources to analyze the data further using various tools in Excel 2019. By multiple sources, we mean all the import options offered under the **Get & Transform** feature and in the analysis tools used in Excel 2019. In the previous sections, you learned how to use the PivotTable and PivotChart tools and you were introduced to the **Data** tab of the Excel environment, where you can get and transform data from different sources. Data models are created in a workbook; you can only have one data model per workbook. Any table that exists in Excel can be added to the data model and table relationships can be defined across them. So, essentially, a data model is the loading of tables into Excel's memory. It is important to note that you do not physically see a data model in your worksheet.

Large data models affect the performance of memory negatively, impacting reports and applications that share the same resources. Make sure that the data you need to use is clean and does not contain any irrelevant fields or data that you do not need to compute in the data model.

The following list outlines the benefits of using a data model:

- Data models can have unlimited rows of data in memory, whereas Excel has a limit. The only limiting factor in a data model is the system resources and the memory available on the system.
- The actual manipulation of data in a data model is much faster than is possible in Excel, as it can handle large volumes of data and calculations without slowing down the computer system.
- New data is automatically loaded into an existing data model.

Let's create a data model from some Excel data as a simple example of how it works:

1. Open the `SSGSchool.xlsx` workbook. This workbook consists of a number of sheets with fictional data relating to students and marks. We want to analyze this data across multiple fields from the different worksheet's data. Note that the data on each worksheet is already formatted as a table (you learned about this skill already in previous topics). Formatting as a table is recommended to allow any new data entered into the worksheets to be included automatically in the table range. The data in the worksheets is not yet related.

2. To create a data model, let's send the data to **Power Query**. **Power Query** is a tool used to transform and shape data, as well as to produce queries. Click on any cell in the worksheet. Then, go to **Data** | **From Table/Range**, located under the **Get & Transform Data** group:

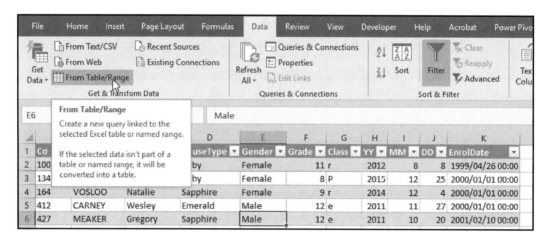

3. The **Power Query** interface opens in a separate window and the table data loads as a query in the middle section of the interface. This tool has vast capabilities as you can use it to discover, connect, combine, and refine data. The aim of this example is not to teach you everything about **Power Query**, but to show you how data is loaded into a model behind the scenes in Excel. We will, however, make a few small tweaks to the data and then send it back to Excel.

4. Right-click on the `Class` column and select **Transform** | **UPPERCASE**. This converts all the data in the column into uppercase letters:

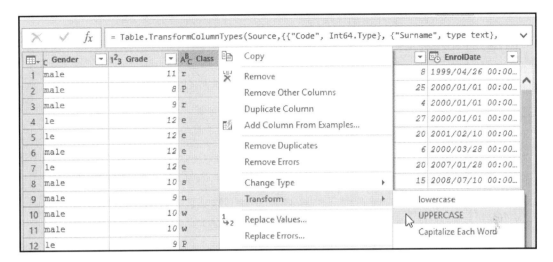

5. Next, we will split up the `EnrolDate` column so that we can separate the date and time. Select the `EnrolDate` column, then go to **Home** | **Split Column** | **By Delimiter**:

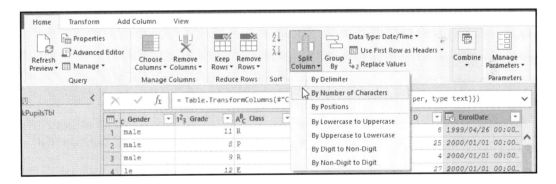

6. Now, choose **Space** as the **Select or enter delimiter** option from the drop-down list and then **Left-most delimiter** for the **Split at** option:

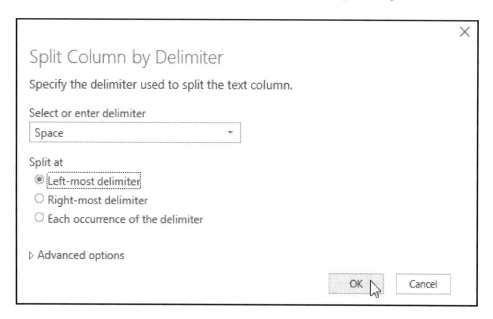

7. Click on the **OK** button to confirm these settings and the column splits into two columns. Right-click on the `EnrolDate.2` column and select **Remove** from the shortcut list to delete it. Double-click on the `EnrolDate.1` column heading and rename it to `Enrol Date`.

8. We have made changes to the data and it is now time to send it back to Excel. This is where the data model comes into play. Go to **File | Close & Load To...**.

9. In the **Import data** dialog box, select **Only create connection** to indicate that this is how you would like to view your data in Excel. Locate the **Add this data to the Data Model** checkbox and make sure it is selected as this is the option that lets you place the data into the data model in Excel. Note that we are only working with the table on the first worksheet in Excel and the process needs to be repeated for all the other worksheet data to load it into the model:

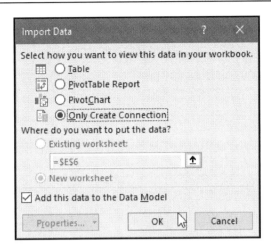

10. Click on **OK** to confirm the settings.

11. You are now taken back to Excel and the **Queries & Connections** pane appears on the right-hand side of the workbook, which now displays the connection. Repeat the preceding steps to add all the other tables from the remaining worksheets into the data model. There are, of course, easier ways to complete this task, but the aim of this example is to understand data models, so manually adding the remaining worksheets to the data model gives you good practice.

12. You should now have four items listed in the **Queries** pane and one item listed in the **Connections** pane in Excel. This means that you have four queries in one connection loaded into the data model.

13. As mentioned previously, the data in each worksheet is not yet related. Relationships do not currently exist between the tables. We will now create these relationships using **Power Pivot** so that we can query data across tables and pull out information from more than one table at one time. Click on **Power Pivot | Manage** from the **Manage Data Model** group:

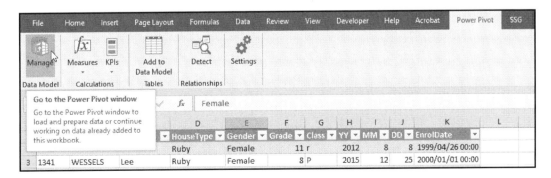

14. When **Power Pivot** loads in a separate window, click on **Design** | **Manage Relationships** to see any existing relationships. Click on **Create** to add a new relationship between two tables linking a common field. In our scenario, we will use the student Code as the link. ElkPupilTbl will be present at the top of the **Create Relationship** dialog box. Choose PupilMarks from the drop-down list in the second part of the window. Make sure that both of the tables have Code selected, as in the following screenshot, as the column to connect between the two tables:

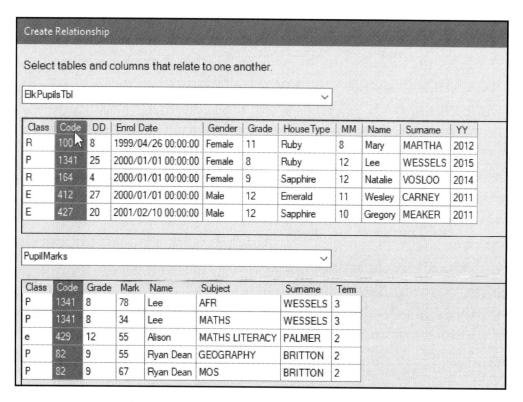

15. Click on **OK** to confirm the relationship, then repeat the process for the other tables, finding a common field between two tables such as ResultsTbl and SubjCodes, linking the SubjCodes field between the two, then link the Code field between ElkPupilsTbl and ResultsTbl. Click on **Close** when done to complete the relationships.

16. To view the relationships you have created visually in Power Pivot, go to **Home** | **Diagram View**. Click on **Home** | **Datasheet View** to see the table data once again:

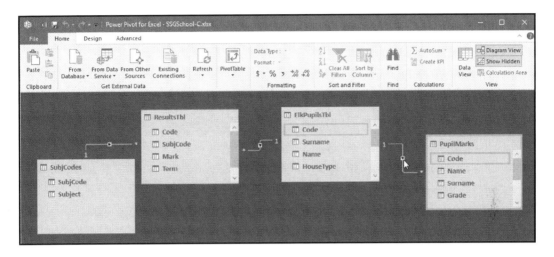

17. Click on the **Save** icon to update the data or use the *Ctrl + S* keyboard shortcut.
18. To return to the workbook, click on the **Switch to Workbook** icon or go to **File** | **Close** to exit Power Pivot and return to Excel:

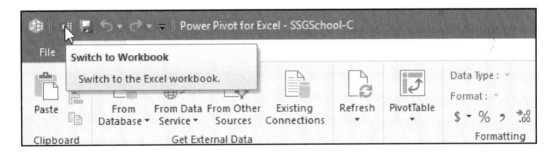

Now that you have your worksheet data loaded into the data model and have set relationships between tables, you are ready to create PivotTables and PivotCharts, as well as to query the data model in memory using Power Query.

Summary

You have now learned valuable skills for visualizing and analyzing data in this chapter, using powerful tools such as PivotTable to create slicers and timelines, and you can now group PivotTable data. We applied these skills to create PivotCharts and also summarized data across worksheets using the **Consolidate** feature. With the ability to install the Analysis Toolpak, you are now able to analyze data using descriptive statistics and use the what-if analysis tools. We discovered the new **3D Maps** feature and are now equipped to create a timeline tour. You also learned how to create macros and add them to a new tab in Excel, and you have a thorough understanding of data models. We also saw an introduction to Power Pivot and Power Query.

In the next chapter, we'll see a variety of common tasks that are applicable to Word, PowerPoint, and Excel.

Section 4: Common Tasks

This section includes all the common tasks that are associated with Word, PowerPoint, and Excel, and the basic things that you need to learn before starting off with the application-specific operations.

In this section, we will cover the following chapters:

11
Exporting and Optimizing Files and the Browser View

In this chapter, you will learn how to export Office 2019 documents, presentations, and workbooks using different formats. You will then learn how to compress images and optimize presentation compatibility using different systems. You will also learn to save workbooks in the comma-delimited format or **comma-separated values** (CSV) files and work with the browser view.

The following list of topics are covered in this chapter:

- Exporting files by changing the file type
- Optimizing files and compressing media
- Investigating the browser view options

Technical requirements

Before working through this chapter, you should be able to save presentations, documents, and worksheets and have good knowledge of file management (that is, of files, folders, and file types). You should also be familiar with the different ribbon options in the Office 2019 applications and be able to navigate with ease around the environment, as well as be skilled at inserting and formatting graphic elements.

The examples used in this chapter can be accessed from `https://github.com/PacktPublishing/Learn-Microsoft-Office-2019`.

Exporting files by changing the file type

Exporting is such a useful feature when working with documents, presentations, and workbooks. All of these files can be saved as templates and to previous versions; the process for doing so is exactly the same for all.

Although the exporting methods for each of the Office 2019 applications are the same, some applications obviously have additional export methods due to the nature of the application.

For instance, PowerPoint 2019 has a number of export methods; not only are you able to export presentations to previous versions of PowerPoint or as a template, but you can also save presentations as a show so that the presentation starts playing automatically in slideshow view when clicked on. You can also save a presentation as a picture presentation and export slides as image files for use in other applications or presentations. We will cover all of these processes in this section.

Moreover, we will work with videos to package a presentation for a CD and automatically update handouts in Microsoft Word 2019 to edit a presentation.

We will demonstrate these processes (and more) using one of the Office 2019 applications, but you can replicate the processes in the other applications by following the same steps!

Exporting a file as a previous version

1. Open the `SSGreenGroupCC.pptx` presentation.
2. Click on **File** | **Export**.
3. Click on **Change File Type**.
4. Choose a **Presentation File Types** option from the list provided. For this example, we will choose **PowerPoint 97-2003 Presentation (*.ppt)**:

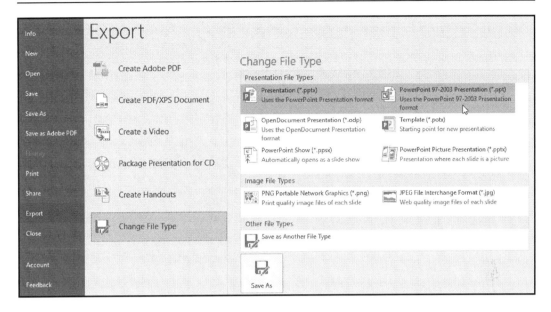

5. Click on **Save As**, then navigate to a folder location to save the presentation to.

6. Change the name of the presentation (if required) and click on **Save** to save the changes. The compatibility checker populates with any errors that may be found due to elements of PowerPoint not being available in previous versions.

7. Click **OK** to continue:

The presentation title bar reflects that the presentation is saved in a previous version (**.ppt**) in the filename and **[Compatibility Mode]** is noted after the filename. Please note that the preceding explanation applies to Word, Excel, PowerPoint, and Access 2019.

 A presentation that contains SmartArt, 3D models, master slide elements, or any new functionality that is not available in previous versions of PowerPoint will not be exported. You will be notified about which elements are troublesome and they will be removed from the presentation or converted into static elements.

Checking the compatibility mode of a file

If you have different versions of a Microsoft office file installed on your computer or receive a workbook saved in a previous version, it will open in **compatibility mode**. Compatibility mode uses a checker to list areas of your document that may not be supported or that perform differently in previous versions.

Sometimes, the checker doesn't convert these changes, even though you used compatibility mode. These changes could affect **charts**, **WordArt**, **text effects**, **shapes**, **text boxes**, **embedded objects**, and so on.

If you open a workbook that was created in an earlier version of Excel, compatibility mode is turned on and is visible on the title bar after the filename and extension. This is to protect the previous versions of the workbook so that if you want to make changes to the document, no new features in Excel 2019 are available.

To check which mode a document that you have opened uses, take the following steps:

1. Open the `YearlyProductSales.xls` workbook.
2. Notice that the **[Compatibility Mode]** text appears after the filename on the Excel title bar. This means that the workbook is saved in a previous version of Excel.
3. Go to **File | Info**.
4. From the **Check for Issues** drop-down button, select an option from **Inspect Document**, **Check Accessibility**, and **Check Compatibility**:

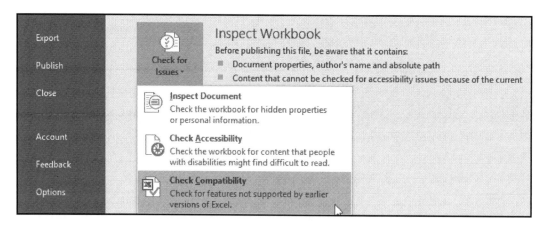

5. Click on **Check Compatibility**. A dialog box pops up, indicating any compatibility issues.

If any compatibility issues are found, then they are itemized in the dialog box, which offers the option to fix them. The easiest way to fix these issues is to convert the document into the newest version of Excel. We will explain how to do this in the next section.

Converting a file using compatibility mode

Converting a document into the new file format clears all the compatibility issues and the layout of the document appears as if it was created in Excel 2010. When working in compatibility mode, you will not have access to the features in the current Excel 2010 program and will not be able to use these features until compatibility mode is turned off. Please note that this explanation and the following steps relate to all of the Office 2019 applications.

Take the following steps to convert a document into the new file format:

1. Open up the workbook you used in the previous topic.
2. Go to **File** | **Info** | **Convert**.
3. Save the document to a location on your computer.
4. An information box will show up on your screen indicating that the workbook will be converted into the newest file format. Click on **OK** to convert the document.
5. The next dialog box indicates that the conversion was successful and that you need to close and open the workbook to use the advanced features. Click **Yes** to close the dialog box:

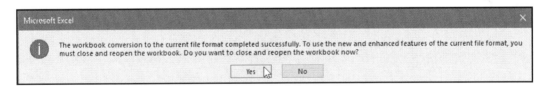

6. The title bar now displays the name of the document without **[Compatibility Mode]**.

Let's look at how to export a workbook into **comma-separated values** (CSV) in the next section so that we can use the data in other applications after exporting it from Microsoft Excel 2019.

Exporting a file in .csv format (Excel only)

At times, you may want to save workbook data in the CSV file format. CSV is a simple file format that can be used to store tabular data. It is used to export workbook data without any formatting or styles so that it can be easily imported into various applications and then transformed and analyzed. In the next section, we'll take a look at how to save data in a CSV-formatted file so that we can prepare data for export.

Often, we need to share workbooks with others, whether within the same organization or externally. It is important to share workbooks in the correct format to prevent loss of functionality.

To save a workbook in `.csv` format, we can take the following steps:

1. Open a workbook. For this example, we will use `YearlyProductSales.xlsx`.
2. Go to **File** | **Export**.
3. Choose the **Save as Type** option.
4. Select the **CSV (Comma delimited) (*.csv)** option and then click on the **Save As** button:

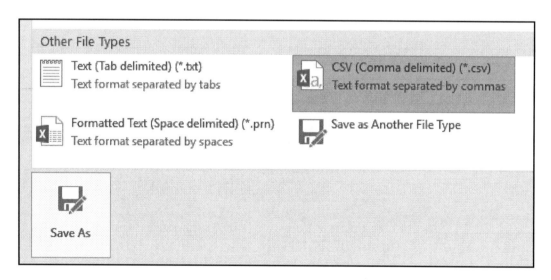

5. Select a location to save the file to, then click on **Save**.

You will see an information bar at the top of the workbook after saving it as a `.csv` file. This information highlights to the user that there could be a loss of certain features in the workbook if they continue working in `.csv` mode.

Note that when saving workbooks with multiple sheets in the `.csv` file format, multiple sheets are not accommodated. Only the first worksheet is saved as `.csv`. In order to save the other sheets in the workbook, each individual sheet needs to be saved in the `.csv` file format separately.

Exporting files as a PDF

If you would like to save files in a read-only format that has a smaller file size, then the export as PDF option is perfect for this purpose. You do not need additional software to do this with the new Office 2019 programs, as the export as PDF feature is integrated within the application so that the file formatting is retained when viewing it online or when the file is printed.

To view a PDF file, you must have a PDF reader installed on your computer, such as Adobe Reader or Foxit PDF Reader; alternatively, PDF presentations can also be opened in Adobe Reader Touch. This is an option for users who do not have Adobe PDF licenses and are therefore still able to read a PDF using the default generic reader available for non-touch and touch devices.

It is also useful to save presentations in this format when you need to visit a printing company as it is a widely used format, so you shouldn't face any compatibility issues.

There are multiple methods that you can use to save files as a PDF, such as the **Save As...** command, the **Export** option, or the **Print to PDF** option:

1. Open a presentation. We will use the `SSGreenGroup.pptx` presentation for this example.

2. Click on either **Create Adobe PDF** or **Create PDF/XPS Document**. Note that you will need an Adobe Acrobat license to complete the **Create Adobe PDF** option, so if you are presented with an error, this is the reason for it and you will need to use the **Create PDF/XPS Document** option instead:

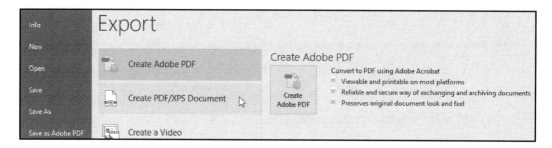

3. From the **Save As** dialog box, choose a location and folder (if necessary) to save the PDF document to.

4. Enter an appropriate filename into the **File name:** text area.

5. You will notice that the **PDF (*.pdf)** option is available in the **Save as type:** dialog box. If you wish to set further options, see the **Optimize for:** and **Options...** sections at the bottom of the **Save As** dialog box:

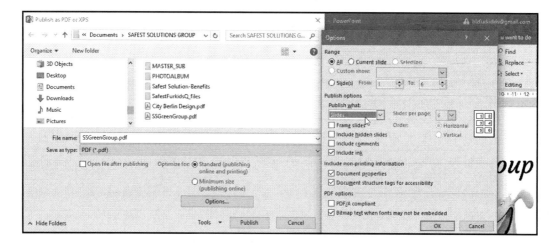

The **Optimize for:** options are used to distinguish between print or online use of the PDF; the **Minimum size** option is the best for reducing the file size of the PDF. If you click on **Options...**, you can specify which slides to create as a PDF, for example, just the first slide or a range of slides.

You will also find an option to set the type of presentation elements, such as slide, handout, outline, notes, or even add a slide border, among other custom settings. Click on **OK** when you have finished selecting the options and then **Publish** to complete the process.

The file is now ready to be distributed via email, as an attachment, or onto the web; to be posted to a SharePoint site, a blog, or a wiki page; or to be uploaded to OneDrive or a social networking site.

 Note that the **Save to PDF** option is also available under the **Share** options, located under the **File** tab list. These options were covered in the preceding sections.

Exporting slides as image files (PowerPoint only)

In addition to exporting a presentation to a picture presentation, we can save presentation slides as image files to use them outside of a presentation:

1. Open a presentation file. We will use the `SSGreenGroup.pptx` presentation for this exercise.
2. Click on the **File** | **Export** | **Change File Type** option from the list provided.
3. Locate the **Image File Types** heading and select either the PNG or JPEG option.

4. The name you specify in the **File name:** text area becomes the folder where all the slide pictures save to. For this example, we will name the file SSGreenGroupPic.png.

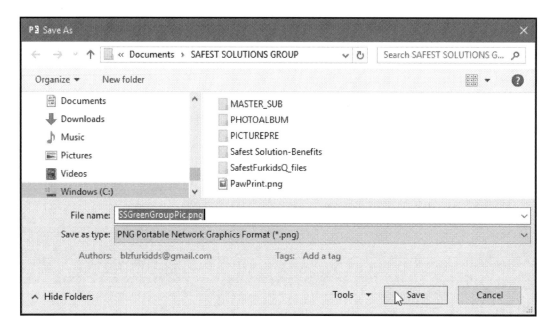

5. Click on the **Save** icon to proceed.
6. A dialog box appears on the presentation screen asking whether you would like to save every slide or just the currently selected slide of the presentation. Choose **All Slides** for this example:

7. When the pictures have finished saving, a further dialog box pops up indicating the location that the pictures have been saved to. Click on **OK** to return to the presentation. Navigate to the destination folder using the file explorer icon on the Windows taskbar to view the result of saving the pictures to SSGreenGroupPic:

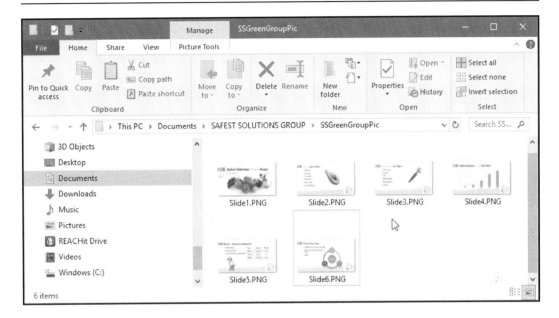

The slides are each saved as individual PNG files in the `SSGreenGroupPic` folder with the `Slide1.PNG`, `Slide2.PNG`, `Slide3.PNG`, `Slide4.PNG`, `Slide5.PNG`, and `Slide6.PNG` names.

Exporting presentations as a video (PowerPoint only)

PowerPoint 2019 allows you to convert videos into large-screen playback using the **Ultra High Definition** (**UHD**) or 4K formats. In this section, you will create a video from an existing presentation and learn how to set the video size and quality output. Creating a video from your presentation offers you the ability to publish your presentation to the web, send it via email, or save it to a DVD or CD.

PowerPoint 2019 allows you to save presentations in the **Windows Media Video** (`.wmv`) format. The beauty of this format is that you do not need PowerPoint installed on your computer to play the video or any additional transitions, effects, voices, and timings:

1. Open a presentation to save as a video. For this example, we will use the `Project Analysis.pptx` presentation.
2. From the **Export** options, select **Create a Video**.

3. Choose the desired video quality. Note that PowerPoint 2019 has the **Ultra HD (4K)** ultra-high quality option:

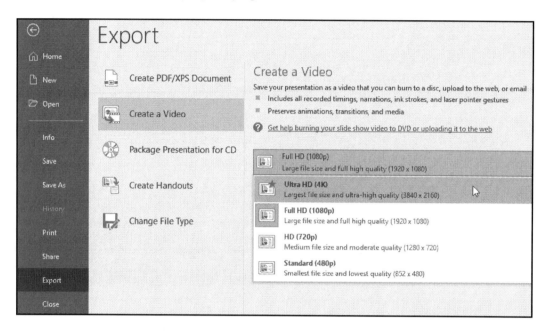

4. Choose whether to record slide timings and whether to set a time in seconds on each slide:

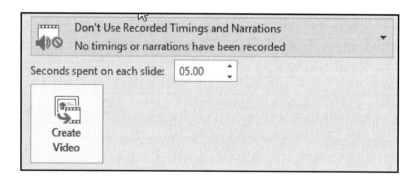

5. If you choose to record slide timings, the **Record** window opens up, showing the presentation in a form that is ready to add the video audio, slide timings, annotations, inking, and notes. This feature was previously referred to as Office Mix, an add-in for Microsoft Office, but has now become part of the **Recording** tab and is available when exporting to video for extra video enhancement:

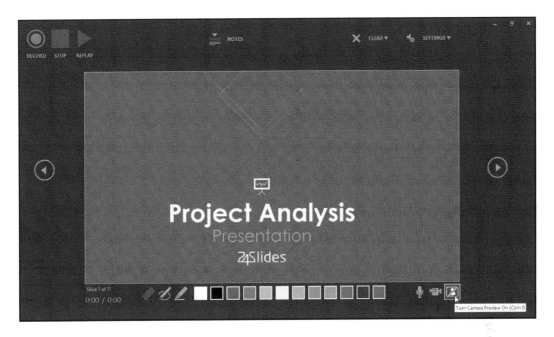

6. Once you have added any extra video enhancements and recorded the timings, the presentation ends and you are taken back to the video export options. Click on the **Create Video** icon.

7. Select a file location and filename in the **Save As** dialog box. Note that the **Save as Type:** option has already been selected as **Windows Media Video (*.wmv)**.

8. Click on **Save**. You can continue to work in PowerPoint while the video is saving. Note that in the PowerPoint status bar, a progress indicator for the video-saving process is shown.

Packaging a presentation for transfer

Packaging a presentation for transfer is solely applicable to PowerPoint and allows you to save a presentation along with all of its content (such as video, audio, and links) to a folder with the PowerPoint viewer ready for presenting. Before packaging a presentation, make sure you have inspected your file for hidden data and personal information. Ask yourself whether you are comfortable with your name and company information, as well as any possible hidden slides in your presentation, being viewed when the presentation is packaged.

Before we learn how to inspect a document, we need to look at the elements we will need to inspect when checking a document for hidden data and personal information. Hidden data and personal information are stored in every file you create. This information is called **metadata**.

In the next section, we will learn about metadata and how to inspect files so that we can remove these properties from files before sharing them with organizations, individuals, or online.

Document properties (metadata)

Another name for document properties is metadata. Metadata is similar to the identification details that exist in a document created in Word 2019.

 The identification details could include the author's name, the date the document was created or edited, or keywords and tags that describe the file or the company.

Document properties are entered as you work on a document either automatically, or manually by the user or owner of the document. An example of automatic metadata is a username or the date the file was modified or created. Manually entered metadata includes a company name, the manager's name, document tags, and keywords.

Document properties are accessed via the **File** | **Info** option in Word, Excel, PowerPoint, and Access 2019. When you choose **Info**, the main properties are listed on the right-hand side of the window. To access even more properties, click on the **Properties** heading at the top of the existing properties, then click on the **Advanced** tab. The following is a screenshot of the Word 2019 **Info** options, displaying the **Properties** list to the right of the window:

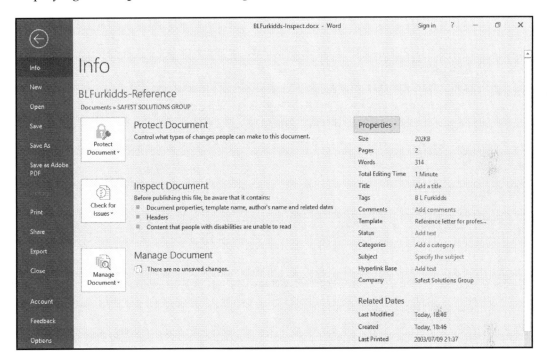

Now that you know where to locate the document properties in Word 2019 and understand what metadata is, the next section looks at how we can inspect documents for personal information and hidden properties and remove them before sharing documents with others.

Inspecting a file

If you are sharing a copy of an Office file electronically with others, you might want to review the file for hidden data and/or personal information. This information is stored in the file's **Properties** list. The function of the document inspector is to find this information and remove it. Always save a copy of the presentation first before inspecting it. Never use the original file as you may not be able to restore any removed hidden data from the file:

1. Open a copy of an original presentation (we will use a presentation as an example for this exercise).
2. Click on the **File | Info** icon to open the options available.
3. From the **Inspect Presentation** heading, select the **Check for Issues** icon.
4. From the drop-down list provided, choose **Inspect Document**:

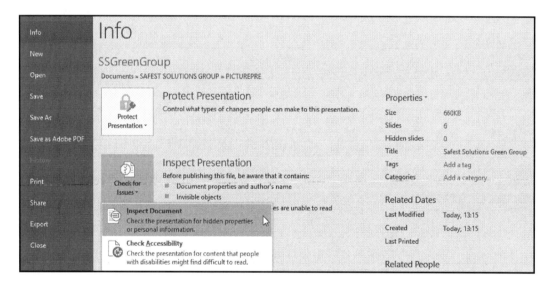

5. A dialog box will open, offering options to inspect the document with. Select which elements you want to inspect by clicking on the checkbox to the left of an item:

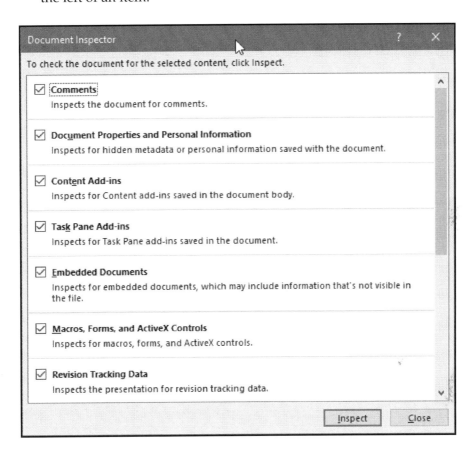

6. Click on **Inspect** to continue. A dialog box will present you with an indication of where any hidden data is located in the presentation:

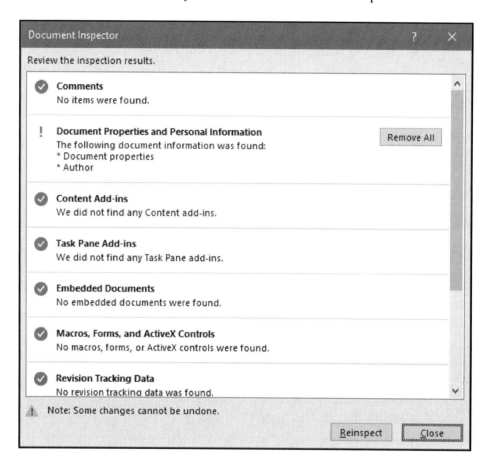

7. Click on **Remove All** next to each instance found to exclude the metadata from the presentation. The document properties and personal information will no longer be present in the document.
8. Click on **Close** to return to the document and don't forget to save it.

Packaging a presentation (PowerPoint only)

This feature is solely applicable to PowerPoint and allows you to save a presentation along with all of its content (such as video, audio, and links) to a folder with the PowerPoint viewer ready for presenting. You do not have to have a CD drive to package a presentation as you can send the output to your local computer, copy it to a flash drive, or upload it online:

1. Save your presentation before you package it in case errors occur and you lose the original presentation. We will use the SSGreenGroup.pptx presentation for this example.
2. Click on the **File** tab and select **Export**.
3. Choose **Package Presentation for CD**.
4. Make sure, at this point, that you have a CD in the drive if you are going to send the package to CD; alternatively, send the package to a folder on your computer.
5. Click to choose **Package for CD**:

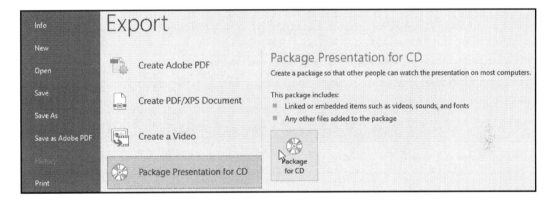

The packaging includes all the videos, fonts, sounds, and any additional files, as well as the PowerPoint viewer to play the presentation in if the destination computer does not have PowerPoint 2019.

6. Name the presentation package in the **Name the CD:** text area and add any other files that need to be sent with the package:

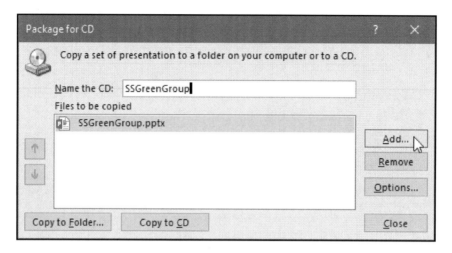

7. Click on the **Options...** button if you would like to add any protection passwords to open the package.

8. Choose to copy the package to a folder on your hard drive or to the CD directly. We will send the package to a folder on the computer for this example:

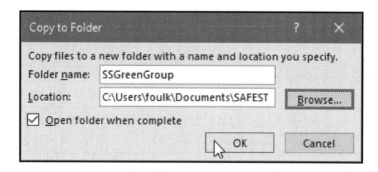

9. Click on **OK** to continue. Once the package is created, click on **Close**.
10. Open the folder to view the packaged presentation:

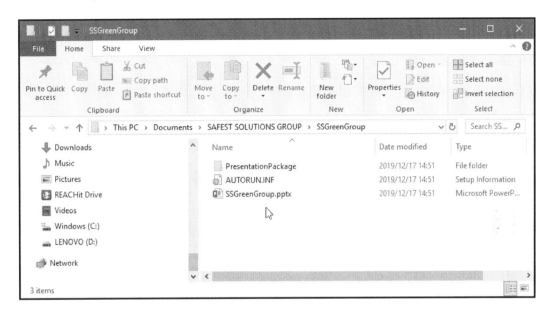

11. The folder contains the **PresentationPackage** folder, containing all the supporting files and the viewer, as well as the original PowerPoint presentation.

Sending handouts from PowerPoint to Word

You can send handouts created in PowerPoint directly from PowerPoint to Word. This is a great feature as it sends the PowerPoint slides and any associated notes into Word automatically and allows you to edit the content. It creates a link from PowerPoint to Word and automatically updates the slides in the Word document after making changes in the original linked presentation:

1. Go to **File | Export**, then choose **Create Handouts** from the list.

2. Click on **Create Handouts** to create a Word document with the notes and slides from the existing presentation:

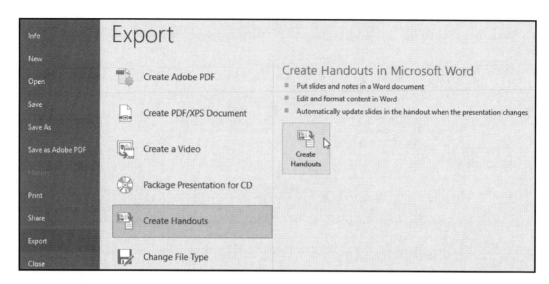

3. A dialog box appears with two options—the first to choose a page layout in Microsoft Word for the document from the choices available and the second to paste a link to the slides in to the Microsoft Word document. This latter option is a must if you want the handout to update each time the presentation changes or is updated:

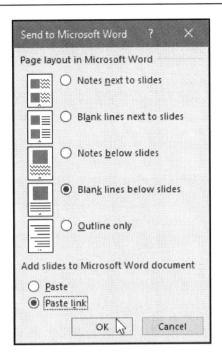

4. Click on **OK** to continue and the handout document opens up in Microsoft Word:

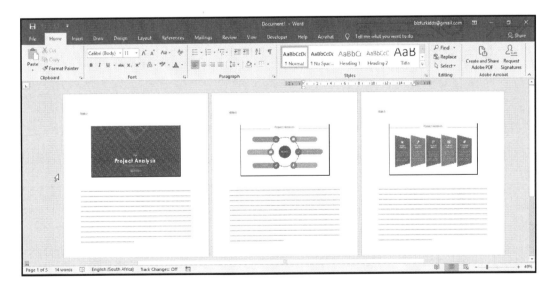

5. Save the document to a location on your computer, making sure it is in the same location as the existing presentation in order to update it if the **Paste Link** option is selected.

6. If you have any broken links in your document, the changes will not update. You can troubleshoot this by visiting the **Linked Slide Object** options by right-clicking on the content in Word 2019, then going to **Update Link** from the shortcut menu:

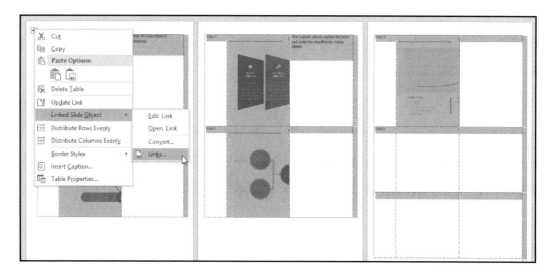

7. For more options or to set automatic or manual updates, go to the **Linked Slide Object** option, then choose **Links**:

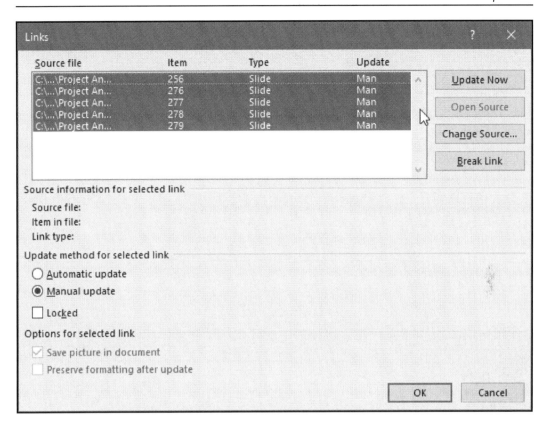

8. In this dialog box, you can choose to break any existing links to the Word document by clicking on **Break Link**, update the source presentation, or change the update options.

Optimizing and compressing media in PowerPoint

Compressing media is another huge factor when exporting a file or if you need to keep a presentation's file size down when working on a file or sending a file as attachments. So, we will learn how to manipulate image compression.

Improving your playback experience is vital when you have audio and video files embedded in your presentation. Compressing these files saves disk space. Please note, however, that 3D models in PowerPoint 2019 increase the file size incredibly and there is currently no way to compress them—static image replacements reduce the file size considerably:

1. Open a presentation that contains pictures and video content. For this example, we will use the SSG Travel.pptx presentation.
2. Click on the **Info** menu item from the **File** tab:

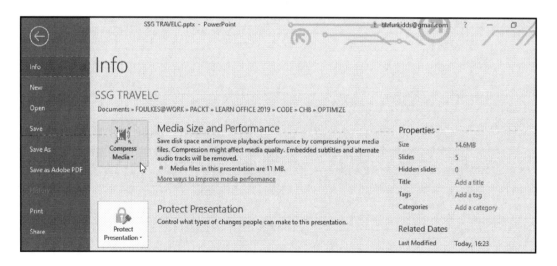

3. Select **Compress Media**:

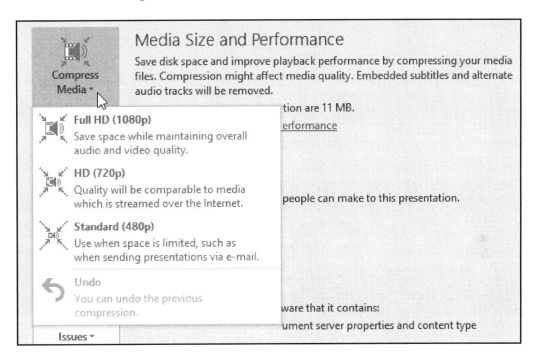

4. Choose the compression you require from the list provided.
5. Once you have chosen an option, the **Compress** dialog box opens and compression begins:

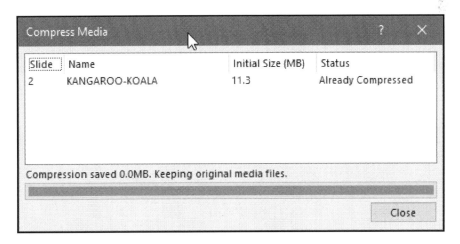

6. Close the dialog box when complete.

7. Pictures can take up a large amount of space within a presentation, especially if you have cropped a picture as the cropped out part of the picture will remain in the presentation unless you compress the images correctly. Please note that once you have removed the unwanted cropped areas of pictures and saved the presentation, you will no longer be able to edit or get back those unwanted areas of the pictures.

8. Select a picture in the presentation to compress.

9. Click on the **Format** tab, then from the **Adjust** group, select **Compress Pictures**:

10. The **Compress Pictures** dialog box populates, where you can choose to compress the selected picture—or all the pictures—by leaving the checkbox blank.

In addition, notice the **Delete cropped area of pictures** option. This reduces the file size considerably if you have a lot of cropped pictures throughout the presentation:

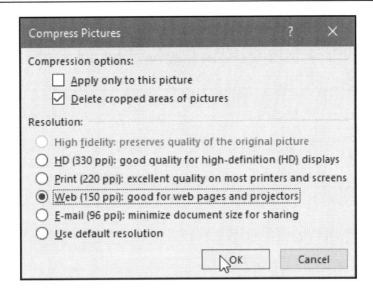

11. Select a **Resolution:** option for the pictures in the presentation, depending on how you intend to use the presentation once it is compressed. Click on the **OK** button when done to confirm the settings, then save the presentation to save the changes.

Investigating the browser view options (Excel only)

If you want to share a workbook with colleagues, Excel 2019 offers browser view options when displaying data through a browser window. Browser view allows you to display Excel workbook data—for example, as a single-screen visual dashboard layout (such as tables and charts) that you prefer the user to interact with. So, instead of just sharing a normal workbook, you can be more creative by pushing content to users by sharing with different browser methods. There are different view options available, such as **Worksheet View**, **Gallery View**, and in an Excel Web Access part on SharePoint.

Follow these steps to learn about and set up **Browser View Options** in Excel:

1. Open the `ChoclatoBrowse.xlsx` workbook. Notice that there are two sheets containing the worksheet data.
2. Go to **File** | **Info**.

3. Locate **Browser View Options** at the bottom of the Backstage view:

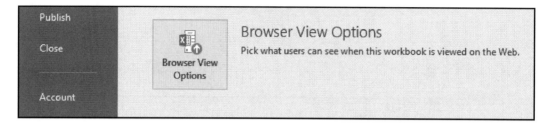

4. Click on the **Browser View Options** button to see the options.
5. Choose the relevant workbook item from the drop-down list. I prefer the **Items in the Workbook** option as it shows all the elements and you can then choose which options you would like to display when viewing it in a browser:

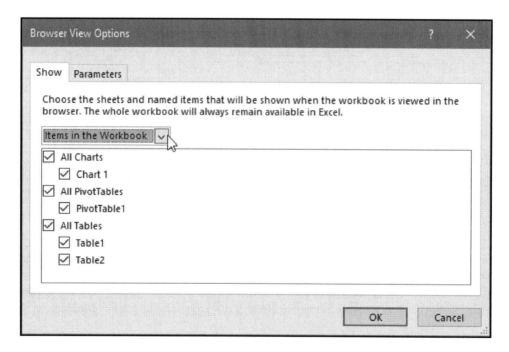

6. Under the **Parameters** tab, you can choose the items that you can edit on ranges within the displayed workbook:

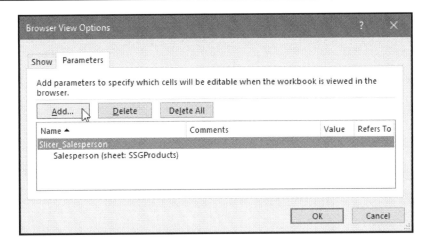

7. Click on **OK** to set the options.

8. If you do not have SharePoint and would like to see the output, save the workbook as a web page, then open the `.html` file to view the file in the browser. Here is an example of what you would see after viewing the browser options:

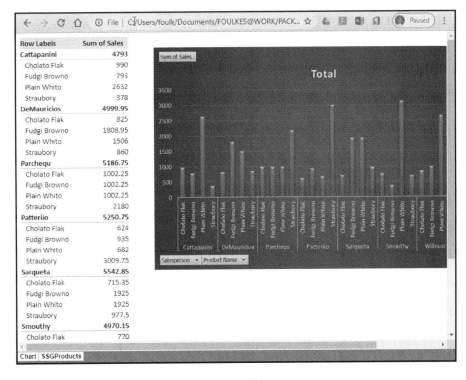

Now that you can set **Browser View Options** in Excel, you can share your workbook data, specifying the editable ranges and elements so that others can interact with your creations.

Summary

You mastered an enormous set of skills in this chapter and now know all the ways that you can export Office 2019 documents, worksheets, and presentations. In addition, you can compress media in different Office files and know about the browser view options in Excel.

In the next chapter, you will learn how to share and protect files in Office 2019.

12
Sharing and Protecting Files

Office 2019 includes several features for sharing and collaborating on documents, presentations, and worksheets. In this chapter, you'll learn how to share files via different sharing methods and locations.

We will look at the **Share with People** option; saving files to OneDrive; the different methods of sharing directly through email using the **Portable Document Format (PDF)**; and attachment options. We will also look at sharing options for Skype for Business and how to present online, as well as via email and blog posts.

Sharing allows you to collaborate with others on documents, by way of commenting and editing, either online or via a link.

The following topics are covered in this chapter:

- Sharing and collaborating in Office 2019
- Presenting online
- Protecting files in Office 2019

 This chapter will use examples from Excel, Word, and PowerPoint 2019 as the steps are exactly the same to achieve the desired output in all three applications, and any deviation from this will be explained in the actual topic.

Technical requirements

Prior to starting this chapter, you should be equipped with file management skills, and be able to save files and interact with the Office 2019 environment comfortably. The examples used in this chapter are accessible from the following GitHub URL: `https://github.com/PacktPublishing/Learn-Microsoft-Office-2019`.

Sharing and collaborating in Office 2019

In this topic, you will learn how to share files in different file formats. The following screenshot displays the various sharing options available in Microsoft Excel 2019. These options are accessible by visiting the **File | Share** window. Let's look at the sharing via email attachment option first, which is illustrated in the following screenshot:

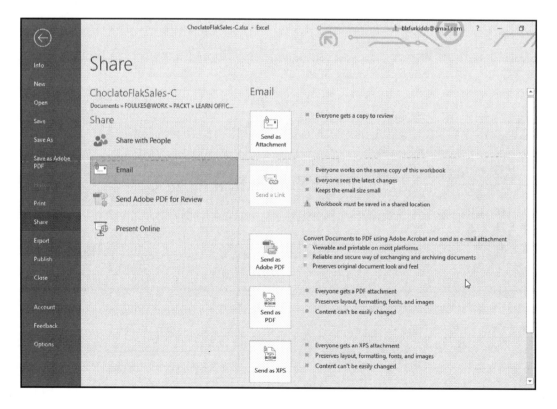

Sharing a file via email

This feature is often overlooked while working in Office 2019 applications. Instead of opening two applications on your desktop (for example, Word and Outlook), simply send an email from within the Office 2019 application directly. Not only does this feature save on system resources, but this will also have a huge impact on your productivity for the day. Let's look at the steps on how to achieve this using a Word 2019 example, as follows:

1. Open the `BLFurkidds_Reference.docx` file. We would like to send the Word document via email to an employment agent, for example.
2. Click on the **File** | **Share** | **Email** option.
3. You will be presented with quite a few options to choose from when sending an email, as can be seen in the following screenshot:

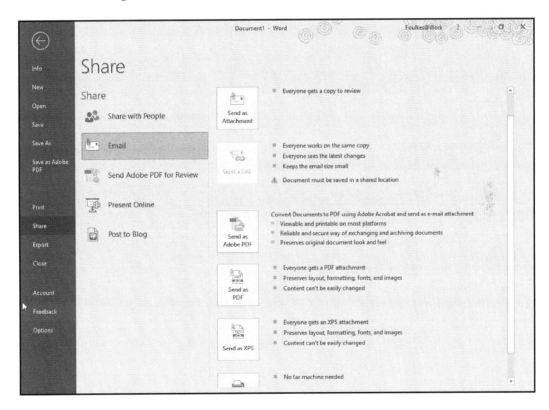

4. Click on the relevant option. For this exercise, we will use **Send as Attachment.**

5. Microsoft Outlook will open a new email message dialog box, including the document as an attachment and the document name as the subject. Complete the email by entering the email address of your intended recipient, set any other mail options, then press **Send**, as illustrated in the following screenshot:

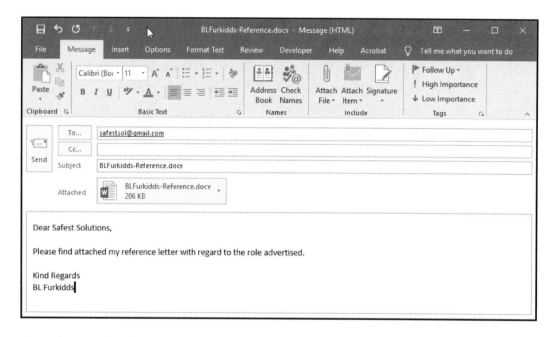

Now that we have learned how to send a document directly from Word 2019 to an email recipient, let's check how to send an email, but as a PDF attachment this time.

Sending as an attachment

We will demonstrate this using an Excel 2019 workbook. This option will attach the workbook to an email message and send it to recipients. Each recipient receives a copy of the workbook to review. The following steps will guide you in sharing a workbook directly via email within Excel 2019:

1. Open the `ChoclatoFlakSales.xlsx` workbook.
2. Click on the **File** tab to access the Backstage view.

3. Select **Share** from the list provided.

4. Select **Email**, and then choose the **Send as Attachment** icon.

5. Add a recipient email address to the email.

6. The **Subject** of the message is already entered as the workbook name, as can be seen in the following screenshot:

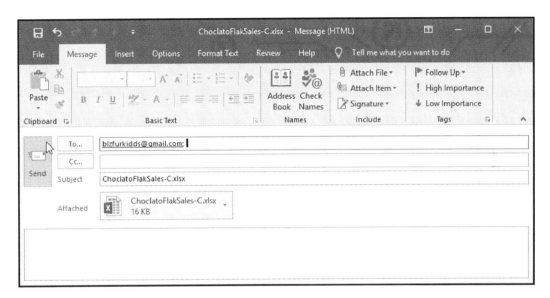

7. As we can see from the previous screenshot, you just need to edit the **Subject** as required, then press the **Send** icon.

We'll now move on to learn about the sharing via a link option in the next topic.

Sharing via an email link

In order to share a file via a link with others, you would need to save the workbook to a *shared location*. The shared location would be OneDrive. Once shared with the recipients via a workbook link, all recipients will be able to work on the same copy via the link and will see all the changes made by all recipients.

A benefit of using this method is the small file size. There are numerous ways of sharing via OneDrive within Excel 2019—we can use the **Share** icon to the right-hand side of the ribbon or the **Share with People** option, or we can do this through the **File | Save As | OneDrive** location, as follows:

1. Open the `ChoclatoFlakSales.xlsx` workbook.

2. Save the workbook to OneDrive using the **File | Save As** option, then choose the **OneDrive** location. If you do not see the **OneDrive | Personal | Documents** folder location, you will need to click on **Add a Place** from the **Save As** options to set this up by logging in first, as illustrated in the following screenshot:

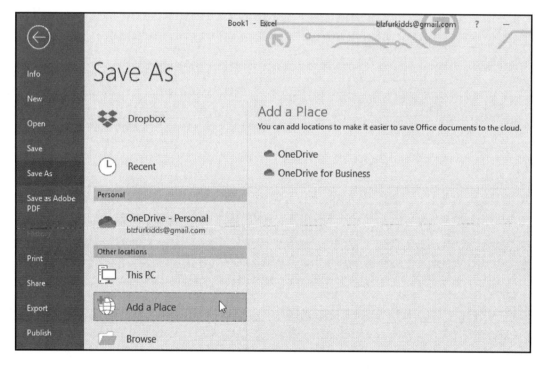

3. Once you have signed in to your OneDrive account, the folder will be visible for you to select in order to place your document online.

4. You will now notice that the **Save** icon located at the beginning of the **Quick Access Toolbar (QAT)** has changed to display the **Refresh** icon, which when pressed automatically updates all changes made by authors who have access to the document, as illustrated in the following screenshot:

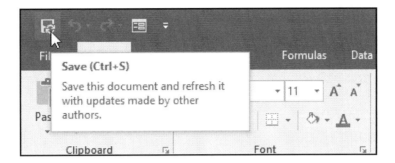

5. Click on the **File** | **Share** | **Email** | **Send a Link** option.
6. The new email message window will open, where you will enter the recipient's email address, check the **Subject** line, add a message to the recipient, and press **Send**, as illustrated in the following screenshot:

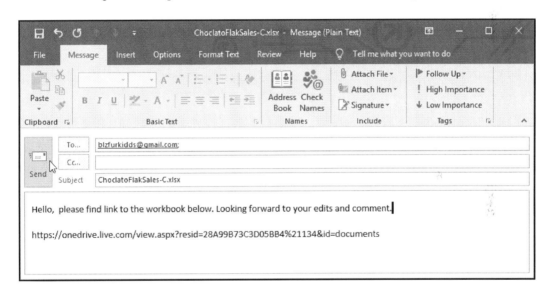

Now that you are competent with the sending via a link option, we will move on to the topic that explains the sharing via a PDF option.

Sharing as a PDF

Normally, you would save a file as a PDF and then attach it to an email message outside of the application—for instance, Word 2019. This feature allows you to do everything you need right within any of the Office 2019 applications.

You can share a document directly to email via a PDF attachment within any of the Office 2019 applications. For this option, you do not require an Adobe Acrobat license. We will demonstrate this using a Word 2019 document, as shown next. Follow these steps to send your Word document as a PDF file attachment to email recipients:

1. Open the document to save as a PDF file.
2. Click on **File** | **Share** | **Email** | **Send as PDF**, as illustrated in the following screenshot:

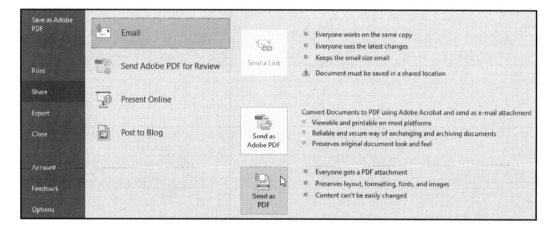

3. The new email message dialog box will open within Word 2019, with the attached PDF file created from your open Word document. Add your email details and send, as illustrated in the following screenshot:

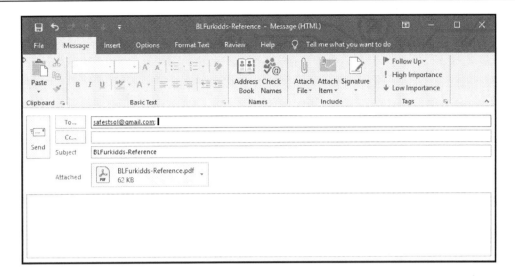

We will now look at the second method of sharing via a PDF file.

Sharing via the Adobe Acrobat license (Adobe PDF)

Sharing a document directly to an email recipient as a PDF file is possible via the **Send Adobe PDF for Review** option, but you will require an Adobe Acrobat license in order to complete the action. Here are the steps to use this feature:

1. Open the document to save as a PDF.
2. Click on the **File** | **Share** | **Email** | **Send Adobe PDF for Review** option from the menu provided, as illustrated in the following screenshot:

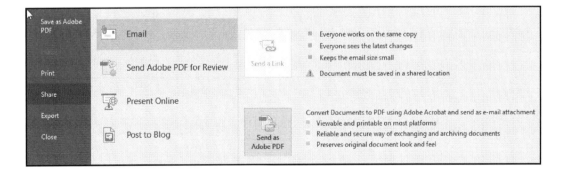

3. Once you have selected a folder and a filename for the PDF file, press the **Save** icon.

4. If you are presented with an **Acrobat PDFMaker** error, then you do not have an Adobe Acrobat license for your computer. This means that you will not be able to use this method to convert the document to PDF. The error message is shown in the following screenshot:

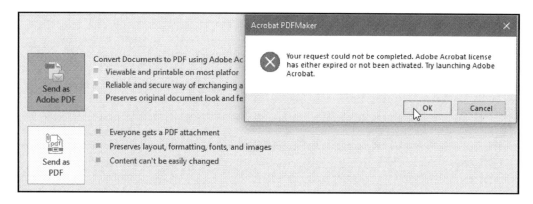

5. Click on the **OK** command to return to the **Share** options.

Sharing a file to OneDrive

Saving and sharing an existing document to OneDrive means that you will send a document (for storage and for sharing with others) to a centralized secure location on the web. With OneDrive, each person is able to contribute by editing or viewing the actual file using Office web applications within the web browser, or locally through desktop versions of the applications. For example, if there is an important presentation with a client and suddenly your laptop stops working, then having important documents stored in OneDrive would help.

You do not need to bother with flash keys or multiple copies of documents. OneDrive is accessible by means of a Microsoft account such as Outlook, Hotmail, Live, Xbox, or Skype.

You can connect to OneDrive and sync files on your computer to OneDrive through the Microsoft OneDrive client, as well as using the following steps:

1. Open the document in Microsoft Word 2019 that you wish to share with people via OneDrive.

2. Click on **File** | **Share** | **Share with People**.

3. Save the document to the cloud and share the document with others, as illustrated in the following screenshot:

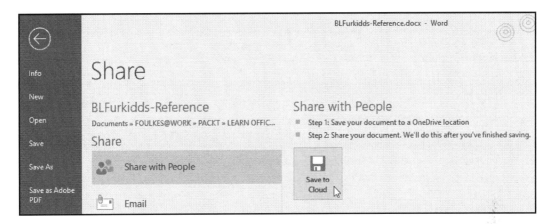

4. Click on **Save to Cloud.**
5. Make sure that you have OneDrive connected to your computer. You will notice that once you have clicked on the **Save to Cloud** icon, your **Personal** folder will be present with the sign-in information, such as the email address shown in the following screenshot under **OneDrive - Personal**:

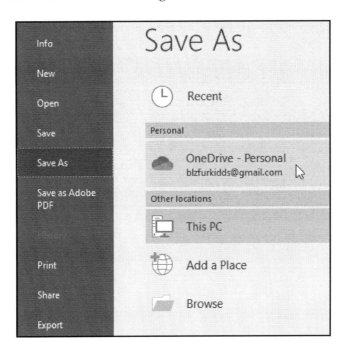

6. If the OneDrive folder is not set up, you can sort this out by choosing the **Add a Place** option, and then selecting the **OneDrive** option on the right of the screen, as illustrated in the following screenshot:

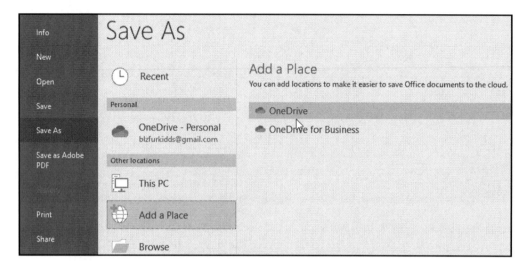

7. Enter the email address associated with your OneDrive account and press **Next**, as illustrated in the following screenshot:

8. Enter your password to sign in to your OneDrive account. Once you have connected to your OneDrive account, you will notice that the **OneDrive - Personal** folder reflects the email address, and the **Documents** folder will appear to the right of the window as the **Current Folder**, as illustrated in the following screenshot:

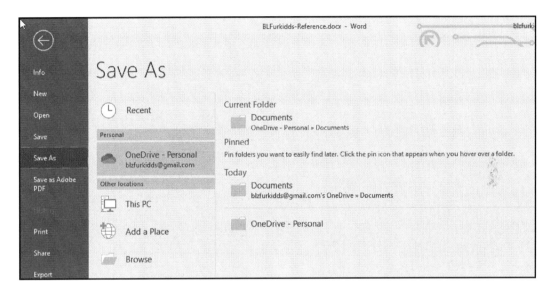

9. To save the document to the `OneDrive` folder, click on **OneDrive - Personal.**

10. The **Save As** dialog box populates. Click on **Save** to send the file to the OneDrive `Documents` folder, as illustrated in the following screenshot:

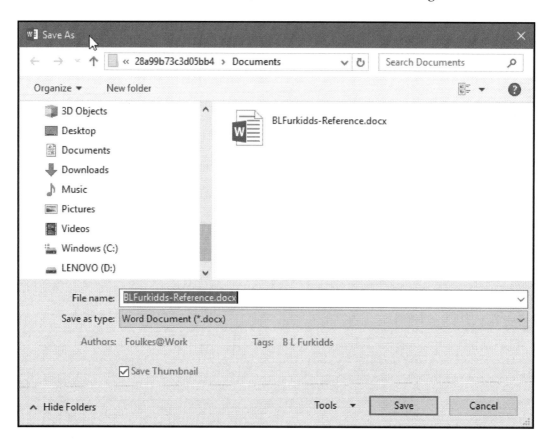

 Note that once you are returned to the Microsoft Word document, the **Save** icon on the QAT reflects the OneDrive connection.

11. Clicking on the **Save** icon allows the `OneDrive` folder to be refreshed, and any collaborator updates are displayed in the document, as illustrated in the following screenshot:

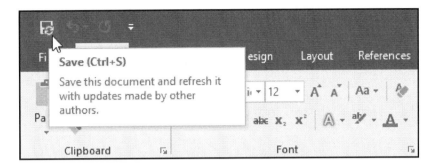

12. The document is now saved to OneDrive; although viewable through the Word 2019 interface, the document is actually stored online in OneDrive. See the following screenshot of the OneDrive account with the document saved under the `Documents` folder:

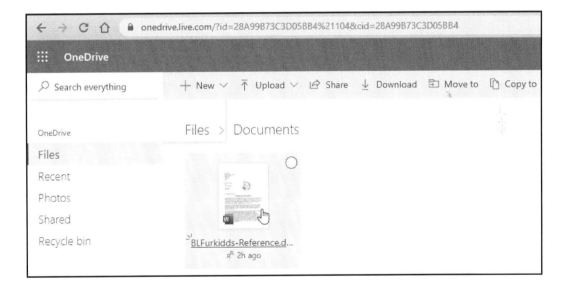

13. Once the document is saved, you can return to the **File** | **Share** option to share the document with others, as illustrated in the following screenshot:

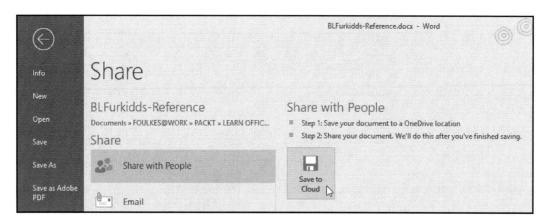

14. The **Share** pane will open to the right of the Word document, where you are able to see any existing collaborators, invite other collaborators, or get a sharing link to share the document with others, as illustrated in the following screenshot:

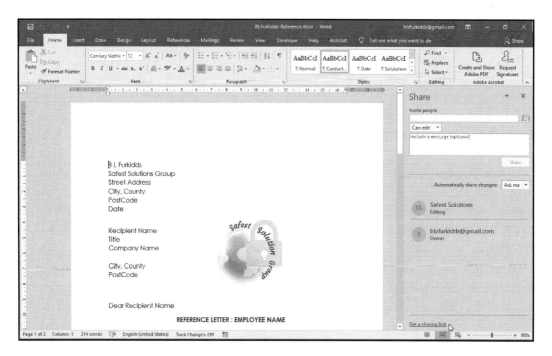

15. The **Get a sharing link** control will offer the option to share the document and allow collaborators to edit the document, or view the document without any editing rights. You need to simply click on the **Copy** icon and then share the link with others via email, a website link, or a document link, as illustrated in the following screenshot:

Let's learn how to send a blog post in the next topic.

Sending a document as a blog post

This option allows you to publish (send) content to the internet or an intranet site. You must have a blog account with one of the following service examples: SharePoint Blog, WordPress, Blogger, Windows Live Spaces, Community Server, or Typepad.

If this is the first time you are using the **Blog** feature from Microsoft Word, you will need to register your blog account (you may have more than one blog account at any one time), as follows:

1. Open a document to save as a blog post.
2. Click on **File | Share | Post to Blog.**
3. Notice the change on the ribbon once you have clicked on **Post to Blog.**
4. A **Blog Post** tab is now visible with the required icons, and the document view has changed automatically to the **Web Layout** view.
5. If this is the first time you are blogging using Word, then you need to register your blog account. If you do not have a blog account, then visit the provider to set one up (for instance, visit `http://wordpress.com` to start a free blog).
6. Click on the **New** icon within the **Blog Accounts** dialog box.
7. Select the blog-type provider from the list provided under the **New Blog Account** dialog box, as illustrated in the following screenshot:

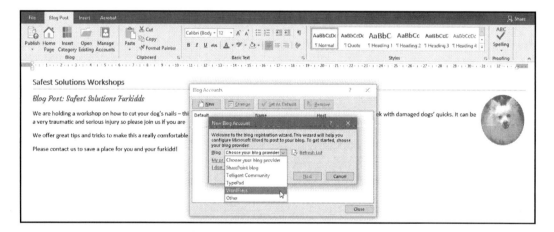

8. In this case, we will select **WordPress.**
9. Click on **Next** to continue.
10. Add the blog address in the space provided.

11. Enter your username and password to log in to your WordPress blog account, as illustrated in the following screenshot:

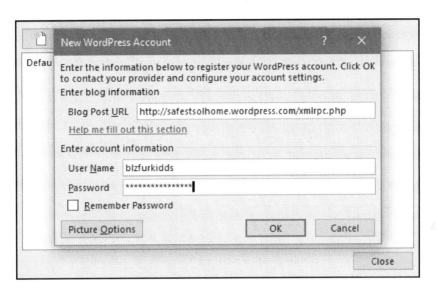

12. Click on **OK** to connect to your blog.
13. Click on the **Publish** icon to send the blog post to the blog provider, as illustrated in the following screenshot:

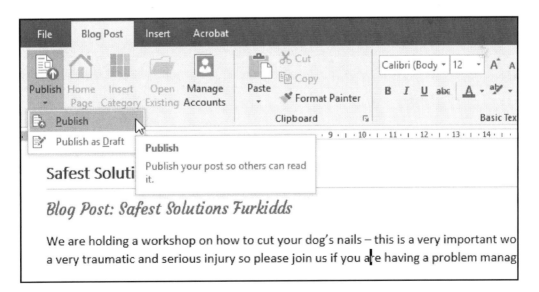

14. The blog post is then sent to the WordPress site, as illustrated in the following screenshot:

Now that you have learned how to publish a Word document to a blog post, you will be able to efficiently and regularly send content from within Word 2019 directly to your website to attract an audience interaction.

Sending a copy of a document via instant messaging

This feature allows you to send a copy of a document that you have opened in Word via an **instant messaging (IM)** service. The recipient addresses are located in your global address book and are existing contacts. You would need to add contacts if they do not appear in your contact list. To send a copy of a document via an IM service, proceed as follows:

1. Open the document you wish to send via IM.
2. Click on **File | Share | Send by Instant Message**, as illustrated in the following screenshot:

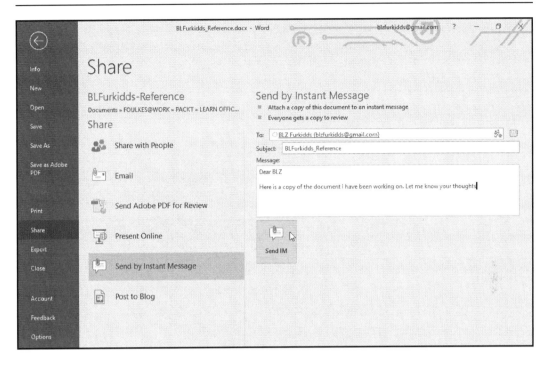

3. Fill in the details of the person you wish to send the copy to.
4. Edit the subject line, if applicable, and type the message to accompany the document.
5. Click on **Send IM**.

Please note that you must be signed in to your instant messaging service for this to work.

Sharing workbooks with others (Excel only)

A shared workbook needs to reside on a shared drive in order for others to collaborate on it. When a shared workbook is edited and then saved, users connected to the same workbook will see the changes automatically. If you created the workbook, then you can control the user access as the owner of the workbook and have the option to stop sharing the workbook at any time.

Sharing and Protecting Files

 Please note that certain functionality is not available after the workbook becomes a shared workbook, so it is best to make sure that all formatting is complete prior to sharing it.

The following steps demonstrate how you would share a workbook with others in order to collaborate together on the same workbook:

1. Use the `ChoclatoFlak.xlsx` workbook for this example.
2. Click to select the **Share** icon, on the very right-hand side of the **Home** tab, as illustrated in the following screenshot:

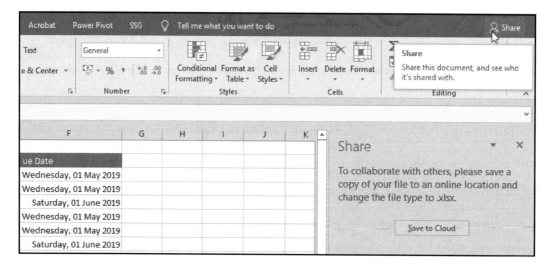

3. The **Share** pane will open to the right of the worksheet, with an icon named **Save to Cloud**. Click on this icon.

4. Add recipients from saved contacts or add email addresses into the **Invite people** recipient placeholder provided. Choose whether to grant edit view privileges and then select either **Ask me**, **Always**, or **Never** from the **Automatically share changes** heading, as illustrated in the following screenshot:

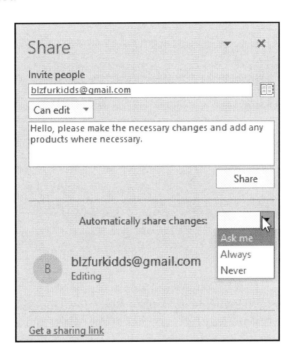

5. Click on **Share** to complete the process, or use **Get a sharing link** at the bottom of the dialog box to send the link to recipients via email.

6. The recipients will receive the email, after which they will click on **Open** to access the shared workbook, as illustrated in the following screenshot:

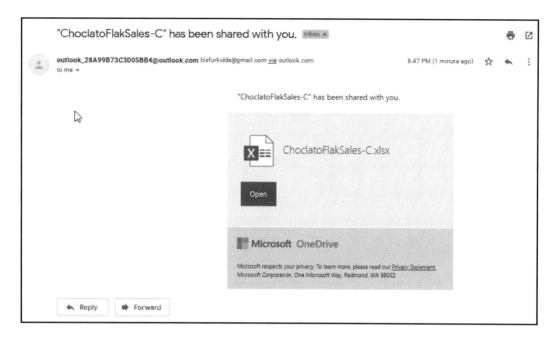

Those recipients sharing the workbook will be displayed near the bottom of the Excel **Share** pane. Only one contributor can edit the workbook at one time, so you will see that you can only view the workbook when another contributor closes the file.

Presenting online

Sharing a file via **Present Online** allows you to collaborate in real time and choose who you would like to give the file control to. There are two options available under **Share** | **Present Online**. The free option would be to use the *Office Presentation Service*, which would only allow users to view the document while you keep control during the presentation. You can, however, allow the audience to download the document you are presenting. The second option is to present through *Skype for Business*. If we chose the *Skype for Business* option, we would need to have a *Skype for Business* subscription so that we could present the document online by sharing our screen with the audience.

Let's go through the steps to discover these options.

Presenting online via Skype for Business

Sharing a document via the *Skype for Business* platform has a lot more features and collaboration benefits than the *Office Presentation Service* by allowing the presenter to view and interact with the audience desktops and through the ability to give control by sharing screens. Let's learn how to present online using *Skype for Business*, as follows:

1. Open the document you wish to present online.
2. Click on the **File** | **Share** | **Present Online** option.
3. Make sure that **Skype for Business** is selected as the preferred method.
4. Click on **Present.**
5. You will be asked to sign in to Skype for Business. For this, you will need an account and a subscription to the service, as illustrated in the following screenshot:

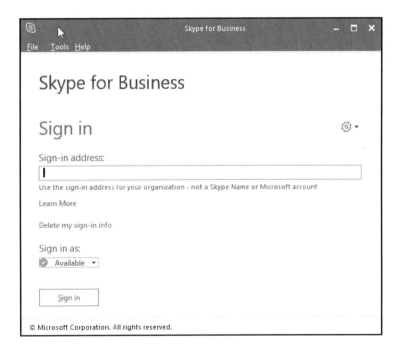

6. Once you have signed in to your account, you will be able to present your document online to others via a link that is sent to the audience contacts (who you would specify during this step).

7. The document will load into the **Skype for Business** window where you will see the online invited contacts, after which the document presentation can begin.

You have now learned how to share and present a document online through the *Skype for Business* interface. In the next topic, we will look at the free version of presenting online using the *Office Presentation Service* interface.

Presenting online via the Office Presentation Service

The Office Presentation Service is a free tool and requires absolutely no setup or sign-in. It allows the owner of a document to share the document online with others. It is really useful for presenting content such as training, marketing, or a presentation walk-through.

The owner can edit the document, and then resume the presentation and push the changes, making them viewable to the audience. After presenting, the updated document or notes can be sent to the meeting participants via OneNote.

Let's learn how to present online using the *Office Presentation Service*, as follows:

1. Open the document you wish to present online.
2. Click on the **File** | **Share** | **Present Online** option.
3. Choose the presenting service you have access to—in this case, **Office Presentation Service**.
4. Choose whether to allow the document to be downloaded by the viewers.
5. Click on **Present Online**, as illustrated in the following screenshot:

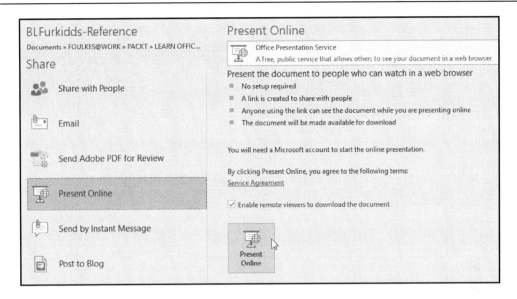

6. Your document will open in the **Office Presentation Service**.
7. The **Present Online** dialog box will display the sharing link options.
8. Choose either to copy the link and send it to participants via email in your own time or send an email right within the Word environment. For this example, we will choose the **Send in Email...** option, as illustrated in the following screenshot:

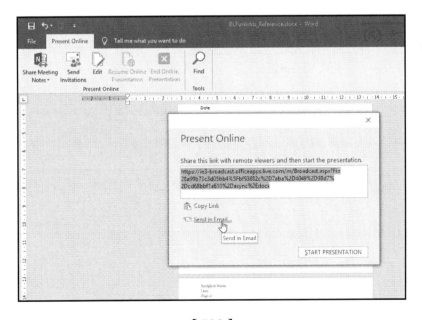

9. Add the email recipients and send your email, as follows:

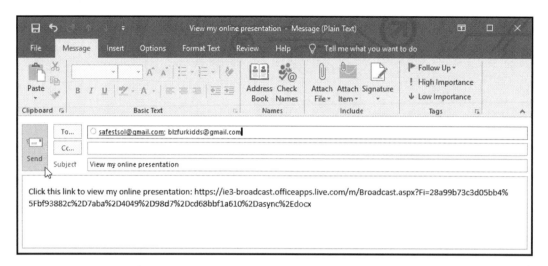

10. Click **START PRESENTATION**, located on the previous dialog box shown in *Step 8*, which will now appear after sending the invitation emails, and wait for others to join you.

11. The recipients will receive an email with the link you have sent. They need to simply click on the link within the email to start watching your presentation.

12. You will see the presenter move through the document.

13. Any changes made to the document are updated to the participants after the presenter has made the changes.

14. The presenter will make changes to the document by clicking on the **Edit** button on the ribbon, as illustrated in the following screenshot:

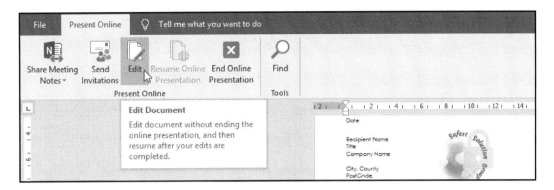

15. Once the change is made, the presenter will resume the presentation and update the changes, as follows:

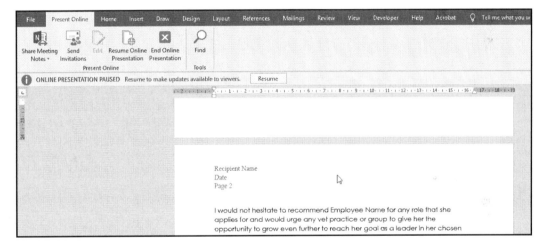

16. Meeting notes can be shared with participants through OneDrive, and the participants can also download the document from within the presentation service (if made active by the presenter at the start of the meeting).

17. To end your online presentation, click on the **End Online Presentation** icon located in the **Present Online** group of the **Present Online** tab at the top of the document.

18. You will be presented with a Microsoft Word notification dialog box, indicating that audience participants still connected will be disconnected if you exit the online presentation.

19. Click on **End Online Presentation** to confirm, or **Cancel** to continue presenting the document to the audience, as illustrated in the following screenshot:

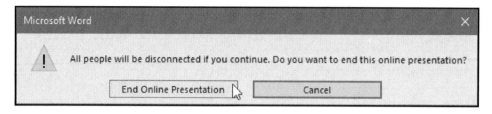

You have now learned how to present a document online using the Office Presentation Service through Word 2019.

Protecting files in Office 2019

We will now learn how to control the types of changes you can make to a workbook. We will cover tools such as the read-only option; encrypt with a password so that you restrict access to a file; and learn how to protect cells, worksheets, or workbooks, and restrict access to certain parts of a worksheet. Although this particular section relates to Excel, the steps for Word and PowerPoint are very similar to this.

Marking a file as final

This feature makes the file read-only and identifies to readers or reviewers that it is a shared workbook that has reached completion, which prevents any further changes being made to it. You are able to mark Word, Excel, and PowerPoint 2019 files as final. The following steps guide us in utilizing this feature:

1. Open the worksheet to mark as final. For this example, we will use the YearlyProductSales.xlsx workbook.

2. Click to select the **File | Info | Protect Workbook | Mark as Final** option, as illustrated in the following screenshot:

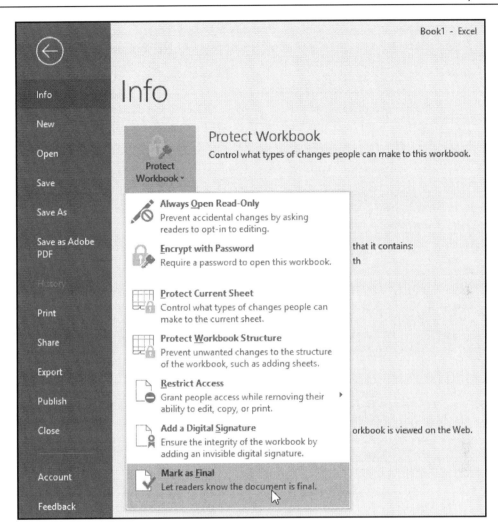

3. A dialog box will indicate that the document will be marked and saved. Click on **OK** to continue.
4. A further dialog box will notify the user that the document is now final and that a read-only file has been created.

No editing is possible after this point unless you choose the **Edit Anyway...** option on the notification panel at the top of the workbook. The workbook would then need to be saved using a different filename.

5. The document filename is updated to reflect **Read-Only** in the title bar at the top of the Excel screen. The protect document permissions update to reflect the change.

We will now learn about the **Protected** mode in the following topic.

Using Protected View

At times, you will find a message on the screen indicating that there is a problem with the file and that it will be opened in read-only mode (**Protected View**). This disables editing in the workbook you are trying to open. As there are many reasons why this could happen, the document can only become a trusted document again once you decide that it requires editing and you wholeheartedly trust the file.

To open a file in a different mode, follow these steps:

1. Open Excel and click on the **File | Open** tab.
2. Locate the file you wish to open by choosing **Browse**—for this example, we will use the `ChoclatoFlakSales.xlsx` workbook.
3. At the bottom right of the dialog box, you will find various options for the opening of the file.
4. Click on the drop-down arrow next to **Open**.
5. Choose the **Open in Protected View** option, as illustrated in the following screenshot:

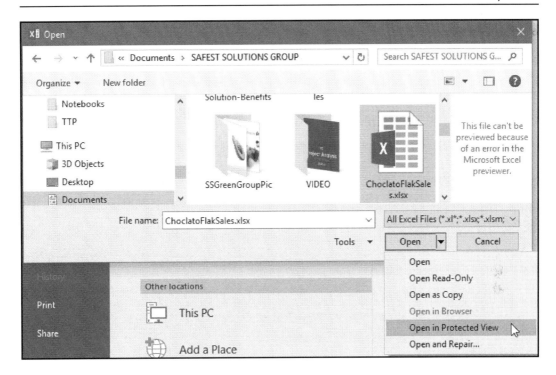

6. If **Protected View** is selected, the following error will appear below the ribbon and on the title bar:

7. If you trust the file, click **Enable Editing** below the ribbon to continue working on and editing the workbook.

Applying file protection

It is possible to protect an Excel workbook or worksheet in a number of ways. You can use the **Save As** dialog box or the **Protect Document** option, as well as using the **Review** tab.

 Please note that if you forget a password, it is not possible to retrieve it.

Requiring a password to access a file

We will now learn how to protect a workbook so that the user is required to enter a password to gain access to the file, as follows:

1. Open the YearlyProductSales.xlsx workbook.
2. Click **File | Info | Protect Workbook** to access the drop-down list.
3. Click on **Encrypt with Password**.
4. Enter a password into the dialog box provided.
5. Click **OK** and then re-enter the password.
6. A permissions message is displayed under the **Info** heading, indicating that a password is required to open the document and save the document.
7. On opening the document, a password dialog box will appear, asking for the password before being able to access the file.
8. To remove a password from a protected document, click on the **File | Info | Protect Workbook** icon. Select the **Encrypt with Password** option from the drop-down list, then remove the password from the dialog box and save the workbook, as illustrated in the following screenshot:

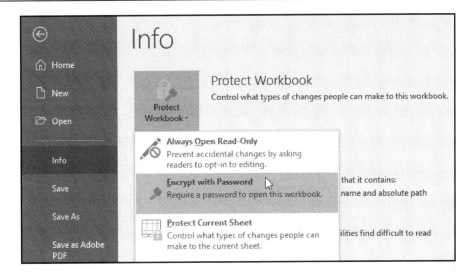

Protecting a workbook is also possible via the **Save As** dialog box when saving a workbook. Click on **Tools** | **General Options**, then enter a password.

Removing a password from a file

In the previous topic, you went through the steps to password-protect a document. We will now learn how to remove password protection from a document. Note that you will require the document password to open the document prior to removing it. Follow these steps:

1. Open a document that is password protected. We will continue with the file from the previous topic.

2. While opening the password-protected document, a **Password** dialog box will appear, as illustrated in the following screenshot:

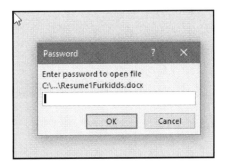

3. Enter the password to open the document.
4. Click on **File** | **Protect Document**.
5. Click on **Encrypt with Password**.
6. Delete the password from the dialog box.
7. Click **OK** and save the document.
8. Protecting a document is also possible via the **Save As** dialog box when saving a document.
9. Click on **Tools** | **General Options...**, as illustrated in the following screenshot:

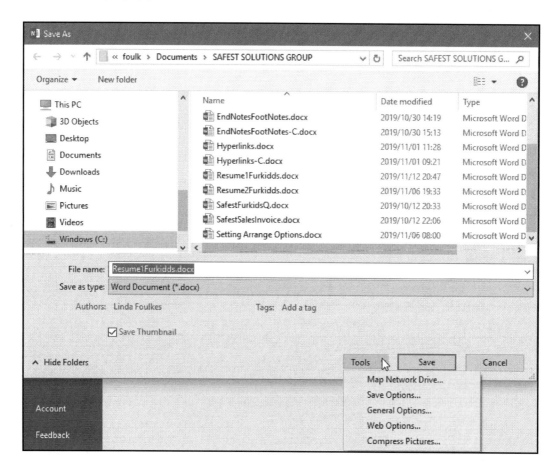

10. In the **General Options...** dialog box, locate the **Password to open** heading (see the following screenshot of the **General Options...** dialog box).

11. Enter the document password to the right of the heading—this is the password you entered when you first protected the document. To remove protection from the document, you will first be required to enter that same password into the **Password to open** placeholder, as shown in the following screenshot:

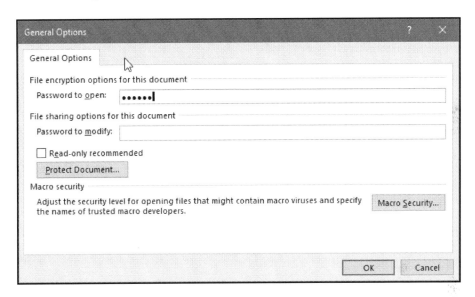

12. Click on the **OK** command to commit the changes, then save the document.

You have now completed the steps to password-protect a document, and understand that you would require the password to open the document from this point unless the password is removed from the document.

When sharing a workbook via **SharePoint** or through a browser window, there are browser view settings in Excel that can enable users to interact with data elements online.

Summary

You now have the skills to work collaboratively in Office 2019, are able to protect documents, workbooks, and presentations, and can set specific ranges as editable once protection is in place. You are also able to export these files in different formats.

In the next chapter, we will learn about the Access 2019 interface and how to work with it.

Section 5: Access

5

Microsoft Access 2016 is included as part of the desktop productivity offering in Microsoft's latest suite. This section introduces end users to Access 2019 and its enhancements and demonstrates how to structure and construct a database, thereby creating and modifying tables, queries, forms, and reports. This section also covers program customizations and contains everything you need to know, from the initial setup to analyzing data.

In this section, we will cover the following chapters:

- Chapter 13, *Database Organization and Setting Relationships*
- Chapter 14, *Building Forms and Report Design*
- Chapter 15, *Constructing Queries to Analyze Data*

13
Database Organization and Setting Relationships

In this chapter, you will be introduced to database theory and will understand the difference between data and information. You will also become familiar with the task of planning a database, learning how to structure a database to ensure speed and accuracy when working with data. Additionally, you will learn how to personalize Access 2019 by setting database options, and will be able to distinguish between database objects such as tables, queries, forms, and reports, as well as learning how to switch between them.

You'll learn how to organize your table data and properties to set primary keys, thereby forming relationships between objects in a database. You will gain an understanding of the different relationship types and when they should be applied, and will learn the rules for setting up relationships between two or more tables in a database.

In this chapter, we're going to cover the following main topics:

- Introduction to Access and the settings options
- Constructing tables and manipulating data
- Building relationships
- Defining the primary key, join type, and referential integrity

Technical requirements

Before going through this chapter, you need to be a confident user of Excel, who is able to construct formulas and use filters and analysis tools. Having worked through previous chapters of this book, you will have the necessary formatting and navigational skills to navigate around the Access application. You will know how to locate and launch Access 2019 from the desktop. The examples used in this chapter are accessible from `https://github.com/PacktPublishing/Learn-Microsoft-Office-2019`.

Introduction to Access and the settings options

In this chapter, you will learn how to structure and construct a database design for a particular purpose. You will also learn the elements that make up the Access environment and set up options applicable to database setup. We will create a new database and learn about the different objects available on the Shutter Bar Navigation Pane.

A database allows for information related to a particular purpose to be entered and manipulated in a systematized way, so that the desired output can be quickly reported and accessed. An example of database content would be, for instance, a library catalog, a music or recipe collection, or student and parent information for a school environment. A database is used to store large amounts of information. The information is organized in such a way that it is fast and easy to extract *only* the information you need. Planning is an absolute necessity and is crucial to the success of your database.

A **database management system (DBMS)** is a piece of computer software used to manage and query a database. A database **schema** describes database objects and the relationships present between objects in the database. There are numerous ways of modeling a database, known as **database models**. The relational database model is the most common type as it characterizes all the information in table format (rows and columns) and signifies relationships created by values common to more than one table within the database.

A database is managed from a single database file. Even though you work with different objects (tables, queries, forms, and reports) within a database, you still work with only one file.

An example of a database program is Microsoft Access. You can recognize an Access 2019 database file by its file extension, `.accdb`:

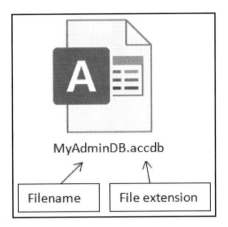

Advantages of using a database

A database is fast and efficient and can store an enormous amount of data. Once the database is set up, data can be entered, edited, and retrieved without effort. Data can be classified, organized, filtered, and combined according to specific criteria. Calculations can be performed and data shared between other office applications or imported into Power Query for further transformation and presentation.

Planning the database design

Planning is an extremely valuable step before you even think of launching the database program.

Follow these easy steps:

1. Define your database clearly.
2. Ask yourself what you would like to get out of using the database – for example, a weekly printout of students' results, attendance, termly reports, or school finances.

3. Think about what information you will need to put (store) into the database to get the results you want. Write down this information on a huge sheet of paper. In order to produce results, you would need to plan backward from the result you would like to reach. Brainstorm the number of tables you need, the purpose and fields within the tables, as well as the field types (such as numeric, text, or date/time). Will you need calculations to be performed? Will the information be sorted? Must the data in different tables be connected via relationships?

4. Plan your tables so that you are able to store your information and decide on the fields you will need for each table. tables are the foundation of the database. It will be easier to create other objects if the tables are set up properly from the outset.

For instance, if you were creating a database for a school environment, you would draw up some sample data with which to start. If you look at the following table, you will notice that the information in six out of the eight columns is being repeated unnecessarily. Every time you would like to enter a student's result, you will have to repeat the student's details again, leading to a lot more wasted time by typing duplicate data. Not to mention a greater chance of making errors when capturing data! You will also waste valuable space on the computer as the database file will be considerably larger:

PUPIL ID	NAME	SURNAME	ADDRESS	CLASS	DOB	LA	MARK
1	Stuart	Smith	14 Cross Road	7Q	15 July 1994	Maths	90
1	Stuart	Smith	14 Cross Road	7Q	15 July 1994	English	84
1	Stuart	Smith	14 Cross Road	7Q	15 July 1994	Human Biology	92
2	Deidre	Optsman	25 Silverside Crescent	8P	2 Sept 1995	Maths	54
2	Deidre	Optsman	25 Silverside Crescent	8P	2 Sept 1995	English	38
2	Deidre	Optsman	25 Silverside Crescent	8P	2 Sept 1995	Physics	42

The problem with the preceding table can be solved by dividing the eighth column table into two tables, one for pupil information and the other for pupils' marks. This way, information can be retrieved very quickly and can be linked by one common, unique field (a relationship) between the tables:

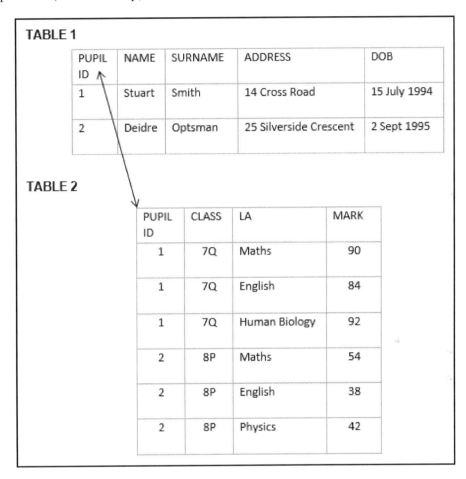

TABLE 1

PUPIL ID	NAME	SURNAME	ADDRESS	DOB
1	Stuart	Smith	14 Cross Road	15 July 1994
2	Deidre	Optsman	25 Silverside Crescent	2 Sept 1995

TABLE 2

PUPIL ID	CLASS	LA	MARK
1	7Q	Maths	90
1	7Q	English	84
1	7Q	Human Biology	92
2	8P	Maths	54
2	8P	English	38
2	8P	Physics	42

This relationship type would be considered a **one-to-many** relationship. This means that we would enter **one** student who will have **many marks** recorded against their name.

You are also able to break up a field in a table. An address field could be divided into street address, city, and postcode. When such fields are divided, it is more beneficial as we are able to sort by data individually.

It is important to discuss the difference between data and information at this point. Information is the output that we receive out of a database. Data is the raw material, for instance, a number, word, or symbol. Data is facts used for reasoning and analysis. Data is stored in the database, not information.

Operating a database

Many people are usually involved in the operation of a database. A large-scale database would require designers, creators, users, and administrators. A database specialist will cost you a small fortune but the database will be professionally created and in good working order. Database specialists can also be employed to maintain the database. Database structures are available for purchase over the internet and through software companies—it depends on the company's needs and requirements as to whether this would be the route to go down.

The person that enters and retrieves data is known as the user. This person (or people) maintains the data by entering, retrieving, and editing the data. Sometimes the user can create queries and pull reports and print them. The user interface is compiled by the database designer who restricts certain objects with permissions. Access to more complex manipulation of objects should be left to the database designer or specific people within the organization.

The database administrator is the person (or people, for large organizations such as insurance companies) who determines and creates the access or permissions to certain parts of the database.

The structure of a database is very important and will ensure speed and accuracy when using the database. Keep it simple and always refer to the basics to make a successful database.

Orientation in the Access environment

The following screenshot outlines the important parts of the Access screen. These parts are referred to throughout the book. Common interface elements were discussed in `Chapter 1`, *Exploring the Interface and Formatting Elements*; this refers to all applications within Microsoft Office 2019:

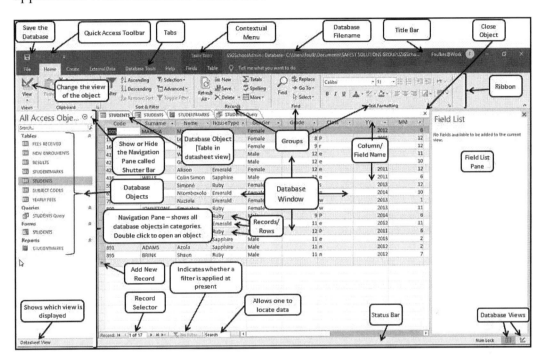

Now that you have an overview of the elements that make up the database window, we will learn to work with each of the elements located on the Access Objects pane.

Learning about database objects

There are four main database objects that you need to get to know in order to build a database effectively. These are tables, forms, queries, and reports. Let's have a look at each of these.

Investigating tables

There are a few types of objects used to manage information in Access. tables consist of and are used to store information about a topic (for example, customers, products, orders, pupils, or marks). They are the foundation of any database where data is organized into records (rows). Each record in a table consists of a number of fields. Data is stored only once if a separate table for each topic is used, which makes the retrieval of information more efficient:

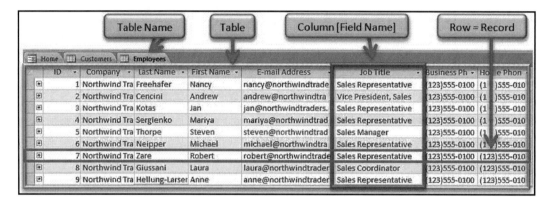

Tables must contain data related to a single subject. This will ensure that the database does not become cluttered or contain repetitive data in more than one table. The **Tables** group is located on the **Create** tab.

Querying data

Queries retrieve information based on certain criteria from one or more tables. It then displays the result in the requested order. For example, if you want to see a list of customers who live in Sonnekeliter, you would create a query to display only the customer names whose city is equal to Sonnekeliter. If you were dealing with a database relating to a school environment, you might want to set up a query to filter children within a particular form/class:

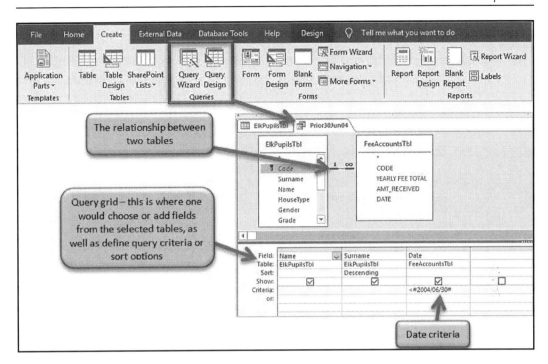

The preceding screenshot displays the Query interface. The Query named
Prior30June04 filters all the first names and surnames of the students who have
paid fee accounts less than or equal to a particular date. There are two ways to create
Queries, the first by using the Query Wizard and the second through the Query
Design view.

The two tables used in the query are ElkPupilTbl and FeeAccountsTbl, showing
that the relationship between the two tables is a one-to-many relationship. As the
fields are related by **Code**, we are able to query fields from both tables to produce a
result. We are also able to perform calculations using a query. Query results from
more than one table are possible only if the tables are related.

Presenting with forms

A form is a frontend tool to view information stored in a table. A form is used to view, enter, modify, and display data in the table. It is used to display the information on screen or in print:

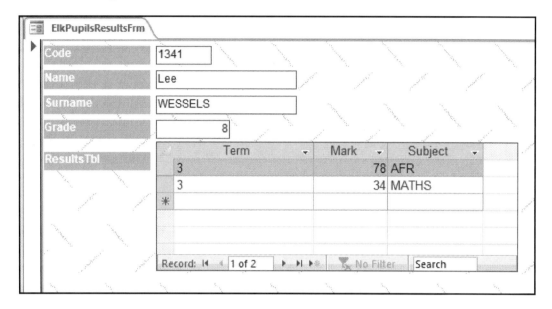

Information typed into a form will be placed automatically into the relevant table. Let's understand what a report is in the next topic.

Creating reports

A report is used to analyze data and display or print the output in the required customized layout:

Class Report				
Grade	**Surname**	**Code**	**Name**	**Class**
8				
	WESSELS	1341	Lee	P
9				
	BRITTON	82	Ryan Dean	P
	JONONO	65	Ntomboxolo	N
	VOSLOO	164	Natalie	R
10				
	FATAAR	794	Naziela	W
	HOWARD	593	Simoné	S
	JOHNSTONE	800	Emmalee	W
11				
	ADAMS	891	Azola	N

You can also group records, show totals for records, and show grand totals for the entire report.

Creating a new database

1. Open Microsoft Access 2019.
2. Click on **File | New**.
3. Under the **Available Templates** heading, click on **Blank Database**.
4. Type a filename into the text area provided to the right. Be sure to click on the **Browse** icon to select a drive and folder to save the new database. For this example, we will create a database named `SSGSchoolAdmin.accdb`.
5. Click on **Create**. A new database is created, including a new table ready for input.

Setting up Access options

In this topic, we will address the application options specific to Access only. The generic application options were addressed in `Chapter 1`, *Exploring the Interface and Formatting Elements,* of this book.

Setting up tabbed mode

When opening different objects in Access 2019, they will overlap on the screen unless they are displayed in tabbed mode. Tabbed mode is normally set up as a default in the Access 2019 environment. Follow these steps to change this option. For the following examples, we have a database named `MyAdminDB.accdb` open in Access:

1. Click on **File | Options | Current Database**.
2. Locate the **Application Options** heading.
3. Select **Tabbed Documents** under the **Document Window Options** heading.
4. Click on **OK** to continue.
5. A dialog box will appear, asking the user to close and reopen the database for the option to take effect. Close the current database and open it again to see the changes.

Switching objects

If you are working without the tabbed view selected, then you will not be able to see all open objects in the database window. The **Switch Windows** icon is perfect for this purpose (note that the **Switch Windows** option will only appear when you are working with **Overlapping** windows):

1. Open a few tables using the Navigation Pane.
2. Click on the **Switch Windows** icon on the **Home** tab along the ribbon.
3. Select an option from the drop-down list to arrange the open windows as desired.

Setting Shutter Bar options

The Shutter Bar is the area to the left of the database window. As with most parts of the program environment, the Navigation Pane can be customized:

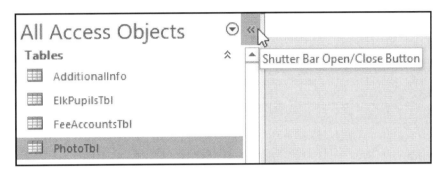

As there is always more than one way to perform an operation in an application, we will address the most common method of accessing the Shutter Bar options as follows:

1. Position the mouse pointer over the text reading **All Access Objects** on the Shutter Bar, then right-click with the mouse.
2. From the shortcut menu, select the desired option:

    *   **Category**: This allows the user to show different categories of objects in the Navigation Pane.
    *   **Sort By**: This allows the user to sort A-Z, Z-A, by name or type of object, and so on.
    *   **View By**: This shows database objects in either icon, list, or detail views. This is the same as the Windows Explorer views options.
    *   **Navigation Options**…: This allows the user to show or hide objects or add objects to the Navigation Pane, as well as to set options relating to how an object is opened by a double or single click.
    *   **Search Bar**: This enables the user to add the search bar to the top of the Navigation Pane, where we can search for objects if working on a huge database.

To change the display of the Shutter Bar, click on the drop-down arrow alongside **All Access Objects** on the Shutter Bar. Click to choose the element you wish to display.

Renaming objects

If you would like to rename an object in the Shutter Bar, do the following:

1. Right-click on an object in the Navigation Pane to rename it.
2. Choose **Rename** from the shortcut menu. The object will open up in edit mode to allow the user to edit the name.
3. Type the new name into the space provided. Click on another object to take the focus off the edited object or press *Enter* on the keyboard:

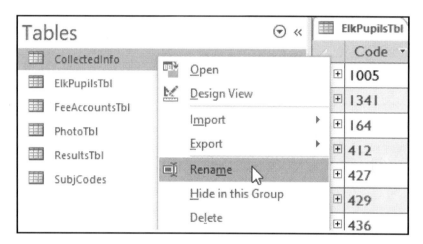

To delete an object, simply select the object and press *Delete* on the keyboard. Make sure your object is not dependent on any other relationships in the database beforehand! You will be prompted again before selecting **OK** to delete the table from the database.

Switching between view modes

Moving between different views is most important in the Access database. Certain functions are performed in **Design View**, while other functions are applicable only in another Access view. The view types are discussed later in this book:

1. Open the relevant table, query, form, or report.
2. On the **Home** tab, in the **Views** group, click the **View** drop-down arrow. A list of the available views will appear. Note that these will differ depending on the object selected. Click on a **View** to select it, after which you can make the relevant changes:

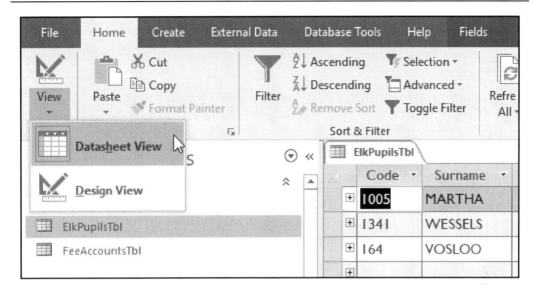

View modes can also be achieved by right-clicking on the title bar of the object in question and choosing the relevant view option.

Applying application parts

Application parts are templates used to create objects and data types within an Access database. Once selected, depending on the application part you choose, a part of a database (such as a single table, form, query, or report, for example) or a complex database (tables, queries, forms, reports, macros, and modules) is created:

1. Click to select the **Create** tab. At the very left-hand side of the ribbon, locate the **Application Parts** icon.
2. Once selected, the icon will present a drop-down list of application parts to choose from. Hover over each icon to gain more information from the tooltip as to what the part will produce. Note that if connected to the internet, you can access content updates from the Office website at `https:/ /www.office.com/?auth=2` for these parts.

Constructing tables and manipulating data

Once you have completed this topic, you will be confident at creating Access tables using the design or Datasheet Views, saving and selecting table views, applying and modifying data types, and setting table field properties.

Creating tables in Datasheet View

Datasheet View is very similar to a spreadsheet. Access saves all data entered into a field automatically. Once you have finished entering data into a record and the focus is moved off that record onto the next, the row (record) is saved automatically. One way of checking whether the record is saved is to make sure that the pencil icon is not visible to the left of a record, as seen in the following screenshot:

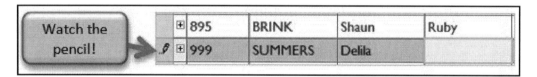

The only type of change not saved automatically is any structural change. An example of a structural change would be sorting and moving fields. Tables should be created in design view as this gives us the opportunity to edit data types and field properties where necessary, and this cannot be achieved in Datasheet View:

1. Open the database to which you would like to add a table.
2. Click on **Create | Table** to design the table in **Datasheet View**.
3. A new table tab will open on the database window labeled Table1. The new table will consist of a default field called **ID** that can be changed/edited at a later stage.
4. Select the **Click to Add** icon to choose a data type for the field. The data type is the type of data that will be stored in the field (date, text, number, currency, or time). These are discussed in detail under the *Modifying data types* section:

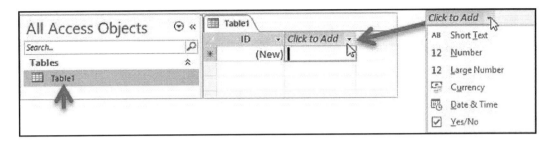

5. The default field name will appear as a column header after choosing the data type. Type the field name into the column header area. If you use reserved names for column headings, such as Name, you will be alerted by the application to change it due to errors that could appear. Reserved names are specific words that Microsoft uses in the database engine. Edit the header to something similar, such as First_Name or FName. Continue in this manner until you have entered all the field names and data types for the new table. As we are only learning the theory at this stage, we will not continue to add names.

6. The next step is to save the table by clicking on the **Save** icon. If you try to change views before saving, you will be prompted to save as well. Once saved, you would normally enter records into the table.

Creating tables using the design view

The purpose of **Design View** is to create or set up a table structure with data types and field properties. In **Design View**, we can add new fields to a table; set indexes, assign primary keys and data types as well as edit the field properties. So, if you are wanting to edit any structural changes to the table, **Design View** is the view to navigate to. Data cannot be added in **Design View**, only the structure. Adding records needs to be completed in **Datasheet View** after the table structure is set up:

1. We will continue with SSGSchoolAdmin.accdb. Click on the **Create | Table Design** icon.

2. The new table opens up in **Design View**, after which you can enter field names into the relevant columns. The **ID** field name is inserted automatically for you.

3. Enter `StudentName` as the second field heading, then choose the short text data type from the drop-down list.

4. Save the table structure by clicking on the **Save** icon. Enter `EnrolledStudentsTbl` as the table name. Note that the ribbon has changed to reflect the **Design View** icons and **Table Tools** contextual menu.

Inserting table fields and data types

When creating a table, field size is extremely important. Field size means the number of characters allocated to each field. If we allocate 50 characters to a field size, but we know there will be no more than five characters per field when inputting data, then the database is going to be larger than we need and the effect on performance (slower) will be huge. Spaces should not be used to separate a field name if it consists of more than one word. Rather, use uppercase letters to differentiate between the words, as in the following example.

A data type must be assigned to each field in a table. The data type determines what kind of data can be entered and stored in a single field. It also has a big effect on what can be done to the data once the data type has been assigned. For instance, if you are going to use the field to perform calculations, then the number data type will be used. Each data type will have its own restrictions so be sure to check out the field properties at the bottom of the **Design View** pane:

1. Open the `EnrolledStudentsTbl` table in **Design View**.
2. Type a field name into the space provided.
3. Assign a data type to the field name by selecting a type from the drop-down list in the **Data Type** column.
4. Press *Tab* on the keyboard to move to the description field or tab again to move to the next field to be entered:

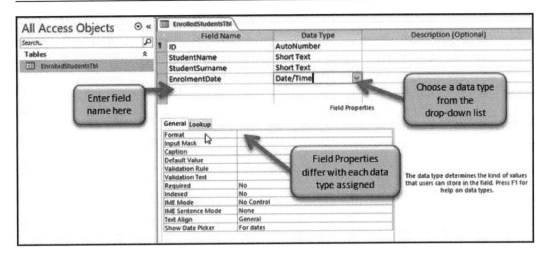

5. Enter the field names and data types as per the example in the preceding screenshot to complete the table fields, then save the table.

Planning your database prior to physically working in Access is extremely important. If you change the data type once the database is set up, a loss of data can occur.

Building relationships

With this section, you will come to understand the term *relationship*, and be able to outline the different types of relationships and when they should be applied. We will look at the rules for creating relationships between tables in a database.

Access is a relational database, which means that tables that are related will have fields that have a common association between them. Related fields do not have to have the same names, but it is obviously easier to identify the relationship if they are the same. Related fields are required to have exactly the same data type unless the primary key field is set to **AutoNumber**. This will only work if the field size property is the same on both matching fields, for example, **Long Integer**.

A relationship is a join (or link) between related fields in the database.

If we think of a company when creating a database, we would create a table for each of the following—employees, customers, products, orders, and order details. There would normally be orders with more than one product, so the linking of tables would be necessary. If we consider the company example, the tables listed would have the following relationships between them:

- Employees sell to a customer.
- The customer orders products.
- The order will contain a number of order details.

A relationship needs to be created in order for data to be used from more than one table at a time. For example, when creating a query, you would need to have access to more than one table so that the data can be combined to produce a specific query result. Relationships are also used to maintain referential integrity, which will be discussed later in this book.

Learning relationship types and rules

In the following bullet list, you will find the three types of relationships we can set from one table to another in a database. The most common of these relationship types is the one-to-many relationship. When we drag the primary key to create a relationship from one table to the other, the relationship is determined automatically by the data contained in the tables and defined by the primary key:

- **One to many**: A field in one table can have many identical fields in the second table, but a field in the second table has only one identical field in the first table (this relationship type is the most common where the field in the first table is the table's primary key):
    - **Rule**: The relationship can only be created if one of the related fields is a primary key or a unique index.
- **One to one**: A field in the first table can have only one identical field in another table and vice versa. This relationship is not a common one:
    - **Rule**: This relationship is only created if both related fields are primary keys or have a unique index.

- **Many to many**: A field in one table can have many identical fields in another table, and so on. For example, one order can have many products, with each product appearing on many orders. A junction table a third table is normally required when using this relationship. So, it contains the primary keys from both tables:
    - **Rule**: It must have two one-to-many relationships, including a third table whose primary key consists of two fields (one from each table).

The following screenshot displays the tables within a database in the relationship window:

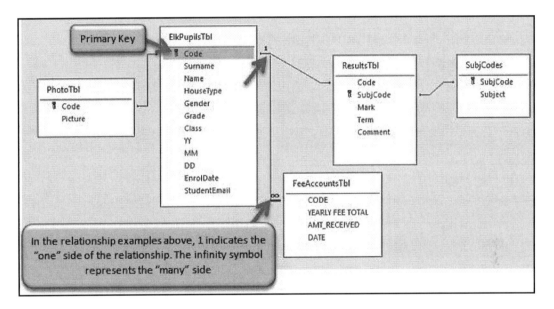

This is where you can edit relationships between tables by right-clicking on the lines in between each table connection. In the next section, we will learn how to define a primary key so that relationships can be formed between tables.

Defining the primary key, join type, and referential integrity

You'll learn what a primary key is, choose a primary key from table fields, and set relationships between tables. We will learn how to delete a relationship, understand the inner and outer join types, and understand what referential integrity means and how important it is to keep your database error-free. There is also a section on cascade updates, which are important when wanting any changes to be drilled down through the database design.

Defining primary keys

A primary key distinctively identifies each record (row) in the table. An example of a primary key is CustomerID—this would be a unique number for each customer. This is very similar to an ID number. The **Data Type** that can be used is AutoNumber, which automatically increments by one each time so that the user does not have to think up a new number for each customer. Access will also prevent duplicates or null values from being entered into the primary key field by alerting the user. If you don't define a primary key whilst designing the table, it will prompt you to do so when saving the table.

Records in a table are sorted according to the value in the primary key field. It is recommended that each table contains a primary key. Primary keys can be based on alphanumeric values as well:

1. Open the SSGEmployees.accdb database. You will see two basic tables. Open the **Employees** table in **Design View** to edit the properties of the field.

2. Click on the **ID** field, then right-click on the field and choose **Primary Key** or click on the **Table Tools Design** contextual menu, then select **Primary Key** from the **Tools** group:

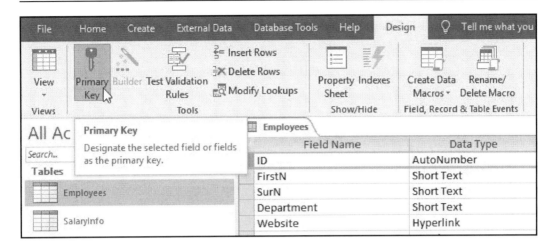

Let's learn how to set a relationship between two tables using the primary key.

Using a primary key to create a relationship

Once a primary key is assigned to a field in a table, you can connect two or more tables using the **Relationships** windows. Let's try this now:

1. We will continue with the previous database example. Click on **Database Tools | Relationships**:

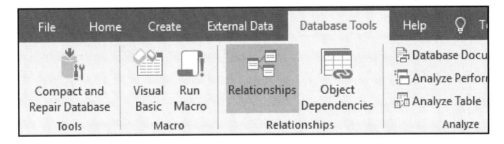

2. If the **Relationships** window does not contain any tables, you will need to add them to relate them to each other. Click on the **Show Table** icon to select the relevant tables from the list. For this example, we will add both the **Employees** and the **SalaryInfo** tables. Tables may be added individually or selected using the *Ctrl* key on the keyboard. Click on the **Add** icon to place the tables onto the relationship window.

3. Locate the **Employees** table. This table contains a primary key called **ID**. It is indicated via the primary key icon to the left of the **ID** field. Click on the **ID** field, and while holding down your left mouse button, drag the **ID** field out of the **Employees** Table over the **ID** field in the **SalaryInfo** table, then let go of the mouse:

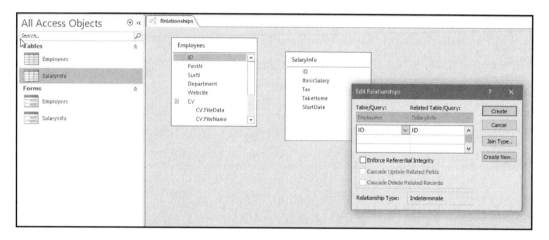

4. The **Edit Relationships** dialog box will appear and the correct tables and relationship will be identified unless the user had made a mistake. Click on **Create** to complete the relationship. The relationship is evident in the Relationship Window by a solid line from one table field to the next. Click on the **Close** icon on the ribbon to exit the relationship window.

5. Click **Yes** to save the relationship when prompted by the dialog box.

Deleting or editing relationships

1. Click on **Database Tools | Relationships**.

2. Select the **line** between the two related tables you wish to edit the relationship of. Click on the **Edit Relationships** icon on the ribbon or right-click on the line between the two related tables and choose **Edit Relationship...**:

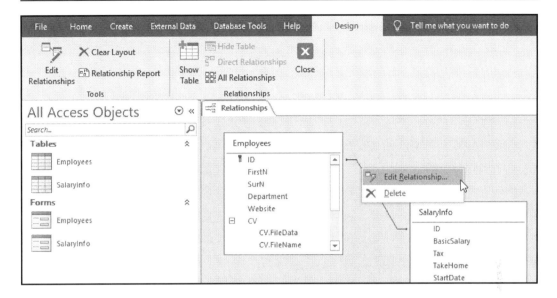

3. Make the desired changes in the **Edit Relationships** dialog box. Click on **OK** to exit and return to the **Relationships** window.
4. Click on the **Close** icon to exit the window.

Discussing join types

There are two basic types of join types in a relationship:

- **Inner joins**: This is the default join type that is set automatically when a new relationship is created. They only include rows where the joined fields from both tables are equal.
- **Outer joins**: All records from the left table and only those records in the right table that have a matching value in the left table (a one-to-many relationship, or many to one). There are two types in this category and it depends on the direction of the join as to whether they are left or right join types.

Changing join types

1. Click on the relationship line between two tables, then select **Edit Relationships** | **Join Type.**

2. Choose the required join:

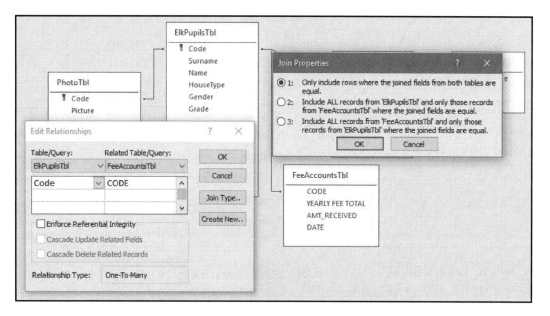

3. Click **OK** to confirm, then click **OK** again to return to the **Relationships** window. Click **Close** to exit the **Relationships** window.

Setting up referential integrity

Referential integrity ensures that records that are related between tables in a database are bound by monitoring the manipulation of data stored in the related tables.

This relationship can only be enforced under the following conditions:

- Related fields need to have the same data type.
- Both fields must belong to the same database.
- The matching field from the primary table is assigned as the primary key or is defined as a unique index.

How will referential integrity change my database?

- If the value in a matching field already exists as the matching field of the related table, then a record (row) can only be added to the related table.
- If any matching records exist in a related table, then records cannot be deleted from the primary table. An exception to this would be when the **Cascade Delete Related Records** option is selected.
- The matching field in the primary table cannot be modified if any matching records exist in the related tables unless the **Cascade Update Related Fields** option is selected.

Setting up referential integrity is done as follows:

1. Click on **Database Tools | Relationships**.
2. Select the **line** between the two related tables you wish to edit the relationship of. Click on the **Edit Relationships** icon on the ribbon or right-click on the line between the two related tables and choose **Edit Relationship...**.
3. Locate the **Enforce Referential Integrity** checkbox and click on it to select it:

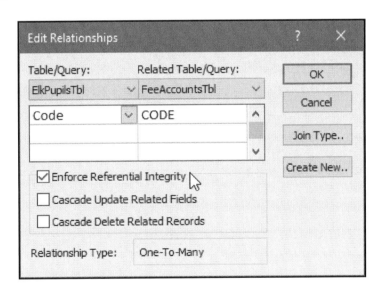

4. Click on **OK** to commit to the change.

Cascading and updating

Cascading means that if you change the content of a primary key field, then the updates to that field will ripple throughout the database. If you don't use cascading, and you try and edit a primary field that is connected to other related fields, you will receive an error. When you enforce referential integrity, the delete and update functions are normally prevented – unless the **Cascade Update** or **Cascade Delete** options are enforced, then the delete and update functions (called cascading) are allowed.

To set referential integrity and the cascade update or delete options, right-click or double-click the relationship line between two tables in the **Relationships** window.

We will open the database named MyAdminDB.accdb for this example in order to enforce referential integrity and cascade updates:

1. Click on **Database Tools** | **Edit Relationships**.
2. Double-click on the line between **ElkPupilsTbl** and **FeeAccountsTbl** to access the **Edit Relationships** dialog box.
3. Click on **Enforce Referential Integrity** and **Cascade Update Related Fields**. Click on **OK** to confirm and return to the **Relationships** window. Close the **Relationships** window:

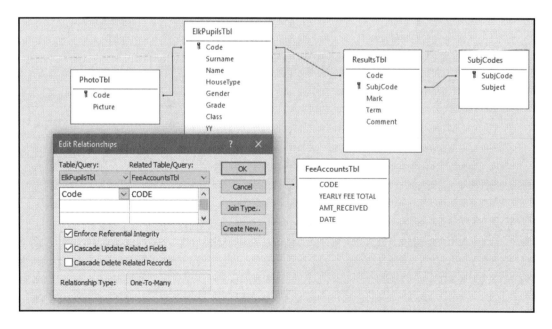

4. The relationship is updated, along with any changes to the primary key: for instance, if a pupil code is edited, it will also change all the related fields in the other tables.

Summary

In this chapter, you have been introduced to the Access 2019 environment and have gained the required theoretical background to be able to make informed design decisions when planning a new database. You have learned about the different objects that make up a database and how they fit together. You should now be confident enough to create a database and add tables using different views, set up fields and data types, and create relationships confidently using primary keys within tables. You also possess theoretical knowledge about referential integrity and cascading updates.

The next chapter will concentrate on building forms and report design, where you will be entering data and using the relevant formatting tools and learning about the different views when working with both forms and reports. You will learn to modify report headers and footers and manipulate report controls.

14
Building Forms and Report Design

In this chapter, we will take you on a journey through the creation of forms and reports. You will enter and modify data in a form and use the relevant formatting tools located on the different views of a form, as well as understand the impact that deleting records could have on a data table. You will create and modify report designs, work with different **Report View** modes, create reports based on a table or query, and master report headers and footers, as well as manipulate controls.

In this chapter, we will cover the following main topics:

- Building forms
- Form customization and layout
- The report design, controls, and output

Technical requirements

Before starting this chapter, you should be a confident user of Excel and be able to construct formulas and use filters and analysis tools. Having worked through the previous chapters of this book, you will have the necessary formatting and navigational skills to navigate the Access application. You will know how to locate and launch Access 2019 from the desktop. The examples used in this chapter can be accessed from `https://github.com/PacktPublishing/Learn-Microsoft-Office-2019`.

Building forms

In this section, you will learn how to create forms using the wizard, become familiar with form views, insert data as a new record using a form, navigate and modify data in form view, create form headers and footers, and use a form's search facility. You will also learn how to add existing fields to a form.

Once you have set up tables on a database and entered the relevant information into a **Datasheet View**, you will be ready to create other objects on the database. If you don't set up tables, you won't have a foundation to create objects on. Entering data into a table is done in exactly the same way as you would in Excel 2019, which we covered in the *Identifying rows, columns, and cells* section in `Chapter 8`, *Formatting, Manipulating, and Presenting Data Visually*.

A **form** is used to enter information, just as you would enter records into a table datasheet, and is typically created for end users who do not have permission to make changes to the table design or field properties. It is a user-friendly way of entering data into a table. It makes the job of the users of the database more pleasant when displaying, entering, and maintaining records. A table structure has to be set up prior to creating a form. When entering data into a form, it is automatically updated to the relevant table.

Using the form wizard

Using the form wizard is the most common method of creating a new form as it takes you through the steps one by one. There are many ways of achieving the same output, such as by using the options under the **Forms** tab. The quickest method is to use the **Form** option—just one click and you have created a simple form that allows you to input information one record at a time:

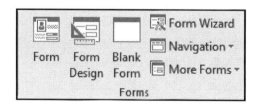

To create a form using the form wizard, follow these steps in the
`SSGSchoolDB.accdb` database:

1. Go to **Create** | **Form Wizard**. The **Form Wizard** page will lead you through the process of creating a form.
2. Follow the steps by clicking **Next >** each time you have completed a step. Select a table from the drop-down list to base your form on. Note that you can select from a list of existing tables or queries. Select the fields to add to the form by either double-clicking on each field or using the double-arrow icon to add all the fields to the form:

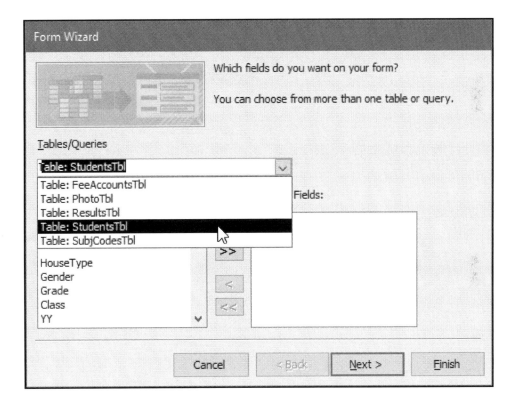

3. To remove fields that you may have added by mistake, simply select the field in the **Selected Fields** box to the right, and then click on the left-facing arrow (<) to move the field back to the **Available Fields** box:

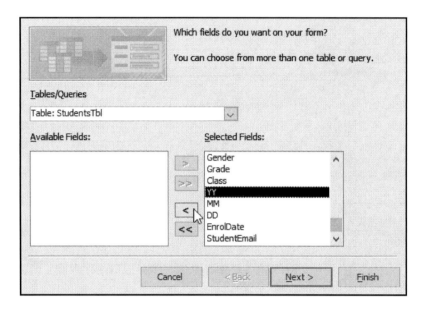

4. Click **Next >** to continue, and then select the desired layout for the form (in our case, **Justified**):

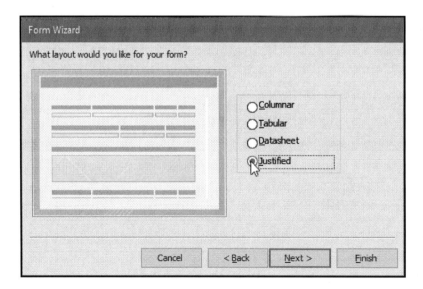

5. Click **Next >** to continue.

6. For the last step, enter a title to be the actual name of the form that will be listed on the Navigation Pane under **Forms**, as well as on the form's header. Click **Finish** to view the completed form.

After you have created the form, it is possible to rename it in the Navigation Pane. Remember that if you rename a form that has macros and other reports connected to it, this renaming could cause serious errors to the macros and reports, which could end up not working.

Working with form views

A form has three different views, which are as follows:

- **Form view**: A user-friendly way of displaying and entering data. Data, as well as records, can be changed and deleted. The structure of the form cannot be changed here. Data entered on a form is updated to the underlying table that was used to create the form.

- **Layout view**: This view is similar to **Design view**, except some tasks are easier to perform in one view than the other. **Layout view** is best for changing the look and feel of the form as you can rearrange fields and change sizes or apply custom styles while viewing the data. In **Design view**, you would not be able to preview these changes. It is easy to control the alignment of items in this view. If a particular design change cannot be performed in **Layout view**, Access will prompt you to switch to **Design view**.

- **Design view**: The layout of the form is altered in this view. This is where all the structural changes are made. New fields can be added to the form in this view from the field list box. **Field Properties** can also be changed here. Data cannot be added to **Design view**. More experienced users will design forms from scratch here.

These views are accessible using one of the following methods:

- Click on the **Home** tab and select the drop-down arrow on the **View** icon to the very left of the window, or right-click on the form's title bar:

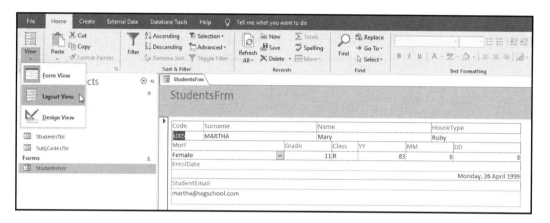

- Right-click on the form name from the Navigation pane.

Adding a new record to a form

1. Open the desired form from the Navigation Pane by double-clicking on it. The form will automatically open in **Form view**.
2. Click on the new (blank) record icon under the **Record** navigator panel displayed at the bottom of the form. Alternatively, click on the **New** icon located under the **Records** tab:

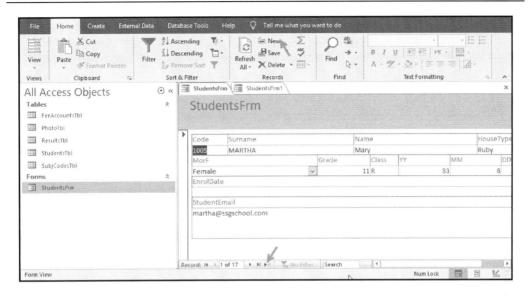

3. Enter data into the first field at the top of the form and press *Tab* or *Enter* on your keyboard to navigate to the next field, and so on.

4. Press *Enter* on your keyboard to save the record automatically and move to the next new record.

Navigating and deleting form records

The following screenshot identifies the different options on the **Record** bar, which is located at the bottom of a form:

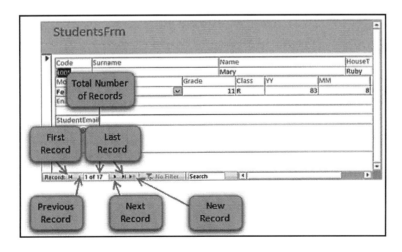

To delete a record, make sure you are viewing the form in **Form view**, and then locate the record to delete it using the **Record** bar. Go to **Home** | **Delete** | **Delete Record**. A dialog box will pop up on over the form to ask you whether you are completely sure you would like to delete the record. Click on Yes to confirm and delete the record.

Applying and editing form headers

Just as we add headers to documents and workbooks, we are able to add a header to a form or report on Access 2019. The header area is located at the top of the form or report, where the main heading is displayed:

1. Open `StudentsFrm` in **Design view** so that you can apply or edit the header. If the form's header is not visible in **Design view**, either right-click with your mouse at the top of the form and choose **Form Header/Footer** from the drop-down list or place the mouse pointer in between the form's header text and page's header text. A double arrow will appear. Hold your mouse down and drag downward to create a space for the form's header:

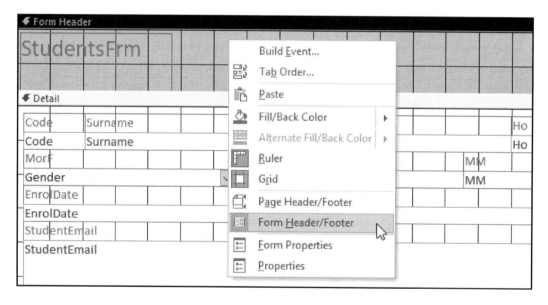

2. Click on the label icon located under the **Design** contextual tab in the **Controls** group.
3. Click and drag to create a label control in the desired position on the form. Type the form's header text into the label control:

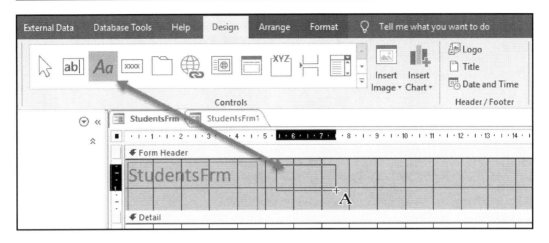

4. Save the form and return to **Form view** to see the changes. To edit the header text, simply navigate back to **Design view** and make the changes. Edit the **StudentsFrm** header to read **Student Database**. Use the **Format** tab of the contextual menu to make changes to the font face, size, alignment, colors, and line types, just as you would do in any other Office 2019 application. You can also add a background image using the **Format** tab or by right-clicking on the form's background to change the fill color.

Adding existing fields to a form

If you have created a form and left out an important field when using the wizard, it is possible to add the field to the form after the form is created, as follows:

1. Open StudentsFrm in **Layout view**. You can add fields in **Design view**, but it is much easier to see the changes when using **Layout view**.

2. Click on the **Design** tab in the **Form Layout Tools** contextual menu and then locate the **Tools** group.

3. Click on the **Add Existing Fields** icon. A **Field List** box will display to the right-hand side of the database window.

4. Before we add the new field to the form, we should place our form controls in the **Stacked** mode so that while we are adding the new field, it will slot into place without us having to separate the label and field by trying to line it up to existing fields on the form. Select all the fields on the form by holding down the *Shift* key and selecting each field on the form, then go to **Arrange | Stacked**.

5. Double-click on the field you would like to add to the form from the **Field List** pane. You can also use alternative methods, such as right-clicking on the field and choosing **Add Field to View** or simply dragging the field to the form yourself by holding down the left mouse button. The following screenshot shows you how to do the drag method:

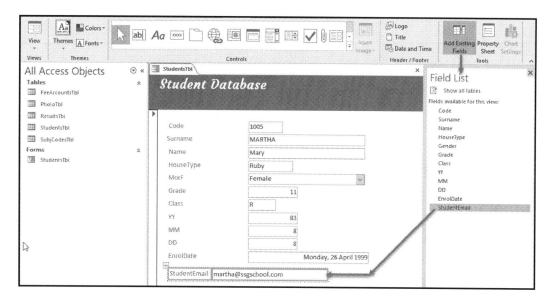

6. The new field will be placed at the top of the form. You then need to drag it into position using your mouse. Note that a field has two parts—the label, and the field. The label is the column header and the field is the actual data contained in the column for a particular row.

Searching for data on a form

Open StudentsFrm. Normally, we would have thousands of records in a database, so you would want to be able to search the records really quickly to locate a certain record. In this example, we will use the quickest method to locate a student in the database:

1. First, click on the **Name** field on the form.

2. Locate the **Search** box at the bottom of the form, which is located to the right of the **Record** bar. Type `Naziela` into the **Search** box. As you start typing, the record will be found immediately:

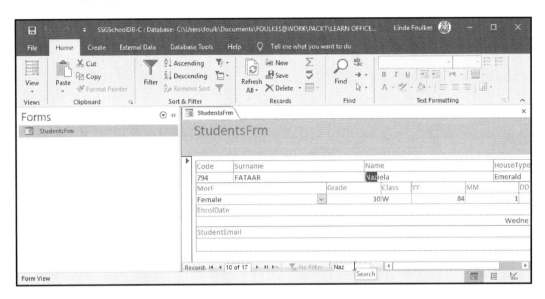

3. For a more comprehensive search option, such as to replace data, go to the **Find** group under the **Home** tab, where you will see more options, which work much the same as in other Office 2019 applications.

Form customization and layout

In this section, you will learn how to change the size of a field textbox on a form to accommodate more text and to investigate various formatting options to create a professional-looking form for user input. You will insert form images and work with the form's background elements to customize its design. You will also become familiar with the form's design tools to control padding, margins, and the table's layout.

Resizing and moving form fields

1. Open `StudentsFrm` in **Design view**.

   The existing fields on the form are neatly arranged, but if we need to add another field to the form, it might not slot into place. Let's see how we would resize fields.

2. Drag a field onto the form, and then click on the field to resize it. You will see that the label and the field can be separated by dragging the gray square to the top-left side of the label or field:

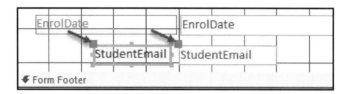

3. Around the edges of the selected label or field, you will notice sizing handles. Place your mouse pointer on one of the sizing handles and a double arrow will appear. Click and drag the field to resize it:

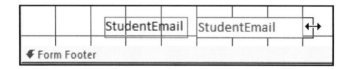

4. Alternatively, go to the **Sizing & Ordering** tab and click on the **Size/Space** icon. Select **To Fit** from the drop-down list.

Inserting a form's background image

When adding an image to the form's background, you need to decide where you would like it to be displayed. If we use **Design view** to add a background image, the image will appear in the background behind the form fields. In **Layout view**, the image will be added alongside the form fields. Although the image is seen in different positions in **Design view** and **Layout view**, the image in **Form view** will appear to the right of the data:

1. Open `StudentFrm` in **Design view** or **Layout view**.
2. Click on the **Format** tab located under the **Form Layout Tools** contextual menu.

3. Select **Background Image**, and then select an image from the recently used list provided or browse for an image on your computer to add to the background of the form. Click on **Open** and the background will apply to the form:

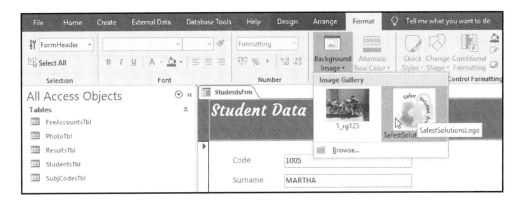

4. To remove the image from the background, right-click on the form's background in **Design view**. Select **Form Properties** from the provided list. The **Form Properties** list will appear to the right of the form. Click on the **All** category tab, and then scroll down to locate the **Picture** element:

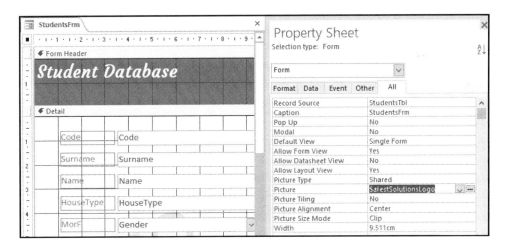

5. Delete the filename of the image—in this example, SafestSolutionsLogo. A dialog box will appear, prompting you to confirm whether you want to delete the image. Click **Yes** to continue and save the form.

Note that there is also an **Insert Image** option, which is located on the **Design** tab of the **Form Design Tools** contextual menu. This option will allow you to draw the image onto the form's header, should you wish to have more control over the image placement.

Changing the form's background color

The form's background color can be edited in exactly the same way as any other element you format—using the fill bucket. The view you choose will determine the method used:

1. Continue to use the example form from the previous section. View the form in **Design view** or **Layout view**.
2. Click on the background of the form. Do not click on a field textbox or object as the options you require will not be present.
3. Click on the **Fill/Back Color** drop-down arrow, and then select the background color of your choice to apply to the form. Alternatively, use the fill bucket located in the shortcut menu when you right-click your mouse to choose a color:

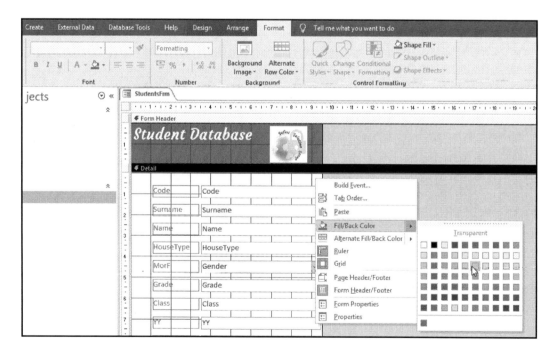

You have now learned how to add a background color to a form. These skills work in exactly the same way in forms and reports in Access 2019. We will now learn how to apply a theme to a form.

Applying a theme to a form

Themes are extremely useful when you do not have the time to format a form. They consist of a combination of colors and fonts that are preassembled for your use. We will follow this example using the form from the previous example:

1. Open the form that you want to apply a theme to from the Navigation Pane.
2. Make sure the form is in **Layout view** so that you can see the changes immediately. **Design view** can also be used, but you would need to change the view to see the changes:

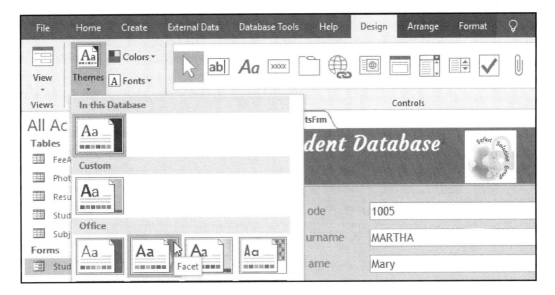

3. Under the **Form Layout Tools** | **Design** tab, locate the **Themes** group.
4. Select a theme from the drop-down list on the **Themes** icon to apply to the form. Changes are made to the background, textboxes, fonts, sizes, and alignments. You can see the changes to the form in **Layout view**.

Using the Position options on a form

The **Position** group is located under the **Arrange** tab of the **Form Layout Tools** contextual menu in Access 2019. It houses the options that relate to the anchoring of form cells, the spacing between labels and data, and the placement of data in the form cells. Let's take a closer look at each of these options:

1. Using the form from the previous example, make sure you are in **Layout view**.
2. Locate the **Control Margins** option, located at **Arrange | Position**.
3. Select the table cells by clicking on the table select icon, located at the top-left corner of the selected table.
4. Select **Medium** from the drop-down list provided. The margins around the top and left of the labels and data cells will adjust accordingly:

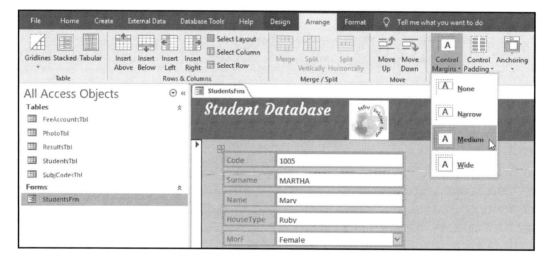

5. Experiment with the other **Control Margin** options.
6. Next, we will investigate the **Control Padding** option. **Control Padding** affects the amount of space between table cells in Access. Make sure the table is selected, then go to **Arrange | Control Padding**. Apply the **Wide** setting to the table.

7. Lastly, let's see what the **Anchoring** option does to the selected list. Click on the **Anchoring** icon to access the drop-down list of options. Choose **Stretch Down and Across** and note that the table is now positioned to the right of the window. This is particularly useful when you need to add an image or another control to the left. It anchors the table to a certain section or control on the form and will move when the control or section is re-positioned:

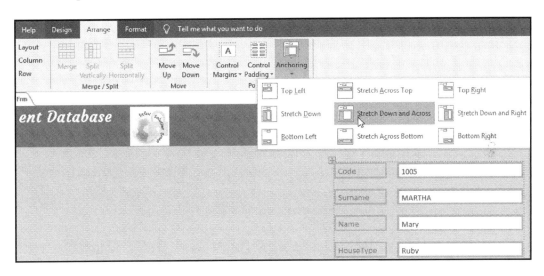

8. Experiment with the other **Anchoring** options.

You have now learned how to format and work with the **Arrange** options when using forms in Access 2019. In the next section, we will look at the report design options and investigate the controls and output options.

The report design, controls, and output

In this section, we will introduce you to the different **Report View** modes and you will create a report based on a table or query and learn how to calculate records in a report and format values. In addition, you will master the creation of report headers and footers, as well as grouping and sorting. You will also learn how to apply report formatting using the **Format** tab options and, finally, you will learn how to add controls to a report and look at the report output.

A report is used to present information in a neat and organized format, which is then normally printed out. If you have successfully created a form, you will also be able to create a report as the process is the same. Reports can also be previewed in different formats, such as labels, invoices, lists, and form letters. You can create a report on a table or a query.

The Report View modes

A report can be displayed in **Design view** or **Report View**. Changes are always made in **Design view** and **Report View** shows the print layout of a report. Structural changes are carried out in **Design view**. Please remember that you cannot edit records in **Design view**.

Report View is user-friendly and is used to display data in the way that it will look when printed out—similar to the **Print Preview** option on other Microsoft Office programs. No changes can be made to the structure and no records can be added, edited, or deleted in **Report View**. You will need to switch to **Design view** to make these changes.

Creating a report based on a table or query

Reports can be created in **Design view** using the wizard. It is always recommended that tables and queries are created in **Design view**, and that reports and forms are created with **Report Wizard**:

1. Open the database that you would like to create a report for. We will continue to use SSGSchoolDB.accdb, as in the previous example.

2. Click on the **Create** tab and locate the **Reports** group. Choose the **Report Wizard** icon and the report wizard will open:

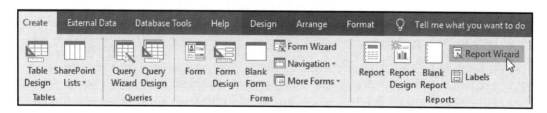

3. Select a table to create the report on using the drop-down arrow at the top of the dialog box.

4. Select the fields for the report from the **Available Fields:** box by double-clicking on the field name. Alternatively, select a field and click on the arrow to place it in the **Selected Fields:** area. One thing to be aware of is that the fields are added in order of selection. So, if you want the Name field to be listed on the report before the Surname field, then you need to select that field first.

5. Click on **Next >** to continue:

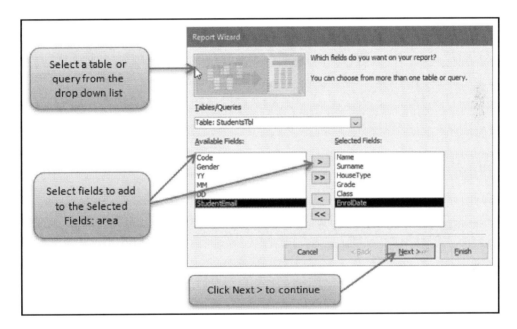

6. Click to select a field to group the report by. In this case, we selected Grade, so the report will group the data by grade. Double-click on the field to add it to the preview pane:

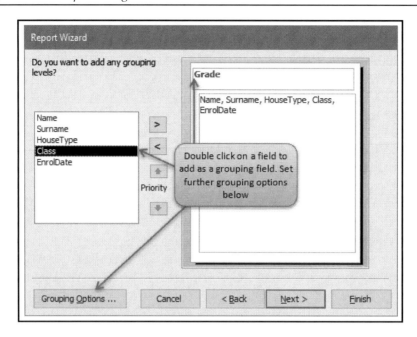

7. Click **Next >** to move on to the next step. The next step allows the user to sort fields in either **Ascending** or **Descending** order:

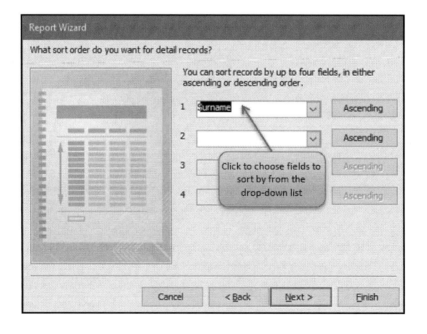

8. Choose a layout for the report and whether you want it to be presented in a **Landscape** or **Portrait** layout.

9. Click **Next >** to continue. The last step is to name the report before previewing it. Click on **Finish** to view the report.

10. The finished report, grouped by Grade, is displayed in the database window:

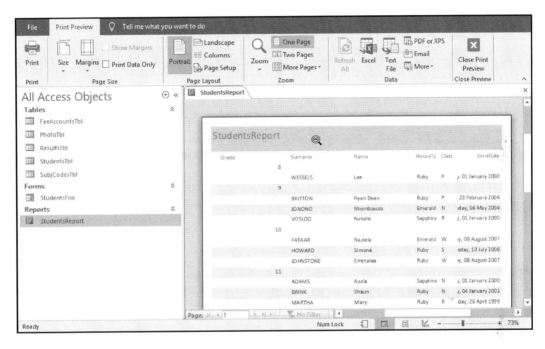

11. To view the report in **Design view**, click on the **Close Print Preview** option located at the top right-hand side of the window to exit the preview.

12. After exiting, the report will automatically move to **Design view**. To change the view to **Report View**, click on the **View** icon (located directly below the **File** tab). To view the report in **Layout view**, click on the **View** icon again. **Layout View** allows you to preview changes as they are made to the report:

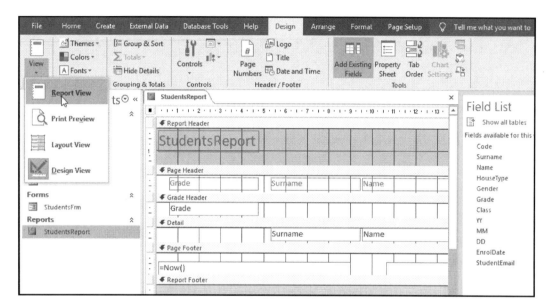

13. When creating a report from a table that contains values, you can perform summary calculations (such as sum, average, maximum, and minimum) automatically through the wizard. When this option is chosen, the calculation results are also added automatically in the form. The **Summary Options...** option is located at the bottom of the sort options step in the wizard:

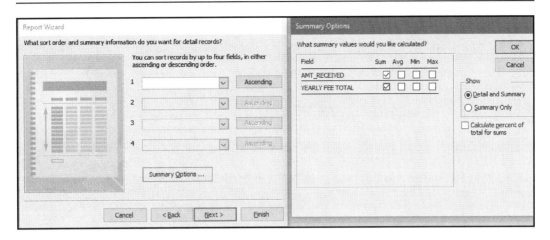

You have now learned how to create a report using **Report Wizard** in this section. We will learn how to perform calculations on a report in the next topic.

Calculating in a report

Records can be calculated in a report by grouping values based on specific fields. Calculated fields can be included in a report. You can work out the total sum of the amount received, the maximum and minimum values, the averages, or the count of a number of items. The calculation that is performed determines where the calculated field will be positioned in the report.

Here are some examples:

=sum([amt_received])	Calculates the sum of the received payments from parents
=average([salary])	Calculates the average salary
=maximum([salary])	Displays the highest salary
=minimum([salary])	Displays the lowest salary
=count([surname])	Counts the number of students
=[salary]*12	Multiplies the value by 12
=[amt_received]/12	Divides the amount received by 12
=[salary]+[bonus]	Adds the salary to the bonus
=[salary]-[bonus]	Subtracts the salary from the bonus

When using the preceding calculations, note the following:

- Brackets are extremely important, just as they are when used in Excel to construct formulas. Just like in Excel, we use square brackets to identify field names on a report.
- Field names are case sensitive.
- Field names must be typed exactly as they appear in the original field.
- Uppercase, lowercase, and spaces must correspond.

Let's go through an example of calculating a report together:

1. Open a report to edit in **Design view**. We will use the StudentsRPT report created in the previous example.
2. Create a textbox in the report's footer:

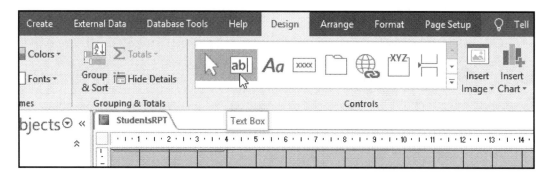

3. Once the **Text Box** control has been inserted onto the report, the two textboxes may appear to overlap:

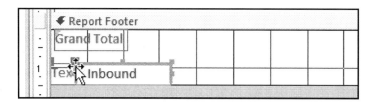

4. Separate the **Text Box** control by dragging the unbound box away from the label. Change the name of the **Text** label to `Number of Payments`. Resize if necessary:

5. Click on the **Unbound** control and type `=count(*)`. Change the font, if necessary, using the **Format** tab on the top ribbon.

6. Preview your report to check the changes. Then, change back to **Design view**.

7. Edit your report's footer to contain a `=sum([AMT_RECEIVED])` function to calculate the total amount of fee payments received per student:

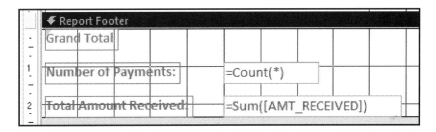

8. Change the view to **Report View**. Note that the calculations are visible at the very end of the report in the footer section:

Number of Payments:	20
Total Amount Received:	171530
Thursday, 19 March 2020	

In the next section, we will look at formatting values to display the currency format on a report.

Formatting values on a report

1. Open the StudentRPT report in **Design view**, and then click on the unbound control. Locate **Property Sheet** to the right of the database window and scroll down until you find the **Format** heading.

2. Click on the drop-down list to locate **Currency,** then click on it with your mouse. Press *Enter* on your keyboard to apply the format to the selected field. Change the **Decimal Places** value (found below the **Format** property to 0 decimal places). A quick way to scroll through the options in a drop-down list is to double-click repeatedly until you land on the desired field format:

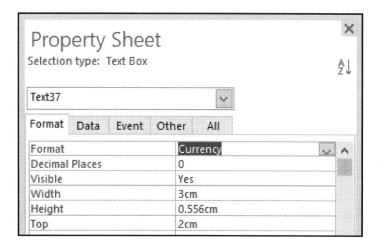

3. Close the **Property Sheet** window, if necessary.

Creating a report header or footer

A **header** is the area at the top of a form or report, while the footer is located at the bottom of a form or report. When text is entered into the header or footer of a report, it will repeat at the top or bottom of the report and is visible when in the **Print Preview** mode or in **Report View**. There are many sets of headers and footers that you can use in Access forms and reports.

These are explained in the following table:

Report Header	Appears only once on the very first page of the report and will most likely contain elements such as company logo, the main report title, or the date.
Page Header	Appears at the top of every page in the report and will contain elements such as a report's title or page number.
Report Footer	Displays directly after the last row of data and above the report's page footer on the very last page of the report.
Page Footer	Shown at the bottom of each page in the report and can contain elements such as the date or page numbers.
The **Group Header** section	This is the field that is grouped on and displays just before a group of rows (records).
The **Group Footer** section	This contains elements such as group totals, sums, averages, counts, and minimum and maximum values, and appears just after a group of records.

Let's take a visual look at the options available and where they are situated on a report:

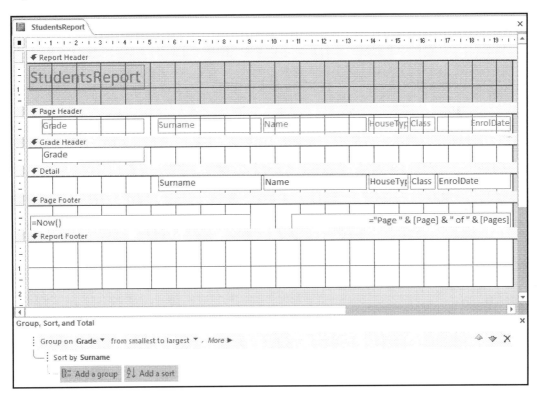

Now that we have an understanding of the header and footer elements, let's put this into practice:

1. Open StudentsReport from the previous example and make sure you are in **Design view**.
2. If **Report Header** is not visible in **Design view**, right-click at the top of the report and choose **Report Header/Footer** from the drop-down list:

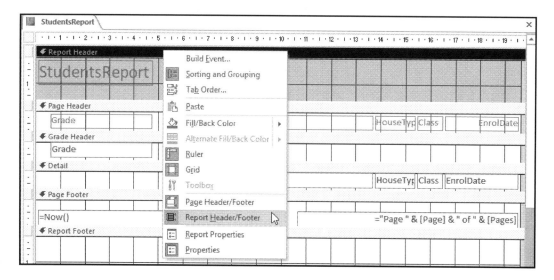

3. Alternatively, place your mouse pointer in between the **Report Header** and **Page Header** text. A double arrow will appear. Hold your mouse down and drag downward to create a space for the report header:

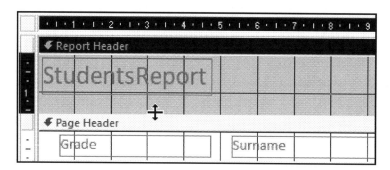

4. Click on the **Controls** icon and select the **Label** control, located in the **Controls** group.

5. Click and drag to create a **Label** control in the desired position, and then type the header text into the control box.

6. Format the **Label** control just as you would any other text, but make sure that you select the control first. Once the label is selected, click on the **Format** tab to access all the formatting options. Click the **Save** icon on the QAT to save the changes.

7. Click on **Report View** to see the changes made. To create a report footer, you will need to follow these steps exactly.

Applying the report formatting options

The formatting of a report in Access is exactly the same as how you would format any other element in the Office 2019 environment. The formatting options are located on the **Format** tab, or by right-clicking on the element or report's background. The options available depend on the view that you select, but you will become familiar with these as you get used to formatting reports.

First, to add color, we'll have to follow these steps:

1. Open a report in **Design view**, and then click on the textbox that you wish to change the color of.

2. Select the arrow next to the **Fill/Back Color** icon under the **Format** tab in the **Font** group. Select a color to apply to the textbox by clicking on it.

Next, we'll check on adding borders to a textbox or label:

1. Open a report in **Design view**, and then select the **Shape Outline** icon under the **Format** tab in the **Control Formatting** group.

2. Select a color from the palette.

Lastly, we'll see how to change the border line width:

1. Open a report in **Design view**, and then select the **Shape Outline** icon under the **Format** tab in the **Control Formatting** group.

2. Place the mouse pointer on the **Line Thickness** option, and then select the line thickness of your choice from the side menu.

Now that you have been through the skills that you need to format a report, the next section will concentrate on the page setup options.

Applying the report's page setup tab options

Print Preview is a view that shows you how a report will look once printed—this view provides you with a snapshot of the entire document. You can zoom in and out of the document, print, or change the layout options of the page:

1. Open the report you want to preview. We will continue to use the `SSGSchoolDB.accdb` database for this purpose.
2. Click on the **File** tab, select **Print** from the drop-down list, and then choose **Print Preview**.
3. Note that the **Print Preview** ribbon is now displayed and various options are presented to change the layout of the report.
4. To exit the **Print Preview** mode, click on the **Close Print Preview** icon on the **Close Preview** group. A quicker method to view the report in the **Print Preview** mode is to choose the **Print Preview** option when you right-click your mouse:

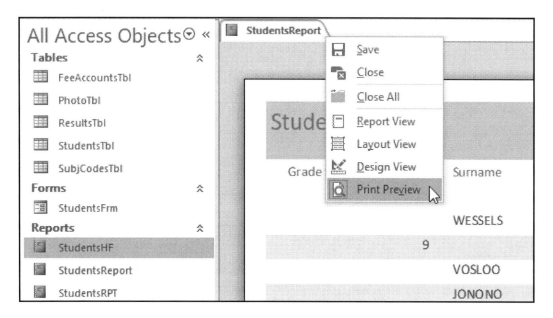

5. The print preview zoom icon displays on the report so that you are able to increase or decrease the size of the preview:

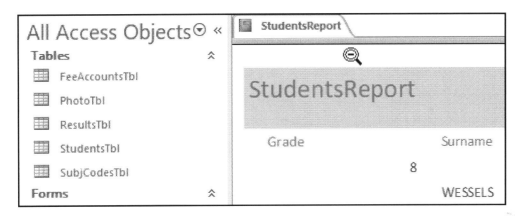

The default orientation in Access is **Portrait**. In this section, we will change the orientation of the report to accommodate any rows that don't fit on a **Portrait** page. This is particularly useful when including charts alongside data on a report:

1. Select the table, form, query, or report that you want to print by double-clicking on the object in the Navigation Pane.
2. Once the object is open, click on the **File** tab, and then go to **Print | Print Preview**. The **Print Preview** tab will display on your screen.
3. In the **Page Layout** group, locate the **Landscape** icon to change the layout from **Portrait** to **Landscape**.
4. To change the paper size, click on the **Size** icon to access the drop-down list. The recommended size is **A4**.

To print a report, open the report from the Navigation Pane that you want to print, and then click on the **File** tab and go to **Print | Print**. All the data will be printed unless you change the default settings in the **Print** dialog box. Click on **OK** to print the table once you have selected the printer, the number of copies, and the page range.

Summary

In this chapter, you acquired the skills to work with forms and reports in Access 2019. You should be comfortable enough to create forms and reports using the wizard and to customize them to suit your output requirements by changing the form and report elements using the options located in the form and the report's **Design view** and **Layout view** modes.

In addition, you learned how to add controls to a form or report and perform calculations to work out totals and count values in a report footer. You have also learned how to add images to a form or report and how to use control padding, anchors, and control margins on a form.

In the next chapter, we will look at queries—the heart of Access 2019—which allow us to search and extract information from tables for analysis. You will learn how to construct queries using **Design view** to analyze data and understand different query types and their functions.

15
Constructing Queries to Analyze Data

Queries, being the heart of Access 2019, allow for the searching and extraction of information from tables for analysis. In this chapter, you will learn how to construct queries using **Design View** to analyze data and become knowledgeable about different query types and their function. You will learn how to create a simple Select query and add tables and fields to the query grid, and become familiar with different views and how to manipulate fields and criteria on the query grid. We will also cover advanced query construction.

In this chapter, we're going to cover the following main topics:

- Constructing basic queries
- Manipulating query fields and the **Total** row
- Constructing advanced queries

Technical requirements

Having worked through previous chapters of this book, you will have the necessary formatting and navigational skills to navigate around the Access application. You will know how to create tables, forms, and reports, as well as how to edit and format elements adding controls and calculations on a report. The examples used in this chapter are accessible from the following GitHub URL: `https://github.com/PacktPublishing/Learn-Microsoft-Office-2019`.

Constructing basic queries

You will gain a solid overview of the different query types in Access 2019 and learn to create and run a Select query in **Design View**.

Queries are used to retrieve information from a database. Queries allow you to search and extract information from tables for analysis. Calculations are possible when constructing queries, and the results are normally displayed in a report. A Select query is when you ask questions of data and extract the answers. You can decide to see certain fields from a table, all records, and fields; or, just fields. Queries can be performed on more than one related table in one single query. A relationship must exist between the tables to allow them to be used together to extract information in a query result. Queries can additionally be used to update fields automatically when run, and also to delete data in fields automatically.

There are different types of queries that can be constructed in Access 2019. Some examples of these are highlighted here:

- **Select query**: Data is extracted from one table, more than one table, from other queries, or from tables for analyzing.
- **Parameter query**: This allows the user to input data depending on the required field or fields. When the query is run, a parameter dialog box will appear, asking the user to input the required criteria to produce a result. For example, to produce a class list for a particular grade and class, you would create a parameter query, requesting the user to enter the grade and class they wish to query. The query result will be based on the input from the user.
- **Update query**: Updates data in fields automatically.
- **Append query**: Performs a query based on user input, and then adds the result to another table automatically.
- **Make Table query**: As the name suggests, you create a query from a table or multiple tables and then create a new table from the results.

Creating a Select query in Design View

1. Open the database to base the queries in. We will continue with the `SSGStudents.accdb` database.

2. On the **Create** tab, locate the **Queries** group, and click the **Query Design** icon, as illustrated in the following screenshot:

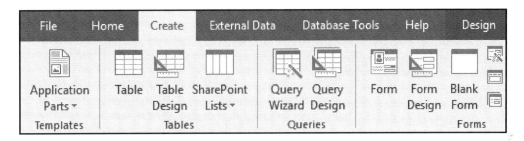

3. The **Show Table** dialog box will present itself, where you will need to select the table on which you wish to base the new query. Choose **StudentsTbl**.

   If one table is used in a query, then it is called a **single table query**.

4. Click **Add,** then click on **Close**.

5. Select the fields from the table list by double-clicking to add them to the query grid. For this example, we will select **Name**, **Surname**, **HouseType**, and **Gender**.

6. Add the criteria for the specific query requirements in the **Criteria:** row. We will use **Sapphire** for the **HouseType** field and **Male** for the **Gender** field. Notice that once you enter the criteria, the text is automatically formatted to include inverted commas before and after the field. This is because the field is a text entry field. The criteria can be viewed in the following screenshot:

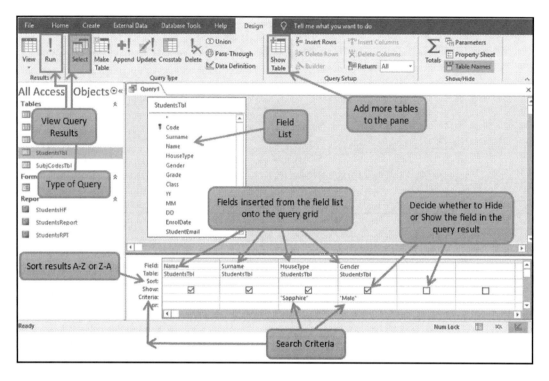

7. From the **Design** tab, locate the **Results** group. Click the **! Run** icon to view the results (see the preceding screenshot to view this), which can be seen in the following screenshot:

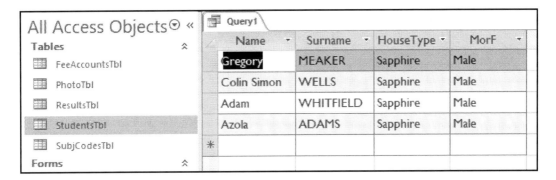

8. The results open up in **Datasheet View**, named **Query1**. Save the query as
   HouseQry, using the **Quick Access Toolbar (QAT)** or by right-clicking on
   the **Query1** tab. Enter the name of the query into the dialog box, which
   populates. Remember that naming is very important in this instance as the
   name will notify the user as to the type of information it will produce when
   run, as illustrated in the following screenshot:

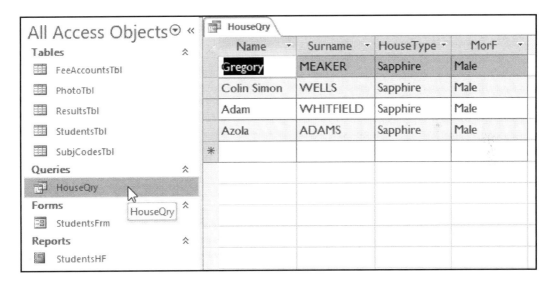

9. The **HouseQry** query appears under the **Queries** object heading in the **All
   Access Objects** Navigation Pane, as illustrated in the preceding screenshot.

Creating a Select query using the Query Wizard

1. We will continue with the example from the previous section. Locate the **Query Wizard** on the **Create** tab from the **Queries** group.

2. Choose the type of query to design from the dialog box. For this exercise, we are using the **Simple Query Wizard**, as illustrated in the following screenshot:

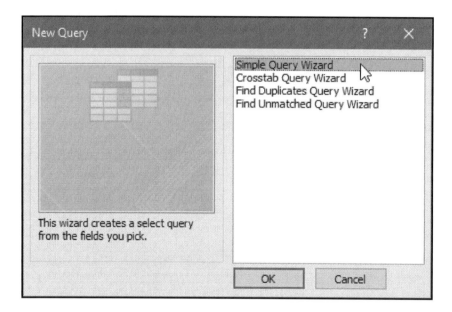

3. Click on **OK** to continue, then choose the table on which to base the query from the drop-down list under **Tables/Queries**. Choose **StudentsTbl**.

4. Add fields from the **Available Fields:** area to the **Selected Fields:** area. For this example, we will add **Name**, **Surname**, **HouseType**, and **Grade**, as illustrated in the following screenshot:

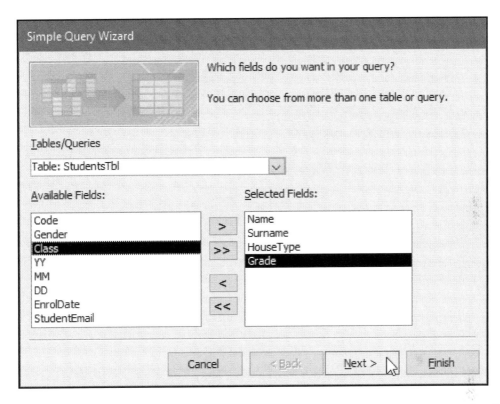

5. Click on **Next >** to continue. Choose whether to produce a summary for the query or use all the fields (detailed).

6. Click on **Next >** to continue. Name the query StudentsQuery. Click on **Finish**. Note that there will be no criteria entries added to the query. This would need to be done using the **Query Design** grid after using the wizard.

7. Click on the **Home** tab to change to **Design View** so that the query can be edited. Add the criteria for the specific query requirements in the criteria row. We would like to search for all the Grade 12e students. Enter this criterion into the query grid. You will need to add the **Class** field to the grid in order to search for all the students in the **e** class, as illustrated in the following screenshot:

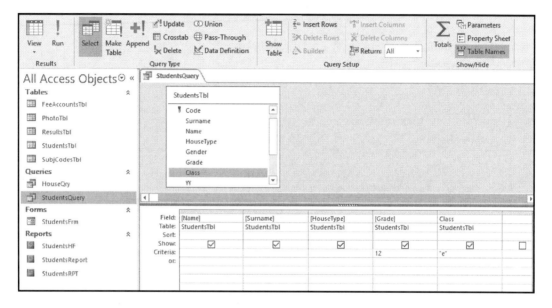

8. From **Design | Results**, click the **Run** icon. The query results are displayed in **Datasheet View**. Close the query, then rename the query by right-clicking on the query name in the **All Access Objects** pane, selecting **Rename**, and entering `Grade12E`. Press *Enter* on the keyboard to commit the change.

In the next section, we will look at more complex queries that you would use to analyze data in Access 2019.

Manipulating query fields and the Total row

In this topic, you will learn how to manipulate fields in a query by adding, removing, and rearranging fields, and we will look at sort and show options, compiling query criteria, using wildcards in a query, and calculating totals.

Adding fields

In this topic, you will learn how to add fields to an existing query. Follow these steps:

1. Open the query to add a field. For this example, open the **HouseQry** field.
2. Make sure that you are viewing the query in **Design View**.
3. Click into the next open column.
4. Select the field you would like to place onto the query grid by locating it from the aforementioned table(s) and double-clicking to add it to the grid, or click on the drop-down arrow to add a field from the table by selecting it from the list provided. We will add the **YY** field.
5. Make sure that the checkbox contains a tick; otherwise, the field will not show up on the query result when run. This is shown in the following screenshot:

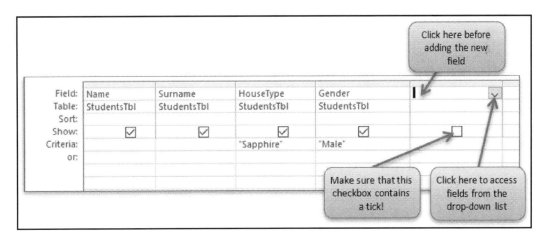

6. Run the query to make sure you are getting the results you need, then save changes to the query by clicking on the **Save** icon on the QAT.

Removing and rearranging fields

If you add a field to the query grid and decide that you no longer need it, simply click on the query grid and select the field you no longer require by clicking on the gray area just above the field name. A black downward-pointing arrow will appear before clicking. Once the column is selected, press *Delete* on the keyboard. The field is removed from the query grid but still remains as one of the fields in the table list above the grid, as illustrated in the following screenshot:

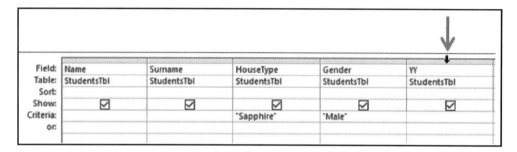

You can rearrange fields on the query grid if you did not add them in the correct order from the **Show Table** dialog box when you first created the query. On the query grid, select the field you wish to move by clicking on the gray area just above the field name. A black downward-pointing arrow will appear before clicking. Hold down the left mouse button and drag the column to a new location on the grid. This step will rearrange the columns in the preferred order and will produce the query output you require once you click on the **! Run** icon to see the result.

Sorting query data

1. On the query grid, select the down arrow on the field you wish to sort.
2. Make sure that you have selected the **Sort:** row. Click to choose to sort in either **Ascending** or **Descending** order, as illustrated in the following screenshot:

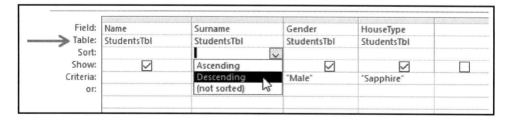

3. The query results will be sorted once the **Run** icon is clicked. Don't forget to save the query.

Compiling query criteria

There are many different types of criteria that you can use to query table data in Access 2019. It all depends on the field types and output you require. Query criteria can consist of dates, text, functions, and so much more. The following table shows some examples and explanations of different criteria that can be used in a query. Try these examples on the `SSGSchool.accdb` file you have been using for the topics in this chapter:

Criteria	Explanation	Example
Text	Simple text results—for example, company or area name.	HouseType StudentsTbl ☑ "Sapphire"
=	Equal to displays query results where the amount is equal to **5000**.	AMT_RECEIVED FeeAccountsTbl Sum ☑ =5000
<>	Not equal to displays query results for all house types except **Emerald**.	[HouseType] ElkPupilsTbl ☑ <>"Emerald"
<	Less than displays query results for all birth months before July.	MM ElkPupilsTbl ☑ <7

<=	Less than or equal to displays query results where the date of payments in the **FeeAccounts** table is less than or equal to June 30, 2004.	DATE FeeAccountsTbl ☑ <=#2004/06/30#
>	Greater than displays query results where the amount paid by parents is greater than **7000**.	AMT_RECEIVED FeeAccountsTbl ☑ >7000
>=	Greater than or equal to displays query results where the enrollment date is greater than or equal to January 28, 2007.	EnrolDate ElkPupilsTbl ☑ >=#2007/01/28#
Yes/No	Displays query results where the child received a scholarship.	Scholarship ▼ FeeAccountsTbl ☑ Yes
Like	Displays query results where the surname field contains text that starts with **W**.	[Surname] ElkPupilsTbl ☑ Like "W*"
Between	Displays query results between two amounts in the **AMT_RECEIVED** column.	AMT_RECEIVED FeeAccountsTbl ☑ Between 2000 And 6000
AND	AND criteria must be placed on the same line on the query grid.	[HouseType] / [Grade] / Gender — ElkPupilsTbl / ElkPupilsTbl / ElkPupilsTbl — ☑ / ☑ / ☑ — "Emerald" / / "Male"

OR	OR criteria must be placed on different lines on the query grid.		
		Field:	Surname	AMT_RECEIVED
		Table:	ElkPupilsTbl	FeeAccountsTbl
		Total:	Group By	Sum
		Sort:		
		Show:	☑	☑
		Criteria:		<5000
		or:		>7000
NOT	Shows query results for all students except **MEAKER** in the case of this example.	[Surname] ElkPupilsTbl ☑ Not "MEAKER"	

In the next topic, we will delve further into query criteria, learning how to apply special characters to get the output you need when constructing queries in Access 2019.

Using wildcards in queries

Wildcard characters are special characters that can be used when you are not sure how to spell a word or when you wish to find similar-type words that start with the same character. These characters make your search more powerful and flexible. Here are two examples of wildcard characters:

- *** or %**: Matches any number of characters. The * can be used anywhere in a character string—see the example in the table in the *Compiling query criteria* section.
- **? or _**: Matches any single alphabetical character.

There are many different types of wildcard characters that can be used in queries. The aforementioned examples are just a few to get you thinking! Let's take a look at how to create a parameter query in the next topic.

Calculating totals with a query

In the following screenshot, you will see a table named **FeeAccountsTbl** on the left and a completed totals query named **SumReceived** on the right. This representation will help you understand what the totals query is about in the explanation that follows:

FeeAccountsTbl			
CODE	YEARLY FEE	AMT_RECEIVED	DATE
1005	R 13 200.00	R 6 000.00	28-Jun-04
1005	R 13 200.00	R 5 000.00	26-Sep-04
1341	R 13 200.00	R 12 000.00	30-Jun-04
164	R 13 200.00	R 12 000.00	30-Jun-04
412	R 13 200.00	R 1 000.00	30-Jun-04
412	R 13 200.00	R 2 530.00	03-Apr-04
412	R 13 200.00	R 1 000.00	28-Jan-97
427	R 13 200.00	R 7 000.00	25-Jun-04
427	R 13 200.00	R 2 000.00	02-Jan-95
429	R 13 200.00	R 12 000.00	30-Jun-04
436	R 13 200.00	R 12 000.00	30-Jun-04
593	R 13 200.00	R 12 000.00	30-Jun-04
65	R 13 200.00	R 12 000.00	30-Jun-04
794	R 13 200.00	R 3 000.00	14-Feb-98
800	R 13 200.00	R 12 000.00	30-Jun-04
882	R 13 200.00	R 12 000.00	30-Jun-04
883	R 13 200.00	R 12 000.00	30-Jun-04
890	R 13 200.00	R 12 000.00	30-Jun-04
891	R 13 200.00	R 12 000.00	30-Jun-04
895	R 13 200.00	R 12 000.00	30-Jun-04
*	R 12 000.00		

The completed totals query named **SumReceived** is displayed here, showing the result of using the calculated totals query option, as illustrated in the following screenshot:

Code	Surname	SumOfAMT
891	ADAMS	£12 000.00
895	BRINK	£12 000.00
412	CARNEY	£4 530.00
794	FATAAR	£3 000.00
593	HOWARD	£12 000.00
800	JOHNSTONE	£12 000.00
65	JONONO	£12 000.00
883	LIONS	£12 000.00
1005	MARTHA	£11 000.00
427	MEAKER	£9 000.00
429	PALMER	£12 000.00
882	RAJANAH	£12 000.00
164	VOSLOO	£12 000.00
436	WELLS	£12 000.00
1341	WESSELS	£12 000.00
890	WHITFIELD	£12 000.00

In the table in the preceding screenshot, I have student codes that are repeated more than once, depending on the numbers of payments that have been received. If you look at **Code** number **412**, which belongs to **CARNEY** in the query result, you will notice that if you add up the three records that are displayed, the total amount received is **£4530.00**, as recorded in the query result. The **Surname** has been displayed in the query result because of the relationship between the **FeeAccountsTbl** table and the **StudentsTbl** table used to generate the query result.

So, how did I manage to sum the amount received so quickly using a query? Let's run through the steps:

1. Using the `SSGSchool.accdb` database, create a new query in **Design View**.
2. Add the two tables (**StudentsTbl** and **FeeAccountsTbl**) to the query grid.

3. Add the **Code** and **Surname** fields from the **StudentsTbl** table and the **AMT_RECEIVED** field from the **FeeAccountsTbl** table to the design grid.

4. From the **Show/Hide** group, select the **Totals** icon.

5. On the query grid, check that the **Total:** row reads **Group By** for the **Surname** field and that the **AMT_RECEIVED** field performs the **Sum** function, as illustrated in the following screenshot:

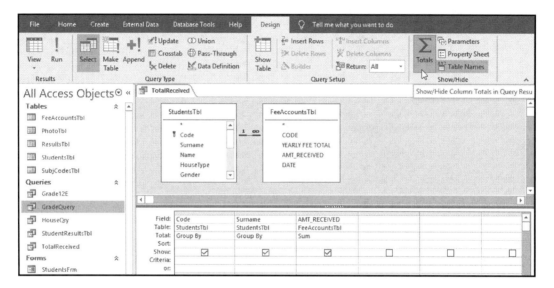

6. Run your query using the **Run** icon on the ribbon. Your query should group the surnames and give the total amount received for each student code.

Constructing advanced queries

In this section, you will create a two-table query and produce output from related fields, and a calculated query. You will discover more about the construction of queries to analyze data in this chapter and will cover the creation of an **Update**, **Make Table**, and **Append** query; create a **Crosstab** query using the wizard; have fun with the Parameter query; and learn how relationships affect a query result.

Creating a two-table query in Design View

When we create a two-table query within Access, we need to ensure that a relationship exists between the two tables prior to creating the query. This is an important rule as the results will neither query nor produce the correct output if the tables are not related via a common key such as **Code**, in the database example we are using for this demonstration. To create such a query, follow these steps:

1. Make sure you have the database open from the previous example. Click on the **Create** tab, then choose **Query Design**.
2. Select the table on which you wish to base the new query. Click **Add**, then repeat the step to add a second table. For this example, we are using the **StudentsTbl**, the **ResultsTbl**, and the **SubjCodesTbl** tables. Click on **Close**.
3. Select fields from both tables' lists by double-clicking to add them to the query grid. As we are requiring a query to produce subject results for all our grades, we will add the following fields from each of the tables listed. Please view the following screenshot to add the relevant fields to the query grid:

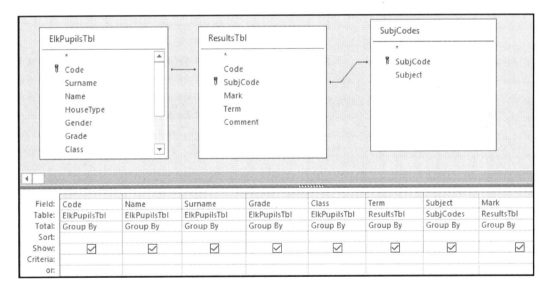

4. Add the criteria for the specific query requirements in the criteria row.
5. From the **Design** tab, locate the **Results** group. Click the **Run** icon. The query results are displayed in **Datasheet View**.

6. Click on the **Save** icon on the QAT and enter a query name called StudentMarksQry.

Use *Ctrl + click* to select more than one table at a time when adding tables from the **Show Table** dialog box.

Constructing a calculated query

It is possible to perform calculations while constructing a query. You can add a new field to the query that calculates, for instance, a 20% markup on products or a 30% increase in outstanding account payments. As long as you have existing fields within the table on which to base the calculation, it's extremely easy. To construct such a query, follow these steps:

1. Open the ElkAdmin.accdb database. Locate the **OutstandingAccounts** query and double-click to open it in **Datasheet View**. Take a few seconds to look at the data provided in the query.
2. View the query in **Design View**.
3. Add a new field called **CHARGES** to the query grid to the right of the **OUTSTANDING** field. The field must calculate a 20% increase in the outstanding amount, as illustrated in the following screenshot:

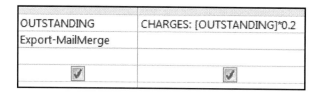

4. There are two methods to enter the calculation into the field, as follows:

   - The first method is to create a new field in the column alongside **OUTSTANDING**. You must insert a colon after the new name—for example, **CHARGES**. When using fields in calculations, you need to surround the field name with square brackets—for example, **[OUTSTANDING]**. To work out 20% of the outstanding amount, you would type *.2. Therefore, the calculation would be as follows: CHARGES: [OUTSTANDING]*.2.

- The second method would be to use the **Builder** button located on the **Query Setup** group to help formulate the calculation. Click on the **Builder** button to launch **Expression Builder**, as illustrated in the following screenshot:

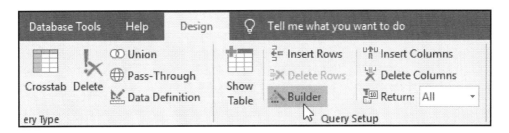

The dialog box contains **Expression Elements** such as the database objects (tables, queries). Click on the ElkAdmin.accdb element to expand the objects underneath it. Click to select the **OutstandingAccounts** query. From **Expression Categories**, choose the field or fields that you require to formulate your calculation by double-clicking on the field to place it into the **Expression Builder**, as illustrated in the following screenshot:

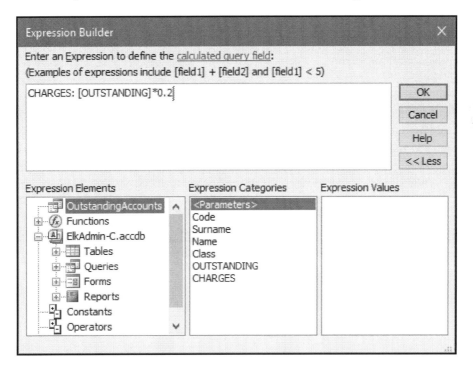

Alternatively, type the expression yourself into the build area provided at the top of the dialog box. Remember to place a colon after typing the field name to separate the name from the calculation.

5. Click the **OK** icon once the expression is complete.
6. The expression appears on the query grid as a new column.
7. To view the complete expression or make any changes, press the *Shift* key on the keyboard. While this key is depressed, also press the *F2* function key. A zoom window will open, showing the expression with enough room for editing.
8. Click on the **OK** icon to return to the query design.
9. Press the **Run** icon located on the **Results** group to see the result of the query.
10. Change the view back to **Design View** to edit the query, if necessary.

Creating a Make Table query

A **Make Table** query is great for copying, archiving, or backing up data. It retrieves data from a query or table and then dumps it into a new table in the same database or a new database, depending on your requirements. Note that you can select data from more than one table or query result to create a new table. To create such a query, follow these steps:

1. We will use the **OutstandingAccounts** query in the example database to create a new table.
2. Click on the **Query Design** icon located on the **Create** tab.
3. The query design will open and will prompt the user, via the **Show Table** dialog box, to select a table or query on which to base the new query. Select the **Queries** tab and choose the **OutstandingAccounts** query. Double-click or click on the **Add** icon to select the query. Click the **Close** icon to return to the query grid.
4. Add the fields that will make up the new table fields to the query grid. You can select all the fields using the *Shift-click* method and drag them out of the table onto the grid.

5. To create the new table, choose the **Make Table** query from the **Query Type** group, as illustrated in the following screenshot:

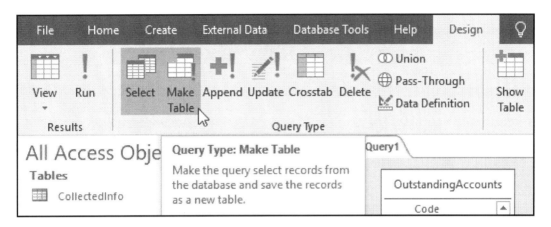

6. Enter a **Table Name** for the new table into the **Make Table** dialog box. Type `OutstandingAcc` into the text area provided, as illustrated in the following screenshot:

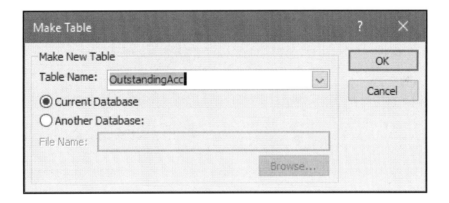

7. Choose whether to create a new table in the current database or a different database. Click on the **OK** icon to continue.

8. The new table will not be created until the **Run** icon is selected. Click the **Run** icon from the **Results** group.

9. The user will be prompted with an information box, indicating how many rows will be sent to a new table. Click on **Yes** to continue, as shown in the following screenshot:

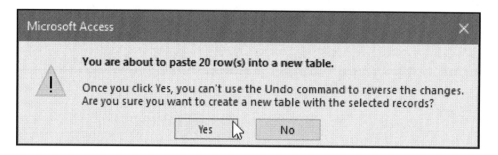

10. The new table called **OutstandingAcc** appears in the **Table** group on the Navigation Pane. Double-click to open the new table and view the contents in **Datasheet View**.

11. Please note that the new table is created but the existing query is not yet saved! Should you be running this query again to make a new table, then save the query design. Save the query as `MakeOutsAcc`. Also, note that running the query again to make the table will first delete the current table and replace it with the new one, as shown in the following screenshot:

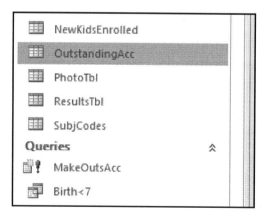

12. The **Make Table** query will reside in the **Query** group on the Navigation Pane. Note the icon it has been assigned, which indicates it is a **Make Table** query.

Using an Update query to replace data

An **Update** query cannot be used to add records or delete records. The query is used to edit, add, or delete data in a single record or multiple records. The concept of an **Update** query is much the same as the **Find and Replace** option, but definitely more potent. As you cannot undo the effects of an **Update** query, you should back up the database prior to running the query. The only way to reverse the effects of an **Update** query is to run another **Update** query or edit the records by hand. To create such a query, follow these steps:

1. Use the same database as the one shown in the preceding example to create an **Update** query. Create a new query in **Design View**.

2. Choose the table on which you will run the **Update** query. Click on **Add** then **Close** to move to the query grid. For this example, we will use **FeeAccountstTbl**.

3. Click on the **Update** icon on the **Query Type** group, as illustrated in the following screenshot:

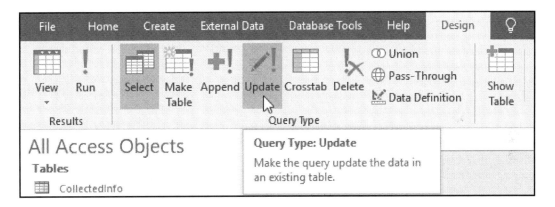

4. Notice that the query grid has changed to include the row called **Update To:**, as illustrated in the following screenshot:

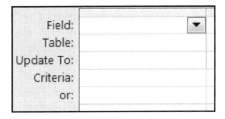

5. Add only the fields that require updating and the fields you would require for criteria purposes from the table onto the grid. Double-click to add the field. For this example, we will update the **YEARLY FEE TOTAL** data located in the **FeeAccountsTbl** table by 10%.

6. Make sure that the **Field:** row contains the **YEARLY FEE TOTAL** field.

7. In the **Update To:** row, enter the following: **[YEARLY FEE TOTAL]*1.1**, as illustrated in the following screenshot:

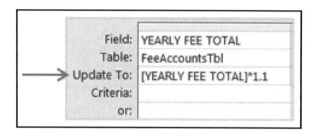

8. Click the **Run** icon on the **Results** group. The **[YEARLY FEE TOTAL]** underlying table field consists of the value **12000.00** at present. We are updating this amount by 10%.

9. You will be prompted with an information box, indicating how many rows will be updated. Click on **Yes** to continue.

10. Double-click to view the **FeeAccountsTbl** table in **Datasheet View**. The **YEARLY FEE TOTAL** field is updated to include a 10% increase from 13200.00 to 14520. Note that if the **Update** query is saved and is run again, it will affect the underlying table once again.

Now that you have seen the possibilities of **Update** queries, we will learn how to add new records to a table by copying and pasting records using **Append**.

Adding new records using an Append query

Use an **Append** query when you wish to add new records to an existing table by way of copying and pasting from one table to another. The field names do not have to be the same, but it is essential that the data is the same. For instance, to copy a value from one table to another table, the data type has to be a number in both tables.

If both tables contain the same field names and field sizes, then the transition is very simple. If the tables contain the same field names but not the same field sizes, then data could be lost in the transition from one table to the next. If the field names are not the same, you can specify which fields in the destination table they would match. To create such a query, follow these steps:

1. Create a new query in **Design View**, using the example database from the previous topic.
2. When prompted by the **Show Table** dialog box, select the **NewKidsEnrolled** table. Click **Add**, and then **Close** to move to the query grid.
3. Click on the **Append** icon, which appears in the **Query Type** group.
4. Select the name of the table into which you want to append the data. For this example, we will use **ElkPupilsTbl**. Click on the **OK** icon to continue, as illustrated in the following screenshot:

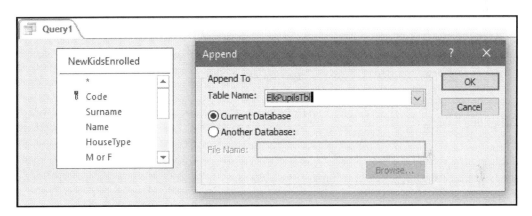

5. Add the fields from the **NewKidsEnrolled** table that you wish to append to the **ElkPupilsTbl** table. Note that you do not have to select all the fields, only those you wish to append. Additionally, note that criteria can also be set using the **Criteria:** row on the query grid. The fields can be seen in the following screenshot:

Field:	Code	Surname	Name	HouseType
Table:	NewKidsEnrolled	NewKidsEnrolled	NewKidsEnrolled	NewKidsEnrolled
Sort:				
Append To:	Code	Surname	Name	HouseType
Criteria:				
or:				

6. If the fields match those of the table you are appending to, then Access will add the corresponding field to match those of the **NewKidsEnrolled** table. If the field names differ from those that are in the appended table, click to specify the field that matches.

7. Click the **Run** icon on the **Results** group to append the data. You will be warned that five rows will be appended from the **NewKidsEnrolled** table to the **ElkPupilsTbl** table. Note that this cannot be undone. The message can be seen in the following screenshot:

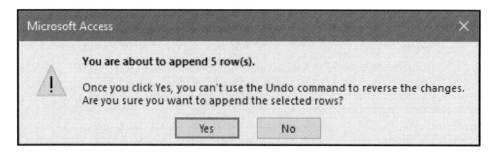

8. Click **Yes** to continue. The **ElkPupilsTbl** table is updated with the new records. Save the query as **AppendNewKids**.

Now that you have learned how to append records, let's investigate Crosstab queries in the next topic.

Building a Crosstab query

A Crosstab query allows the user to summarize data by arranging information into a more readable structure, such as a spreadsheet. Crosstab queries can group information horizontally and vertically, whereas a normal Select query groups information vertically only. You would specify which fields would be displayed in the column format and which would be displayed in the row format.

The following screenshot shows an example of a normal Select query in Access:

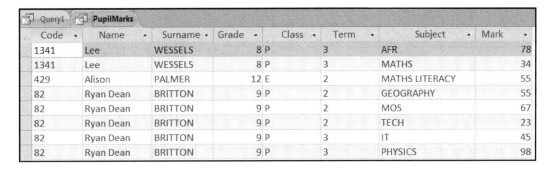

Code	Name	Surname	Grade	Class	Term	Subject	Mark
1341	Lee	WESSELS	8	P	3	AFR	78
1341	Lee	WESSELS	8	P	3	MATHS	34
429	Alison	PALMER	12	E	2	MATHS LITERACY	55
82	Ryan Dean	BRITTON	9	P	2	GEOGRAPHY	55
82	Ryan Dean	BRITTON	9	P	2	MOS	67
82	Ryan Dean	BRITTON	9	P	2	TECH	23
82	Ryan Dean	BRITTON	9	P	3	IT	45
82	Ryan Dean	BRITTON	9	P	3	PHYSICS	98

Here is an example of a **Crosstab** query (using the same table and data converted to a **Crosstab** query):

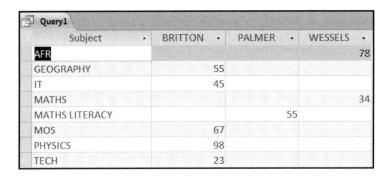

Subject	BRITTON	PALMER	WESSELS
AFR			78
GEOGRAPHY	55		
IT	45		
MATHS			34
MATHS LITERACY		55	
MOS	67		
PHYSICS	98		
TECH	23		

Let's go through the steps together, as follows:

1. Using the database from the previous example, click to create a new query in **Design View**.
2. When prompted by the **Show Table** dialog box, select the **Query** tab, and then double-click on the **PupilMarks** query to add it to the query grid. Click **Close** to move to the query grid.
3. Click the **Crosstab** icon, which appears in the **Query Type** group.
4. Notice that the grid updates to display the **Total:** row as well as the **Crosstab:** row.
5. Add the **Subject**, **Surname**, and **Mark** fields from the **PupilMarks** query to the query grid.

6. In the **Subject** column, in line with the **Crosstab:** row, select **Row Heading**.
7. In the **Surname** column, in line with the **Crosstab:** row, select **Column Heading**.
8. From the **Mark** column, in line with the **Crosstab:** row, select **Value**. Change the **Total:** row to reflect **Sum** for the **Mark** column, as illustrated in the following screenshot:

Field:	Subject	Surname	Mark
Table:	PupilMarks	PupilMarks	PupilMarks
Total:	Group By	Group By	Sum
Crosstab:	Row Heading	Column Heading	Value
Sort:			
Criteria:			
or:			

9. Click the **Run** icon on the **Results** group to see the output of the **Crosstab** query.
10. Click the **Save** icon to save the query. Enter **Crosstab** as the query name into the dialog box provided.
11. The **Crosstab** query will appear under the **Queries** group on the Navigation Pane.

How relationships affect a query result

In the explanation that follows, we will learn how to delete records from a table using a **Delete** query. It is important to note that you would need to make sure that **Enforce Referential Integrity**, as well as **Cascade Delete Related Records**, is selected in the table relationships before you create the **Delete** query. This ensures that all records relating to code 417 (**MEAKER**) are removed from all tables throughout the database:

1. Click on the **Relationships** icon on the **Database Tools** tab, as illustrated in the following screenshot:

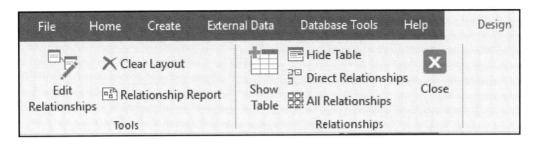

2. The **Relationships** window will launch and display all related tables, indicating the relationships between them. If the relationship window is empty, click the **Show Table** icon to add tables to the window and relate them to each other using the primary keys from each table, as illustrated in the following screenshot:

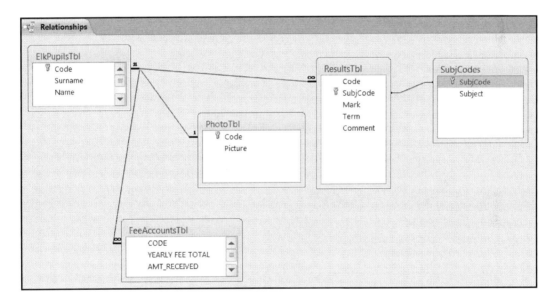

3. To enforce referential integrity, right-click on the relationship line between the **ElkPupilsTbl** table and the **ResultsTbl** table.
4. Select the **Edit Relationship...** option from the drop-down list provided. Alternatively, click on the line between the two tables and select the **Edit Relationship** icon on the **Tools** group.

5. The **Edit Relationships** dialog box will open. Click the checkboxes to select **Enforce Referential Integrity** and **Cascade Delete Related Records**, as illustrated in the following screenshot:

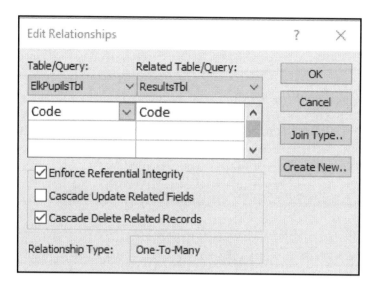

6. Click the **OK** button to confirm. Select the **Close** icon on the **Relationships** group.

Using a Delete query

A Delete query enables you to delete large quantities of information quickly:

Important:

If you want to delete data from related tables, you may need to edit the table relationships so that **Enforce Referential Integrity**, as well as **Cascade Delete Related Records**, is selected. This ensures that related data is deleted on the one-and-many side of the relationship. If, however, you are just deleting records on the many sides of the relationship, you do not have to enforce referential integrity.

1. Using the `ElkAdmin-DeleteMe.accdb` database from the previous example, select the **Query Design** icon located on the **Queries** group of the **Create** tab.

2. When prompted by the **Show Table** dialog box, double-click on the **ElkPupilsTbl** table to add it to the query grid. Click **Close** to move to the query grid.

3. Click the **Delete** icon, which appears in the **Query Type** group. Notice that the grid updates to display the **Delete:** row. Double-click on the **Code** field from the table to add it to the grid.

4. Enter =427 into the **Criteria:** row, as we would like to delete all instances of the surname **MEAKER**, who belongs to code **427**, as the child no longer attends the school. This information can be seen in the following screenshot:

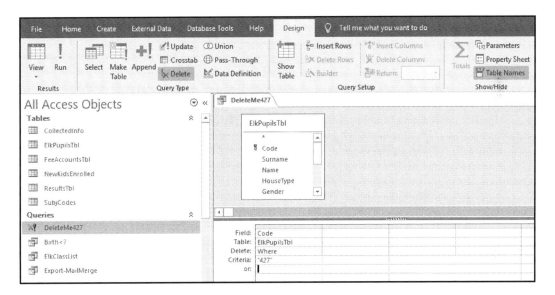

5. A dialog box will appear, warning you that one row will be permanently deleted from the table. Click **Yes** to continue, after which code **427** is removed from the database.

6. Save the query, should you wish to run it at another time. The saved query will be visible in the Navigation Pane, under the **Queries** group.

Creating a Parameter query

When you create a query using Access, there will be times when you would like your query to prompt you for an item to search for, instead of committing to one specific set of criteria for a single result. Normally, you would set up queries to run automatically according to the criteria defined in the query—for example, a specific grade and class, as illustrated in the following screenshot:

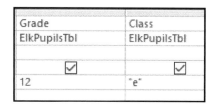

You would not want to have to edit your query every time you need to generate a class list for each different grade in a school setting. Instead, we set up a Parameter query to solve this problem. An example of such a query can be seen in the following screenshot:

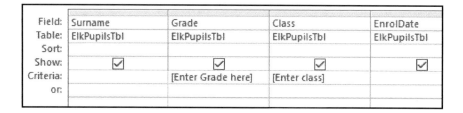

To differentiate between a normal Select query and a Parameter query, we add square brackets around the criteria we require. In the preceding screenshot, you will see **[Enter Grade here]** and **[Enter class]**, which will, when run, prompt the user to enter a grade and class to show a particular output, as illustrated in the following screenshot:

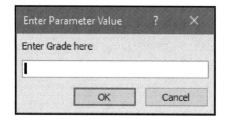

The first screenshot in this section displays **12** and **"e"**, as the criteria will only return results for a single grade and class—for instance, *12e*—and it would be very time consuming to have to edit the query each time to get the results you require.

The only difference between typing normal text into the **Criteria:** section for a field is that a parameter query requires square brackets around the question you ask the user from the relevant field. A Parameter query displays a dialog box prompting you for information. A report can also be based on a Parameter query so that it prompts the user for a particular month to print.

Summary

You now have the skills to construct basic queries and manipulate output using different criteria. We have been on a tour of many of the basic and advanced queries in Access 2019, and you are now confident about creating **Append**, **Delete**, **Crosstab**, **Parameter**, **Update**, and **Make Table** queries with which to analyze data. You have learned how to manipulate relationships in order to delete cascaded records by setting referential integrity and are able to work with fields and enter criteria to fit the query purpose.

The next chapter concentrates on the Outlook 2019 interface. You will learn how to manipulate item tags and arrange the content pane. In addition, we will apply some search and filter tools and learn how to print Outlook items. We will configure send and delivery options to improve productivity in the Outlook application, and learn to attach content to an email.

Section 6: Outlook
6

Outlook 2019 is a personal information manager and part of the Office 2019 suite of applications. In this part of the book, you will learn step by step the different offerings of Outlook, such as the email application, calendar, task manager, contact manager, note-taking functionality, and the journal.

In this section, we will cover the following chapters:

- Chapter 16, *Creating and Attaching Item Content*
- Chapter 17, *Managing Mail and Contacts*
- Chapter 18, *Calendar Objects, Tasks, Notes, and Journal Entries*

16
Creating and Attaching Item Content

This chapter will take you through the important parts of the Outlook 2019 interface and show you how to configure objects such as mail, contacts, tasks, notes, and journals. You will set some advanced options and language options in the interface, and learn how to manipulate item tags and arrange the content pane.

In addition, we will apply some search and filter tools, and print Outlook items. You will learn best practices for sending email messages, as well as configure send and delivery options to improve productivity in the Outlook application. You will also learn to professionally format item content and to attach content to an email.

The following topics are covered in this chapter:

- Investigating the Outlook environment
- Manipulating item tags
- Working with views, filtering, and printing
- Creating and sending email messages
- Creating and managing Quick Steps
- Attaching item content

Technical requirements

You do not need any prior knowledge of an email application to learn how to use Outlook 2019. It is, however, imperative that you are able to launch the Outlook 2019 interface from your computer desktop. You should be confident with minimizing and maximizing the Outlook window and should have some knowledge of the general purpose of an email application such as Outlook 2019. Any examples used in this chapter are accessible from GitHub at `https://github.com/PacktPublishing/Learn-Microsoft-Office-2019`.

Investigating the Outlook environment

You will take a tour around the Outlook 2019 interface and explore elements that are applicable to Outlook, such as the Mini formatting toolbar, the **Focused** inbox, and the **To-Do Bar**, and learn how to view Outlook items. In the previous chapters of this book, we have already familiarized you with the generic interface options applicable to all of the Office 2019 applications.

In this chapter, you will also learn program options for all the objects in the Outlook 2019 interface such as **Mail**, **Calendar**, **Tasks**, **Notes**, **Journals**, advanced options, and language options. We will cover the creating, formatting, and attaching of content to email messages, as well as how to set up Quick Steps to automate repetitive Outlook tasks.

Outlook is a better choice to use than web-based email for business or work-related emails, tasks, calendars, and contacts as you will have considerably more functionality and access to a productivity workflow. Multiple email accounts can be configured within Outlook, such as Gmail, Yahoo, and many more mail providers.

Accessing the Mini toolbar

The Mini toolbar is a formatting toolbar that pops up above selected text when editing an email message. It is automatically activated by double-clicking on a word, or after selecting a sentence or paragraph. If you move the mouse pointer away from a selected area of a message or click away from the selected text, the Mini toolbar will disappear. The Mini toolbar can be seen in the following screenshot:

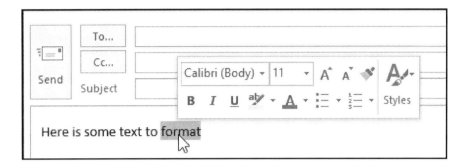

This toolbar is an efficient way of changing text attributes, instead of moving the mouse pointer to the top of the Outlook screen to access the relevant format group.

Using the To-Do Bar

The **To-Do Bar** is formed of separate peek windows that can be populated to the right of the Outlook screen. The **To-Do Bar** can display the calendar, tasks, and people either all at the same time or separately. Note that when you add items from the **To-Do Bar** options, they will appear in order of selection to the right of the Outlook environment.

Note that only the contacts you have marked as favorites will appear in the **Contacts To-Do** peek. These little square windows are called **peeks**. To the right of each peek added to the Outlook environment, you will see a **Remove the peek** icon, as illustrated in the following screenshot:

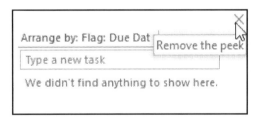

Change the **To-Do Bar** display properties by locating the **Layout** group on the **View** tab. Click the **To-Do Bar** icon to add or remove options. Use the **To-Do Bar** to create new tasks quickly by adding task details directly into the peek shown to the right of the Outlook environment, as illustrated in the following screenshot:

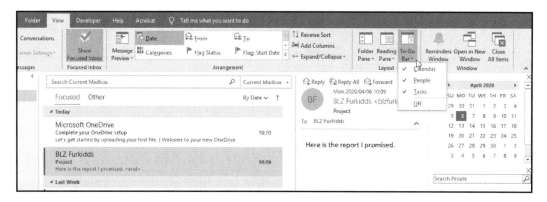

You will also be able to view any emails that have been marked for action (flagged) in your mailbox on the **To-Do Bar**.

Outlook stores each type of information it manages in separate Outlook folders. A single piece of information is known as an **item**. An email message would be an item stored in the **Inbox** folder, and a single appointment would be an item stored in the calendar, and so on. It is also possible to create additional folders to store items.

In the following table, a description of the default Outlook folders is provided:

Default Outlook folders	Description
Focused inbox	This option separates items into two separate tabs in Outlook—the **Focused** tab and the **Other** tab.
Outlook Today	The Outlook screen that shows the user's appointments, tasks, and emails in one window.
Inbox	All incoming messages are received here, allowing the user to send messages and manage mail.
Calendar	The **Calendar** is a folder where the user schedules appointments and events.
Contacts	The user keeps track of business and personal contacts in this folder, and can also enter new contacts. The Contact Activities page tracks contact history emails and does not require the Journal to do so.
Tasks	This folder allows the user to create and manage tasks for themselves or to assign to others.
Journal	The **Journal** tracks all items as you work in Outlook.

Notes	Sticky notes store text information enabling reminders to the user.
Deleted Items	Stores any items the user deletes in Outlook. Users must remove/delete these permanently from the **Deleted Items** folder.
Sent Items	Keeps copies of the user's sent messages.
Outbox	Stores messages very temporarily until delivered. If connection problems occur, sent messages are stored here until the connection is restored.
Drafts	This allows you to save incomplete messages so that the user is able to edit them and send them off at a later stage.

Using the Message pane to display folder items

To view a folder, you need to click on the folder name to open it, after which Outlook displays the folder items in the Message pane of the Outlook window. Once the Message pane lists the contents of the current folder, the ribbon will change to reflect the options available to manage the information in the current folder. For instance, if I select the **Calendar** folder, the **Home** tab will display calendar icons along with the ribbon, and so on.

The Navigation Pane

The Navigation Pane exists to the left of the Outlook screen. It allows you to select the default folders in Outlook (**Calendars**, **Tasks**, **Inbox**, **Sent Items**, and so forth). It is possible to drag an existing folder—for example, the **Inbox**—to the **Favorites** section of the Navigation Pane to enable quick access to the **Inbox** or other mail folders.

The Peek bar

At the bottom of the Navigation Pane, you will find the Peek bar with default icons (Mail, Calendar, Contacts, Tasks, and three dots). You are able to change the options on the Peek bar by visiting the three dots to the right of it, after which a shortcut menu will open, allowing access to **Notes**, **Folders**, **Options**, and **Shortcuts**, as illustrated in the following screenshot:

This bar is named Peek as it allows the user to hover over the icons on the bar to display a peek preview of an item. The **Shortcuts** section resides at the bottom of the Navigation Pane. Users are able to create shortcuts to open favorite and most frequently used folders quickly.

Creating a shortcut to an item

1. Click the three dots on the Peek bar located on the Navigation Pane. From the list of options, choose **Shortcuts**.
2. The **Shortcuts** folder will appear in place of the Navigation Pane. Right-click on the word **Shortcuts**, then choose **New Shortcut** to launch the dialog box to select a folder to which you would like to create a shortcut, as illustrated in the following screenshot:

3. Select a folder from the list—in this case, **Notes**. Then, click on **OK** to add the folder to the **Shortcuts** folder. To return to your **Inbox**, click on the **Mail** icon on the Peek bar.

Previewing Outlook items

You are able to set the number of lines to view per email message in the Message pane. This allows you to view the contents of an Outlook item without opening the entire item, by presenting the user with a view of the first few lines of a message on the main Outlook screen. Another way to view items is to set the properties of the **Reading Pane**, which shows the contents of an email without having to change the view with the mouse to open the entire message.

Previewing emails in the Message pane

Click on the **View** tab, and then locate the **Message Preview** icon. Select the drop-down list arrow and choose the desired number of lines to view per email message. You will receive a notification, asking whether you would like to change the preview setting for all mailboxes or just the current folder. Alternatively, turn off the preview altogether by selecting **Off** from **Message Preview.** When the **Message Preview** is set to **Off**, then the text that is displayed in the preview will refer to the message subject. For instance, **Project** is the subject of the email from **BLZ Furkidds**, as shown in the following screenshot:

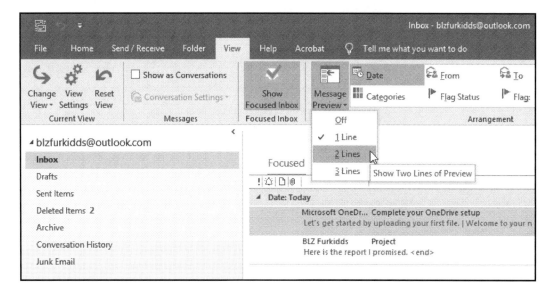

The default preview is set to display **1 Line** of text per email received.

Using the Reading Pane

The **Reading Pane** allows the user to view the contents of an email message quickly without actually double-clicking on the email to open it. When set, you can use the down arrow on the keyboard (or click on each email message) to move from one email to another in the Message pane, and each mail message will display its contents in the **Reading Pane**.

Options to position the **Reading Pane** to the right or bottom of the Outlook screen are available, or, alternatively, choose to turn it off completely. To use the **Reading Pane**, follow these steps:

1. Click on the **View** tab. Select the **Reading Pane** icon from the **Layout** group.
2. Choose where you would like the **Reading Pane** positioned on the Outlook screen (**Right** or **Bottom**), or click on the **Off** icon should you wish to not display it, as illustrated in the following screenshot:

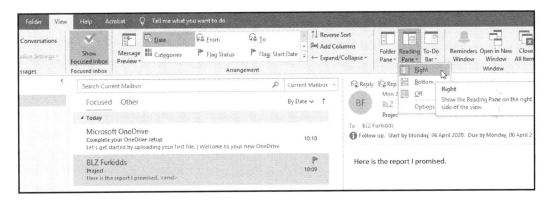

3. Click on the **Options...** icon to display the dialog box, where more changes to the **Reading Pane** are possible.

Manipulating Outlook program options

Outlook is a powerful information management application that allows you to do the following:

- Use email (a mailbox) for communication
- Use the calendar for time management
- Manage tasks, workload, employees, and projects
- Put notes as reminders to yourself

- Organize and track contacts and people you deal with every day by phone, email, distribution lists, or just reaching out
- And, lastly, create a timeline of actions for particular contacts using the journal

Once the Outlook installation is complete, the setup program will look for the user's profile (a group of settings that define the setup of Outlook for a specific user). The transport application called Exchange allows the flow of information and needs installing in order to use the email feature of Outlook.

Using the Focused inbox option

The **Focused** inbox is a new feature of Outlook. It allows you to view the most important emails in a separate view. The **Inbox** is now separated into two tabs, one for the **Focused** items and one for **Other** items, as illustrated in the following screenshot:

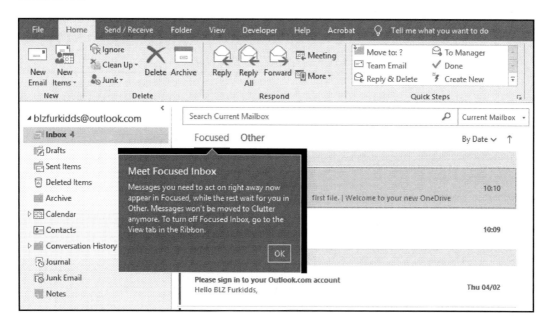

The **Focused** tab is set as the default. Should you wish to alter these settings, visit the **View** tab on the ribbon to either activate the **Show Focused Inbox** setting or deactivate the **Focused** inbox setting, as illustrated in the following screenshot:

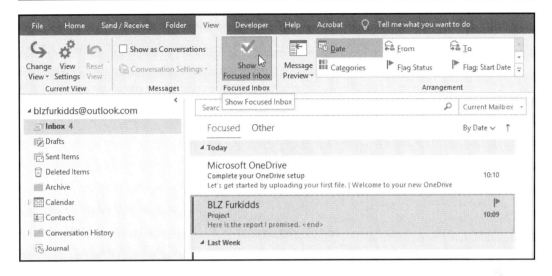

To move important messages into the **Focused** inbox, simply right-click on the message you would like to move from the **Other** folder, then choose the **Move to Focused** option, as illustrated in the following screenshot:

The message is moved to the **Focused** inbox. To move messages from **Focused** to **Other**, simply repeat the step on the relevant tab.

Investigating mail options

Mail options in Outlook have the greatest range of settings in the program. There are so many ways to configure message options using this dialog box. As you work through the chapters on Outlook 2019, we will cover items from this dialog box. When composing email messages, the body of the email uses a Word 2019-based editor. This gives you a huge amount of functionality from the Office 2019 Microsoft Word program. You can set the importance of a message, set delivery receipt options, and set expiry dates for messages. Some of the settings can be seen in the following screenshot:

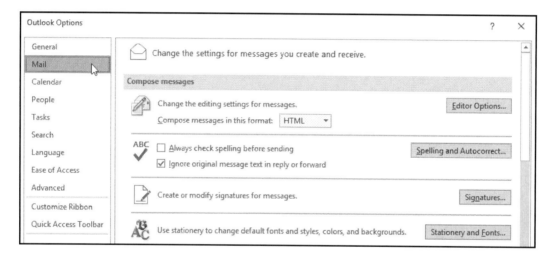

To access interface options, click on the **File** tab, then select **Options** from the drop-down menu provided. The following sections—namely, the **Mail**, **Calendar**, **Tasks**, and **Advanced** options—are all listed in the **Outlook Options** dialog box under separate categories.

Another way to access options for all the items within Outlook is to right-click on an item on the Peek bar, located at the bottom of the Navigation Pane. Choose **Options...** from the shortcut list to launch the **Outlook Options** dialog box, as illustrated in the following screenshot:

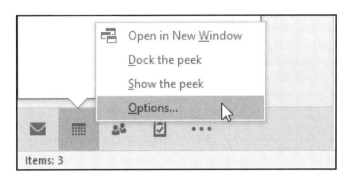

The following table shows a list of **Option** categories and their descriptions:

Calendar options	This category in the dialog box allows the setting up of start and end times for working hours and calendar reminders, colors, and resource scheduling.
Task options	Options relating to setting and assigning tasks to others using Outlook are located under the **Tasks** menu in the **Outlook Options** dialog box. Task colors and reminder settings are of importance here.
Journal options	The journal can be set up to record all the information it can (such as emails, meeting information, tasks, and program usage) for specific contacts, and adds these to a timeline. The journal is accessible as one of your **Inbox** folders. If you cannot see the journal, visit the three dots on the Peek bar, located at the bottom of the Navigation Pane. Choose **Folders** to make the journal visible in the folder pane.
Advanced options	Advanced options in the **Outlook Options** dialog box include settings for reminders and sounds, and for customizing different parts of the Outlook environment (screen layout). It is possible to add additional languages to edit documents in Outlook. To change language settings, visit the **Language** menu in the **Outlook Options** dialog box.

Manipulating item tags

In this section, you will learn how to categorize items by adding a color, as well as go through the options to rename; assign categories to items; and remove a category from an Outlook item. You will also be able to set a Quick Click, work with flags, mark items as read or unread, and view message properties.

Categorizing items

To understand what categorizing items mean, you would need to understand the following:

- **What is meant by an item?** An item is an email message, a task, a calendar entry, a contact, or a note.
- **What is meant by categorizing?** Categories are keywords assigned by a color that helps you keep track of items.

Categorizing items allows you to filter, sort, and group with ease, according to categories. **Categorize** is located on the **Tags** group on the ribbon and is part of the **Home** tab. Click on the **Categorize** icon from the **Tags** group, then from the drop-down list, a few default categories will populate. Click on the **All Categories...** option to access the full list, as illustrated in the following screenshot:

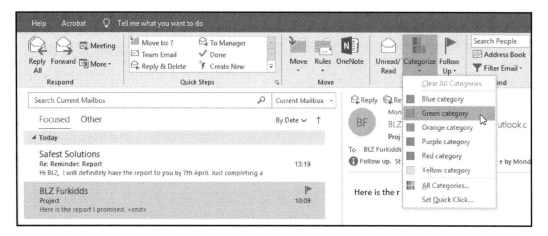

Category names can be changed to suit your working environment and the nature of the emails you deal with daily.

Color categories are not available when Outlook is configured using the **Internet Message Access Protocol (IMAP)** setting.

Renaming categories

1. Click on the **Categorize** icon, then choose **All Categories...** from the drop-down list.
2. In the **Color Categories** dialog box, click on the color category to rename. In this case, the **Blue category** color category is chosen.
3. Click on the **Rename** button on the right of the dialog box, as illustrated in the following screenshot:

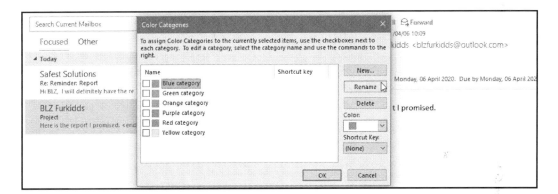

4. The **Blue category** is in edit mode. Type the name of the new category in its place (in this case, **Projects**). Click on **OK** to confirm, or continue to rename the other categories in the dialog box.
5. To add your own custom category, click on the **New...** button to the right of the dialog box. Click on **OK** to confirm. The new category is added to the list.
6. To change the category color, choose a color from the **Color:** drop-down list in the **Color Categories** dialog box.

Assigning categories to items

1. Click on the item (in this case, an email message). Locate the **Tags** group, then click to open the **Categorize** menu.

2. Select a category to assign to the email message by clicking on the tick box to the left of the category name you have chosen, as illustrated in the following screenshot:

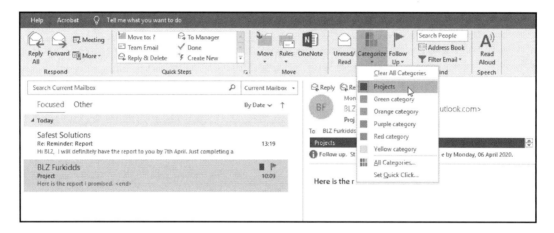

3. Click on **OK** to return to the mailbox. Note that the email message now has a category color assigned in the Message pane. The size of the Message pane depends on what you will see when you add a category (either the color block plus the category name will display or just the color block). If you open the email by double-clicking on it, you will also see that the message header section contains the category you have assigned, as well as the color.

4. You can assign more than one category to one email message. Remember to click on a category to remove it from the email message if you decide to change to a different category color.

5. Color categories can also be applied to calendar events. Right-click on a calendar entry to access the **Categorize** option, then select a color category to assign to the item, as illustrated in the following screenshot:

6. By adding calendar category colors this way, we can focus on important, or urgent, must-attend events in our calendar.

Setting up a Quick Click

If you use a certain category and color more than you use any other, you can set this up as a Quick Click option, which means that if you click with the mouse in the category column next to the email message, it will assign the default category. To do this, follow these steps:

1. Click on the **Categorize** | **Set Quick Click** option from the bottom of the menu.

2. In the dialog box, select a category to assign as the Quick Click option, then click on **OK** to confirm, as illustrated in the following screenshot:

3. In the Message pane, click in the **CATEGORIES** column next to a message to assign the Quick Click category (called **Project**, in this case). Note that the **CATEGORIES** heading will only display if you have the Outlook screen set to not display the **Reading Pane** and/or remove the Peek **To-Do Bar** windows from the environment. The following screenshot illustrates the process:

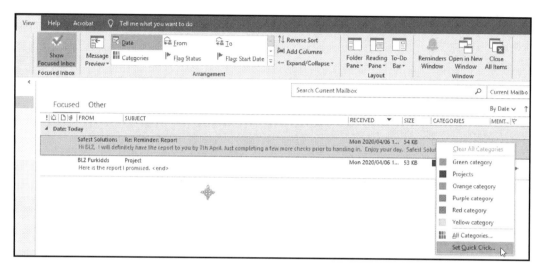

We have learned how to set up a Quick Click so that we can assign categories quickly to mail items. To use the Quick Click option, simply click on the category block under the **CATEGORIES** heading in the Message pane, as illustrated in the following screenshot:

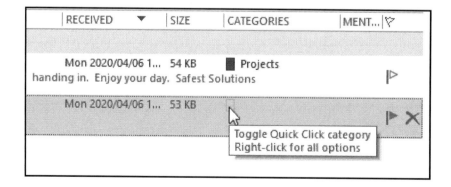

This will assign the default Quick Click to messages easily. Note that if you have a busy screen, the **CATEGORIES** heading might not be visible. To remove a category from an Outlook item, select the mail message from which you wish to remove the category. Click on **Categorize | Clear All Categories**. The color indicator and the category are removed from the message. You can also use the right-click method to remove categories, or you can click on the category block to the right of the email message to remove the Quick Click option.

Setting flags

A **flag** is a visual reminder to follow up a contact or message in Outlook. You are able to customize your flags with specific dates. Once a flag is assigned, it appears in the email view, the **To-Do Bar**, the **Daily Calendar Task List**, and the **Tasks View**. The default flag color is red and, when assigned, it will appear next to the **Categories** icon to the right of the email message. In the following screenshot, the flag is seen in the email and in the task list (located to the right of the screen positioned under the calendar):

If you assign a flag to an email message that must follow up a task on the same day, then the time that the reminder will pop up on your screen will depend on the workday default settings in Outlook.

Consult the Outlook **Help (Tell me what you want to do)** feature for an explanation of how the default dates work for follow-ups, as illustrated in the following screenshot:

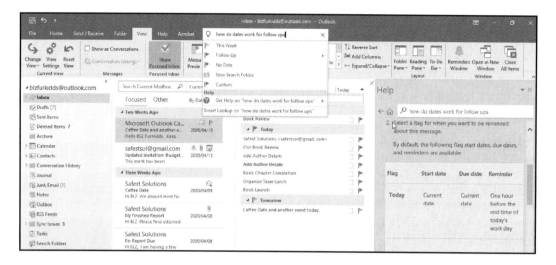

Click on the **Tell me what you want to do** text just to the right of the light bulb at the end of the ribbon tabs. Type the following into the placeholder provided: how do dates work for follow ups. The **Help** pane will open to the right of the Outlook window, displaying information on follow-up default reminder settings.

In the next topic, we will look at options to add flags to messages and contacts.

Adding a flag to a message and contact

1. To the right of an email message (in the Message pane), you will notice little white flag outlines. Click on the flag to add a reminder to the message for a follow-up.

2. By default, the flag is assigned for **Today** and will remind you an hour before the end of the working day (as set in Outlook).

3. If you would like to change the follow-up date to **Tomorrow**, for instance, right-click on the flag to set further options, as illustrated in the following screenshot:

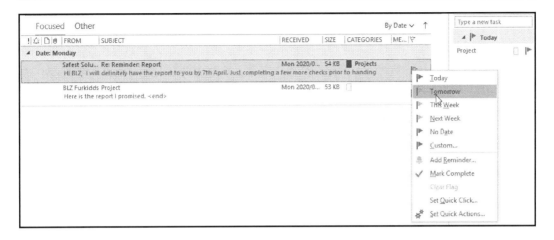

4. To add a flag to a contact, open the Contacts pane located at the bottom left-hand corner of the Outlook window, as illustrated in the following screenshot:

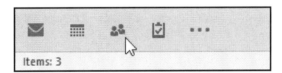

5. Click to select a contact, as illustrated in the following screenshot:

6. Right-click on the contact to add a follow-up reminder using the **Follow Up** option.

Sending out a flag for recipients

The **Follow Up** icon can be used to encourage recipients to respond to a request or email message. The **Follow Up** flag can be set on a new mail message, a contact, or from the **Follow Up** icon flag at the end of the Message pane:

1. Click on the **Home | New Email** icon to compose a new message. In the **Untitled - Message (HTML)** dialog box, click on the **Follow Up** icon to set options for the message. Choose **Custom...** from the drop-down list.

2. In the **Custom** dialog box, remove the check mark for **Flag for Me** as you do not need to flag yourself.

3. Click on the **Flag for Recipients** checkbox and enter the details of your message into the **Flag to** text area. Set a reminder date and time. Click on **OK** to return to the message, as illustrated in the following screenshot:

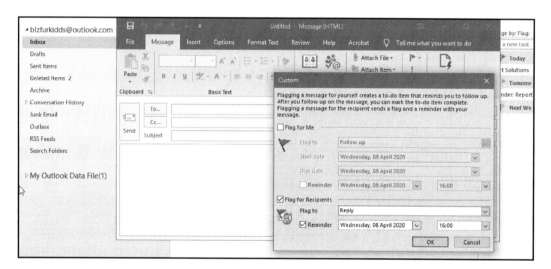

4. In the **To...** text entry area of the message, remember to add an email address or group name for your recipients, as illustrated in the following screenshot:

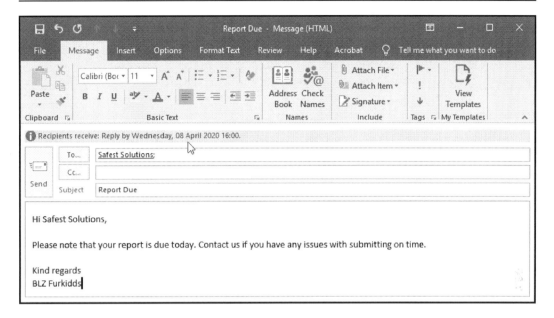

5. Type the body of the email message, then click on the **Send** icon. Note that above the **To...** button in the message, you will see the flag information. This message notification bar highlights to the recipient that a reply is requested by **Wednesday** at **16:00**.

Marking mail items as read/unread

At times you may read an email, or click on it to open it, and would like to refer to it later. Until you refer to it again, you might want it to appear in your **Inbox** as unread. This option gives the user information at a glance, as new email messages are always highlighted in bold text. Here's how we do this:

1. Click on the message you wish to mark as unread. Locate the **Tags** group on the **Home** tab. Click on the **Unread/Read** icon.
2. This icon is a toggle icon; press once for unread and once again for read.

Note: Right-clicking on the message to mark it as unread is another way to achieve this.

Checking for new messages

1. Click on the Send/Receive All Folders icon on the Quick Access Toolbar, located at the very top-left corner of the Outlook environment, to check for new mail, as illustrated in the following screenshot:

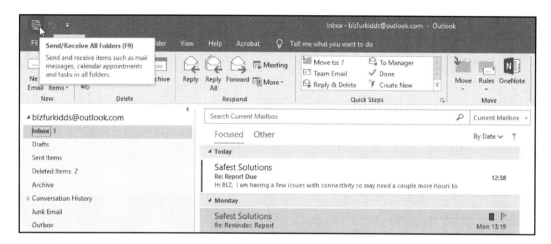

You can also use the *F9* function key to refresh the **Inbox** to bring through any new messages. In the following topic, we will learn how to work with content views, and filtering and printing of Outlook items.

Working with views, filtering, and printing

This topic will cover content on the content page—such as changing the view type—and will take a look at the **Reminders Window**. You will become confident in using built-in search folders, and search and filter facilities. In addition, you will learn to print attachments, calendars, multiple messages, contact records, tasks, and notes.

Changing the view type

There are three main views on the **View** tab that can be managed or saved as a new view in order to customize the layout of your Outlook application—namely, **Compact**, **Single**, and **Preview**:

1. To change the current view, click on the **View** tab and select **Change View**, as illustrated in the following screenshot:

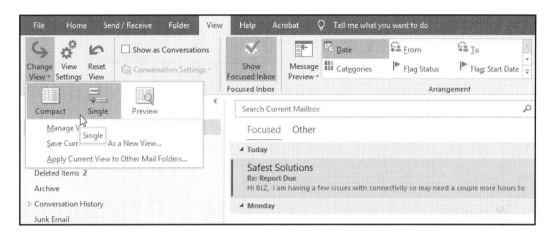

2. From the drop-down list, select a view to see the change on the screen. Each view (**Compact, Single,** and **Preview**) has a certain arrangement of fields that can be modified using the **Manage View...** icon. Explore this option to find the view that works best for you.

Using the Reminders Window

The **Reminders Window** opens (pops up on screen) while you are working to remind yourself of important meetings and/or tasks you need to attend to. The **Reminders Window** can be manually opened by visiting the **View** tab and clicking on the **Reminders Window**, located under the **Window** group. These reminders are set on an item when creating a reminder flag for an item by right-clicking on an item. The **Reminders Window** option can be seen in the following screenshot:

Once the **Reminders Window** pops up on your screen, you can open the item to view its content, snooze the item for a further selected time period, or dismiss the reminder, as illustrated in the following screenshot:

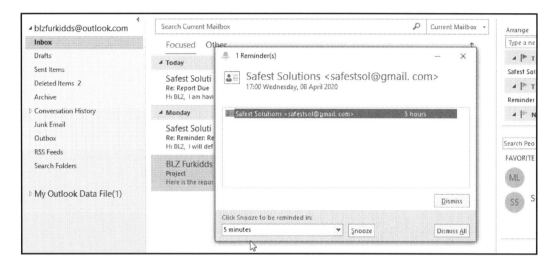

We will now look at ways to locate and filter for Outlook content in the next topic.

Applying search and filter tools

To quickly find items in Outlook, you can use the Instant Search facility, which is a built-in search. This facility is available on every one of the Outlook folders (**Mail**, **Calendar**, **Tasks**, and **Contacts**):

1. Click on a folder in the Navigation Pane in which to search—for instance, **Mail**, **Calendar**, **Tasks**, or **People**. In the Instant Search text box, enter the information you are looking for. You will see gray text named **Search Current Mailbox** in the search box—this will disappear when you start typing your search criteria. Notice that there is a drop-down list to the right offering more choices, such as a search through **All Outlook Items**. The Instant Search text box can be seen in the following screenshot:

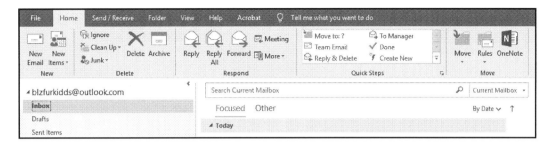

2. Press *Enter* to start your search. An example of the search results can be seen in the following screenshot:

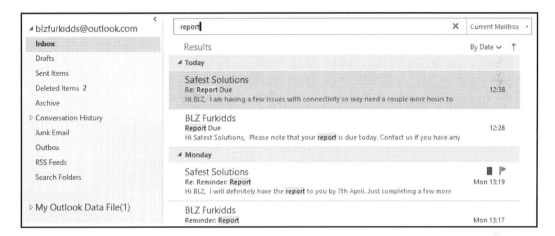

3. The search results are highlighted in yellow in the Message pane. Notice that the ribbon has changed to reflect options to refine the search. The **Search Tools** contextual menu is now visible on the ribbon. Experiment with these options.

4. The **Recent Searches** icon along the ribbon allows you to reuse a previous search. The **Search Tools** icon must also not be ignored as you will be able, for instance, to have the located items displayed in a color other than yellow. Note that you will need to restart Outlook if you change these options, for them to take effect. The **Recent Searches** icon can be seen in the following screenshot:

5. To clear a search, click on the **X** located at the right side of the Instant Search box or click on **Close Search** at the right of the ribbon.

Printing Outlook items

You can print Outlook items such as attachments, calendars, tasks, contacts, or notes. The procedure for each option is very similar to choosing the **Print** facility within the relevant icon on the Backstage view.

Printing attachments

1. Open the email containing the attachment, then click on the drop-down arrow to the right of the attachment, just below the subject. In the case of this example, we have a Word document as an attachment.

2. Choose **Quick Print** from the shortcut menu, after which you will receive a trust notification warning, highlighting the importance of opening only trustworthy attachments. Click on **OK** to print the document to the default printer. If you prefer to save the attachment first to the computer and then print using the relevant application options, choose **Save As** from the drop-down list instead, as illustrated in the following screenshot:

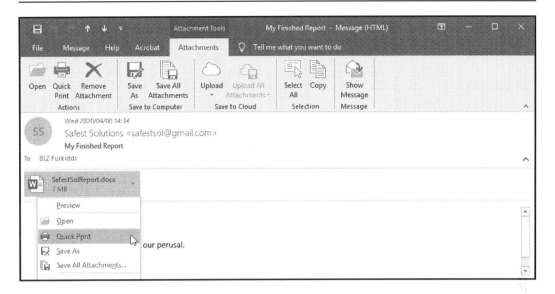

3. Please note that this option will use the current default printer as well as the default options, and will send the attachment straight to the printer without previewing the document or allowing you to set printing preferences).

Printing calendars

1. Click on the **Calendar** icon located at the bottom of the Navigation Pane. Click on the **File** tab to access the Backstage view.
2. Choose the **Print** icon from the menu. From the Backstage view, select the style of the **Calendar** printout.
3. To access more options, click on the **Print Options** button. Use the **Define Print Styles** dialog box to edit a particular print style if you would like to customize it and keep the changes for the next time the calendar is printed using the same style.

Printing tasks, notes, and contacts

Click on the relevant task, note, or contact icon on the Navigation Pane to open the item. Select items using the *Ctrl + click* method. Click on **File** | **Print** from the menu. In **Preview**, select multiple pages so that you can see all tasks in the **Preview** pane. Set **Print Options**, and print as usual.

You will discover more about each one of the preceding items in the chapters that follow.

Creating and sending email messages

In this section, you will learn how to specify a message theme, and understand the use of the **Bcc...** field when sending mail. We will delve into configuring message delivery options. We will look at how to set voting and tracking options, and also proofing and sorting mail messages.

Specifying a message theme

A theme helps you create professional-looking emails. When themes are applied to documents, their fonts, styles, backgrounds, colors, tables, hyperlink colors, and graphics are all affected:

1. Click on the **New Email** icon to create a new message. On the **Options** tab, select the **Themes** group to apply to the email message, or set the **Colors**, **Fonts**, and **Effects** yourself by using the relevant icons, as illustrated in the following screenshot:

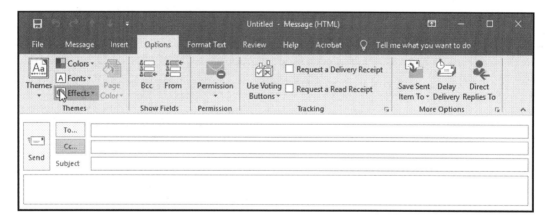

2. The **Page Color** is also changeable via the drop-down arrow. You would need to click into the body of the message (the white space area under the **Subject** of the email message) to activate the **Page Color**.

Showing/hiding the From and Bcc... fields

The **To...** and **Cc...** fields are displayed on a new mail message by default. The **Bcc...** field is not part of an email message by default. This option needs to be activated to appear in the email headings. The **Bcc...** field is located by clicking on the **Options** tab in the new mail message dialog box. This applies to the **From** field as well as the **Bcc...** field:

1. Click on the **Bcc...** field to send a copy of the email to the person specified in the **Bcc...** field without the main recipient of the email knowing, as illustrated in the following screenshot:

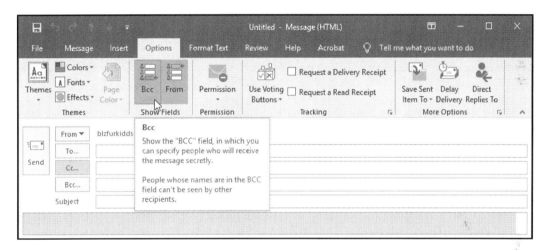

2. Click on the **From** field icon to select an email address of the person you would like to send the email to. This only works if you have delegate access to that person's account.

Configuring message delivery options

In this topic, we will learn how to set the importance option for an email message to highlight to a recipient that the message is urgent.

Setting the level of importance

Setting the level of importance of a mail message identifies to the recipient, when receiving the message in the **Inbox**, how important the contents of the message are and how promptly they are expected to respond to the message. The example in the screenshot indicates that the message is of high importance (with a red exclamation mark). This also helps to sort email messages by importance in the message list.

To set this option, follow these steps:

1. Click on the **New Email** option to create a new message. Select the **Message** tab and locate the **Tags** group, as illustrated in the following screenshot:

2. Click on **High Importance** to set the level, as illustrated in the preceding screenshot.
3. The red exclamation mark indicating that the email is of high importance will be visible in the **Inbox** or **Sent Items** folders, as illustrated in the following screenshot:

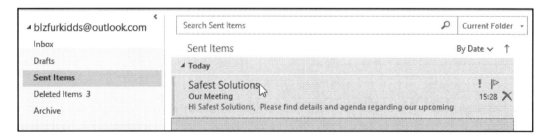

4. You can also set a delivery receipt to show when a recipient has read or received your email. Use the **Options** tab to set this under the **Tracking** group, as illustrated in the following screenshot:

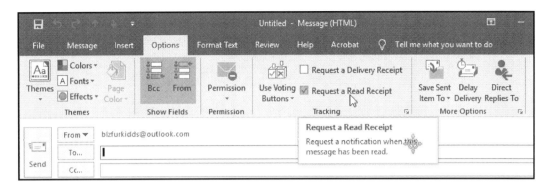

5. Click on **Request a Read Receipt** to request a notification when the message has been read by the recipient.

Configuring voting and tracking options

Creating a poll in Outlook 2019 is a stunning feature. It allows you to quickly gather replies to a question sent to recipients via an email message. It is, however, always best to make sure that all recipients are using the same version of Office as you are:

1. Click on the **New Email** message icon. From the **Options** tab, select the **Use Voting Buttons** icon from the **Tracking** group.

2. Select one of the default tracking buttons or click on **Custom...** to create your own, as illustrated in the following screenshot:

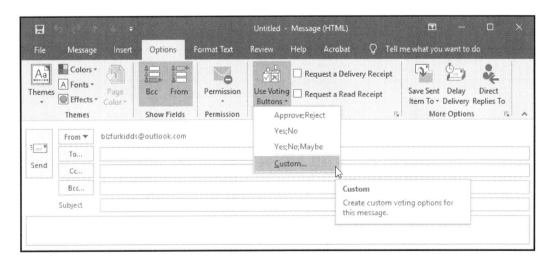

3. In the **Properties** dialog box, make sure you have located the **Voting and Tracking options** heading. Click on the checkbox for **Use Voting Buttons** to make it active.

4. Type your own custom text into the space provided. In the example, I have used **Monday; Wednesday; Thursday** as I would like to obtain a poll on when colleagues could attend a training session. Remember to put a semicolon in between each voting choice, and not a comma, as illustrated in the following screenshot. Click on **Close** to confirm:

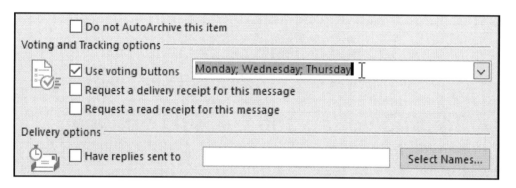

5. Your email header will now display an information bar with the text **You added voting buttons to this message**.

6. The recipient will receive an email with voting buttons in the message header, on which they will click to select the day that suits them for the training, as illustrated in the following screenshot:

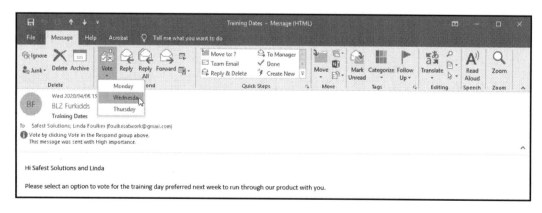

7. The response is then sent to the sender.

Sending a message to a contact group

1. Click the **New Email** icon to create a new message.

2. In the message header, click on the **To...** icon to access the address list, or type the contact group name into the **To...** text area. From the **Address Book** drop-down list, select **Contacts**. Click on **OK** to add the group information to the email message.

3. A group is identified by a two-people icon and will display a bold attribute, as illustrated in the following screenshot:

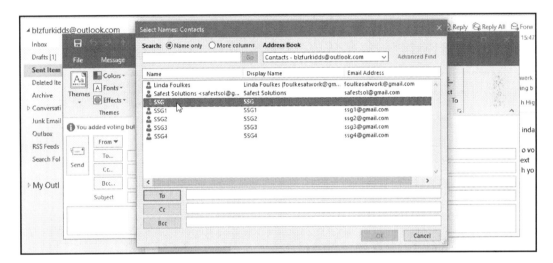

4. Select a group to send the email to by double-clicking on the group name. The group name will appear at the bottom of the dialog box in the **To** heading. A contact group will also display a **+** sign next to the contact name, indicating that it is a group. Click on **OK** to add the contact group to the email message.

Moving, copying, and deleting email messages

Copying or moving information from one email to another is exactly the same concept as in any other Microsoft Office application. Select the element to cut or copy, then use the right-click method over the selected element to cut or copy. Move to the destination email message and right-click once again to paste the information into the email. To delete an email from your **Inbox**, simply click on the email and press the *Delete* key on the keyboard.

Replying to and forwarding email messages

1. Select an email message in the **Inbox**. Click on the **Reply**, **Reply All**, or **Forward** options to respond to the message you have received:

    *   **Reply**: To only the person who sent you the email
    *   **Reply All**: To the sender and all other recipients in the message
    *   **Forward**: To send the email message on to someone else to action

2. Edit the subject, if necessary, and then send the email.

Sorting email messages

Click on the column headings just under the **Focused** and **Other** inboxes in order to sort in an ascending and descending fashion, or right-click on the column headings to access the shortcut menu arrange options, as illustrated in the following screenshot:

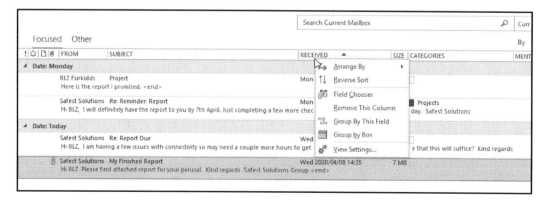

There are numerous options to sort email messages in the sub-menu when choosing the **Arrange By** option at the top of the shortcut list provided.

Creating and managing Quick Steps

You will be proficient at performing Quick Steps by creating, editing, deleting, and duplicating Quick Steps after completing this topic. Quick Steps help you to quickly manage your mailbox by selecting multiple options to apply to mail messages at once. An example would be if you frequently send emails to certain folders or forward emails to a certain person regularly. You are also able to formulate and customize your own Quick Steps for actions that you need to be done quickly. There are some default Quick Steps available to get you started:

1. Locate the **Quick Steps** group on the **Home** tab.
2. There are a number of default Quick Steps, some of which are outlined here:

   - **Move to** moves a new mail message to another folder and then marks the message as read.
   - **To Manager** will forward an email to the manager specified in the dialog box that populates.
   - **Done** moves the message to a specified folder and marks it as read and complete.
   - **Reply & Delete** opens a reply to the selected message and deletes the original message.

The aforementioned options can be seen in the following screenshot:

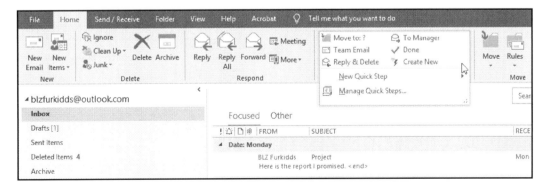

3. Be careful of the **Reply & Delete** option. It happens so fast you hardly see it and realize it's deleted the original!

4. To apply a Quick Step, click on the mail message to apply the step to. The first time you use a Quick Step, it will ask you to enter the details. Thereafter, it will not prompt you again until you right-click and edit the step. Enter the name of the manager you wish to use as the Quick Step. In this case, we will enter the manager's name as `BLZ Furkidds`. Click on **Save**, as illustrated in the following screenshot:

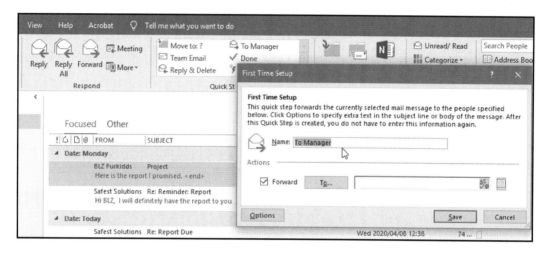

5. Once the Quick Step has been edited, you will notice that the item has been updated in the **Quick Steps** group, as illustrated in the following screenshot:

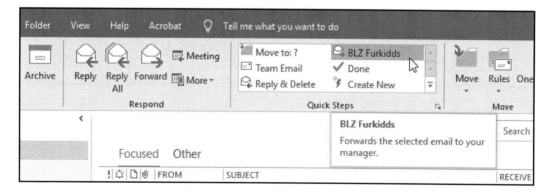

6. When you next use the Quick Step, simply click on the **BLZ Furkidds** Quick Step to forward the selected email to this manager.

Attaching item content

By the end of this topic, you will have learned how to attach an Outlook item and various external file types to an email.

Attaching an Outlook item

At times, it might be required of you to attach another email message, task, calendar item, or contact to a message you are sending. Here is the quickest way to attach multiple items of this nature:

1. Open a **New Mail** message. From the **Insert** tab, locate the **Include** group, then click on **Outlook Item**, as illustrated in the following screenshot:

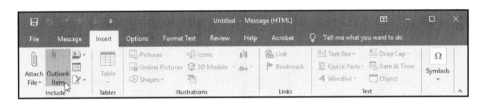

2. From the **Insert Item** dialog box, locate the folder (**Task**, **Contact**, **Calendar**, and **Email**), then the item you wish to attach to the existing email message. Alternatively, use the **Business Card** dropdown to insert a contact as an email attachment by clicking on the **Insert Business Card** icon from the **Include** group on the **Insert** tab. The former option is highlighted in the following screenshot:

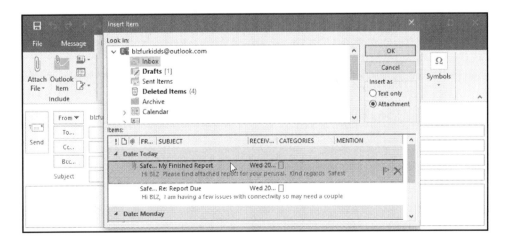

3. Click on the item, and then click on **OK** to insert the item into the mail message.

4. In the email message, the inserted item will appear in the **Attached** area in the message header, as illustrated in the following screenshot:

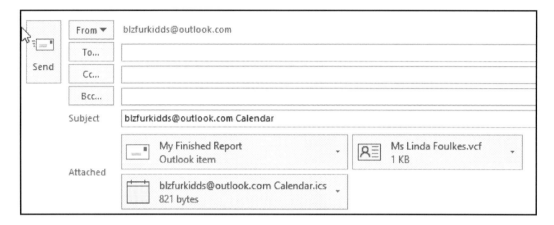

5. Don't forget to click on **Send** once you have added the recipients and attached the item content to the email.

Attaching external files

1. Open an existing email or a **New Mail** message to add an attachment. From the **Message** tab, locate the **Include** group.

2. Click on the **Attach File** icon. You will see a drop-down list populate, containing the most recently worked-on files, as well as an option to **Browse this PC...** to locate the file you wish to add to the email.

3. Once you have located the file attachment on the PC, click on **Open** to place the document into the email message. The file is inserted below the **Subject** line, into the **Attached** section. To remove an attachment, if you have inserted it in error, simply click on the drop-down arrow at the end of the inserted filename attached, then select **Remove Attachment**.

Summary

Throughout this chapter, you have collected the skills to create and send email messages within the Outlook 2019 application. You are able to attach item content from different items in Outlook, and can confidently add and remove file attachments and content. Quick methods to enhance productivity have also been learned, and you will now be able to apply Quick Steps and item tags and set a message as being of high importance. You will be able to set a message so that the sender receives a notification that the message has been read by the recipient. We have also learned how to search, print, and filter mail messages in the **Inbox**.

In the next chapter, we will cover best practices while working with message attachments and will learn about keeping your mailbox clean and streamlined. You will learn how to set up rules and manage junk mail options, and create or modify signatures within the Outlook application. The next chapter will also teach you how to set up and manage contacts and contact groups.

17
Managing Mail and Contacts

This chapter will introduce you to best practices while working with message attachments, to keep your mailbox clean and streamlined. You will learn how to set up rules and manage junk mail options, and how to create or modify signatures within the Outlook application. This chapter will also teach you to be proficient at creating business cards for contacts, and you will learn how to set up and manage contacts and contact groups.

The following topics are covered in this chapter:

- Cleaning up the mailbox and managing rules
- Managing junk mail and automatic message content
- Creating contact information and groups

Technical requirements

To work through this chapter, you need to have prior knowledge of navigating around the Outlook 2019 interface and setting options. In addition, you will need to be confident in creating, sending, and managing the mail environment. You should be able to insert and attach item content to elements within the interface, and also be able to format email content, just as you have learned in previous chapters of this book. Any examples used in this chapter are accessible from GitHub at: https://github.com/PacktPublishing/Learn-Microsoft-Office-2019.

Cleaning up the mailbox and managing rules

Keeping the mailbox clean is a task you should do regularly. With the amount of digital correspondence and attachments that come into your mailbox daily, it is imperative to manage your workflow. We will learn how to clean up the mailbox and where to locate the mailbox size. We will learn how to work with message attachments and save a message in an external format. We will also learn how to ignore conversations, and we will use the cleanup tools available in Outlook 2019. We will learn how to access the rule options in Outlook and create a basic rule, then apply the rule to a selected email message. We will also cover deleting, modifying, and running a rule on a specific folder.

Cleaning up the mailbox

Our mailboxes often get extremely cluttered with messages from subscriptions to sites, that are delivered daily, weekly, and monthly. This can get out of control very easily, and we normally only start to worry about this once we are reaching the full mailbox capacity. Let's look at how to view the mailbox size in Outlook 2019.

Viewing the mailbox size

1. Click on **File | Tools**.
2. Locate the **Mailbox Settings** heading, just to the right of **Tools**, as illustrated in the following screenshot:

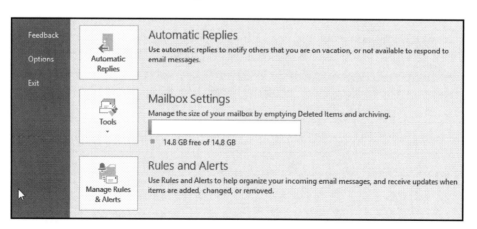

3. You will see the mailbox capacity and the amount of free space available, and the slider shown in the preceding screenshot will depict this graphically.

Saving message attachments

It is important to keep the mailbox size down by saving email message attachments to your computer, instead of leaving them attached to email messages in the Inbox. This will reduce the mailbox size considerably:

1. Open an email that contains an attachment to download, then click on the attachment to open it.
2. The **Attachment Tools** contextual menu opens. Click on **Save As** to save the file to a location on the computer.
3. Note that to return to the message, you simply need to click on **Back to message** or use the **Show Message** icon at the end of the ribbon, as illustrated in the following screenshot:

4. A **Remove Attachment** option is also available, and a **Save All Attachments** option allows you to save attachments to a specific location if the message contains more than one attachment. Note that, if connected, you can also use the **Upload** icon in the **Save to Cloud** group to save attachments to an online location (such as *OneDrive*).

Saving a message in an external format

1. Open a message you wish to save to an external format, then click on **File | Save As**. In the **Save As** dialog box, select the drive and folder to save the message into, then enter a filename into the relevant text area. The default save option in Outlook is **Outlook Message Format - Unicode (*.msg)**, as illustrated in the following screenshot:

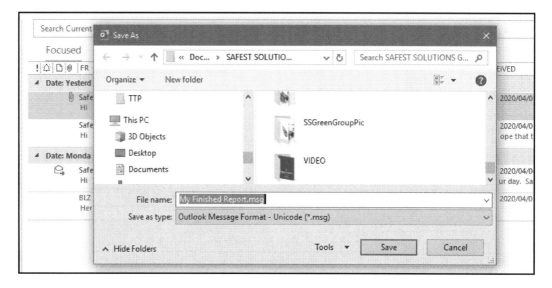

2. Click on **Save**. Saving in this message-type format will open up the email message in Outlook when the user double-clicks on the `My Finished Report.msg` file after saving it.

3. Other options are available in the **Save as type:** drop-down list, such as **Text Only**—this saves the message as a `.txt` file and will remove any pictures, graphics, and formatting from the message. The **Outlook Template (*.oft)** option works exactly the same as a Word template, for example, it allows you to save the formatting of a message so that you can apply this message template to a new email at a later stage. The **HTML (*.htm; *.html)** option will save the message in web format (with the code, images, and text in a separate file to accompany the message), and will open in a browser when opened after saving. The **MHT files (*.mht)** option is a web page archive file format that also opens in a web browser.

All the preceding options can be seen in the following screenshot:

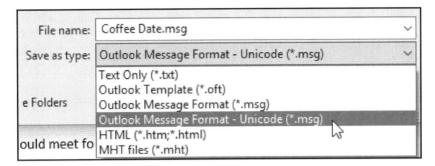

4. If you prefer, you can save your email in `.pdf` format for safekeeping on your computer, then use the **File** | **Print** | **Microsoft Print to PDF** option, as illustrated in the following screenshot:

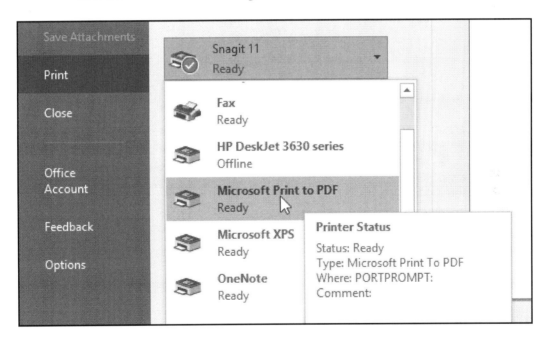

You have now learned how to save messages in external formats for safekeeping. This is purely a personal choice, and many companies will have their own policies on how your Inbox is stored, or alternatively have additional software to integrate with your Outlook mail application.

Ignoring a conversation

The **Ignore** feature is available to remove unwanted conversations in your inbox. Please note that an ignored conversation will land up in the **Deleted Items** folder, and if you delete it from that location, you will not be able to recover it. Be careful to select the correct message you select prior to clicking on the **Ignore** feature:

1. Click on the message header (but do not open the message). Click on the **Home** tab, then choose the **Ignore** option from the **Delete** group, as illustrated in the following screenshot:

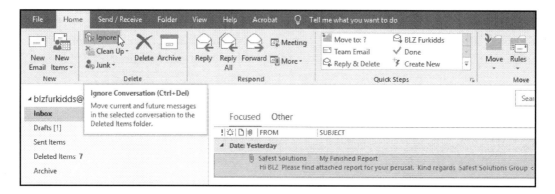

2. A dialog box will open on screen with the following warning:

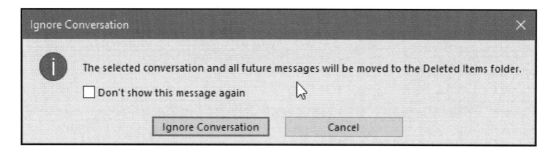

3. Click on **Ignore Conversation** to confirm. This feature is also available in an open email but is located on the **Message** group.

4. If you decide to stop ignoring a conversation, do the following: Locate the email in the **Deleted Items** folder, then double-click to open the email. Click on the **Ignore** icon on the **Message** tab, after which a dialog box will open on the screen. Click on **Stop Ignoring Conversation**, as illustrated in the following screenshot:

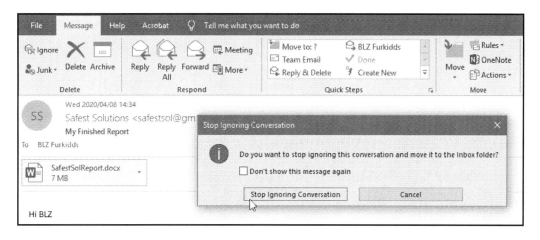

5. The email will return to the Inbox.

Using cleanup tools

Mailbox cleanup tools are located on the Backstage view. You would use this option to find out the size of your mailbox and the folders within it. Other features under this heading enable you to empty the **Deleted Items** folder and archive old items to the Outlook Data File (`*.pst`) archive.

1. Click on **File** | **Tools** | **Mailbox Cleanup...** to view the mailbox size, as illustrated in the following screenshot:

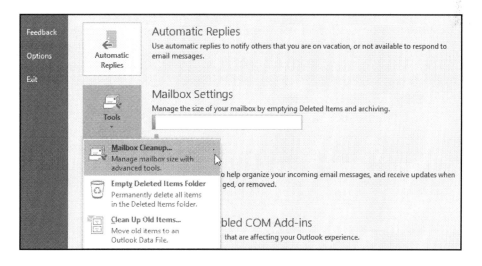

2. The **Mailbox Cleanup...** dialog box will launch with a range of options, as illustrated in the following screenshot:

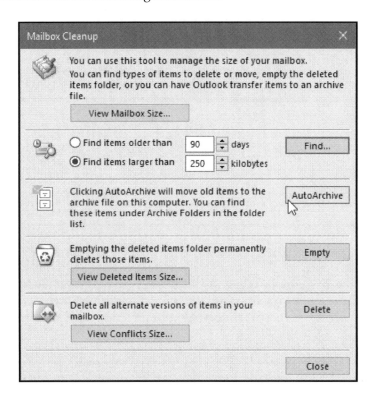

3. In this dialog box, you will be able to view mailbox size categorized by Outlook item and **find** items based on the number of days and size. **AutoArchive** will move all old items to the Outlook Data File, which is normally located in the `Documents\Outlook Files` folder on your hard drive. You can also empty the **Deleted Items** folder and delete versions of items from this dialog box.

Creating and managing rules

Messages can be managed by creating rules on them automatically, every time an email is received or sent. When creating a rule, it can be based on your own rules, templates, or from an existing message:

1. On the **Home** tab, locate the **Move** group, then click on **Rules**.

2. Choose **Create Rule...** or choose **Manage Rules & Alerts...** to edit an existing rule, as illustrated in the following screenshot:

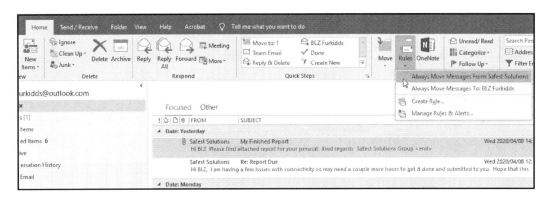

3. In the **Create Rule** dialog box, set the conditions for the message. For this exercise, we will set up a rule to send all emails received from **Safest Solutions** to a folder named **Safest Solutions** in my inbox. You can click on **Advanced Options...** to set further conditions, if required. To create a folder for all the **Safest Solutions** emails, click on the **Select Folder...** option at the bottom of the dialog box, and then click on **New...** to create a new folder called **Safest Solutions** in the Inbox, as illustrated in the following screenshot:

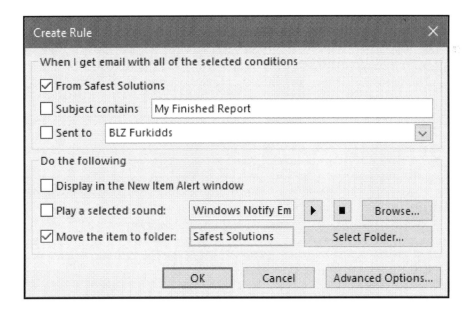

4. Click on **OK** to set up the rule. You will receive a message on the screen, indicating the rule has been created. The option to **Run this rule now on messages already in the current folder** is also visible on this information box, as illustrated in the following screenshot:

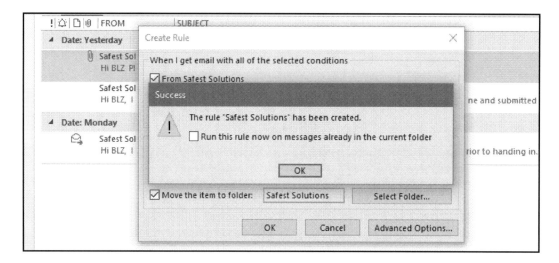

5. Click on the **Run this rule now on messages already in this current folder** checkbox, and then click on the **OK** button to see the results.

Note: When a rule is applied, all delivery receipts, read receipts, voting responses, and automatic replies are also based on the criteria upon which the email message is sent and, when received, are acted upon automatically by that applied rule. Tracking is affected by voting responses and tally responses if moved automatically to another folder.

Modifying rules

There are many rules to select from the **Edit Rules** option. Remember that setting too many rules on incoming messages in your inbox could lead to confusion, and you may miss very important emails needing attention! Only create rules when they are absolutely necessary and can help you with your productivity or workflow.

1. On the **Home** | **Rules** | **Manage Rules & Alerts** option, click on **Change Rule** at the top of the dialog box.
2. Choose **Edit Rules**.

3. From the **Rules Wizard** dialog box, adjust the settings by selecting a new condition, or click on the blue highlighted underlined words to change the criteria to suit your requirements. In this case, we will choose **with specific words in the body** for **Step 1: Select condition(s)**, and **with Report in the body** from **Step 2: Edit the rule description (click an underlined value)**. Click on **Next**, then **OK**, as illustrated in the following screenshot:

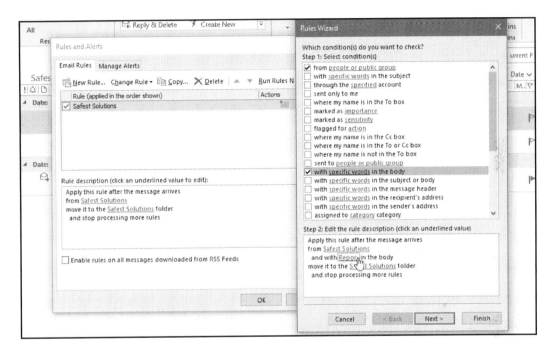

4. Click on **Next >** until you have completed making relevant changes. Then, click on **Finish**.

Deleting rules

1. Click on **Home** | **Rules** | **Manage Rules & Alerts**.

2. Select the rule to remove, as illustrated in the following screenshot:

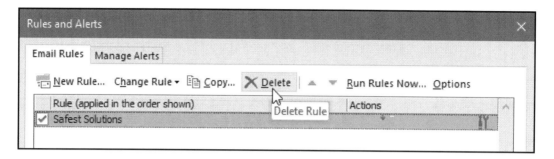

3. Choose the **Delete** icon to remove the rule.

Changing Rule order

Rules are run on incoming messages in your Inbox according to how they are set in the list when creating the rule. We can change the priority of which rules will run first by reordering their position in the Rules area:

1. To reorder rules, visit **Rules | Manage Rules & Alerts...**
2. Simply click on a rule you wish to move from the **Rules and Alerts** dialog box, then click on the **Move Up** or **Move Down** arrow to reorder.

Note that you can also **Stop processing more rules** by selecting the option on the **Rules Wizard** when creating a Rule. This will allow rules to be stopped if more than one rule is applied to the same email.

Managing junk mail and automatic message content

In this topic, you will be directed to the junk mail options, such as allowing a specific message to be not junk; filtering junk mail with an option that never blocks the sender; viewing a list of safe senders; learning how to block a sender. You'll learn how to create and manage signatures; assign a signature to an email message manually; specify font options for new HTML messages; set options for replying to and forwarding mail messages; and, lastly, set a default theme for all HTML messages.

Allowing a specific message (not junk)

Sometimes, mail messages are sent to the **Junk Email** folder by mistake. To mark the message as not junk, do the following:

1. In the Navigation Pane, click on the **Junk Email [1]** folder, as illustrated in the following screenshot:

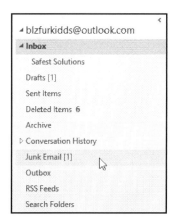

2. In the Message pane to the right, click to select a message that you want to mark as not junk. Click on **Home | Junk | Not Junk**.

3. A dialog box will notify you that the message will be moved back to the **Inbox** folder and messages from the recipient will always be trusted, as illustrated in the following screenshot:

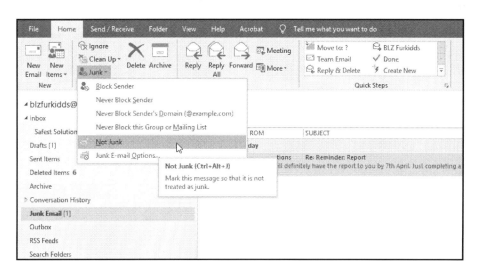

4. A mail message that is sent to the `Junk Email` folder is saved as plain text, and all links contained in it are removed. Moving a message out of the `Junk Email` folder restores the message to its format and links.

Filtering junk mail with Never Block Sender

It is possible to mark a recipient in your Inbox as a safe sender. If you do not want to allow just a single email address from a large company and would prefer to allow receipt of all user addresses from a company, then use the **Never Block Sender's Domain** option (for example, `@packt.com`). In addition, if you belong to a mailing list, you can add this to the safe senders' list too. The steps are exactly the same for each of these options, and are illustrated here:

1. In the Message pane, click on a message received from a recipient you trust. Click on **Home** | **Junk** | **Never Block Sender**, as illustrated in the following screenshot:

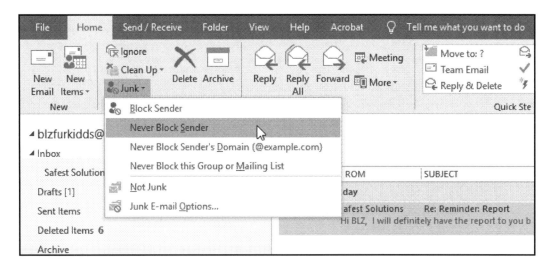

2. A dialog box appears, informing you that the sender of the selected message is added to the **Safe Senders**' list.
3. Click on **OK** to confirm.

Viewing the safe senders' list

1. Click on **Home** | **Junk Email Options…**.

2. In the dialog box, select the **Safe Senders** tab, as illustrated in the following screenshot:

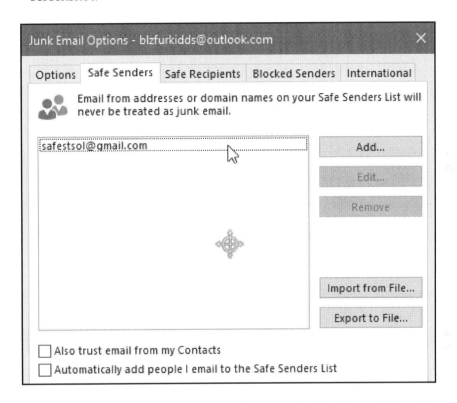

3. The addresses of safe senders are shown in the list. You will be able to add and edit the list there.

Blocking senders

If you receive messages in your inbox that look suspicious or are spam, you can ensure that you don't receive such messages in the future by marking this recipient as blocked:

1. In the Navigation Pane, click on a message from a recipient you trust. Then, click on the **Home | Junk | Block Sender** option, as illustrated in the following screenshot:

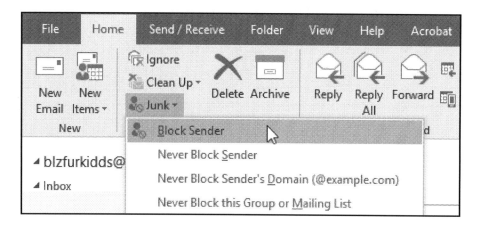

2. A dialog box appears, informing you that the sender of the selected message has been added to the blocked senders' list and moved to the `Junk Email` folder. Click on **OK** to continue.

Managing signatures

A personal business card can be added automatically to every email message you send, or manually on the messages you choose. This is called a **signature**. It contains contact information that will appear in the body of each new email message you create in Outlook 2019.

Creating a signature

1. Open a new email message, then click on **Signature**. In the list, you will see any existing signatures.

2. To create a new signature, choose **Signatures...** from the drop-down list, as illustrated in the following screenshot:

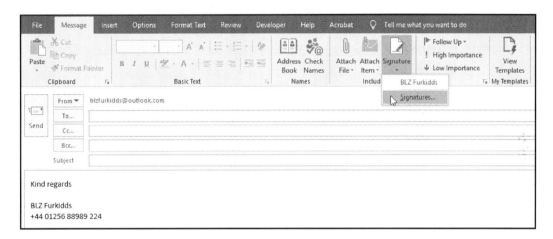

3. Click on the **New** icon to create a new signature. In the textbox that populates, enter a name for the signature. The name of the signature is not going to appear in the email; it is just a name given to the signature to identify it.

4. Click on **OK** when done.

5. In the **Edit signature** text body area, type the contact details, and format the text using the options provided. Note that you can also insert a picture and a hyperlink, as well as a business card. These options can be seen in the following screenshot:

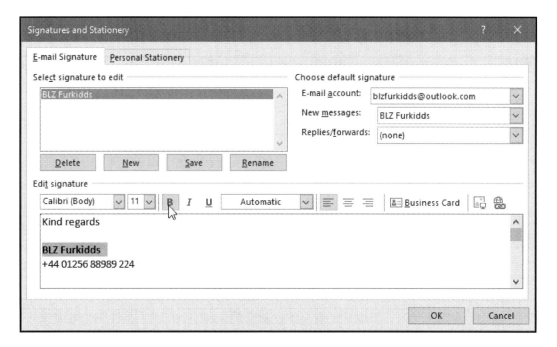

6. To the right of the dialog box, you will see the **Choose default signature** heading. If you do not want to add the signature you have just created to every new email message you compose, then you would need to change the option in the drop-down list next to **New messages:** to **(none)**. Also, note that this can be changed using **File | Options | Mail | Signatures**. You can set a separate signature for the **Replies/forwards:** option as well.

7. Click on **OK** to confirm.

Specifying the font for new HTML messages

You can specify the fonts for traditional-style documents—namely, the HTML-type message as a default in Outlook 2019. By traditional-style documents, we mean those that contain bullets, fonts, colors, and images. Plain-text messages are also available but, of course, will not support bold or italics or any formatting:

1. Click on **File | Options**, then, in the **Outlook Options** dialog box, make sure you are on the **Mail** category to the left to access the options.
2. Under the **Compose messages** heading, select the **Stationery and Fonts...** button.
3. Click on the **Font...** icon under the **New mail messages** heading to specify the font for new HTML messages.
4. In the **Font** dialog box, choose the formats you would like to apply to every new mail message by default. For this example, the font face and font color were changed. For reference, font face refers to the font type that you choose from the **Font:** drop-down list.

Refer to the following screenshot to view the preceding information:

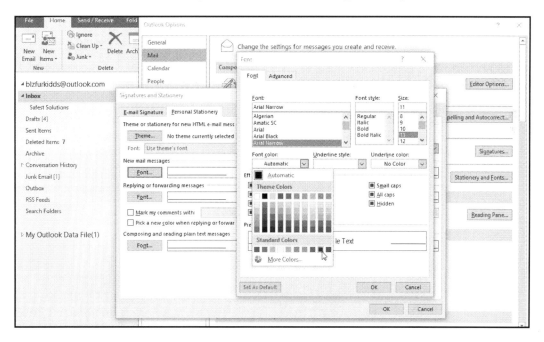

5. Click on **OK** to confirm, and **OK** again, and once again to exit the dialog box. The sample text has updated in the preview window, and, when typing in a new mail message, the changes will be noted.

Specifying options for replies and forwards

You can set a different font and attributes for replying and forwarding messages, as follows:

1. Click on **File | Options**, then, in the **Outlook Options** dialog box, make sure you are on the **Mail** category to the left to access the options.
2. Under the **Compose messages** heading, select the **Stationery and Fonts...** button.
3. In the **Signatures and Stationery** dialog box, locate the **Replying or forwarding messages** heading.
4. Click on the **Font...** button to change the attributes, then click on **OK** when done. Note that there are two other options on the dialog box, relating to replying and forwarding messages.

Setting a default theme for all HTML messages, stationery, and fonts

1. Click on **File | Options | Mail | Signatures and Stationery.**
2. In the **Signatures and Stationery** dialog box, locate the **Theme...** icon on the **Personal Stationery** tab, as illustrated in the following screenshot:

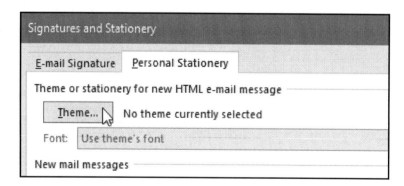

3. In the **Theme or Stationery** dialog box, select a theme to apply to all messages by default. Choose whether to display background graphics at the bottom left-hand corner of the dialog box. Click on **OK** to confirm. All this is illustrated in the following screenshot:

4. Click on **OK** to confirm.

Creating contact information and groups

In this topic, you will learn how to create a contact business card and modify it. You will also master the forwarding of contacts and updating of a contact in the Outlook address book. We will look at creating contact groups and how to manage the contact group membership, show notes about a contact group, and delete a contact group. In addition, we will look at the search features in order to search for a specific contact or group in order to send a meeting to the contact or group.

Modifying a default business card

A business card provides contact information for a contact within Outlook:

1. From the Navigation Pane, select the **People** icon located on the Peek bar.
2. Double-click on an existing business card to edit it. Edit the business card by clicking in the relevant text area to type new information or edit existing information.
3. Click on **Save & Close** when complete.

 Once an email is opened, you can right-click on the sender's email address to save the contact to the address book, or drag the message from the inbox to the **People** icon on the Peek bar at the bottom of the Navigation Pane to create a new contact.

Forwarding a contact

1. Click the **People** icon on the Peek bar at the bottom of the Navigation Pane.
2. Locate the **Share** group on the **Home** tab, then select **Forward Contact**, as illustrated in the following screenshot:

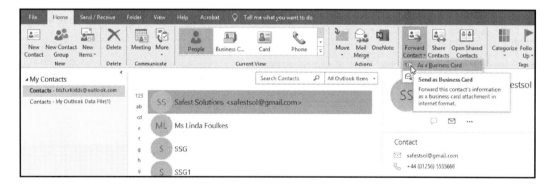

3. Choose the relevant option from the drop-down list, as follows:

   - The **As a Business Card** forwarding option will insert the business card into a new mail message and attach the *.vcf file to the email.
   - The **As an Outlook Contact** forwarding option will attach the business card to the message.

4. You can also **Share Contacts** using the icon on the **Share** group. This option grants other users access to your contact list in Outlook and/or permission to access other people's contact lists.

Creating and manipulating contact groups

When emailing contacts regularly for a specific purpose—such as conference attendees, a list of parents, or a list of meeting attendees—it is much simpler when you have a group of contacts set up. That way, when emailing all of the contacts, you would just use the group name as the recipient, and each contact listed in the group would receive the email message sent.

Creating a contact group

Let's create a contact group using the **People** icon, as follows:

1. At the bottom of the Navigation Pane, locate the **People** icon.
2. Click on **New Contact Group** from the **Home** tab, as illustrated in the following screenshot:

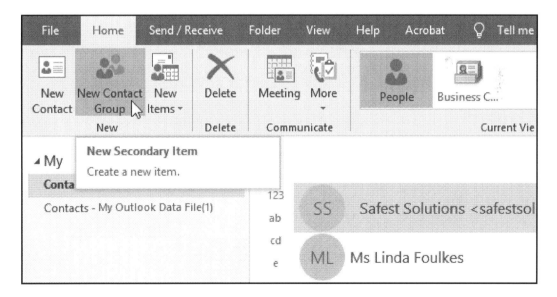

3. In the dialog box, name your new contact group in the **Name** text area. For this example, let's create a **SafestContacts** group.

4. To add the email address of all the members of the group, click on the **Add Members** icon.

5. Choose **New E-mail Contact**, **From Address Book**, or **From Outlook Contacts**, as illustrated in the following screenshot:

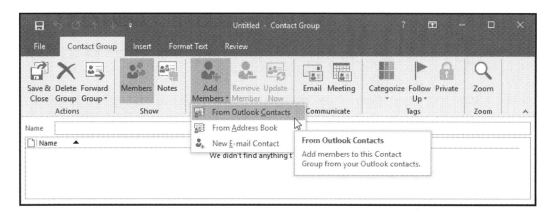

6. For this example, we will use **New E-mail Contact**. In the dialog box, enter a display name into the text area, and type the contact's email address into the space provided. Click on **OK**.

7. Keep on adding contacts in this way until all the required members are in the group. Click on **Save & Close** when done.

8. In the **Contacts** window, the new group called **Safest Contacts** (in the case of this exercise) should be seen.

Managing contact group membership

Managing a group is very simple using the ribbon. All the relevant icons are displayed for ease of use, as can be seen in the following screenshot:

Using these ribbon options, you are able to do the following:

- Add new members using the **Add Members** icon (members can be added from email, the address book, or the Outlook contact list).
- Remove any members from the list by clicking on the display name and then choosing **Remove Member** from the ribbon.
- Update the group by clicking on **Update Now**, if you have made changes
- Add **Notes** about the distribution list.
- **Categorize** your group according to a specific category and color.
- Use the **Private** lock at the end of the ribbon to mark the group as private so that no one else can see the details thereof.
- Set a **Follow Up** reminder to remember to do something related to the contact group.

We will now have a look at how to work with the **Notes** feature in the next topic.

Showing notes about a contact group

1. In the **People** contacts window, locate the contact group for which you want to create a note.
2. Double-click on the group name to open it. We will open `SafestContacts`, as created in the preceding topics, for this example.
3. On the **Contact Group** tab, click to select **Notes**. Add a note for the current group by typing text into the notes area. We will add a note by adding the following text—**This client is one of our acquisitions for September**, as illustrated in the following screenshot:

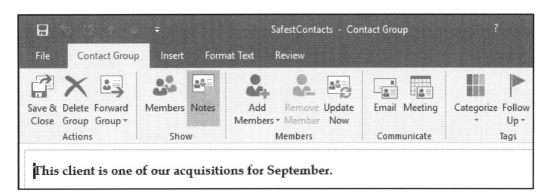

4. Click on **Members** to return to the contact group email list. To view the notes for the group, click on the **Notes** icon again.

5. Click on **Save & Close** when complete.

Deleting a contact group

1. Open the contact group, as shown in the preceding section. From the **Contact Group** tab, click on the **Delete Group** icon to move it from the list.

2. A dialog box will prompt you, asking if you are definitely sure you want to delete the group.

3. Click on **Yes** to confirm.

Sending a meeting to a contact group

1. At the bottom of the Navigation Pane, click to select **People**.

2. Locate the contact group you would like to invite to a meeting. Open the contact group by double-clicking on it.

3. Locate the **Meeting** icon on the **Contact Group** tab, as illustrated in the following screenshot:

4. A new meeting request is opened, where you are able to confirm the date(s) and time of the meeting request, as illustrated in the following screenshot:

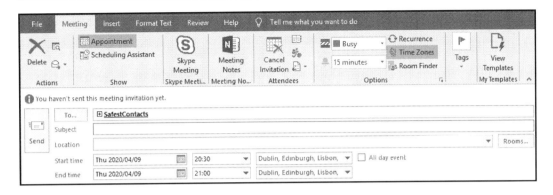

5. Fill in the details, and then click on **Send**.

Searching for a contact

1. Click to select **People** from the bottom of the Navigation Pane.
2. Locate the search box at the top of the contacts list. Type into the search text area the name of the contact you wish to find.
3. Click on **All Outlook Items** to view the drop-down list of search destinations, as illustrated in the following screenshot:

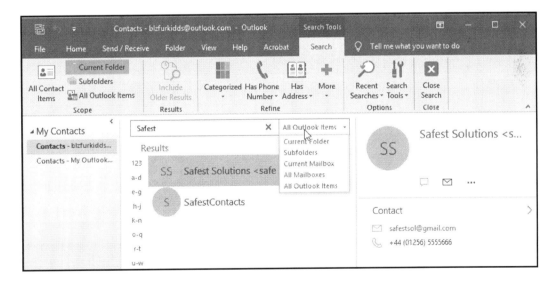

4. The search will return the results from the criteria you entered. Note that the ribbon contains a number of search options, including a list of **Recent Searches**, and **Search Tools** to investigate. When you are done searching, click on **Close Search** at the end of the ribbon, or click on the **X** located at the end of the search entry text area.

Summary

In this chapter, you have learned all about keeping the mailbox clean, and are knowledgeable about where to check the mailbox size and how to add messages to the safe senders or blocked senders list. You can set and manage rules on your mailbox and folders, and are able to work with the junk mail options. You have also mastered the setting up of signatures when sending new email messages, as well as when replying to and forwarding mail. Specifying font options for new HTML messages, and the setting up of fonts for replying to and forwarding mail, are now skills you have also acquired. In addition, you are able to set up a theme for all HTML messages and work with contact groups in Outlook 2019.

In the following chapter, you will work with calendars, appointments, and events. You'll learn to set meeting response options and arrange calendars and calendar groups. You will also create tasks and assign them to other Outlook users, as well as track them via the **Status Report** tool. There is also a topic on the **Journal**, where you will learn to create items such as telephone calls and use this method to record the time taken on particular tasks, using Outlook 2019.

18
Calendar Objects, Tasks, Notes, and Journal Entries

In this chapter, you will learn how to work with calendars, appointments, and events, as well as setting meeting response options and arranging calendars and calendar groups. You will also learn how to work with tasks and how to assign them to other Outlook users, as well as track them via the status report tool.

This chapter also includes a section on journal entries, which you can use to create and track items such as telephone calls, tasks, and documents relating to a specific client on a timeline. This is particularly useful if you need to record the time spent on certain tasks in Outlook.

The following topics are covered in this chapter:

- Working with the calendar, appointments, and events
- Modifying meeting requests and manipulating the calendar pane
- Creating and managing tasks
- Creating and manipulating notes and journal entries
- Setting out-of-office options

Technical requirements

To work through this final chapter, you need to have prior knowledge of the Outlook 2019 interface and setting options. In addition, you need to be confident in creating and sending mail and managing the mail environment. You should be able to insert, format, and attach items to elements within the interface. All of the examples used in this chapter can be accessed from `https://github.com/PacktPublishing/Learn-Microsoft-Office-2019`.

Working with the calendar, appointments, and events

This section will cover setting up appointments and options, forwarding and printing appointments, scheduling a meeting with a message sender, and sharing a calendar.

Creating and manipulating appointments and events

In this section, we will look at how to set up an appointment, as well as using the recurring appointment option. We will also learn how to print the appointment details, as well as forwarding an appointment to another recipient.

Setting the appointment options

1. Locate the calendar icon on the Peek bar at the bottom of the Navigation Pane:

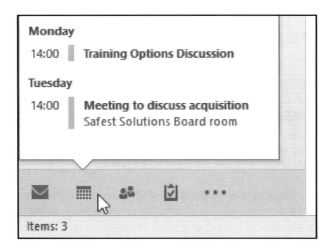

2. From the **Home** tab, locate the **New** group. Click on **New Appointment**. Note you can right-click or double-click directly on a day in the calendar to create a new appointment.

3. To enter a start and end time of the appointment, make sure that **All day event** is not active (remove the tick from the option). Be careful to watch the AM and PM timeslots as you could end up setting your appointment to the wrong hour of the day. If your appointment will occur at the same time on certain days of the week for a certain period of time, then the recurring appointment option is perfect. Click on **Recurrence** under the **Appointment** tab to set the recurring appointment options. Click on **OK** to confirm the changes:

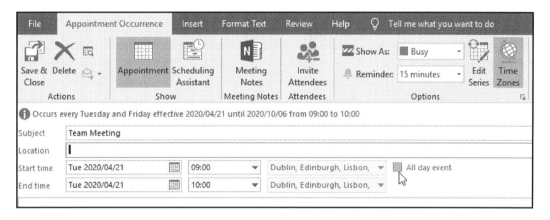

4. To remove a recurring appointment, you need to open an appointment that the recurrence occurs on. From the **Appointment** tab, select the **Recurrence** icon. At the bottom of the dialog box, choose **Remove Recurrence**.

5. For **Reminders**, you will receive a pop-up reminder **15 minutes** before an appointment begins. This reminder can be turned off or set for a longer period of time. You would probably miss someone's birthday party if you only have 15 minutes to get there or buy a gift! You can also assign a sound to your reminders.

6. To format appointments, have a look at the **Format Text** tab when you create an appointment. All the options from the Word 2019 environment that you are used to can be accessed from here. **WordArt** can be inserted, as well as files, Outlook items, tables, charts, pictures, clip art, **SmartArt**, screenshots, textboxes, drop caps, and objects. In addition, the horizontal line icon is available here. Click on **Save & Close** to add the appointment into the calendar.

Printing the appointment details

1. Double-click on an appointment to view its details.
2. From the **File** tab, choose the **Print** menu item.
3. The appointment is displayed in **Memo Style**. Look at the preview pane to see the appointment details:

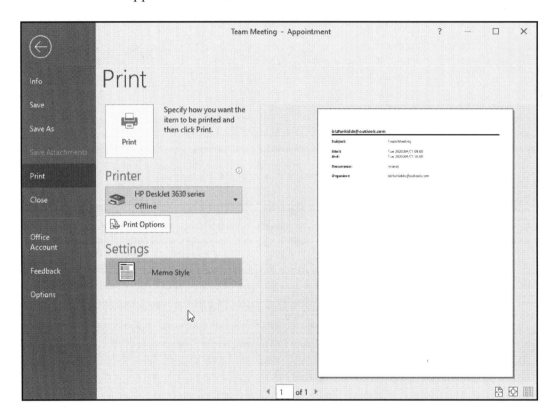

4. Check that you are happy with the print settings and click on the **Print** icon to send it to the printer.

Forwarding an appointment

1. Navigate to the calendar and click on an appointment to select it.
2. From the **Appointment** tab, click on the **Forward** icon:

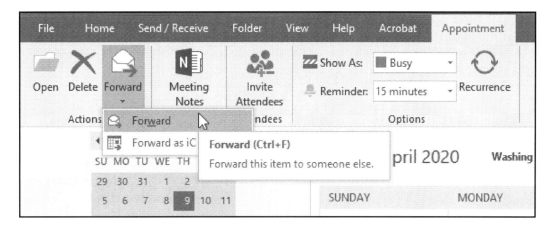

3. A new email will open, listing all the information about the meeting.
4. Enter a recipient in the **To:** text area. Click on the **Send** icon to forward the message.

Scheduling a meeting with someone who sent a message

1. If you receive an email message from someone, for example, asking you for a coffee date, you can create a meeting from the message. Double-click on the message to open it.
2. Under the **Home | Respond** tab, click on the **Meeting** icon to create an appointment in your calendar:

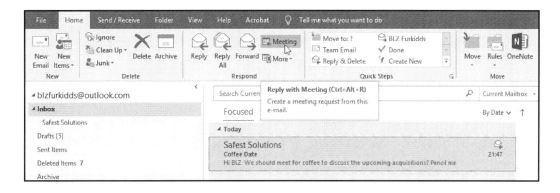

3. The name of the recipient will automatically be inserted in the **To:** text area. Click on **Send** to add the appointment to your diary, as well as to send the meeting request to the recipient (that is, the person who sent you the email message in the first place).

Sharing a calendar

It is possible to share your calendar with other contacts as well as to ask permission to gain access to their calendars. When sharing your calendar, you can choose to share only certain details, such as the **Availability Only**, **Limited Details**, or **Full Calendar** details:

1. Open your calendar by clicking on the calendar icon at the bottom of the Navigation Pane.
2. Click on **Share Calendar** on the ribbon.
3. Enter the name of the contact that you would like to grant access to your calendar.
4. Choose a sharing option from the **Details** drop-down list—either **Availability Only**, **Limited Details**, or **Full Details** access. For this example, we will choose **Availability Only**:

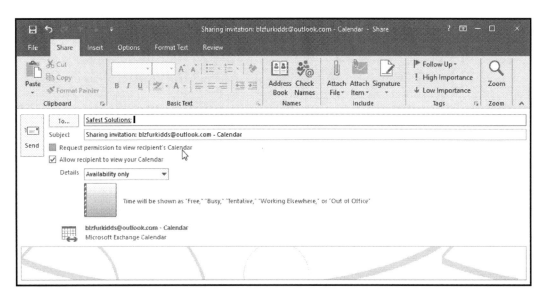

5. When you have finished, click on **Send**:

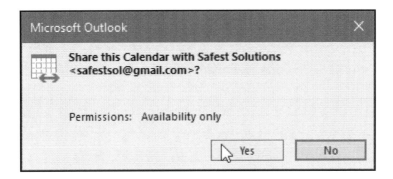

6. A notification will pop up on the screen asking whether you are sure you want to share the calendar with the permissions you have granted. Click **Yes** to continue.

Modifying meeting requests and manipulating the calendar pane

You will now learn how to set a meeting request and look at the meeting response options. After sending out a meeting request, you can change the options to update or cancel a meeting, allowing recipients to propose a new time for the meeting. We will look at how to view the tracking status and how to edit a meeting series. This section will also equip you with the skills to arrange your calendar views, change the calendar formats, display or hide calendars, and create a calendar group.

Setting the response options

Before sending a meeting request, you can set the response options. If you would like the recipient to be prompted to accept, reject, or tentatively accept the meeting request, then you need to check whether these options have been selected. You can also request a new timeslot if the meeting time does not suit you. By default, both of these options should be activated in the Outlook program:

1. Open your calendar and then select **New Meeting** from the **New** group. Once you have filled out the meeting details, you can set the response options:

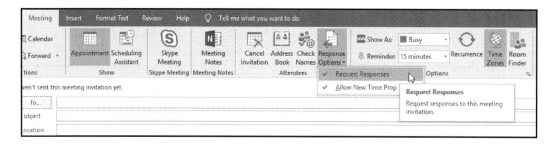

2. From the **Attendees** group, select **Response Options**. You can choose **Request Responses** and/or **Allow New Time Proposals**. Both of these options are turned on by default.

Updating a meeting request

To update a meeting request, double-click on the appointment in your calendar. Once the appointment is open, change the details to update them:

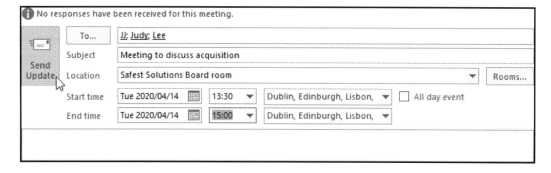

Once you are done, you need to click on the **Send Update** icon to resend the meeting to all of the recipients so that their calendars adjust accordingly.

Canceling a meeting or invitation

1. Open the meeting that you need to cancel from your calendar.
2. Click on the **Cancel Meeting** icon under the **Meeting** tab. Don't forget to click on **Send Cancellation** to send the email to the recipients:

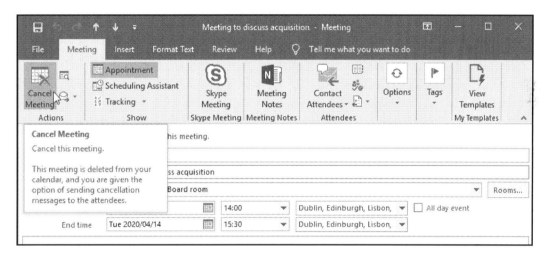

Proposing a new time for a meeting

If you are unable to make the time of a meeting request, a new time can be proposed and sent to the sender:

1. Open the meeting request from your inbox.

2. Click on the **Propose New Time** icon under the **Meeting** tab:

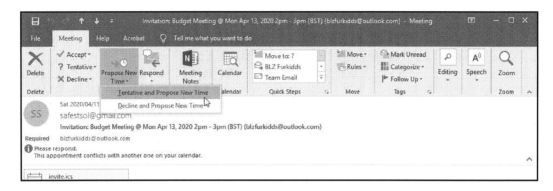

3. Choose either **Tentative and Propose New Time** or **Decline and Propose New Time** to choose a time that you are available:

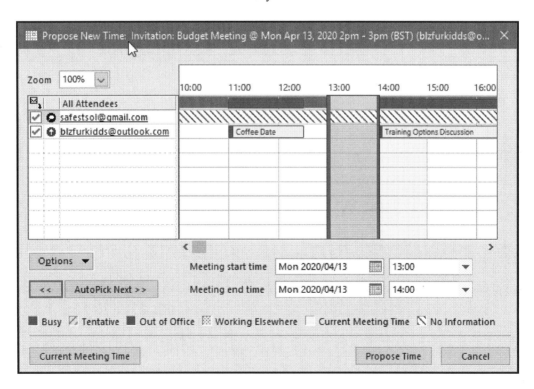

4. Once you have selected a new proposed time using the drop-down arrows next to **Meeting start time** and **Meeting end time**, or you have used the **AutoPick Next >>** button to find the next available time slot, click on **Propose Time** to reply to the meeting request:

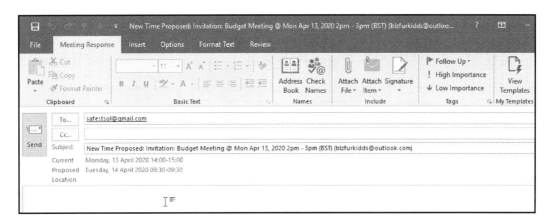

5. Check the invitation email and then click on **Send**.

Viewing the tracking status of a meeting

If you have sent a meeting request to a number of people and would like to see whether they have responded without having to check your email countless times, the **Tracking** feature is a wonderful tool to use:

1. Click on the meeting entry in your calendar.
2. Under the **Meeting** tab, select the **Tracking** icon:

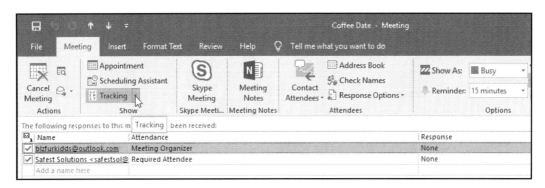

3. Choose to either click on the drop-down arrow and select **View Tracking Status** for the meeting request or simply click on the **Tracking** icon. The **Tracking** pane will open, where you will see a summary of who has and hasn't responded to your meeting request. Close the pane when you are finished.

Editing a meeting series

If you have set a recurring appointment and wish to edit the entire series, simply open the appointment. A dialog box will prompt you to choose whether you would like to edit the series or just the appointment you clicked on:

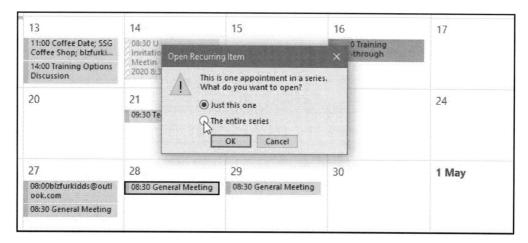

Click on **The entire series**, then make the changes to the appointment. Click on **Save & Close** when done to update the series.

Manipulating the calendar pane

Just like any other view in Outlook, we can manipulate the calendar's elements, such as the font settings and the color, as well as arrange the way the calendar entries are displayed. Let's investigate these options in the following sections.

Arranging the calendar view

The default calendar view in Outlook is set to **Month**. When you open the calendar from the bottom of the Navigation Pane, you will notice that the **View** tab is available for the calendar arrangement. Click on **Day**, **Work Week**, **Week**, **Month**, or **Schedule View** to display the calendar in your preferred format:

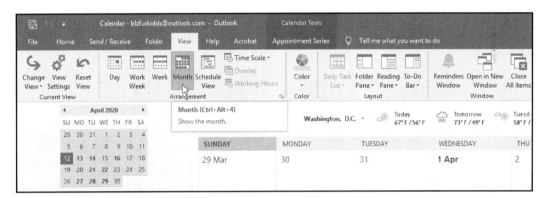

Schedule View displays the calendar horizontally. You can use **Schedule View** when viewing multiple calendars as this view allows more space on the interface window. The calendar arrangement options are also available under the **Home** tab. Take a look at the **Go To** group to set even more options.

Changing the calendar color

1. Click on the calendar icon at the bottom of the Navigation Pane to access the calendar.
2. From the **Color** group under the **View** tab, select the **Color** icon. A drop-down list of colors will appear. Select a color to apply to your calendar:

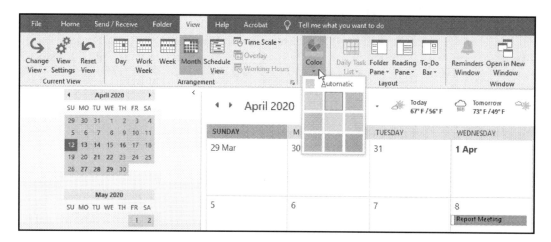

3. The calendar will update to the chosen color. The color of the calendar can also be set in the Outlook **Options** dialog box.

Changing the calendar's font settings

To change the calendar's font settings, as well as other **Day**, **Week**, and **Month** view settings, click on the **View Settings** icon when viewing the calendar. Choose **Other Settings...** from the **Advanced View Settings: Calendar** dialog box that appears on your screen. From the **Format Calendar** dialog box, choose **Font...** to apply changes to the font and size attributes. You can also set **Time scale:** for **Day and Week View** here:

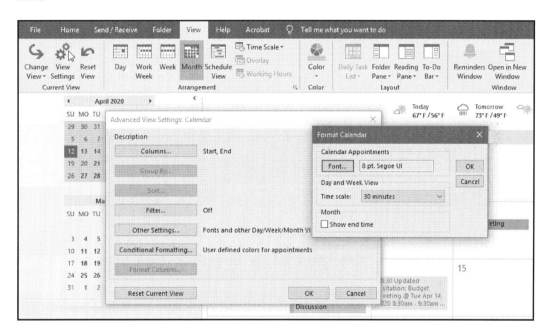

In the next section, we will look at displaying and hiding calendars.

Displaying or hiding calendars

It is extremely useful to be able to hide or show calendars when working with others from the same or external organizations. If you have access to someone's calendar, you can show or hide it in your calendar view:

1. At the bottom of the calendar folder pane, you will see a number of different calendar headings. The first is **My Calendars**, the second is **Other Calendars**, and the third is **Shared Calendars**. In the following screenshot, **Calendar - blzfurkidds@outlook.com** is visible because that calendar has been selected:

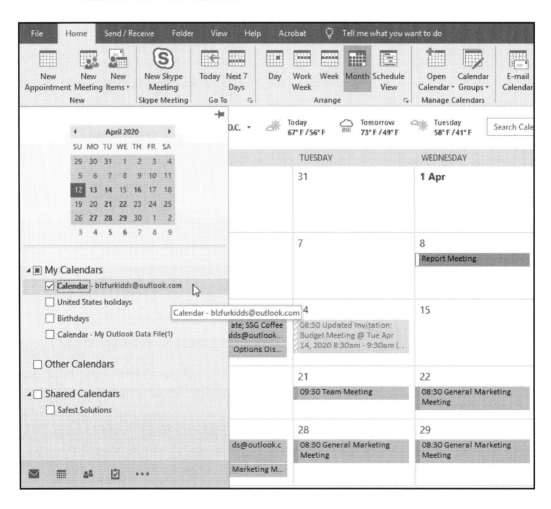

2. To view another calendar alongside your personal calendar, click on it from the **Shared Calendars** folder to view it. You will notice that we have access to the **Safest Solutions** calendar, as it is listed under **Shared Calendars**:

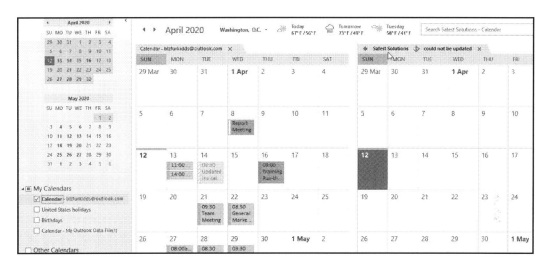

3. Once you check a calendar (in this example, **Safest Solutions**), the calendar is shown to the right of your personal calendar.

4. To hide the selected calendar, click on the **x** icon at the end of the **Calendar** tab, right-click on the tab and choose **Hide This Calendar**, or click on the name of the calendar under **Shared Calendars** to hide it from view:

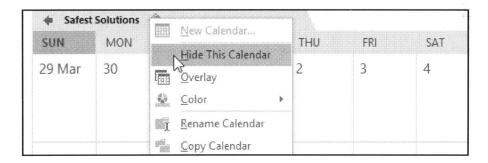

5. Calendars can also be set to **Overlay**. This is very useful when you want to view multiple calendars at the same time in one calendar view. Right-click on a **Calendar** tab, then choose **Overlay**.

6. If you can't see a calendar that you need under the **Shared Calendars** heading to the left of the calendar view, click on **Open Calendar** from the top ribbon. You can choose to open a calendar using the **From Address Book...**, **Create New Blank Calendar...**, or **Open Shared Calendar...** options:

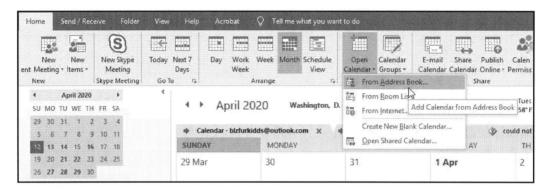

Certain calendars will require permission from the owner to open them.

Creating a calendar group

1. Open the calendar view by clicking on the icon at the bottom of the Navigation Pane.
2. From the **Home** tab, locate the **Manage Calendars** group.
3. Click on **Calendar Groups**, then from the drop-down list, click on **Create New Calendar Group**:

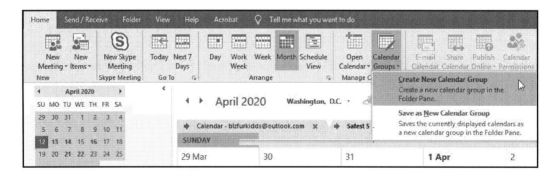

4. In the dialog box, type a name for the new calendar into the text area provided. For this example, we will create a calendar group called `SSG Calendar`. Click on **OK** when you are done:

5. Select **Contacts** from the address book to view all of the available contacts. Double-click on each contact to add them to the **Group Members** section at the bottom of the dialog box. Click on **OK** when done:

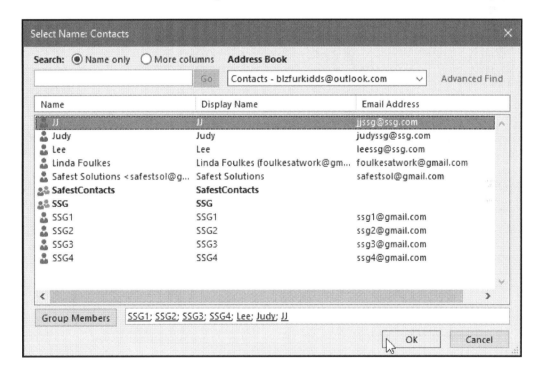

6. The calendar information will display on your screen. If someone from your group has not shared their calendar, then you will not be able to view it. Click on the **Send a sharing request to see more details for this calendar** icon at the bottom-right corner of each of the contacts in the calendar to request to see more details for the calendar:

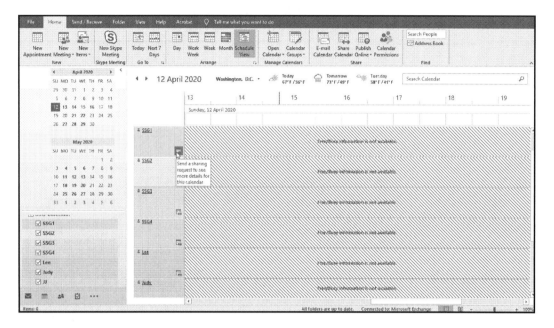

Each person is displayed in a different color on the calendar and you can hide or display individual calendars using the group list to the left under the folder pane.

Creating and managing tasks

In this section, you'll learn how to create and manage a task so that you receive a reminder of items you need to complete by a certain date and a status report. We will also cover marking tasks as complete and assigning a task to another Outlook user. Accepting and declining task assignments will also be covered in this topic.

Creating tasks

1. Click on the tasks icon at the bottom of the Navigation Pane:

2. In the task window, you will see any follow-up messages you have received, as well as any outstanding tasks or to-do list items.

3. Click on the **Home** tab, then select the **New Task** icon:

4. Fill out the details for the task:

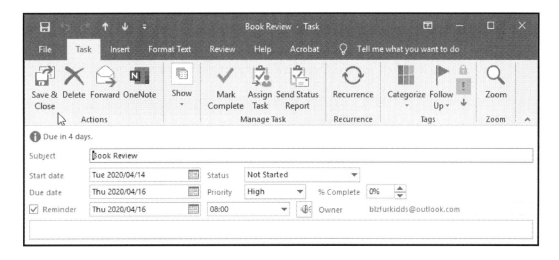

5. Click on the **Save & Close** icon.

Note that Outlook items can be dragged to the tasks icon on the Navigation Pane to create a task from the item. This is the quickest way to create a task as it fills in all required information from the Outlook item. You can also set a reminder for a task as you would with appointments.

Managing the task details

1. Open a task to view its contents. Take a look at the **Task** and **Details** options under the **Show** group of the **Task** tab. This area is used to enter any secondary information about the task or to update the task:

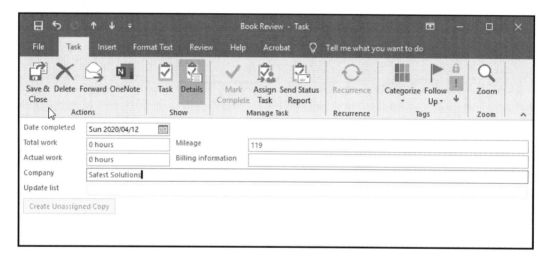

2. Click on the **Save & Close** icon to update and close the task.

Sending a status report

To send an email to someone to let them know how far you have got with a task is really simple:

1. Open the task, then select the **Task** tab.
2. Click on the **Send Status Report** option under the **Manage Task** group.
3. A new email is created with **Task Status Report: Book Review** as the subject (**Book Review**, in this case, is the name of the task):

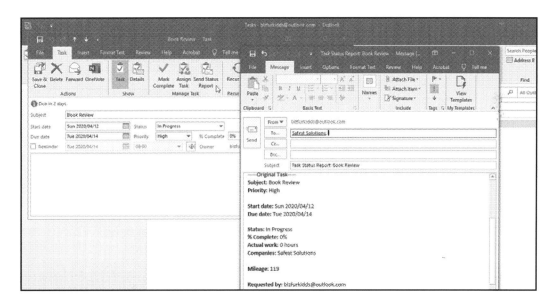

4. In the body of the message, the task details are listed, indicating the percentage of completion. Note that the % **Complete** option will not work unless you diligently update the task as you work on it. Enter a recipient into the **To...** text area. Click on **Send**.

Assigning a task to another Outlook contact

1. Create a task to assign to a colleague.
2. Click on the **Assign Task** icon under the **Manage Task** group, located under the **Task** tab:

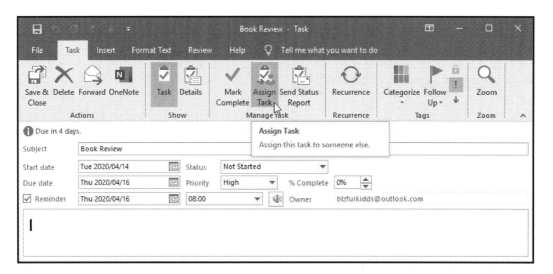

3. In the **To...** text area, type in an address to send the task to or click to populate the address book to select a contact. Make sure the task details have been filled in correctly. Click on **Send**.

Marking a task as complete

1. Open the task that you want to update.
2. Under the **Task** tab, locate the **Mark Complete** icon and click on it:

3. The task is marked as complete with strikethrough lines in the task pane and a green tick at the end in the flagged section of the view.

Accepting or declining a task assignment

1. In your inbox, open a task that you have received:

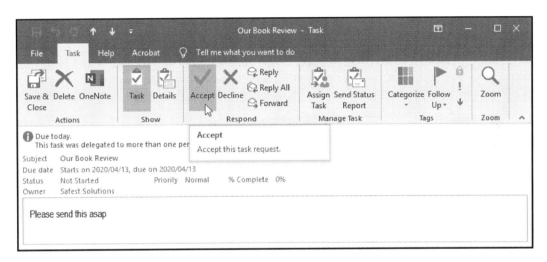

2. Click **Accept** or **Decline** using the icons under the **Respond** ribbon.

Creating and manipulating notes and journal entries

In this topic, you will learn how to create a note, change the current view, and categorize notes.

Creating a note

A **note** is a useful space to jot down thoughts and ideas within Outlook 2019. You can drag notes from Outlook 2019 to your Windows desktop so that they are always visible, even when you are not in the Outlook application. Notes can be categorized in the same way as any other item within Outlook:

1. Click on the three dots at the bottom of the Navigation Pane to access the **Notes** option:

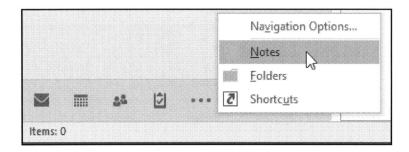

2. The notes window will open. Click on the **New Note** icon to create a new note:

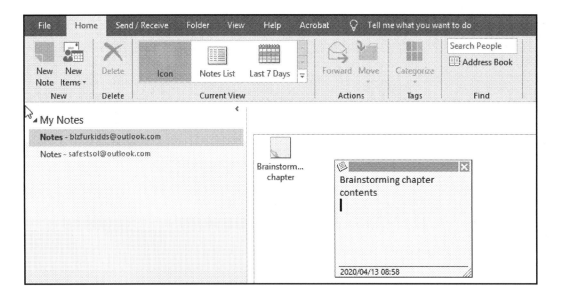

3. The **New Note** icon opens at the top of the Outlook window in a separate window and can be moved to the desktop while Outlook is open:

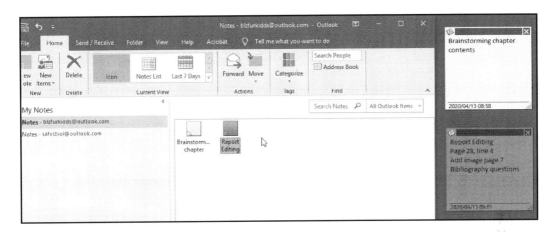

4. Type some text into your new note, then close the note using the **X** symbol at the top-right corner of the screen. The note is added to the **Notes** pane. The first line of the note's text becomes its title.

Changing the current view

Notes can be viewed in icons, lists, and the last 7 days' view. Click on the Last 7 days icon to change the view in the **Current View** group.

Categorizing notes

Notes are categorized just like other items in Outlook:

1. Select the note you want to categorize.
2. Click on the **Categorize** icon under the **Home** tab.
3. Select an existing category or click on **All Categories...** to assign a different category to the new note.

Working with journal entries

In this section, we will look at how to manipulate journal entries by recording Outlook items and folders and learn how to edit a journal entry. The journal records actions that you choose that relate to different contacts and enters the information into a timeline. The journal can track meetings and email messages, as well as other Office program files. The timeline shows all the items that have been sent, received, created, saved, or opened, as well as items that you have made changes to.

Tracking Outlook items and files

1. Click on the three dots at the bottom-right of the Navigation Pane.
2. Choose **Folders**, then locate **Journal**. In this view, you will see any previously tracked items and you will be able to create new ones:

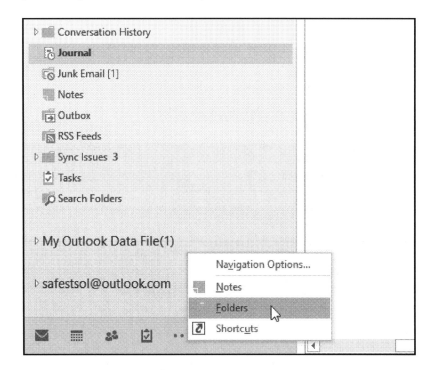

3. Click on the **Home** tab, then select **Journal Entry** from the **New** group to create a new entry. Enter a subject for the journal entry. Add details about the journal entry, such as **Entry type** and **Start time**.

4. **Start Timer** is a very useful tool to track the amount of time a task takes—for example, you might track a client business call so that you can bill the client for your time:

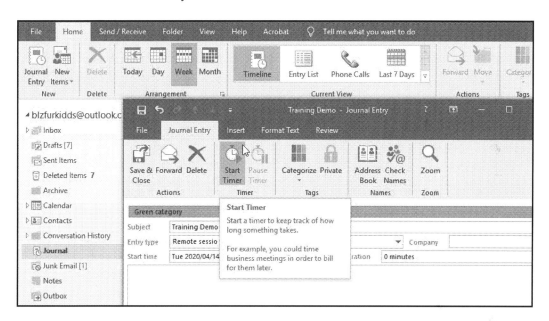

5. Click on **Save & Close** to view the entry in the timeline. You can change the view to display the entries in a list by clicking on the **Entry List** icon under the **Current View** group. To edit a journal entry, simply double-click on the entry in **Timeline View** or the **Entry List** view. Make changes to the entry, then click on the **Save & Close** icon again to update it.

Setting out-of-office options

If you are going to be away from your desk or office for a long period of time (for example, if you are going on holiday or to a conference), you can set up an automatic reply that notifies others that you are unable to respond to incoming email messages:

1. Click on **File**, then choose **Automatic Replies** from the Backstage view.

2. In the **Automatic Replies** dialog box, click on **Send automatic replies**. Make sure that **Only send during this time range:** is selected if you are only going to be out of the office for a set amount of time—for example, for annual leave or maternity leave.

3. Enter the **Start time:** and **End time:** criteria, then add an explanatory note in the space provided under the **Automatic replies** section. Note that you can format your message using the formatting options located just under the **Automatic replies** tab. Click on **OK** to set the automatic reply:

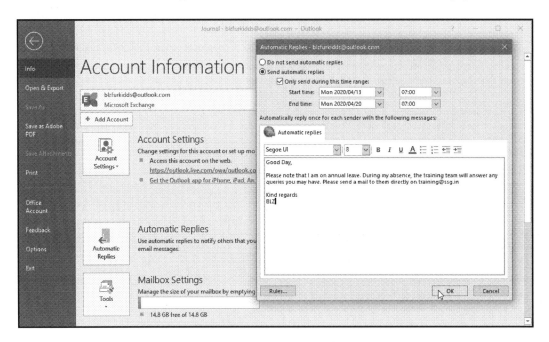

4. The automatic reply is set and all messages that you receive are automatically responded to with this message, highlighting that you are away from the office and for how long.

5. When you visit your inbox, you will see a yellow notification, just under the ribbon, indicating that you have an automatic reply set on your mailbox:

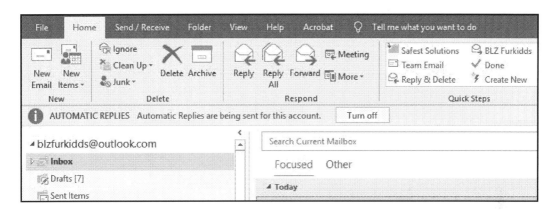

6. Click on **Turn off** to remove the setting from your mailbox so that others do not receive the out-of-office return email anymore. The out-of-office message is stored in the **Automatic Replies** area if you wish to use the same message again in the future—just remember to change the dates, times, and message.

Summary

In this final chapter, you mastered working with notes, tasks, the calendar, and the journal in Outlook 2019. You will now feel confident in creating and managing these items and working with the different views and options available. When you are out of the office, you know how to set up the option to send automatic replies to recipients and how to turn this setting off on your return. You have learned how to manipulate calendar views, change the calendar color, and set up a calendar group. You should also now be proficient with creating and categorizing notes and changing the notes view.

Other Books You May Enjoy

If you enjoyed this book, you may be interested in these other books by Packt:

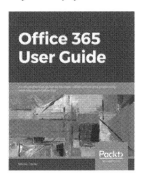

Office 365 User Guide
Nikkia Carter

ISBN: 978-1-78980-931-2

- Understand the UI of Office 365
- Perform a variety of email functions through Exchange
- Communicate using Skype for Business and Microsoft Teams
- Explore file management using OneDrive for Business
- Collaborate using SharePoint
- Understand how to leverage Office 365 in your daily tasks

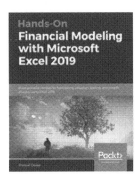

Hands-On Financial Modeling with Microsoft Excel 2019
Shmuel Oluwa

ISBN: 978-1-78953-462-7

- Identify the growth drivers derived from processing historical data in Excel
- Use discounted cash flow (DCF) for efficient investment analysis
- Build a financial model by projecting balance sheets and profit and loss
- Apply a Monte Carlo simulation to derive key assumptions for your financial model
- Prepare detailed asset and debt schedule models in Excel
- Discover the latest and advanced features of Excel 2019
- Calculate profitability ratios using various profit parameters

Leave a review - let other readers know what you think

Please share your thoughts on this book with others by leaving a review on the site that you bought it from. If you purchased the book from Amazon, please leave us an honest review on this book's Amazon page. This is vital so that other potential readers can see and use your unbiased opinion to make purchasing decisions, we can understand what our customers think about our products, and our authors can see your feedback on the title that they have worked with Packt to create. It will only take a few minutes of your time, but is valuable to other potential customers, our authors, and Packt. Thank you!

Index

Z

Made in the USA
Middletown, DE
29 November 2020